taste of home

the ULTIMATE
POTLUCK
COOKBOOK

taste of home

the ULTIMATE
POTLUCK
COOKBOOK

Taste of Home is a registered trademark of
The Reader's Digest Association, Inc.

INTERNATIONAL STANDARD BOOK NUMBER (10):
0-89821-864-0

INTERNATIONAL STANDARD BOOK NUMBER (13):
978-0-89821-864-0

LIBRARY OF CONGRESS CONTROL NUMBER:
2010943106

Printed in U.S.A.
1 3 5 7 9 10 8 6 4 2

PICTURED ON FRONT COVER:
Hearty Chicken Lasagna (p. 166)
Italian Subs (p. 98)
Zinfandel Strawberry Trifle (p. 266)
Crunchy Apple Salad (p. 71)
Chocolate-Peanut Butter Cupcakes (p. 260)

PICTURED ON BACK COVER:
Elegant Green Beans (p. 84)
Virginia Box Bread (p. 225)
Crispy Fried Chicken (p. 133)

VICE PRESIDENT, EDITOR IN CHIEF: Catherine Cassidy
VICE PRESIDENT, EXECUTIVE EDITOR/BOOKS: Heidi Reuter Lloyd
CREATIVE DIRECTOR: Howard Greenberg
FOOD DIRECTOR: Diane Werner, RD
SENIOR EDITOR/BOOKS: Mark Hagen
EDITOR: Amy Glander
ASSOCIATE CREATIVE DIRECTOR: Edwin Robles, Jr.
ART DIRECTOR: Gretchen Trautman
CONTENT PRODUCTION MANAGER: Julie Wagner
LAYOUT DESIGNER: Emma Acevedo
PROOFREADER: Linne Bruskewitz
RECIPE ASSET SYSTEM MANAGER: Coleen Martin
RECIPE TESTING AND EDITING: Taste of Home Test Kitchen
FOOD PHOTOGRAPHY: Taste of Home Photo Studio
ADMINISTRATIVE ASSISTANT: Barb Czysz
COVER PHOTOGRAPHER: Rob Hagen
COVER FOOD STYLISTS: Shannon Roum, Kaitlyn Besasie
COVER SET STYLISTS: Melissa Haberman, Stephanie Marchese

NORTH AMERICAN CHIEF MARKETING OFFICER: Lisa Karpinski
VICE PRESIDENT/BOOK MARKETING: Dan Fink
CREATIVE DIRECTOR/CREATIVE MARKETING: Jim Palmen

THE READER'S DIGEST ASSOCIATION, INC.
PRESIDENT AND CHIEF EXECUTIVE OFFICER: Mary G. Berner
PRESIDENT, NORTH AMERICAN AFFINITIES: Suzanne M. Grimes

For other Taste of Home books and products, visit
ShopTasteofHome.com

table of
contents

Grab a plate and dig into our
biggest collection
of potluck recipes!

What's not to love about a potluck dinner? A few hours of laughter and camaraderie with friends and family and the opportunity to indulge in a lineup of sensational foods make potlucks one of America's most celebrated traditions. The latest book to join ranks with Taste of Home's popular Ultimate Series, **THE ULTIMATE POTLUCK COOKBOOK** is your **BIGGEST** and **BEST** source for **445** impressive feed-a-crowd dishes, all guaranteed to have guests piling their plates high and begging for the recipe!

SOMETHING FOR EVERY OCCASION

There are so many events that call for an unforgettable dish...church suppers, family reunions, holiday dinners, brunch buffets, backyard barbecues, game-day parties, birthday and anniversary celebrations, showers, luncheons and classroom parties, for example. Divided into 10 easy chapters, this book contains all of your crowd-pleasing favorites...hot, savory appetizer nibblers, comforting casseroles, delicious sunrise specialties, oven-fresh breads, colorful salads and sides, even luscious desserts to put a finishing touch on a fabulous spread. You'll also find dishes suitable for specific holidays and themed parties as well as slow cooker recipes that cut down on prep time in the kitchen.

COOK WITH CONFIDENCE

When it comes to bring-a-dish recipes, many cooks are left wondering just that...what should I bring? Finding the perfect recipe is no longer "luck of the pot" because we've collected the best-of-the-best in potluck fare to help you find a mouthwatering dish everyone will love. Each of these versatile large-yield specialties has been tested and approved by our staff of Test Kitchen experts so you can trust that every dish is a winner. You'll also find potluck pointers for transporting food safely and saving time in the kitchen plus other handy how-to tips for making the most of your culinary creations.

POTLUCK FAVORITES FROM READERS LIKE YOU

With *THE ULTIMATE POTLUCK COOKBOOK*, you can serve up all the classic potluck pleasers you've come to know and love as well as fun new twists on old favorites. Almost every recipe is from a home cook just like you and many call for everyday ingredients or can even be made ahead to save precious time at the last minute. So whether you just need a dish to pass or are hosting a special gathering in your home, rely on this colossal collection to make your next potluck experience truly unforgettable!

p. 17

p. 20

p. 26

appetizers
snacks & beverages

VEGETABLE APPETIZER PIZZA

PREP: 15 min. | **BAKE:** 10 min. + chilling

- 4 tubes (8 ounces *each*) refrigerated crescent rolls
- 2 packages (8 ounces *each*) cream cheese, softened
- 2/3 cup mayonnaise
- 1 tablespoon dill weed
- 4 medium tomatoes, seeded and chopped
- 2 cups chopped fresh broccoli
- 3 green onions, thinly sliced
- 2 cups sliced fresh mushrooms
- 1/3 cup chopped green pepper
- 1/3 cup chopped sweet red pepper
- 1 can (2-1/4 ounces) sliced ripe olives, drained
- 2 cups (8 ounces) shredded cheddar cheese

Unroll two tubes of crescent dough and press into each of two ungreased 15-in. x 10-in. x 1-in. baking pans; seal the seams and perforations.

Bake at 375° for 8-10 minutes or until lightly browned. Cool the crusts completely on a wire rack.

In a small bowl, beat the cream cheese, mayonnaise and dill until smooth. Spread over crusts. Sprinkle with vegetables, olives and cheese. Cover and refrigerate for at least 1 hour.

Cut into squares. Refrigerate leftovers.

YIELD: 4 dozen.

marcia tiernan
MADRID, NEW YORK

My sister brought home this recipe after she visited California. We served it at a family get-together, and everyone simply loved it. Now it's my go-to appetizer for potlucks.

CARAMEL FRUIT DIP

PREP/TOTAL TIME: 10 min.

- 2 packages (8 ounces *each*) cream cheese, softened
- 1 cup packed brown sugar
- 1/2 cup caramel ice cream topping
- Assorted fresh fruit

In a small bowl, beat cream cheese and brown sugar until smooth. Beat in caramel topping until blended. Serve with fruit. Refrigerate leftovers.

YIELD: 3 cups.

trish gehlhar
YPSILANTI, NORTH DAKOTA

This creamy, melt-in-your-mouth dip, served with assorted fruits, makes a refreshing accompaniment to any snack tray. It's also a sweet treat in the fall when apples are in season.

SWEET starters

Most appetizer buffets feature a lineup of items that are warm and savory. Shake things up with a light, cold item like Caramel Fruit Dip to appeal to anyone with a sweet tooth.

CRAB SALAD TEA SANDWICHES

PREP/TOTAL TIME: 1 hour

  4 celery ribs, finely chopped
  2 cups reduced-fat mayonnaise
  4 green onions, chopped
1/4 cup lime juice
1/4 cup chili sauce
1/2 teaspoon seasoned salt
  8 cups cooked fresh *or* canned crabmeat
  6 hard-cooked eggs, chopped
 48 slices whole wheat bread
1/2 cup butter, softened
 48 lettuce leaves
1/2 teaspoon paprika
Green onions, cut into thin strips, optional

In a large bowl, combine the first six ingredients; gently stir in crab and eggs. Refrigerate until assembling.

With a 3-in. round cookie cutter, cut a circle from each slice of bread. Spread each with 1/2 teaspoon butter. Top with lettuce and 2 rounded tablespoonfuls of crab salad; sprinkle with paprika. Garnish with onion strips if desired.

YIELD: 4 dozen.

edie despain
LOGAN, UTAH

I make these sandwiches for showers, weddings, luncheons and special family events. They are so delicious, you can't stop at just one.

CHICKEN TACO RING

PREP: 25 min. | **BAKE:** 20 min.

2 tubes (8 ounces *each*) refrigerated reduced-fat crescent rolls

2/3 cup finely crushed tortilla chips, *divided*

2 cups finely chopped rotisserie chicken

3/4 cup shredded reduced-fat Mexican cheese blend

1/2 cup reduced-fat mayonnaise

1 can (4 ounces) chopped green chilies, undrained

1/4 cup chopped pitted ripe olives

1 plum tomato, seeded and chopped

1 tablespoon taco seasoning

1 tablespoon lime juice

GARNISH:

1 cup (8 ounces) reduced-fat sour cream

1 cup salsa

2 plum tomatoes, sliced

1 medium lime, halved and sliced

Grease a 12-in. pizza pan. Unroll crescent dough. Sprinkle with 1/4 cup tortilla chips; press down gently. Separate dough into 16 triangles.

Place wide end of one triangle, chip side down, 3 in. from edge of prepared pan, with point overhanging edge of pan. Repeat with remaining triangles, overlapping the wide ends (dough will look like a sun when complete). Lightly press wide ends together.

In a small bowl, combine the chicken, cheese, mayonnaise, chilies, olives, tomato, taco seasoning, lime juice and remaining tortilla chips. Spoon over wide ends of dough. Fold points of triangles over filling and tuck under wide ends (filling will be visible).

Bake at 375° for 20-25 minutes or until golden brown. Garnish with sour cream, salsa, tomatoes and lime.

YIELD: 16 servings.

kathy martinez
ENID, OKLAHOMA

Try this eye-catching appetizer the next time you want to wow your guests with Southwestern flavor. I serve it with salsa, sour cream and other toppings served in small homemade tortilla bowls.

CURRIED CHICKEN TRIANGLES

PREP/TOTAL TIME: 30 min.

2 tubes (8 ounces *each*) refrigerated crescent rolls

1 can (8 ounces) sliced water chestnuts, drained and chopped

1 cup (4 ounces) shredded Swiss cheese

1/2 cup chopped green onions

1/3 cup mayonnaise

1 teaspoon lemon juice

1/2 teaspoon curry powder

1/2 teaspoon garlic salt

1 can (5 ounces) chunk white chicken, undrained

Paprika, optional

Separate crescent dough into triangles. Cut each piece into four triangles. Place on greased baking sheets. In a large bowl, combine the water chestnuts, cheese, onions, mayonnaise, lemon juice, curry powder and garlic salt. Crumble chicken over mayonnaise mixture; stir to coat.

Place rounded teaspoonfuls in the center of each triangle. Sprinkle with paprika if desired. Bake at 350° for 12-15 minutes or until the edges are lightly browned. Serve appetizers warm.

YIELD: 64 appetizers.

anne marie cardilino
KETTERING, OHIO

Guests love these little bites that get some zip from curry powder. The savory triangles work well for any occasion, big or small.

LAYERED SHRIMP DIP

PREP/TOTAL TIME: 15 min. + chilling

1 package (3 ounces) cream cheese, softened

6 tablespoons salsa, *divided*

1/2 cup cocktail sauce

3 cans (6 ounces *each*) small shrimp, rinsed and drained

1 can (2-1/4 ounces) sliced ripe olives, drained

1 cup (4 ounces) shredded cheddar cheese

1 cup (4 ounces) shredded Monterey Jack cheese

Sliced green onions

Tortilla chips

In a small bowl, combine cream cheese and 3 tablespoons salsa; spread into an ungreased 9-in. pie plate. Combine cocktail sauce and remaining salsa; spread over cream cheese.

Arrange shrimp evenly over top. Sprinkle with olives. Combine the cheeses; sprinkle over top. Add the onions. Chill. Serve with tortilla chips.

YIELD: 12-16 servings.

sue broyles
CHEROKEE, TEXAS

You'll see eyes light up when you set this special shrimp dip on the buffet table. It has a fantastic combination of flavors and makes a colorful addition to any spread.

MAKE ahead

If you're hosting the potluck or party, include appetizers on your menu that can be made ahead and require little last-minute fuss so that you can spend more time with your guests.

HOT CRAB DIP

PREP: 15 min. | **BAKE:** 25 min.

 1 package (8 ounces) fat-free cream
   cheese
 1/2 cup fat-free sour cream
 2 tablespoons fat-free mayonnaise
 1 teaspoon Worcestershire sauce
 1/2 teaspoon seafood seasoning
 1/2 teaspoon spicy brown mustard
 1/2 teaspoon reduced-sodium soy sauce
 1/8 teaspoon garlic salt
 2 cans (6 ounces *each*) crabmeat, drained,
   flaked and cartilage removed *or* 1/2
   pound imitation crabmeat, flaked
 1/3 cup plus 2 tablespoons shredded
   reduced-fat cheddar cheese, *divided*
 1/3 cup plus 2 tablespoons shredded
   part-skim mozzarella cheese, *divided*
Melba rounds *or* crackers

In a large bowl, beat cream cheese until smooth. Add the sour cream, mayonnaise, Worcestershire sauce, seafood seasoning, mustard, soy sauce and garlic salt. Stir in the crab, 1/3 cup cheddar cheese and 1/3 cup mozzarella cheese.

Transfer to a greased shallow 1-qt. baking dish. Sprinkle with remaining cheeses. Bake at 350° for 25-30 minutes or until bubbly around the edges. Serve warm with melba rounds or crackers.

YIELD: 2-1/2 cups.

cammy brittingham
CAMBRIDGE, MARYLAND

I lightened up a recipe for traditional crab dip with reduced-fat and fat-free sour cream and cheeses. Feel free to experiment with different cheeses to suit your tastes. This is great for parties because you can make it a day in advance.

SMOKY CHICKEN SPREAD

PREP: 10 min. + chilling

 3 cups finely chopped cooked chicken
 1/2 cup finely chopped celery
 1/2 cup coarsely chopped smoked almonds
 3/4 cup mayonnaise
 1/4 cup finely chopped onion
 1 tablespoon honey
 1/2 teaspoon seasoned salt
 1/8 teaspoon pepper
Crackers

In a large bowl, combine the first eight ingredients. Cover and chill at least 2 hours. Serve with crackers.

YIELD: 4 cups.

mary beth wagner
RIO, WISCONSIN

The unique "smoky" flavor in this spread comes from smoked almonds. It makes a hearty treat on your favorite crackers. Don't expect many leftovers!

LEMON ICE TEA MIX

PREP/TOTAL TIME: 5 min.

7-1/2 cups sugar
 2 cups unsweetened instant tea
 5 envelopes (.23 ounce *each*) unsweetened
   lemonade soft drink mix
ADDITIONAL INGREDIENTS:
 1 cup warm water
Cold water

In a large bowl, combine the sugar, tea and drink mix. Divide into five equal batches; store in airtight containers in a cool dry place for up to 6 months.

YIELD: 5 batches (8-1/2 cups total).

TO PREPARE TEA: Dissolve about 1-2/3 cups tea mix in 1 cup warm water. Place in a gallon container. Add cold water to measure 1 gallon. Cover and refrigerate.

YIELD: about 16 (1-cup) servings per batch.

linda fox
SOLDOTNA, ALASKA

A friend who has a large family and does a lot of entertaining created this mix. It's inexpensive and makes a tasty, refreshing batch of iced tea perfect for a picnic or barbecue.

SALSA FOR A CROWD

PREP/TOTAL TIME: 30 min.

4 cans (14-1/2 ounces *each*) diced tomatoes

4 large tomatoes, chopped

2 cups frozen corn, thawed

1 can (15 ounces) black beans, rinsed and drained

1 medium sweet onion, finely chopped

1/3 cup lime juice

1/4 cup minced fresh cilantro

2 tablespoons cider vinegar

2 tablespoons hot pepper sauce

1 garlic clove, minced

1 tablespoon coriander seeds, crushed

1 tablespoon ground cumin

1 teaspoon salt

1 teaspoon coarsely ground pepper

Chopped jalapeno pepper, optional

Corn chips *or* tortilla chips

Place two undrained cans of tomatoes in a large bowl; drain the two remaining cans and add tomatoes to the bowl.

Stir in the chopped fresh tomatoes, corn, beans, onion, lime juice, cilantro, vinegar, pepper sauce, garlic and seasonings. Stir in jalapeno if desired. Cover and refrigerate until serving. Serve with chips.

YIELD: 56 servings (1/4 cup each).

betsy sams
JAMESVILLE, NEW YORK

When planning your next fiesta, be sure to set out this colorful salsa on the snack table. The succulent seasoning includes coriander, cumin, garlic and cilantro. Your crowd will definitely say, "Ole!"

PEPPERY HUSH PUPPIES

PREP: 10 min. | **COOK:** 30 min.

 2 cups cornmeal
 1 cup plus 3 tablespoons all-purpose flour
 2 teaspoons baking powder
1-1/2 teaspoons sugar
 1 teaspoon salt
1/2 teaspoon baking soda
 1 egg
2/3 cup water
1/2 cup buttermilk
1/2 cup butter, melted
 1 cup grated onion
 2 jalapeno peppers, seeded and chopped
 1 small green pepper, chopped
Oil for deep-fat frying

In a large bowl, combine the cornmeal, flour, baking powder, sugar, salt and baking soda. In another bowl, whisk the egg, water, buttermilk and butter. Stir in the onion, jalapenos and green pepper. Stir into dry ingredients just until moistened.

 In an electric skillet or deep-fat fryer, heat oil to 375°. Drop batter by teaspoonfuls, a few at a time, into hot oil. Fry until golden brown on both sides. Drain on paper towels. Serve warm.

YIELD: 6 dozen.

carolyn griffin
MACON, GEORGIA

These zesty hush puppies are great fare for a church or community fish fry. You can also serve them alone as a satisfying snack.

BEST BARBECUE WINGS

PREP: 20 min. | **GRILL:** 20 min.

1/2 cup finely chopped onion
1/4 cup canola oil
3 teaspoons minced garlic
1-1/2 cups ketchup
1/2 cup cider vinegar
1/3 cup packed brown sugar
1/3 cup Worcestershire sauce
2 teaspoons chili powder
1/2 teaspoon cayenne pepper
1/2 teaspoon ground cumin
1/8 teaspoon hot pepper sauce
1/4 cup cider vinegar
1/4 cup olive oil
1/8 teaspoon salt
1/8 teaspoon pepper
30 frozen chicken wingettes, thawed

For barbecue sauce, in large saucepan, saute onion in oil until tender. Add garlic; cook 1 minute longer. Stir in the ketchup, vinegar, brown sugar, Worcestershire sauce, chili powder, cayenne and cumin. Simmer, uncovered, for 8-10 minutes, stirring often. Remove from the heat; stir in pepper sauce. Set aside 2/3 cup for serving.

In a large resealable plastic bag, combine the vinegar, olive oil, salt and pepper; add chicken wings in batches and turn to coat.

Using long-handled tongs, moisten a paper towel with cooking oil and lightly coat the grill rack. Grill wings, covered, over medium heat or broil 4 in. from the heat for 12-16 minutes, turning occasionally. Brush with some of the barbecue sauce.

Grill, uncovered, 8-10 minutes longer or until the juices run clear, basting and turning several times. Serve with the reserved barbecue sauce.

YIELD: 2-1/2 dozen.

linda gardner
RICHMOND, VIRGINIA

My husband always calls this recipe finger lickin' good! The sweet-and-spicy flavor really is to die for! The sauce is also great on chicken breasts.

CHICKEN VEGGIE STRUDEL

PREP: 30 min. | **BAKE:** 35 min.

3 cups cubed cooked chicken
3 cups fresh broccoli florets
3 cups fresh cauliflowerets
3 cups finely chopped carrots
2 cups (8 ounces) shredded cheddar cheese
2 cups (8 ounces) shredded Swiss cheese
1 cup chopped onion
3 eggs
2 garlic cloves, minced
2 tablespoons minced fresh parsley
2 teaspoons *each* dried basil, tarragon and thyme
2 teaspoons pepper
2 tablespoons plus 1-1/2 cups butter, *divided*
2 tablespoons all-purpose flour
1 cup milk
24 sheets phyllo dough (14 inches x 9 inches)
1 package (15 ounces) seasoned bread crumbs

In a large bowl, combine the first seven ingredients. In a small bowl, beat the eggs. Stir in the garlic, parsley, basil, tarragon, thyme and pepper. Add to chicken mixture; toss to coat. In a small saucepan, melt 2 tablespoons butter. Stir in flour until smooth; gradually stir in milk. Bring to a boil; cook and stir for 2 minutes or until thickened. Pour over chicken mixture; toss to coat.

Melt remaining butter. Place one sheet of phyllo dough on a work surface (keep remaining dough covered with plastic wrap and a damp towel to avoid drying out). Brush with butter; sprinkle with bread crumbs. Repeat layers five times.

Spread about 3-1/3 cups of filling down the center of dough to within 1 in. of edges. Fold short sides 1 in. over filling. Roll up jelly-roll style, starting with a long side. Brush with the butter. Place seam side down in an ungreased 15-in. x 10-in. x 1-in. baking pan.

Make three more strudels with remaining phyllo, butter and filling. Bake at 375° for 35-40 minutes or until golden brown.

YIELD: 4 loaves (6 servings each).

debra mckim
HASTINGS, NEBRASKA

I often serve this hearty entree at dinner parties and usually keep a few extra strudels in the freezer for unexpected company.

MENU planning

For an appetizer buffet that serves as the meal, offer five or six different items (including some substantial selections) and plan on eight to nine pieces per guest. If you'll also be serving a meal, two to three pieces per person is sufficient.

MINI CORN DOGS

PREP/TOTAL TIME: 30 min.

1-2/3 cups all-purpose flour
1/3 cup cornmeal
3 teaspoons baking powder
1 teaspoon salt
3 tablespoons cold butter
1 tablespoon shortening
1 egg
3/4 cup milk
24 miniature hot dogs
HONEY MUSTARD SAUCE:
1/3 cup honey
1/3 cup prepared mustard
1 tablespoon molasses

In a large bowl, combine the first four ingredients. Cut in butter and shortening until mixture resembles coarse crumbs. Beat egg and milk; stir into dry ingredients until a soft dough forms.

Turn onto a lightly floured surface; knead 6-8 times or until smooth. Roll out to 1/4-in. thickness. Cut with a 2-1/4-in. biscuit cutter. Fold each dough circle over a hot dog and press edges to seal (dough will be sticky). Place on greased baking sheets.

Bake corn dogs at 450° for 10-12 minutes or until golden brown. In a small bowl, combine the sauce ingredients. Serve with the corn dogs.

YIELD: 2 dozen.

geralyn harrington
FLORAL PARK, NEW YORK

Summertime means county fairs and corn dogs! I make my own by wrapping cornmeal dough around mini hot dogs. They're so tasty dipped in the honey-mustard sauce.

TACO DIP

PREP/TOTAL TIME: 25 min.

12 ounces cream cheese, softened
1/2 cup sour cream
1 teaspoon chili powder
1/2 cup salsa
2 cups shredded iceberg lettuce
1 cup (4 ounces) shredded cheddar cheese
1 cup (4 ounces) shredded Monterey Jack cheese
1/2 cup diced tomato
1 can (4-1/4 ounces) sliced ripe olives, drained, optional
Tortilla chips

In a large bowl, beat the cream cheese, sour cream and chili powder until smooth; stir in salsa. Spread cream cheese mixture over a large serving platter. Cover and refrigerate for 15 minutes.

Layer cream cheese mixture with lettuce, cheddar cheese, Monterey Jack cheese, tomato and olives if desired. Serve with the tortilla chips.

YIELD: about 6-1/2 cups.

aleta amick
MADISON, WISCONSIN

This classic dip recipe is one of my favorites. It's so easy to make and always goes over well at parties and get-togethers.

HAM 'N' CHEESE BISCUIT STACKS

PREP: 1 hour | **BAKE:** 10 min. + cooling

2 tubes (12 ounces *each*) refrigerated buttermilk biscuits
3/4 cup stone-ground mustard, *divided*
1/2 cup butter, softened
1/4 cup chopped green onions
1/4 cup mayonnaise
1/4 cup honey
10 thick slices deli ham
10 slices Swiss cheese
2-1/2 cups shredded romaine
40 frilled toothpicks
20 pitted ripe olives, drained and patted dry
20 pimiento-stuffed olives, drained and patted dry

Cut each biscuit in half, forming half circles. Place 2 in. apart on ungreased baking sheets. Spread each with 1/2 teaspoon mustard. Bake at 400° for 8-10 minutes or until golden brown. Remove from the pans to wire racks to cool.

In a small bowl, combine the butter and onions. In another bowl, combine the mayonnaise, honey and remaining mustard. Cut each slice of ham into four rectangles; cut each slice of cheese into four triangles.

Split each biscuit in half; spread bottom halves with butter mixture. Layer with one ham piece, one cheese piece and 1 tablespoon romaine on each biscuit bottom.

Spread mustard mixture over biscuit tops; place over romaine. Thread toothpicks through olives; insert into stacks. Refrigerate any leftovers.

YIELD: 40 appetizers.

kelly williams
MORGANVILLE, NEW JERSEY

Ham and cheese lovers will stand in line for these fancy finger sandwiches. They also add a pretty touch to any table setting.

TEA party

Include these delicate finger sandwiches the next time you're hosting an afternoon tea party or bridal shower luncheon. They pair well with scones, tea cakes, fruit and cheese.

CLASSIC ANTIPASTO PLATTER

PREP/TOTAL TIME: 40 min.

1 pound fresh mozzarella cheese, sliced

1 jar (16 ounces) pickled pepper rings, drained

1 jar (10 ounces) colossal Sicilian olives, drained

4 large tomatoes, cut into wedges

6 hard-cooked eggs, sliced

1 medium cucumber, sliced

1 medium sweet red pepper, julienned

1 can (3-3/4 ounces) sardines, drained

1 can (2 ounces) anchovy fillets, drained

1/2 pound thinly sliced hard salami, prosciutto *or* smoked ham, optional

1/4 cup olive oil

1 teaspoon grated Parmesan cheese

1 teaspoon minced fresh oregano

1/8 teaspoon salt

1/8 teaspoon pepper

On a large serving platter, arrange the first nine ingredients; adding sliced meats if desired. In a small bowl, whisk the oil, cheese, oregano, salt and pepper; drizzle over antipasto.

YIELD: 14-16 servings.

weda mosellie
PHILLIPSBURG, NEW JERSEY

This large antipasto platter is a must-have item on my menu whenever I have friends over for a pasta bar soiree. With delicious food and a little Dean Martin playing in the background, it truly feels like a night in Italy. Mangia!

BEER-BATTERED POTATO WEDGES

PREP: 25 min. | **COOK:** 5 min./batch

    4 medium baking potatoes
    1 cup all-purpose flour
1/4 cup milk
    1 egg
    1 tablespoon seasoned salt
    1 tablespoon canola oil
1/2 teaspoon pepper
1/2 cup beer *or* nonalcoholic beer
Oil for deep-fat frying
Sour cream, optional

Scrub and the pierce potatoes. Microwave, uncovered, on high for 10-12 minutes or just until tender, turning once.

Meanwhile, in a shallow bowl, whisk the flour, milk, egg, seasoned salt, oil and pepper until smooth. Stir in beer; set aside.

When the potatoes are cool enough to handle, cut each into 12 wedges. In an electric skillet or deep-fat fryer, heat oil to 375°. Dip potato wedges into batter. Fry in batches for 3-4 minutes or until golden brown, turning occasionally. Drain on paper towels. Serve with sour cream if desired.

YIELD: 4 dozen.

pat miller
LYNNVILLE, TENNESSEE

These yummy wedges are great for large and small gatherings alike, especially backyard barbecues. The spuds taste just like those you find in retro diners.

MOZZARELLA STICKS

PREP/TOTAL TIME: 20 min.

    12 pieces string cheese
    12 egg roll wrappers
Oil for deep-fat frying
Marinara *or* spaghetti sauce

Place a piece of string cheese near the bottom corner of one egg roll wrapper (keep remaining wrappers covered with a damp paper towel until ready to use). Fold bottom corner over cheese. Roll up halfway; fold sides toward center over cheese. Moisten remaining corner with water; roll up tightly to seal. Repeat with remaining wrappers and cheese.

In an electric skillet, heat 1/2 in. of oil to 375°. Fry sticks, a few at a time, for 30-60 seconds on each side or until golden brown. Drain on the paper towels. Serve with the marinara sauce.

YIELD: 1 dozen.

shirley warren
THIENSVILLE, WISCONSIN

You won't believe something this easy could taste so fantastic! Crunchy on the outside, gooey on the inside...this is a treat everyone will love. Kids can help wrap them, too.

BEER DIP

PREP/TOTAL TIME: 5 min.

> 2 packages (8 ounces *each*) cream cheese, softened
> 1/3 cup beer *or* nonalcoholic beer
> 1 envelope ranch salad dressing mix
> 2 cups (8 ounces) shredded cheddar cheese

Pretzels

In a large bowl, beat the cream cheese, beer and dressing until smooth. Stir in cheddar cheese. Serve dip with pretzels. Refrigerate any leftovers.

YIELD: 3-1/2 cups.

michelle long
NEW CASTLE, COLORADO

Ranch dressing mix flavors this cheesy, fast-to-fix dip. I take it to game-day parties along with a bag of pretzels, and I'm always asked for the recipe. It's one of those snacks that once you start, you just can't stop!

DELIGHTFUL dip

This beer dip can be made with your favorite type of beer, including nonalcoholic. Serve it alongside pretzels, tortilla chips or assorted fresh cut vegetables.

CRUNCHY POTATO MOUNDS

PREP: 30 min. + chilling | **BAKE:** 30 min.

> 1/2 cup Dijon mustard
> 1/3 cup honey
> 2 tablespoons plus 1/2 cup mayonnaise, *divided*
> 3-1/2 cups crushed cornflakes
> 2 cups cold homemade mashed potatoes (without added milk and butter)
> 2 cups finely chopped fully cooked ham
> 1 cup (4 ounces) shredded Swiss cheese
> 1/4 cup finely chopped onion
> 1/4 cup milk
> 1 egg, lightly beaten
> 1 teaspoon yellow mustard

In a small bowl, combine the Dijon mustard, honey and 2 tablespoons mayonnaise until smooth. Cover and refrigerate the mustard sauce until serving.

Place cornflakes in a shallow bowl. In another bowl, combine the mashed potatoes, ham, cheese, onion, milk, egg, yellow mustard and remaining mayonnaise. Shape into 1-in. balls; roll in cornflakes.

Place in three greased 15-in. x 10-in. x 1-in. baking pans. Cover and refrigerate for at least 1 hour.

Bake at 350° for 30 minutes or until golden brown. Serve appetizers warm with mustard sauce.

YIELD: 5 dozen (1 cup sauce).

mary relyea
CANASTOTA, NEW YORK

This is one of my best hors d'oeuvres to bring to potlucks. These crunchy little bites disappear fast!

VEGGIE CHEESE SPREAD

PREP/TOTAL TIME: 15 min.

- 1 package (8 ounces) cream cheese, softened
- 1/2 cup sour cream
- 1/4 cup mayonnaise
- 1 cup seafood cocktail sauce
- 2 cups (8 ounces) shredded part-skim mozzarella cheese
- 1 medium green pepper, chopped
- 3 green onions, chopped
- 1 medium tomato, chopped

Assorted crackers *or* tortilla chips

In a small bowl, beat the cream cheese, sour cream and mayonnaise until smooth. Spread onto a serving plate; top with seafood sauce. Sprinkle with half of the cheese and vegetables; repeat layers.

Cover and chill until serving. Serve with crackers or tortilla chips.

YIELD: 6-1/4 cups.

sue fraser
GRANDE PRAIRIE, ALBERTA

This easy cheese spread is an all-time family favorite. It's an ideal addition to an appetizer buffet and is also a time-saver, as it can be made in advance. If you like, sprinkle tiny shrimp over the seafood sauce for a fancy touch.

MANDARIN SALSA

PREP/TOTAL TIME: 25 min.

- 5 plum tomatoes, chopped
- 1 large sweet onion, chopped
- 2 jalapeno peppers, seeded and chopped
- 2 tablespoons sugar
- 2 tablespoons minced fresh cilantro
- 2 tablespoons lime juice
- 1 teaspoon salt
- 1 teaspoon minced garlic
- 1 can (15 ounces) mandarin oranges, drained

Tortilla chips

In a small bowl, combine the first eight ingredients. Gently stir in mandarin oranges. Chill until serving. Drain before serving if necessary. Serve with tortilla chips.

YIELD: 4 cups.

yvonne opp
GREENVILLE, PENNSYLVANIA

Sweet mandarin oranges temper the boldness of cilantro, jalapeno and onion in this salsa, creating an impressive and colorful combination.

PIZZA FONDUE

PREP/TOTAL TIME: 25 min.

- 1/2 pound ground beef
- 1 cup chopped fresh mushrooms
- 1 medium onion, chopped
- 1 garlic clove, minced
- 1 tablespoon cornstarch
- 1-1/2 teaspoons fennel seed
- 1-1/2 teaspoons dried oregano
- 1/4 teaspoon garlic powder
- 2 cans (15 ounces *each*) pizza sauce
- 2-1/2 cups (10 ounces) shredded cheddar cheese
- 1 cup (4 ounces) shredded part-skim mozzarella cheese
- 2 tablespoons chopped ripe olives
- Breadsticks, bagel chips, baked pita chips *and/or* tortilla chips

In a large skillet, cook the beef, mushrooms and onion over medium heat until meat is no longer pink. Add garlic; cook 1 minute longer. Drain. Stir in the cornstarch, fennel, oregano and garlic powder until blended. Stir in pizza sauce.

Bring to a boil; cook and stir for 1-2 minutes or until thickened. Gradually stir in the cheeses until melted. Stir in the olives. Keep warm.

Serve with breadsticks, bagel chips, pita chips and/or tortilla chips.

YIELD: 5-1/2 cups.

margaret schissler
MILWAUKEE, WISCONSIN

Great for a party or game-day gathering, this hearty appetizer can be made with Italian sausage instead of ground beef if you prefer. Add a little more pizza sauce if the mixture is too thick.

CANNELLINI BEAN HUMMUS

PREP/TOTAL TIME: 5 min.

- 2 garlic cloves, peeled
- 1 can (15 ounces) white kidney *or* cannellini beans, rinsed and drained
- 1/4 cup tahini
- 3 tablespoons lemon juice
- 1-1/2 teaspoons ground cumin
- 1/4 teaspoon salt
- 1/4 teaspoon crushed red pepper flakes
- 2 tablespoons minced fresh parsley
- Pita breads, cut into wedges

Place garlic in a food processor; cover and process until minced. Add the beans, tahini, lemon juice, cumin, salt and pepper flakes; cover and process until smooth.

Transfer mixture to a small bowl; stir in parsley. Refrigerate until serving. Serve with pita wedges.

YIELD: 1-1/4 cups.

marina castle
NORTH HOLLYWOOD, CALIFORNIA

My version of hummus features a delightful nuttiness from tahini, a peanut butter-like paste made from ground sesame seeds. The beans pack a lot of protein so it's a healthy snack to serve kids at birthday parties.

FRIED CHEESE RAVIOLI

PREP: 15 min. | **COOK:** 20 min.

- 1 package (9 ounces) refrigerated cheese ravioli
- 2 eggs
- 2 cups seasoned bread crumbs
- 1/2 cup shredded Parmesan cheese
- 3 teaspoons dried basil
- 1/2 cup canola oil, *divided*

Additional shredded Parmesan cheese, optional

- 1 cup marinara sauce *or* meatless spaghetti sauce, warmed

Cook the ravioli according to the package directions; drain and pat dry. In a shallow bowl, lightly beat the eggs. In another shallow bowl, combine the bread crumbs, cheese and basil. Dip ravioli in eggs, then in bread crumb mixture.

In a large skillet or deep-fat fryer, heat 1/4 cup oil over medium heat. Fry ravioli in batches for 30-60 seconds on each side or until golden brown and crispy; drain on paper towels. Halfway through frying, replace the oil; wipe out skillet with paper towels if necessary.

Sprinkle with additional cheese if desired. Serve with marinara sauce.

YIELD: about 3-1/2 dozen.

kate dampier
QUAIL VALLEY, CALIFORNIA

This crunchy breaded ravioli is bound to be the hit of your party. The golden-brown pillows are easy to pick up and dip in marinara or pizza sauce.

COCOA FOR A CROWD

PREP/TOTAL TIME: 15 min.

- 5 cups baking cocoa
- 3 cups sugar
- 2 teaspoons salt
- 5 quarts water, *divided*
- 10 quarts milk
- 1 quart heavy whipping cream
- 2 tablespoons vanilla extract

Whipped cream and additional baking cocoa

In each of two large stockpots, combine 2-1/2 cups cocoa, 1-1/2 cups sugar and 1 teaspoon salt. Gradually stir 5 cups water into each pot. Bring to a boil; reduce heat. Whisk in the milk, cream and remaining water; heat through. Remove from the heat; stir in vanilla. Garnish with whipped cream and additional cocoa.

YIELD: 65 (1-cup) servings.

julia livingston
FROSTPROOF, FLORIDA

You'll warm hearts with this rich, satisfying cocoa. It's the perfect beverage to indulge in after ice skating, sledding or any outdoor winter gathering.

CHICKEN AND PORK EGG ROLLS

PREP: 2-1/2 hours | **COOK:** 30 min.

1 medium head cabbage, shredded
3 celery ribs, chopped
1 can (8 ounces) bamboo shoots, drained and chopped
1 can (8 ounces) sliced water chestnuts, drained and chopped
5 green onions, chopped
2 tablespoons canola oil
1 to 2 garlic cloves, minced
2-1/4 cups diced cooked chicken breasts
2 cups diced cooked pork
1/4 cup chicken broth
1/4 cup soy sauce
1/4 teaspoon salt
1/4 teaspoon pepper
2 packages (16 ounces *each*) egg roll wrappers
1 egg, lightly beaten
Additional oil for deep-fat frying

SAUCE:

1-1/2 cups unsweetened pineapple juice
3/4 cup cider vinegar
1/2 cup packed brown sugar
1 tablespoon soy sauce
1/8 to 1/4 teaspoon white pepper
3 tablespoons cornstarch
2 tablespoons cold water

In a large nonstick wok, stir-fry the cabbage, celery, bamboo shoots, water chestnuts and onions in oil until crisp-tender. Add the garlic; cook 1 minute longer. Stir in the chicken, pork, broth, soy sauce, salt and pepper. Cook and stir for 1 minute or until heated through.

Position an egg roll wrapper with one point toward you. Place about 1/4 cup meat mixture in the center. Fold bottom corner over filling; fold sides toward center over filling. Roll toward the remaining point. Moisten top corner with beaten egg; press to seal. Repeat with the remaining wrappers and filling.

In an electric skillet or deep-fat fryer, heat oil to 375°. Fry egg rolls, a few at a time, for 1-2 minutes on each side or until golden brown. Drain on paper towels.

In a saucepan, combine the first five sauce ingredients. Bring to a boil. Combine the cornstarch and cold water until smooth; stir into boiling mixture. Cook and stir for 2 minutes or until thickened. Serve warm with the egg rolls.

YIELD: about 3 dozen.

bruce beaver
FLORISSANT, MISSOURI

These egg rolls are a delightful addition to a backyard luau. I developed this recipe after watching my neighbor's wife make crispy egg rolls while I was stationed in Hawaii.

TRY stemware

With the assortment of foods served at potlucks, guests will likely have their plates piled high! Instead of having them juggle already-full plates, use stemware to dish out single-serving portions of the dipping sauce for these egg rolls. Try this for similar dips or shrimp cocktail.

HONEY BARBECUE WINGS

PREP: 40 min. + marinating | **BAKE:** 25 min.

2 garlic cloves, minced
1 tablespoon canola oil
1/2 cup honey
1/4 cup ketchup
2 tablespoons orange juice
2 tablespoons lemon juice
2 tablespoons soy sauce
2 teaspoons ground ginger
2 teaspoons cider vinegar
1 teaspoon Worcestershire sauce
1 teaspoon Dijon mustard
1/4 teaspoon pepper
1/4 teaspoon hot pepper sauce
18 whole chicken wings
 (about 3-3/4 pounds)

In a small saucepan, saute garlic in oil for 1 minute. Stir in the honey, ketchup, juices, soy sauce, ginger, vinegar, Worcestershire sauce, mustard, pepper and hot pepper sauce. Bring to a boil. Reduce heat; simmer, uncovered, for 15 minutes. Remove from the heat; cool to room temperature.

Cut chicken wings into three sections; discard wing tip sections. Place wings in a large resealable heavy-duty plastic bag; add 3/4 cup cooled honey mixture. Seal bag and turn to coat; refrigerate for 2 hours. Cover and refrigerate remaining honey mixture for basting.

Drain and discard the marinade. Place chicken wings on a greased rack in a large baking pan. Bake at 400° for 10 minutes on each side, basting occasionally with the honey mixture.

Broil 4-6 in. from the heat for 2-3 minutes or until browned and juices run clear.
YIELD: 3 dozen.

diane acord
SAVAGE, MINNESOTA

These chicken wings are mild enough to please even the kids at your party. The honey barbecue sauce is the only one you'll need.

BLACK BEAN QUESADILLAS

PREP/TOTAL TIME: 30 min.

2 cans (15 ounces *each*) black beans, rinsed and drained
1-2/3 cups salsa, *divided*
10 flour tortillas (8 inches)
2 cups (8 ounces) shredded Colby-Monterey Jack cheese
2/3 cup sour cream

In a large bowl, mash the beans; add 1 cup salsa. Place the five tortillas on ungreased baking sheets; spread with bean mixture. Sprinkle with the cheese; top with the remaining tortillas.

Bake at 350° for 15-18 minutes or until crisp and heated through. Cut each quesadilla into six wedges. Serve with sour cream and remaining salsa.

YIELD: 30 wedges.

jane epping
IOWA CITY, IOWA

As a time-pressed cook, I rely on this handy recipe when I need a potluck item or just want a quick meal at home. When I have extra time, I add chopped onion, black olives and green chilies to the beans.

FAST FRUIT PUNCH

PREP/TOTAL TIME: 10 min.

1/2 cup orange breakfast drink mix
4 cups water
1 can (12 ounces) frozen pink lemonade concentrate, thawed
1 can (12 ounces) white grape raspberry juice concentrate
1 can (12 ounces) frozen orange juice concentrate, thawed
2 cups chilled cranberry juice
2 cups chilled pineapple juice
2 bottles (2 liters *each*) lemon-lime soda, chilled
Lemon, lime and orange slices

In a large container or punch bowl, dissolve drink mix in water. Stir in the next five ingredients. Add soda and sliced fruit. Serve the punch immediately.

YIELD: 40 servings (7-3/4 quarts).

joanne stark
WABAMUN, ALBERTA

This family recipe is featured at all of our special events. The pink punch is a pretty addition to any spread.

MAKE-AHEAD MEATBALLS

PREP/TOTAL TIME: 25 min.

4 eggs, lightly beaten
2 cups dry bread crumbs
1/2 cup finely chopped onion
1 tablespoon salt
2 teaspoons Worcestershire sauce
1/2 teaspoon white pepper
4 pounds lean ground beef (90% lean)

In a large bowl, combine the first six ingredients. Crumble the beef over mixture and mix well. Shape into 1-in. balls, about 12 dozen.

Place meatballs on greased racks in shallow baking pans. Bake at 400° for 10-15 minutes or until no longer pink, turning often; drain. Cool.

Place about 30 meatballs into each freezer container. Meatballs may be frozen for up to 3 months.

YIELD: 5 batches (about 30 meatballs per batch).

RUTH ANDREWSON
LEAVENWORTH, WASHINGTON

I keep a supply of these frozen meatballs on hand so I can easily prepare a quick, satisfying nibbler. I start with a versatile meatball mix that makes about 12 dozen meatballs, then freeze them in batches for when I host company or need a dish to bring to an event.

NUT 'N' CORN CLUSTERS

PREP/TOTAL TIME: 30 min.

> 5 quarts popped popcorn
> 2 cups mixed nuts
> 1-1/2 teaspoons butter
> 1 cup sugar
> 1/2 cup honey
> 1/2 cup corn syrup
> 1 cup peanut butter
> 1 teaspoon vanilla extract
> 1 teaspoon molasses

Line baking sheets with waxed paper; set aside. Combine popcorn and nuts in a large roasting pan. Bake at 250° for 10-15 minutes or until warm. Meanwhile, grease the sides of a heavy saucepan with 1-1/2 teaspoons butter. Combine the sugar, honey and corn syrup in saucepan. Bring to a boil over medium heat, stirring constantly. Boil for 2 minutes without stirring.

Remove from the heat; stir in peanut butter, vanilla and molasses. Pour over warm popcorn mixture and stir to coat. Working quickly, use buttered hands to form mixture into 1-1/2-in. clusters. Place on prepared baking sheets to dry. Store in an airtight container at room temperature.
YIELD: about 12 dozen.

maryeileen jahnke
SOUTH MILWAUKEE, WISCONSIN

I can tell this recipe has served me faithfully for a long time by the old dog-eared recipe card. Folks love to munch on these crisp caramel corn clusters at holiday gatherings as well as game-day parties.

SUN-DRIED TOMATO DIP

PREP/TOTAL TIME: 10 min.

> 1 package (8 ounces) cream cheese, softened
> 1/2 cup sour cream
> 1/2 cup mayonnaise
> 1/4 cup oil-packed sun-dried tomatoes, drained and patted dry
> 1/2 teaspoon salt
> 1/4 teaspoon pepper
> 1/4 teaspoon hot pepper sauce
> 2 green onions, sliced
> Assorted crackers *and/or* fresh vegetables

Place the first seven ingredients in a food processor; cover and process until blended. Add green onions; cover and pulse until finely chopped. Serve the dip with crackers and/or vegetables.
YIELD: 2 cups.

andrea reynolds
ROCKY RIVER, OHIO

I love to serve this dip for just about any occasion. It's so quick and easy to whip up and full of flavor!

CAESAR SALSA BAGUETTE SLICES

PREP/TOTAL TIME: 25 min.

2 cups chopped seeded tomatoes

3 tablespoons minced fresh chervil
   or 1 tablespoon dried chervil

1 tablespoon minced fresh cilantro

1 tablespoon minced fresh parsley

1 tablespoon capers, drained

1/2 teaspoon hot pepper sauce

2 tablespoons plus 1-1/2 teaspoons olive oil

4-1/2 teaspoons lemon juice

2-1/2 teaspoons red wine vinegar

1 shallot, finely chopped

1 garlic clove, minced

1/2 teaspoon anchovy paste

1/8 teaspoon grated lemon peel

1 loaf (10-1/2 ounces) French bread
   baguette, cut into 1/2-inch slices and
   toasted

In a small bowl, combine the tomatoes, chervil, cilantro, parsley, capers and hot pepper sauce.

In another bowl, whisk the oil, lemon juice, vinegar, shallot, garlic, anchovy paste and lemon peel. Drizzle over the tomato mixture; toss to coat. Serve salsa with toasted baguette slices.

YIELD: 32 appetizers.

jodie gharbi
SHREVEPORT, LOUISIANA

I love throwing themed get-togethers, and this appetizer was the hit of "Mediterranean Night." The garden-fresh flavors in the salsa are outstanding with a crusty baguette.

SHRIMP APPETIZERS WITH SEAFOOD SAUCE

PREP/TOTAL TIME: 20 min.

2 packages (*9 ounces each*) frozen breaded jumbo butterfly shrimp

1/2 cup ketchup

1/2 cup chili sauce

1 tablespoon lemon juice

1 tablespoon prepared horseradish

1/8 teaspoon hot pepper sauce

Bake shrimp according to package directions. Meanwhile, in a small bowl, combine the remaining ingredients. Arrange shrimp on serving platter; serve with sauce.

YIELD: 26 appetizers.

alyce wyman
PEMBINA, NORTH DAKOTA

My husband and I treat ourselves to these once or twice a month when we host dinner parties for friends. The shrimp goes well with other staple items on an appetizer buffet.

SUPER NACHO APPETIZER

PREP: 15 min. | **BAKE:** 20 min.

- 1/2 pound ground beef
- 1/2 pound uncooked chorizo
- 2 cans (16 ounces *each*) refried beans
- 1 can (4 ounces) chopped green chilies
- 3 cups (12 ounces) shredded cheddar cheese
- 3/4 cup bottled taco sauce
- 3 large ripe avocados, peeled and pitted
- 1 tablespoon lemon juice
- 1/4 teaspoon garlic salt
- 1 cup (8 ounces) sour cream
- 1 medium tomato, chopped
- 1/2 cup sliced pimiento-stuffed olives

Additional shredded cheddar cheese
Tortilla chips

Crumble beef and chorizo into a large skillet; cook over medium heat until no longer pink. Drain well. In a greased 13-in. x 9-in. baking dish, layer the meat mixture, refried beans, chilies, cheese and taco sauce. Bake, uncovered, at 400° for 20 minutes.

For guacamole, in a small bowl, mash the avocados. Stir in lemon juice and garlic salt. Cool nacho mixture for 5 minutes. Top with guacamole, sour cream, tomato and olives. Garnish with additional cheese. Serve with tortilla chips.

YIELD: 30 servings.

connie bolton
SAN ANTONIO, TEXAS

Mexican food is popular for potluck gatherings here in South Texas, and this dish always brings oohs and aahs. It's usually served as an hors d'oeuvre, but it's also good as a main course served alongside a salad and Spanish rice.

SPICED NUTS

PREP/TOTAL TIME: 20 min. + cooling

- 1/4 cup butter, cubed
- 1/2 cup plus 3 tablespoons sugar, *divided*
- 2 teaspoons ground cardamom
- 1 cup salted cashews
- 1 cup salted peanuts
- 1 cup pecan halves

In a large heavy skillet, melt butter. Add 1/2 cup sugar; cook and stir over high heat until sugar is dissolved. Meanwhile, place cardamom and remaining sugar in a large bowl; set aside.

Reduce heat to medium; add the cashews, peanuts and pecans to butter mixture. Cook and stir until the nuts are toasted, about 3 minutes. Add hot nuts to reserved cardamom mixture; toss to coat. Spread on foil to cool.

YIELD: 3-1/2 cups.

judi oudekerk
BUFFALO, MINNESOTA

These seasoned mixed nuts make great hostess gifts or mini treats to be tucked in a present or stocking. I like cardamom so I often add another teaspoon to this recipe.

DEVILED EGGS EXTRAORDINAIRE

PREP/TOTAL TIME: 40 min.

24 hard-cooked eggs, peeled
4 ounces cream cheese, softened
1/2 cup mayonnaise
2 tablespoons prepared mustard
1 teaspoon cider vinegar
1/4 teaspoon salt
1/4 teaspoon onion powder

Cut eggs in half lengthwise. Remove yolks; set whites aside. In a small bowl, mash yolks. Add the cream cheese, mayonnaise, mustard, vinegar, salt and onion powder; mix well. Stuff or pipe into egg whites. Refrigerate until serving.

YIELD: 4 dozen.

carol ross
ANCHORAGE, ALASKA

These creamy deviled eggs boast a pleasant mustard flavor. They're perfect for summertime picnics but could also work for formal occasions when garnished with tiny amounts of red or black caviar.

CHEERY CHERRY PUNCH

PREP/TOTAL TIME: 15 min. + freezing

3 packages (3 ounces *each*) cherry gelatin
2 to 3 cups sugar
6 cups boiling water
1 can (46 ounces) unsweetened pineapple juice
1 can (12 ounces) frozen orange juice concentrate, thawed
1 can (12 ounces) frozen lemonade concentrate, thawed
1 gallon cold water
2 bottles (2 liters *each*) ginger ale

In a stockpot, dissolve gelatin and sugar in boiling water. Stir in the pineapple juice, concentrates and cold water.

Transfer to several freezer containers. Cover and freeze for at least 8 hours or overnight, stirring several times. Just before serving, transfer to a large punch bowl; stir in ginger ale.

YIELD: 60 (4-ounce) servings.

florence grewe
LONG PRAIRIE, MINNESOTA

I reach for this recipe whenever I need to quench the thirst of a hungry crowd. It's a refreshing beverage that nicely complements a variety of meals.

TEXAS JALAPENO JELLY

PREP: 15 min. | **PROCESS:** 10 min.

2 jalapeno peppers, seeded and chopped
3 medum green peppers, cut into 1-inch pieces, *divided*
1-1/2 cups white vinegar, *divided*
6-1/2 cups sugar
1/2 to 1 teaspoon cayenne pepper
2 pouches (3 ounces *each*) liquid fruit pectin
About 6 drops green food coloring, optional
Cream cheese and crackers, optional

In a blender or food processor, place the jalapenos, half of the green peppers and 1/2 cup vinegar; cover and process until pureed. Transfer to a large Dutch oven.

Repeat with remaining green peppers and another 1/2 cup vinegar. Add the sugar, cayenne and remaining vinegar to pan. Bring to a rolling boil over high heat, stirring constantly. Quickly stir in pectin. Return to a rolling boil; boil for 1 minute, stirring constantly.

Remove from the heat; skim off foam. Add food coloring if desired. Carefully ladle hot mixture into hot half-pint jars, leaving 1/4-in. headspace. Remove air bubbles; wipe rims and adjust lids.

Process for 10 minutes in a boiling-water canner. Serve over cream cheese with crackers if desired.

YIELD: 7 half-pints.

EDITOR'S NOTE: When cutting hot peppers, disposable gloves are recommended. Avoid touching your face.

lori mcmullen
VICTORIA, TEXAS

This deliciously different jelly is a great complement to a Tex-Mex buffet. The jelly is not too hot and features a surprising sweetness that will tingle taste buds.

SWEET 'N' SOY SNACK MEATBALLS

PREP: 25 min. | **BAKE:** 20 min.

1 egg
1/4 cup finely chopped onion
1 tablespoon ketchup
1-1/2 teaspoons salt
1/2 teaspoon pepper
1/2 teaspoon seasoned salt
1/2 teaspoon Worcestershire sauce
2 pounds ground beef
3/4 cup dry bread crumbs

SAUCE:
2 tablespoons plus 1-1/2 teaspoons cornstarch
1 cup orange marmalade
3 to 4 tablespoons soy sauce
2 tablespoons lemon juice
2 garlic cloves, minced

In a large bowl, combine the first seven ingredients. Crumble the beef over mixture. Sprinkle with the bread crumbs; mix gently. Shape into 1-in. balls.

Place meatballs on a greased rack in a shallow baking pan. Bake, uncovered, at 350° for 20-25 minutes or until meat is no longer pink; drain.

Meanwhile, in a small saucepan, combine the sauce ingredients. Bring to a boil; cook and stir for 2 minutes or until thickened. Transfer meatballs to a serving dish; serve with the sauce.

YIELD: 5 dozen.

jodi klassen
COALDALE, ALBERTA

My mom gave me this recipe when I was a newlywed. The tender meatballs are quick to fix and disappear in a flash.

SPRUCED-UP CHEESE SPREAD

PREP/TOTAL TIME: 20 min.

1 jar (4 ounces) diced pimientos, drained, *divided*

1 small onion, grated

1 cup mayonnaise

1 to 2 tablespoons prepared mustard

1 tablespoon Worcestershire sauce

1 teaspoon celery seed

1/2 teaspoon paprika

1/4 teaspoon garlic salt

3 cups (12 ounces) finely shredded sharp cheddar cheese

2 tablespoons finely chopped pecans

Minced fresh parsley

Assorted crackers

Set aside 2 tablespoons pimientos for the topping. In a large bowl, combine the remaining pimientos and the next seven ingredients. Stir in cheese.

Transfer to a serving bowl; sprinkle with pecans, parsley and reserved pimientos. Serve with crackers.

YIELD: 4 cups.

judy grimes
BRANDON, MISSISSIPPI

Folks will quickly gather around the appetizer buffet when this zippy spread is on the table. It's delicious served on snack rye bread or assorted crackers.

MEXICAN CHEESECAKE

PREP: 20 min. | **BAKE:** 30 min. + chilling

- 2 packages (8 ounces *each*) reduced-fat cream cheese
- 1-1/4 cups reduced-fat sour cream, *divided*
- 1 envelope taco seasoning
- 3 eggs, lightly beaten
- 1-1/2 cups (6 ounces) shredded sharp cheddar cheese
- 1 can (4 ounces) chopped green chilies
- 1 cup chunky salsa, drained

Tortilla chips *or* fresh vegetables

In a large bowl, beat the cream cheese, 1/2 cup sour cream and taco seasoning until smooth. Add the eggs; beat on low speed just until combined. Stir in the cheddar cheese and chilies.

Transfer to a greased 9-in. springform pan. Place on a baking sheet. Bake at 350° for 25-30 minutes or until center is almost set. Spread remaining sour cream evenly over top. Bake 5-8 minutes longer or until topping is set.

Cool the cheesecake on a wire rack for 10 minutes. Carefully run a knife around the edge of the pan to loosen; cool 1 hour longer. Refrigerate overnight.

Just before serving, spread the salsa over the cheesecake. Serve with tortilla chips or vegetables.

YIELD: 24 servings.

sandy burkett
GALENA, OHIO

Guests will rave over this savory cheesecake appetizer. It's great for Mexican-themed potlucks or Cinco de Mayo parties.

PARTY TIME MINI CHEESEBURGERS

PREP/TOTAL TIME: 30 min.

- 1 egg, lightly beaten
- 2 tablespoons dill pickle relish
- 2 tablespoons ketchup
- 2 teaspoons Worcestershire sauce
- 2 teaspoons prepared mustard
- 1/4 cup quick-cooking oats
- 1/4 teaspoon pepper
- 1/8 teaspoon garlic powder
- 1 pound ground beef
- 3 to 4 slices process American cheese
- 10 dinner rolls, split

In a large bowl, combine the first eight ingredients. Crumble beef over mixture and mix well. Shape into 10 patties. Broil 3-4 in. from the heat for 4-6 minutes on each side or until a meat thermometer reads 160° and juices run clear.

Meanwhile, cut the cheese slices into thirds. Immediately place cheese on burgers; serve on rolls.

YIELD: 10 servings.

taste of home test kitchen

Kids and adults alike will love these moist and mouthwatering mini burgers from our home economists. Juiced up with pickle relish and topped with cheese, these sliders will disappear in no time!

p. 54

p. 63

p. 59

brunch
buffets

HAM BUNDLES

PREP: 55 min. + rising | BAKE: 20 min.

1 package (1/4 ounce) active dry yeast
1/4 cup warm water (110° to 115°)
3/4 cup warm milk (110° to 115°)
1/2 cup shortening
3 eggs, lightly beaten
1/2 cup sugar
1-1/2 teaspoons salt
4-1/2 to 4-3/4 cups all-purpose flour

FILLING:
1 large onion, finely chopped
5 tablespoons butter, *divided*
4 cups cubed fully cooked ham, coarsely ground
4 bacon strips, cooked and crumbled, optional
1/4 to 1/3 cup sliced pimiento-stuffed olives, optional
1/2 to 3/4 cup shredded cheddar cheese, optional

In a large bowl, dissolve the yeast in warm water. Add the milk, shortening, eggs, sugar, salt and 2 cups flour; beat dough until smooth. Add enough remaining flour to form a soft dough.

Turn onto a lightly floured surface; knead until smooth and elastic, about 8 minutes. Place in a greased bowl, turning once to grease top. Cover and let rise in a warm place until doubled, about 1 hour.

Meanwhile, in a large skillet, saute onion in 2 tablespoons butter until tender. Add ham and mix well; set aside.

Punch dough down. Turn onto a lightly floured surface; divide into thirds. Roll each portion into a 16-in. x 8-in. rectangle. Cut each rectangle into eight squares. Place a tablespoonful of ham mixture in the center of each square. Add bacon, olives and/or cheese if desired. Fold up corners to center of dough; seal edges.

Place 2 in. apart on greased baking sheets. Cover and let rise in a warm place until doubled, about 45 minutes.

Melt remaining butter; brush over dough. Bake at 350° for 16-20 minutes or until golden brown and filling is heated through. Refrigerate leftovers.

YIELD: 2 dozen.

chris sendelbach
HENRY, ILLINOIS

Whenever I serve ham, I can't wait for the leftovers so I can whip up these yummy breakfast bundles.

SUNSHINE BAKED EGGS

PREP: 15 min. | BAKE: 40 min.

1 pound sliced bacon
14 eggs
1-1/3 cups 4% cottage cheese
1 can (8 ounces) crushed pineapple, drained
1 teaspoon vanilla extract
Minced fresh parsley, optional

In a large skillet, cook bacon over medium heat until crisp. With a slotted spoon, remove bacon to paper towels; drain, reserving 2 tablespoons drippings. Crumble bacon.

In a large bowl, lightly beat eggs; add bacon and drippings, cottage cheese, pineapple and vanilla. Pour into greased 11-in. x 7-in. baking dish.

Bake, uncovered, at 350° for 40-45 minutes or until a knife inserted near the center comes out clean. Let stand for 5 minutes. If desired, sprinkle with parsley.

YIELD: 8 servings.

jane zielinski
ROTTERDAM JUNCTION, NEW YORK

My son-in-law experimented with my standby egg recipe by adding cottage cheese and crushed pineapple. It's so delicious, I now make his version all the time!

FRESH eggs

When purchasing eggs, open the carton at the store to check that none are cracked. Move each egg with your fingers to make sure it isn't stuck onto the carton because of a crack you can't see on the bottom of the egg. Refrigerate eggs as soon as you get home.

BREAKFAST BURRITOS

PREP: 20 min. + freezing

  12 bacon strips, diced
  12 eggs, lightly beaten
Salt and pepper to taste
  10 flour tortillas (8 inches)
1-1/2 cups (6 ounces) shredded cheddar
    cheese
  1/2 cup thinly sliced green onions

In a large skillet, cook the bacon until crisp; remove to paper towels. Drain, reserving 1-2 tablespoons drippings. Add the eggs, salt and pepper to bacon drippings; cook and stir over medium heat until the eggs are completely set.

Spoon about 1/4 cup of egg mixture down the center of each tortilla; sprinkle with cheese, onions and reserved bacon. Fold bottom and sides of each tortilla over filling. Wrap each in waxed paper and aluminum foil. Freeze for up to 1 month.

TO USE FROZEN BURRITOS: Remove foil. Place waxed paper-wrapped burritos on a microwave-safe plate. Microwave at 60% power for 1 to 1-1/2 minutes or until heated through. Let stand for 20 seconds.

YIELD: 10 burritos.

audra niederman
ABERDEEN, SOUTH DAKOTA

Bacon and egg lovers will go crazy for these filling breakfast burritos. The savory hand-held bites are also scrumptious with cooked sausage.

CHEESE-FILLED COFFEE CAKES

PREP: 25 min. + rising | **BAKE:** 20 min. + cooling

4-1/2 cups all-purpose flour

1/2 cup sugar

2 packages (1/4 ounce *each*) active dry yeast

1 teaspoon salt

1 cup (8 ounces) sour cream

1/2 cup butter, cubed

1/2 cup water

2 eggs

FILLING:

2 packages (8 ounces *each*) cream cheese, softened

3/4 cup sugar

1 egg

1 teaspoon almond extract

1/8 teaspoon salt

GLAZE:

2 cups confectioners' sugar

3 tablespoons milk

1/2 teaspoon vanilla extract

In a large bowl, combine 1-1/2 cups flour, sugar, yeast and salt. In a small saucepan, heat the sour cream, butter and water to 120°-130°; add to dry ingredients. Beat on medium speed for 2 minutes. Add eggs and 1/2 cup flour; beat 2 minutes longer. Stir in enough remaining flour to form a firm dough. Do not knead. Cover and refrigerate for 2 hours.

In a bowl, beat filling ingredients until smooth; set aside. Turn dough onto a lightly floured surface; divide into four pieces. Roll each into a 12-in. x 8-in. rectangle. Spread filling to within 1/2 in. of edges.

Roll up jelly-roll style, starting with a long side; pinch the seams to seal and tuck ends under. Place, seams side down, on two greased baking sheets. With a sharp knife, make deep slashes across the top of each loaf. Cover and let rise in a warm place until doubled, about 1 hour.

Bake at 375° for 20-25 minutes. Remove from the pans to wire racks. Combine glaze ingredients; drizzle over warm loaves. Cool. Refrigerate leftovers.

YIELD: 4 loaves (10 slices each).

shirley hartman
COLORADO SPRINGS, COLORADO

Friends and family always feel special when I bake these tender coffee cakes for brunch. A smooth cream cheese filling and a drizzle of white icing on top makes them over-the-top indulgent.

APRICOT KOLACHES

PREP: 40 min. + rising | BAKE: 15 min.

7-3/4 to 8-1/4 cups all-purpose flour
2/3 cup sugar
1 tablespoon active dry yeast
2 teaspoons salt
2-1/2 cups 2% milk
1 cup plus 2 tablespoons butter, cubed, *divided*
4 egg yolks
2 cans (12 ounces *each*) apricot cake and pastry filling

GLAZE:
3/4 cup confectioners' sugar
1 to 2 tablespoons water

In a large bowl, combine 2 cups flour, sugar, yeast and salt. In a saucepan, heat the milk and 1 cup butter to 120°-130°. Add to the dry ingredients; beat until moistened. Add egg yolks; beat on low speed for 30 seconds. Beat on high for 3 minutes. Stir in enough remaining flour to form a soft dough.

Turn onto a floured surface; knead until smooth and elastic, about 6-8 minutes. Place in a greased bowl, turning once to grease top. Cover and let rise in a warm place until doubled, about 1 hour.

Punch dough down. Turn onto a lightly floured surface. Shape into 1-1/2-in. balls; roll each into a 2-1/2-in. circle. Place 2 in. apart on greased baking sheets. Cover and let rise until doubled, about 30 minutes.

Using the end of a wooden spoon, make a 1-1/2-in. indentation in the center of each roll; fill with about 2 teaspoons apricot filling. Melt remaining butter; brush over dough.

Bake at 350° for 15-20 minutes or until golden brown. Remove from the pans to wire racks. Combine the glaze ingredients; drizzle over warm rolls.

YIELD: about 4 dozen.

arlyn kramer
DUMAS, ARKANSAS

These apricot-filled pastries make any gathering special. They take some time to prepare but are well worth the effort.

PEAR-PECAN SAUSAGE QUICHE

PREP: 15 min. | BAKE: 35 min.

1/2 pound bulk hot Italian sausage
1/3 cup chopped sweet onion
1 medium pear, sliced
1 pastry shell (9 inches)
1/3 cup chopped pecans
4 eggs
1-1/2 cups half-and-half cream
1/2 teaspoon salt
1/2 teaspoon dried thyme
1/8 teaspoon ground nutmeg
1 cup (4 ounces) shredded cheddar cheese
8 pecan halves

In a large skillet, cook sausage and onion over medium heat for 4-5 minutes or until meat is no longer pink; drain. Arrange pear slices in crust; top with the sausage. Sprinkle with pecans. In a large bowl, whisk the eggs, cream, salt, thyme and nutmeg. Stir in the cheese. Pour over sausage.

Bake at 350° for 35-40 minutes or until a knife inserted near the center comes out clean and crust is golden brown. Garnish with pecan halves. Let stand for 5 minutes before slicing.

YIELD: 8 servings.

patricia harmon
BADEN, PENNSYLVANIA

This quiche would be a delightful addition to breakfast, especially during the holiday season. It's savory from the Italian sausage yet sweet from the sliced pear.

BAKING a quiche

When baking a quiche, be sure to put the pan on the bottom rack of the oven to avoid a soggy crust. Also, use an oven thermometer to monitor the temperature of the oven.

SAUSAGE-MUSHROOM BREAKFAST BAKE

PREP: 25 min. | **BAKE:** 50 min. + standing

    1 pound bulk pork sausage
    2 cups sliced fresh mushrooms
    6 cups cubed bread
    2 cups (8 ounces) shredded sharp cheddar
        cheese
    1 cup chopped fresh tomatoes
   10 eggs, lightly beaten
    3 cups milk
    2 teaspoons ground mustard
  1/2 teaspoon salt
  1/4 teaspoon pepper

In a large skillet, cook the sausage and mushrooms over medium heat until meat is no longer pink; drain.

Place half of the bread cubes in a greased 13-in. x 9-in. baking dish; top with 2 cups sausage mixture and half of the cheese and tomatoes. Repeat layers. In a large bowl, combine the eggs, milk, mustard, salt and pepper; pour over bread mixture.

Bake, uncovered, at 350° for 50-55 minutes or until a knife inserted near the center comes out clean. Let stand for 10 minutes before serving.

YIELD: 12 servings.

diane babbitt
LUDLOW, MASSACHUSETTS

My mom shared this delicious recipe when I needed to bring a dish to a breakfast potluck. It was devoured in a hurry!

HINT OF MINT FRUIT SALAD

PREP: 20 min. + chilling

      1 cup sugar
      1 cup water
      1 cup loosely packed mint sprigs
  2-1/2 cups chopped apples
  2-1/2 cups chopped ripe pears
      2 cups cubed fresh pineapple
      2 cups sliced fresh strawberries
      1 cup fresh blueberries
      1 cup mayonnaise

In a large saucepan, bring sugar and water to a boil. Reduce heat; simmer, uncovered, for 4 minutes. Remove from the heat. Add mint; cover and steep for 20 minutes. Strain and discard mint. Transfer syrup to a small bowl; refrigerate until chilled.

Just before serving, combine the apples, pears, pineapple, strawberries and blueberries in a large bowl. Stir mayonnaise into mint syrup until blended; pour over fruit and toss to coat.

YIELD: 12 servings.

sue gronholz
BEAVER DAM, WISCONSIN

I love making herbal syrups like the simple dressing for this colorful recipe. It definitely adds pizzazz to any typical fruit salad.

BREAKFAST PIZZA

PREP: 30 min. + rising | **BAKE:** 30 min.

kathy evanko
BLAIRSVILLE, PENNSYLVANIA

1 package (1/4 ounce) active dry yeast
1 cup warm water (110° to 115°)
1 tablespoon sugar
1 teaspoon salt
2-1/2 to 3 cups all-purpose flour
1/2 pound thinly sliced deli ham, chopped
1/2 pound sliced American cheese
1/2 pound bulk pork sausage, cooked and drained
2 eggs
3 tablespoons milk
2-1/2 cups (10 ounces) shredded part-skim mozzarella cheese

In a large bowl, dissolve the yeast in warm water. Add the sugar, salt and enough flour to form a soft dough.

Turn onto a floured surface; knead until smooth and elastic, about 6-8 minutes. Place in a greased bowl, turning once to grease top. Cover and let rise in a warm place until doubled, about 45 minutes.

Punch dough down. Press onto a lightly greased 14-in. pizza pan. Build up edges slightly. Bake at 350° for 10-12 minutes or until very lightly browned.

Sprinkle the ham, American cheese and sausage over the crust. Whisk eggs and milk; pour over toppings. Sprinkle with mozzarella. Bake for 20-25 minutes or until the crust is golden and cheese is melted.

YIELD: 8 servings.

Everyone loves this cheesy breakfast pizza I include on my special-occasion menus. It's filling so it keeps my gang going all day long.

VANILLA CINNAMON ROLLS

PREP: 30 min. + rising | **BAKE:** 20 min.

2 cups cold milk

1 package (3.4 ounces) instant vanilla pudding mix

2 packages (1/4 ounce *each*) active dry yeast

1/2 cup warm water (110° to 115°)

1/2 cup plus 2 tablespoons butter, melted, *divided*

2 eggs

2 tablespoons sugar

1 teaspoon salt

6 cups all-purpose flour

1/2 cup packed brown sugar

1 teaspoon ground cinnamon

FROSTING:

1 cup packed brown sugar

1/2 cup heavy whipping cream

1/2 cup butter, cubed

2 cups confectioners' sugar

In a large bowl, whisk milk and pudding mix for 2 minutes. Let stand for 2 minutes or until soft set; set aside.

In a large bowl, dissolve yeast in warm water. Add 1/2 cup butter, eggs, sugar, salt and 2 cups flour. Beat on medium speed for 3 minutes. Add pudding; beat until smooth. Stir in enough remaining flour to form a soft dough (dough will be sticky).

Turn onto a floured surface; knead until smooth and elastic, about 6-8 minutes. Place in a greased bowl, turning once to grease top. Cover and let rise in a warm place until doubled, about 1 hour.

Punch dough down. Turn onto a floured surface; divide in half. Roll each portion into an 18-in. x 11-in. rectangle; brush with remaining butter. Combine brown sugar and cinnamon; sprinkle over the dough to within 1/2 in. of edges.

Roll up jelly-roll style, starting with a long side; pinch seams to seal. Cut each into 16 slices. Place cut side down in two greased 13-in. x 9-in. baking dishes. Cover and let rise until doubled, about 30 minutes.

Bake at 350° for 20-25 minutes or until golden brown. Meanwhile, in a large saucepan, combine the brown sugar, cream and butter. Bring to a boil; cook and stir for 2 minutes. Remove from the heat. Beat in confectioners' sugar with a hand mixer until creamy. Frost warm rolls. Serve warm.

YIELD: 32 rolls.

linda martin
WARSAW, INDIANA

This is the best recipe I have found for cinnamon rolls. They're so tender with a delightful vanilla flavor and yummy frosting.

NEW ORLEANS BEIGNETS

PREP: 15 min. | **COOK:** 35 min.

1 package (1/4 ounce) active dry yeast
1/4 cup warm water (110° to 115°)
1 cup evaporated milk
1/2 cup canola oil
1/4 cup sugar
1 egg
4-1/2 cups self-rising flour
Oil for deep-fat frying
Confectioners' sugar

In a large bowl, dissolve the yeast in warm water. Add milk, oil, sugar, egg and 2 cups flour. Beat until smooth. Stir in enough remaining flour to form a soft dough (dough will be sticky). Do not knead. Cover and refrigerate overnight.

Punch dough down. Turn onto a floured surface; roll into a 16-in. x 12-in. rectangle. Cut into 2-in. squares.

In an electric skillet or deep-fat fryer, heat oil to 375°. Fry the squares, a few at a time, until golden brown on both sides. Drain on the paper towels. Roll the warm beignets in confectioners' sugar.

YIELD: 4 dozen.

beth dawson
JACKSON, LOUISIANA

These sweet French doughnuts are a traditional breakfast treat in New Orleans. Include them on your menu the next time you are planning a Southern-inspired brunch.

SAUSAGE BACON BITES

PREP: 20 min. + chilling | **BAKE:** 35 min.

3/4 pound sliced bacon
2 packages (8 ounces *each*) brown-and-serve sausage links
1/2 cup plus 2 tablespoons packed brown sugar, *divided*

Cut the bacon strips widthwise in half; cut sausage links in half. Wrap a piece of bacon around each piece of sausage. Place 1/2 cup brown sugar in a shallow bowl; roll sausages in sugar. Secure each with a toothpick. Place in a foil-lined 15-in. x 10-in. x 1-in. baking pan. Cover and refrigerate for 4 hours or overnight.

Sprinkle with 1 tablespoon brown sugar. Bake at 350° for 35-40 minutes or until the bacon is crisp, turning once. Sprinkle with remaining brown sugar.

YIELD: about 3-1/2 dozen.

pat waymire
YELLOW SPRINGS, OHIO

These tasty morsels are perfect with almost any egg dish or as finger foods that party guests can just pop into their mouths. They also make a great accompaniment to fondue.

DOUBLE-CHEESE HAM SOUFFLE

PREP: 15 min. + chilling | **BAKE:** 40 min. + standing

16 slices day-old bread, crust removed and cubed
1 pound cubed fully cooked ham
2 cups (12 ounces) shredded cheddar cheese
1 cup (4 ounces) shredded Swiss cheese
6 eggs
3 cups milk
1/2 teaspoon onion powder
1/2 teaspoon ground mustard
1/8 teaspoon pepper
Dash to 1/8 teaspoon cayenne pepper
1-1/2 cups finely crushed cornflakes
3 tablespoons butter, melted

Place half of the bread cubes in a greased 13-in. x 9-in. baking dish. Top with ham, cheeses and remaining bread cubes. In a large bowl, whisk together the eggs, milk and seasonings; pour over the top. Cover and refrigerate for 8 hours or overnight.

Remove from the refrigerator 30 minutes before baking. Combine the cornflakes and butter; sprinkle over casserole.

Bake, uncovered, at 375° for 40-45 minutes or until a knife inserted near the center comes out clean. Let stand for 10 minutes before serving.

YIELD: 8-10 servings.

aita gattis
HAWKINSVILLE, GEORGIA

I've made this for holiday breakfasts and shower brunches. It's a big hit and also a welcome change at covered-dish dinners at church. There's never another one like it.

VANILLA-ALMOND COFFEE

PREP/TOTAL TIME: 5 min.

- 1 pound ground coffee
- 2 tablespoons almond extract
- 2 tablespoons vanilla extract

Place coffee in a large jar with tight-fitting lid. Add extracts. Cover and shake well. Store in the refrigerator. Prepare coffee as usual.
YIELD: 1 pound.

tina christensen
ADDISON, ILLINOIS

This recipe is perfect for any coffee lover. Instead of buying flavored coffees, I make my own versions using extracts commonly used for baking.

CHOCOLATE CREPES

PREP: 30 min. + chilling | COOK: 45 min.

- 1-1/2 cups milk
- 3 eggs
- 3 tablespoons water
- 2 tablespoons canola oil
- 1-1/2 teaspoons vanilla extract
- 1-1/2 cups all-purpose flour
- 1/4 cup sugar
- 1/4 cup baking cocoa
- 1/8 teaspoon salt

FILLING:
- 1 package (8 ounces) cream cheese, softened
- 1/4 cup sugar
- 1/2 cup sour cream
- 1/2 teaspoon vanilla extract
- 1/3 cup creme de cacao
- 1 carton (8 ounces) frozen whipped topping, thawed

FUDGE SAUCE:
- 3/4 cup semisweet chocolate chips
- 1/4 cup butter
- 1/2 cup sugar
- 2/3 cup half-and-half cream
- 10 mint Andes candies, chopped, optional

For batter, place the first nine ingredients in a blender or food processor. Cover and process until smooth. Refrigerate for 1 hour.

Meanwhile, in a large bowl, beat cream cheese and sugar until light and fluffy. Beat in sour cream and vanilla. Fold in creme de cacao and whipped topping. Cover and refrigerate for at least 1 hour.

For the fudge sauce, in a large saucepan, melt chocolate chips and butter over low heat. Stir in sugar and cream. Bring to a boil. Reduce heat; simmer, uncovered, for 10 minutes. Set aside and keep warm.

Heat a lightly greased 8-in. nonstick skillet; pour 2 tablespoons batter into center of skillet. Lift and tilt pan to evenly coat bottom. Cook until top appears dry; turn and cook 15-20 seconds longer. Remove to a wire rack. Repeat with remaining batter, greasing skillet as needed. When cool, stack crepes with waxed paper or paper towels in between.

Spoon 1/4 cup filling down the center of each crepe; roll up. Top with fudge sauce. Sprinkle with mint candies if desired.
YIELD: 10 servings.

taste of home
test kitchen

These chocolate crepes make luscious breakfast fare. If you want a more refreshing flavor, replace the creme de cacao with creme de menthe and add some of the chopped Andes candies to the fudge sauce.

CINNAMON PEACH KUCHEN

PREP: 25 min. | BAKE: 45 min. + cooling

- 2 cups all-purpose flour
- 2 tablespoons sugar
- 1/2 teaspoon salt
- 1/4 teaspoon baking powder
- 1/2 cup cold butter, cubed
- 2 cans (15-1/4 ounces *each*) peach halves, drained and patted dry
- 1 cup packed brown sugar
- 1 teaspoon ground cinnamon
- 2 egg yolks, lightly beaten
- 1 cup heavy whipping cream

In a small bowl, combine the flour, sugar, salt and baking powder; cut in butter until crumbly. Press onto the bottom and 1-1/2 in. up the sides of a greased 9-in. springform pan. Place pan on a baking sheet. Arrange the peach halves, cut side up, in the crust. Combine the brown sugar and cinnamon; sprinkle over peaches.

Bake at 350° for 20 minutes. Combine the egg yolks and cream; pour over the peaches. Bake 25-30 minutes longer or until the top is set. Cool kuchen on a wire rack. Refrigerate any leftovers.

YIELD: 10 servings.

rachel garcia
ARLINGTON, VIRGINIA

The flaky crust, creamy filling and pretty peach topping make this home-style dessert a delight to serve company.

OVERNIGHT STUFFED FRENCH TOAST

PREP: 20 min. + chilling | **BAKE:** 45 min.

20 slices French bread (1 inch thick)
1 package (8 ounces) fat-free cream cheese
3 cups egg substitute
2 cups fat-free milk
1/3 cup plus 1-3/4 cups sugar-free maple-flavored syrup, *divided*
1 teaspoon vanilla extract
1/4 teaspoon ground cinnamon
2-1/2 cups sliced fresh strawberries

Arrange 10 slices of bread in a 13-in. x 9-in. baking dish coated with cooking spray. Spread each slice with cream cheese. Top with remaining bread. In a large bowl, whisk the egg substitute, milk, 1/3 cup syrup, vanilla and cinnamon; pour over bread. Cover and refrigerate overnight.

Remove from the refrigerator 30 minutes before baking. Bake, uncovered, at 350° for 45-50 minutes or until top is lightly browned and a thermometer reads at least 160°. Serve with strawberries and remaining syrup.

YIELD: 10 servings.

bren childress
BROKEN ARROW, OKLAHOMA

This sunrise specialty is so rich that no one will suspect each generous serving has just 3 grams of fat. I don't like to cook a lot in the morning so this make-ahead dish is perfect.

BAKED OATMEAL

PREP: 10 min. | **BAKE:** 40 min.

3 cups quick-cooking oats
1 cup packed brown sugar
2 teaspoons baking powder
1 teaspoon ground cinnamon
1 teaspoon salt
1 cup milk
1/2 cup butter, melted
2 eggs, lightly beaten
Additional milk

In a large bowl, combine the oats, sugar, baking powder, cinnamon and salt. In a small bowl, combine the milk, butter and eggs. Stir into oat mixture until blended.

Spoon into a greased 9-in. square baking pan. Bake at 350° for 40-45 minutes or until set. Serve warm with milk.

YIELD: 9 servings.

arlene riehl
DUNDEE, NEW YORK

This breakfast treat is like taking a big bite into a fresh-from-the-oven oatmeal cookie. Kids will love the scrumptious flavor while adults will appreciate the nutritional value.

COLORFUL BRUNCH FRITTATA

PREP: 15 min. | **BAKE:** 55 min. + standing

1 pound fresh asparagus, trimmed and cut into 1-inch pieces
1/2 pound sliced fresh mushrooms
1 medium sweet red pepper, diced
1 medium sweet yellow pepper, diced
1 small onion, chopped
3 green onions, chopped
3 tablespoons olive oil
2 garlic cloves, minced
3 plum tomatoes, seeded and chopped
14 eggs, lightly beaten
2 cups half-and-half cream
2 cups (8 ounces) shredded Colby-Monterey Jack cheese
3 tablespoons minced fresh parsley
3 tablespoons minced fresh basil
1/2 teaspoon salt
1/4 teaspoon pepper
1/2 cup shredded Parmesan cheese

In a large skillet, saute the asparagus, mushrooms, peppers and onions in oil until tender. Add garlic; cook 1 minute longer. Add tomatoes; set aside.

In a large bowl, whisk the eggs, cream, Colby-Monterey Jack cheese, parsley, basil, salt and pepper; stir into the vegetable mixture.

Pour mixture into a greased 13-in. x 9-in. baking dish. Bake, uncovered, at 350° for 45 minutes.

Sprinkle with the Parmesan cheese. Bake 10-15 minutes longer or until a knife inserted near the center comes out clean. Let stand for 10 minutes before cutting.

YIELD: 12-15 servings.

kristin arnett
ELKHORN, WISCONSIN

A friend called and asked me for a recipe that could be served at his daughter's wedding brunch. I created this hearty bake for the special day.

GARLIC sprouts

Store-bought garlic is sometimes last year's crop, and if the cloves start to sprout, they pick up a bitter taste. Cut cloves in half before using and remove the green sprout in the middle to get that fresh-picked taste.

CORN FRITTERS WITH CARAMELIZED ONION JAM

PREP: 30 min. | **COOK:** 15 min.

- 1 large sweet onion, halved and thinly sliced
- 1 tablespoon olive oil
- 2 teaspoons balsamic vinegar
- 1/3 cup apple jelly
- 1/3 cup canned diced tomatoes
- 1 tablespoon tomato paste
- 1/8 teaspoon curry powder
- 1/8 teaspoon ground cinnamon
- Dash salt and pepper

FRITTERS:

- 2 cups biscuit/baking mix
- 1 can (11 ounces) gold and white corn, drained
- 2 eggs, lightly beaten
- 1/2 cup 2% milk
- 1/2 cup sour cream
- 1/2 teaspoon salt
- Oil for frying

In a small skillet, saute onion in oil until golden brown. Add vinegar; cook and stir for 2-3 minutes. Set aside.

In a small saucepan, combine the jelly, tomatoes, tomato paste, curry, cinnamon, salt and pepper. Cook over medium heat for 5-7 minutes or until heated through. Add onion mixture. Cook and stir for 3 minutes; set aside and keep warm.

In a small bowl, combine the baking mix, corn, eggs, milk, sour cream and salt just until combined.

In a deep-fat fryer or electric skillet, heat the oil to 375°. Drop batter by heaping tablespoonfuls, a few at a time, into hot oil; fry for 1-1/2 minutes on each side or until golden brown. Drain on paper towels. Serve warm with jam.

YIELD: 2 dozen (3/4 cup jam).

kim cupo
ALBANY, GEORGIA

A friend's husband, who's a chef, came up with these light and fluffy fritters accompanied perfectly by a sweet-tart jam.

FROZEN FRUIT CUPS

PREP: 30 min. + freezing

- 5 packages (3 ounces *each*) lemon gelatin
- 10 cups boiling water
- 5 cans (20 ounces *each*) unsweetened pineapple tidbits, undrained
- 5 cans (11 ounces *each*) mandarin oranges, drained
- 5 cans (6 ounces *each*) frozen orange juice concentrate, partially thawed
- 5 large firm bananas, sliced

In a very large bowl, dissolve the gelatin in boiling water; cool for 10 minutes. Stir in the remaining ingredients.

Spoon mixture into foil cups. Freeze until firm. Remove from the freezer 30 minutes before serving.

YIELD: 9-1/2 dozen.

sue ross
CASA GRANDE, ARIZONA

Add some sparkle to your next get-together or church breakfast with these sunny citrus treats. The refreshing cups burst with color and flavor, plus they look so cute served in shiny foil muffin cups.

BREAKFAST SUPREME

PREP: 20 min. + chilling | BAKE: 35 min. + standing

1 pound bulk pork sausage

1 pound ground beef

1 small onion, chopped

3/4 cup sliced fresh mushrooms

1/2 cup chopped green pepper

1 to 1-1/2 teaspoons salt

1/4 to 1/2 teaspoon pepper

2 tablespoons butter, melted

2 cups (8 ounces) shredded cheddar cheese, *divided*

12 eggs

2/3 cup heavy whipping cream

In a large skillet, cook the sausage, beef, onion, mushrooms and green pepper over medium heat until meat is no longer pink; drain. Stir in salt and pepper; set aside.

Pour the butter into an ungreased 13-in. x 9-in. baking dish. Sprinkle with 1 cup cheese. Beat the eggs; pour over cheese. Top with sausage mixture.

Pour the cream over sausage mixture. Sprinkle with remaining cheese. Cover and refrigerate for 8 hours or overnight.

Remove from the refrigerator 30 minutes before baking. Bake, uncovered, at 325° for 35-40 minutes or until a knife inserted near the center comes out clean. Let stand for 10 minutes before cutting.

YIELD: 12 servings.

laurie harms
GRINNELL, IOWA

Friends shared this recipe with me many years ago, when we spent the night at their home. After one taste, you'll understand why this breakfast is "supreme." It's really that good!

LIVELY leftovers

Put any leftover sausage and vegetables to good use by stirring them into prepared mac 'n' and cheese for a quick and tasty lunch.

STRAWBERRY MASCARPONE CREPES

PREP: 45 min. + standing | **COOK:** 20 min.

BATTER:
  3 eggs
  3/4 cup plus 2 tablespoons milk
  3/4 cup all-purpose flour
  5 teaspoons butter, melted
  1 tablespoon sugar
  1 teaspoon vanilla extract
  1/4 teaspoon salt

FILLING:
  1 cup (8 ounces) Mascarpone cheese
  2 tablespoons confectioners' sugar
  3 to 4 teaspoons minced fresh basil
  1 teaspoon lemon juice
  1-1/2 cups sliced fresh strawberries

STRAWBERRY TOPPING:
  2 cups sliced fresh strawberries
  1/2 cup sugar
  2 tablespoons orange juice
  1 teaspoon strawberry *or* vanilla extract
Dash salt
  4 teaspoons butter, *divided*

In a blender, combine the batter ingredients; cover and process until smooth. Cover and refrigerate for 1 hour.

Meanwhile, for filling, in a small bowl, combine the cheese, confectioners' sugar, basil and lemon juice. Gently fold in the strawberries. Cover and refrigerate for at least 30 minutes.

For topping, in a small bowl, combine the strawberries, sugar, orange juice, extract and salt. Let stand for 30 minutes.

Melt 1 teaspoon butter in an 8-in. nonstick skillet over medium heat; pour about 1/4 cup batter into the center of skillet. Lift and tilt pan to coat bottom evenly. Cook until top appears dry; turn and cook 15-20 seconds longer. Remove to a wire rack. Repeat with remaining batter, greasing skillet as needed. When cool, stack crepes with waxed paper or paper towels in between.

Spoon filling over crepes; roll up. Serve with strawberry topping.

YIELD: 8 crepes.

shannon soper
WEST BEND, WISCONSIN

Greet the day in a luscious way with these tender strawberry-filled crepes. This recipe was my mom's Sunday morning specialty, and I'm happy to now have it in my own collection of favorite brunch recipes.

MAKE-AHEAD SCRAMBLED EGGS

PREP: 15 min. + chilling | **BAKE:** 35 min.

2 cups soft bread cubes (crusts removed)
1-3/4 cups milk
8 eggs, lightly beaten
3/4 teaspoon salt
1/8 teaspoon pepper
3 tablespoons butter, *divided*
2 cups (8 ounces) shredded Swiss cheese
1/4 cup dry bread crumbs
6 bacon strips, cooked and crumbled

In a large bowl, combine bread cubes and milk; let stand 5 minutes. Drain, reserving excess milk. Place bread in a greased 8-in. square baking dish; set aside.

In a large bowl, whisk eggs, salt, pepper and reserved milk. In a large skillet, heat 2 tablespoons butter over medium heat. Add egg mixture; cook and stir until set. Spoon over bread cubes. Top with cheese.

Melt remaining butter; add bread crumbs. Sprinkle over cheese. Top with bacon. Cover and chill 8 hours or overnight.

Remove from the refrigerator 30 minutes before baking. Bake, uncovered, at 350° for 35 minutes or until a knife inserted near the center comes out clean. Let stand 5 minutes before cutting.

YIELD: 8 servings.

diane sackfield
KINGSTON, ONTARIO

When my grown kids and their families come to visit, this egg dish is devoured in a hurry...even if I double it! The Swiss cheese is a nice change from the usual cheddar cheese.

BACON POPOVERS

PREP: 10 min. | **BAKE:** 25 min.

1 cup all-purpose flour
1/4 teaspoon salt
2 eggs
1 cup milk
1 tablespoon canola oil
3 bacon strips, cooked and crumbled

In a large bowl, combine flour and salt. Combine the eggs, milk and oil; whisk into the dry ingredients just until blended.

Using a 12-cup muffin tin, grease and flour five alternating cups. Fill two-thirds full with batter. Sprinkle with bacon. Fill empty cups two-thirds full with water.

Bake at 450° for 15 minutes. Reduce heat to 350° (do not open oven door). Bake 15 minutes longer or until deep golden brown (do not underbake).

YIELD: 1 dozen.

marisa may
FAIRPORT, NEW YORK

Even picky eaters will find the eggs and hint of bacon in these popovers too irresistible to pass up. For a delicious variety, try pairing them with maple syrup or melted cheese sauce.

APPLE FRITTERS

PREP: 15 min. | **COOK:** 30 min.

2-1/2 cups all-purpose flour
1/2 cup nonfat dry milk powder
1/3 cup sugar
2 teaspoons baking powder
1 teaspoon salt
2 eggs
1 cup water
2 cups chopped peeled apples
Oil for deep-fat frying
Sugar

In a large bowl, combine first five ingredients. Whisk eggs and water; add to dry ingredients just until moistened. Fold in apples.

In an electric skillet, heat oil to 375°. Drop batter by teaspoonfuls, a few at a time, in hot oil. Fry until golden brown, about 1-1/2 minutes on each side. Drain on paper towels. Roll warm fritters in sugar. Serve warm.

YIELD: 40 fritters.

katie beechy
SEYMOUR, MISSOURI

My kids love these fritters year-round, but I get even more requests in the fall when there are plenty of apples in season. I like to serve them as a special breakfast treat when they host friends for sleepovers.

LONG JOHNS

PREP: 15 min. + rising | **COOK:** 30 min.

1 package (1/4 ounce) active dry yeast
1/4 cup warm water (110° to 115°)
1 cup warm milk (110° to 115°)
1/4 cup butter, softened
1/4 cup sugar
1/2 teaspoon salt
1 egg
3-1/4 to 3-3/4 cups all-purpose flour
Oil for deep-fat frying
GLAZE:
1-1/4 cups confectioners' sugar
1 tablespoon brown sugar
1 tablespoon water
1/2 teaspoon vanilla extract
1/8 teaspoon salt

In a large bowl, dissolve yeast in warm water. Add the milk, butter, sugar, salt, egg and 2 cups flour. Beat until smooth. Stir in enough flour to form a soft dough.

Do not knead. Place dough in a greased bowl, turning once to grease top. Cover and let rise in a warm place until doubled, about 1 hour.

Punch dough down. Turn onto a lightly floured surface; roll into a 12-in. x 8-in. rectangle. Cut into 3-in. x 1-in. rectangles. Place on greased baking sheets. Cover and let rise in a warm place until doubled, about 30 minutes.

In an electric skillet or deep-fat fryer, heat oil to 400°. Fry doughnuts, a few at a time, until golden brown on both sides. Drain on paper towels. Combine glaze ingredients. Dip tops in glaze while warm.

YIELD: 2-1/2 dozen.

twilla eisele
WELLSVILLE, KANSAS

The tattered recipe in my files is a good indication of how popular these doughnuts have been in our family over the years. They disappear in a hurry, so I typically double the recipe.

KITCHEN tools

Some kitchen tools can be so versatile! The next time you're making these quiche cups, use a curved grapefruit knife to pop the tart shells out of the mini muffin tins.

BACON QUICHE TARTS

PREP: 15 min. | **BAKE:** 20 min.

2 packages (3 ounces *each*) cream cheese, softened
5 teaspoons 2% milk
2 eggs
1/2 cup shredded Colby cheese
2 tablespoons chopped green pepper
1 tablespoon finely chopped onion
1 tube (8 ounces) refrigerated crescent rolls
5 bacon strips, cooked and crumbled

In a small bowl, beat cream cheese and milk until smooth. Add the eggs, cheese, green pepper and onion.

Separate dough into eight triangles; press onto the bottom and up the sides of greased muffin cups. Sprinkle half of the bacon into cups. Pour egg mixture over bacon; top with remaining bacon.

Bake, uncovered, at 375° for 18-22 minutes or until a knife inserted near the center comes out clean. Serve warm.

YIELD: 8 servings.

kendra schertz
NAPPANEE, INDIANA

Flavored with vegetables, cheese and bacon, these memorable morsels are bound to be requested at your house. The tarts are an impressive addition to brunch, but they're quite easy to make.

EGG SCRAMBLE

PREP: 15 min. | **COOK:** 20 min.

1-1/2 cups diced peeled potatoes
1/2 cup chopped sweet red pepper
1/2 cup chopped green pepper
1/2 cup chopped onion
2 teaspoons canola oil, *divided*
2 cups cubed fully cooked ham
16 eggs
2/3 cup sour cream
1/2 cup milk
1 teaspoon onion salt
1/2 teaspoon garlic salt
1/4 teaspoon pepper
2 cups (8 ounces) shredded cheddar
cheese, *divided*

Place potatoes in a small saucepan and cover with water. Bring to a boil. Reduce heat; cover and simmer for 10-15 minutes or until tender. Drain.

In a large skillet, saute half of the peppers and onion in 1 teaspoon oil until tender. Add half of the ham and potatoes; saute 2-3 minutes longer.

Meanwhile, in a blender, combine the eggs, sour cream, milk, onion salt, garlic salt and pepper. Cover and process until smooth. Pour half over vegetable mixture; cook and stir over medium heat until eggs are completely set. Sprinkle with 1 cup cheese. Repeat with remaining ingredients.

YIELD: 10 servings.

vicki holloway
JOELTON, TENNESSEE

Filled with potatoes, ham, cheese and sweet red and green peppers, this easy egg scramble bakes up warm and hearty. It's perfect for a special-occasion breakfast or holiday brunch.

ICED RAISIN BISCUITS

PREP: 20 min. | **BAKE:** 15 min.

2 cups all-purpose flour
1 tablespoon sugar
3 teaspoons baking powder
1 teaspoon ground cinnamon
1/2 teaspoon salt
1/8 teaspoon ground nutmeg
1/2 cup cold butter, cubed
1/3 cup raisins
1/2 cup 2% milk
3 tablespoons maple syrup

ICING:
1/2 cup confectioners' sugar
1/8 teaspoon rum extract
2-1/4 teaspoons 2% milk

In a large bowl, combine the first six ingredients. Cut in the butter until mixture resembles coarse crumbs. Add raisins. In a small bowl, combine milk and syrup; stir into crumb mixture just until moistened.

Turn onto a lightly floured surface; knead 8-10 times. Pat or roll out to 1/2-in. thickness; cut with a floured 2-1/2-in. biscuit cutter.

Place 1 in. apart on an ungreased baking sheet. Bake at 450° for 12-15 minutes or until golden brown.

Meanwhile, combine the confectioners' sugar, extract and enough milk to achieve desired consistency. Drizzle the icing over warm biscuits.

YIELD: 10 biscuits.

taste of home test kitchen

Our home economists help you whip up a warm, mouthwatering breakfast treat in a snap! Sweet raisins and maple syrup bring out the best in this seasonally inspired spice blend.

SPICY BREAKFAST LASAGNA

PREP: 20 min. + chilling | **BAKE:** 35 min.

- 3 cups (24 ounces) 4% cottage cheese
- 1/2 cup minced chives
- 1/4 cup sliced green onions
- 18 eggs
- 1/3 cup milk
- 1/2 teaspoon salt
- 1/4 teaspoon pepper
- 1 tablespoon butter
- 8 lasagna noodles, cooked and drained
- 4 cups frozen shredded hash browns
- 1 pound bulk pork sausage, cooked and crumbled
- 8 ounces sliced Monterey Jack cheese with jalapeno peppers
- 8 ounces sliced Muenster cheese

In a large bowl, combine the cottage cheese, chives and onions; set aside. In a large bowl, whisk the eggs, milk, salt and pepper. In a large skillet, heat butter until hot. Add egg mixture; cook and stir over medium heat until eggs are completely set. Remove from heat; set aside.

In a greased 13-in. x 9-in. baking dish, place four lasagna noodles. Top with 2 cups hash browns, scrambled eggs, sausage and half of cottage cheese mixture. Cover with Monterey Jack cheese. Repeat layers with the remaining lasagna noodles, hash browns and cottage cheese mixture. Top with the Muenster cheese.

Cover and refrigerate for 8 hours or overnight. Remove from the refrigerator 30 minutes before baking. Bake, uncovered, at 350° for 35-40 minutes or until a knife inserted near the center comes out clean. Let stand for 5 minutes before cutting.

YIELD: 12-16 servings.

guthrie torp jr.
HIGHLAND RANCH, COLORADO

It's fun to cook up something new for family and friends—especially when it gets rave reviews. When I brought this dish to our breakfast club at work, people said it really woke up their taste buds!

BIG-BATCH BISMARKS

PREP: 30 min. + rising | **COOK:** 20 min.

- 2 tablespoons active dry yeast
- 4 teaspoons plus 1 cup sugar, *divided*
- 1/2 cup warm water (110° to 115°)
- 4 cups warm milk (110° to 115°)
- 2 eggs
- 1 tablespoon canola oil
- 1-1/2 teaspoons salt
- 11 to 12 cups all-purpose flour
- Additional oil for deep-fat frying
- Strawberry jelly
- Frosting and sprinkles, optional

In a large bowl, dissolve the yeast and 4 teaspoons sugar in warm water. Add the milk, eggs, oil, salt, remaining sugar and 8 cups flour until blended. Stir in enough remaining flour to form a soft dough. Divide dough in half.

Turn onto a floured surface; knead until smooth and elastic, about 6-8 minutes. Place in two greased bowls, turning once to a grease tops. Cover and let rise in a warm place until doubled, about 1 hour.

Punch the dough down. Turn on a floured surface; roll out to 1/2-in. thickness. Place on greased baking sheets. Cover and let rise until doubled, about 30 minutes.

In an electric skillet or deep-fat fryer, heat the oil to 375°. Fry bismarks, a few at a time, for 1 minute on each side or until golden brown. Drain on paper towels. Cool for 2-3 minutes. Cut a small slit with a sharp knife in one side of each bismark; fill with about 1 teaspoon jelly. Decorate with frosting and sprinkles if desired.

YIELD: about 5 dozen.

araminta adams
SOLDIERS GROVE, WISCONSIN

These delicious jelly-filled doughnuts will disappear right before your eyes.

FROSTED bismarks

To keep frosted bismarks from sticking to aluminum foil when you cover them, mold a sheet of aluminum foil over an upturned bowl a little larger than the plate. Remove the foil, place the domed piece over the plate and tuck in the edges.

MARY'S BAKED FRUIT

PREP/TOTAL TIME: 30 min.

1 can (16 ounces) apricot halves, drained
1 can (16 ounces) pear halves, drained
2 cans (15 ounces *each*) plums, drained and halved
1 can (29 ounces) peach halves, drained
1 can (8 ounces) pineapple slices, undrained
1/3 cup packed brown sugar
1 tablespoon butter
1/2 teaspoon ground cinnamon
1/4 teaspoon ground cloves

In a greased 13-in. x 9-in. baking pan, starting at the 9-in. end, arrange rows of fruit in the following order: half of the apricots, pears and plums, all of the peaches, then remaining apricots, pears and plums.

Drain pineapple, reserving 1/2 cup of juice. Lay pineapple over fruit in pan. In a saucepan, combine the pineapple juice, brown sugar, butter, cinnamon and cloves. Cook and stir until sugar is dissolved and butter is melted. Pour over fruit.

Bake, uncovered, at 350° for 20-25 minutes or until heated through.
YIELD: 12-16 servings.

mary neville
FREDERICKTOWN, MISSOURI

A brunch buffet would not be complete without this baked fruit casserole. Feel free to add raisins, pecans or walnuts if you like.

CHEESY EGG CASSEROLE

PREP: 10 min. + chilling | **BAKE:** 40 min.

4 cups (16 ounces) shredded Monterey Jack cheese
1 tablespoon all-purpose flour
2 cups (8 ounces) shredded sharp cheddar cheese
1 pound sliced bacon, cooked and crumbled
12 eggs
1 cup milk

Toss Monterey Jack cheese with flour; place in a greased 13-in. x 9-in. baking dish. Top with cheddar cheese; sprinkle with bacon. Beat eggs and milk; pour over all. Cover and chill for 8 hours or overnight. Remove from refrigerator 30 minutes before baking.

Bake, uncovered, at 325° for 40-45 minutes or until a knife inserted near the center comes out clean. Let stand 5 minutes before cutting.
YIELD: 12-16 servings.

dawn reeve
SALT LAKE CITY, UTAH

You'll love the home-style appeal of this hearty egg bake. It's perfect for holiday gatherings and makes a pretty addition to the table.

FRENCH BREAKFAST PUFFS

PREP: 20 min. | **BAKE:** 20 min.

1/3 cup shortening
1 cup sugar, *divided*
1 egg
1-1/2 cups all-purpose flour
1-1/2 teaspoons baking powder
1/2 teaspoon salt
1/4 teaspoon ground nutmeg
1/2 cup whole milk
1 teaspoon ground cinnamon
6 tablespoons butter, melted

In a small bowl, beat shortening, 1/2 cup sugar and egg until smooth. Combine the flour, baking powder, salt and nutmeg; add to the sugar mixture alternately with milk.

Fill greased muffin cups two-thirds full. Bake at 350° for 20 minutes or until a toothpick inserted near the center comes out clean. Cool for 5 minutes before removing from pan.

Meanwhile, combine cinnamon and remaining sugar in a shallow bowl. Roll the warm puffs in butter, then in cinnamon-sugar. Serve immediately.
YIELD: 1 dozen.

kimberly flora
PERU, INDIANA

Rather than serve typical pastries, I like to make these light, tender treats when I have guests for breakfast. Everyone enjoys the sweet cinnamon and sugar coating.

CHEESE SAUSAGE STRATA

PREP: 15 min. + chilling | **BAKE:** 1 hour

1-1/2 pounds bulk pork sausage
9 eggs, lightly beaten
3 cups milk
9 slices bread, cubed
1-1/2 cups (6 ounces) shredded cheddar cheese
1/2 pound sliced bacon, cooked and crumbled
1-1/2 teaspoons ground mustard

In a large skillet, cook the pork sausage over medium heat until no longer pink; drain. Add the eggs, milk, bread, cheese, bacon and mustard. Transfer to a greased shallow 3-qt. baking dish. Cover and refrigerate overnight.

Remove from the refrigerator 30 minutes before baking. Cover and bake at 350° for 60-65 minutes or until a knife inserted near the center comes out clean. Let stand for 5 minutes before serving.

YIELD: 12 servings.

teresa marchese
NEW BERLIN, WISCONSIN

Sausage provides plenty of flavor in this filling morning casserole. It's easy to make for a brunch buffet as it's assembled the night before, which cuts down on last-minute fuss.

PEPPERONI SPINACH QUICHE

PREP: 25 min. | **BAKE:** 25 min.

- 1 tube (8 ounces) refrigerated crescent rolls
- 1 large sweet red pepper, chopped
- 1 tablespoon olive oil
- 1 garlic clove, minced
- 5 eggs, lightly beaten
- 1/2 cup shredded part-skim mozzarella cheese
- 1/2 cup frozen chopped spinach, thawed and squeezed dry
- 1/4 cup sliced pepperoni, cut into strips
- 1/4 cup half-and-half cream
- 2 tablespoons grated Parmesan cheese
- 1 tablespoon minced fresh parsley
- 1 tablespoon minced fresh basil *or* 1 teaspoon dried basil

Dash pepper

Separate crescent dough into eight triangles; place in an ungreased 9-in. fluted tart pan with removable bottom with points toward the center. Press onto the bottom and up the sides to form a crust; seal seams. Set aside.

In a small skillet, saute red pepper in oil until tender. Add garlic; cook 1 minute longer. Remove from the heat. In another small bowl, combine the remaining ingredients; stir in red pepper mixture. Pour into crust.

Bake at 375° for 25-30 minutes or until a knife inserted near the center comes out clean. Let quiche stand for 5 minutes before cutting into wedges.

YIELD: 8 servings.

elly townsend
SUMMERFIELD, FLORIDA

Several years ago, I brought this colorful quiche to a brunch-style pool party, and it was a hit! It's also great as part of an antipasto platter.

PANCAKES FOR A CROWD

PREP: 25 min. | **COOK:** 35 min.

- 40 cups all-purpose flour
- 3 cups sugar
- 1-1/2 cups baking powder
- 1-1/2 cups baking soda
- 3/4 cup salt
- 28 eggs
- 2 gallons milk
- 1 gallon buttermilk
- 64 ounces canola oil

In several large bowls, combine the flour, sugar, baking powder, baking soda and salt. Combine the eggs, milk, buttermilk and oil; stir into dry ingredients just until blended.

Pour batter by 1/3 cupfuls onto a greased hot griddle. Turn when bubbles form on top; cook until second side is golden brown.

YIELD: 70-80 servings (5 gallons of batter).

penelope hamilton
RIVERSIDE, CALIFORNIA

Let this be your go-to recipe the next time you're feeding breakfast to a crowd. The batter for these buttermilk pancakes comes together easily, and the flapjacks couldn't be any more delightful.

TRADITIONAL ENGLISH MUFFINS

PREP: 30 min. + rising | **BAKE:** 20 min.

- 2 packages (1/4 ounce *each*) active dry yeast
- 1 tablespoon sugar
- 3 cups warm water (110° to 115°), *divided*
- 2 eggs, lightly beaten
- 2/3 cup honey
- 1 teaspoon salt
- 9 to 10 cups all-purpose flour

In a large bowl, dissolve yeast and sugar in 2 cups water. Beat in eggs, honey, salt, 2 cups flour and remaining water. Add enough remaining flour to form a soft dough.

Turn onto a floured surface; knead until smooth and elastic, about 6-8 minutes. Place in a greased bowl, turning once to grease top. Cover and let rise in a warm place until doubled, about 1 hour.

Punch dough down. On a floured surface, roll to 1/2-in. thickness. Cover and let stand for 5 minutes. Cut into 4-in. circles. Place 2 in. apart on greased baking sheets.

Bake at 375° for 8 minutes or until bottom is browned. Turn and bake 7 minutes longer or until the second side is browned. Cool on wire racks.

To serve, split with a fork and toast.

YIELD: about 3 dozen.

loretta kurtz
ALLENSVILLE, PENNSYLVANIA

I often bake up a few batches of these yeast treats and share them with our neighbors. They tell me my muffins taste so much better than store-bought ones!

HAM 'N' CHEESE STRATA

PREP: 20 min. + chilling | **BAKE:** 1 hour

- 15 slices white bread
- 3 cups (12 ounces) process cheese (Velveeta), shredded
- 2 tablespoons dried minced onion
- 3 cups frozen chopped broccoli, cooked and drained
- 2 cups diced fully cooked ham
- 6 eggs, lightly beaten
- 3-1/3 cups milk
- 1/4 teaspoon salt
- 1/4 teaspoon ground mustard
- Paprika

Using a doughnut cutter, cut 15 circles and holes from the bread; set aside. Tear leftover bread into small pieces and place in a greased 13-in. x 9-in. baking dish.

Sprinkle cheese and onion over bread. Layer with broccoli and ham. Arrange bread circles and holes over ham. In a large bowl, combine the eggs, milk, salt and mustard; pour over the bread. Cover and chill 8 hours or overnight.

Remove from refrigerator 30 minutes before baking. Bake, uncovered, at 325° for 50 minutes; sprinkle with paprika. Bake an additional 10 minutes or until golden brown. Let stand 5 minutes before cutting.

YIELD: 12-16 servings.

janet wielhouwer
GRAND RAPIDS, MICHIGAN

I love to make this delicious and attractive dish for special brunches and showers. Because it's made the night before, I can relax in the morning before guests arrive.

EASY APPLE DANISH

PREP: 25 min. + chilling | **BAKE:** 15 min.

1 package (1/4 ounce) active dry yeast
1/4 cup warm water (110° to 115°)
5 cups all-purpose flour
1/4 cup sugar
1 teaspoon salt
1 teaspoon grated lemon peel
1 cup cold butter, cubed
1 cup warm 2% milk (110° to 115°)
2 eggs, lightly beaten

FILLING:
1-1/2 cups chopped peeled tart apples
3/4 cup chopped walnuts
1/3 cup sugar
1-1/2 teaspoons ground cinnamon
2 tablespoons butter, melted

GLAZE:
2 cups confectioners' sugar
3 tablespoons 2% milk
1/2 teaspoon vanilla extract

In a small bowl, dissolve the yeast in warm water. In a large bowl, combine the flour, sugar, salt and lemon peel; cut in the butter until mixture resembles fine crumbs. Stir in the yeast mixture, milk and eggs until blended.

Turn onto a lightly floured surface; knead about 20 times (dough will be slightly sticky). Cover and refrigerate for at least 2 hours.

For filling, combine the apples, walnuts, sugar and cinnamon; set aside. Punch dough down. Turn onto a lightly floured surface; divide in half. Roll each portion into an 18-in. x 15-in. rectangle; brush with butter. Sprinkle the filling to within 1/2 in. of the edges.

Starting with a short side, fold a third of the dough over filling; repeat with other side, making a 15-in. x 6-in. rectangle. Pinch seams to seal. Cut each into 15 slices. Twist each slice a few times; pinch ends together, forming a small circle. Place 2 in. apart on greased baking sheets.

Bake at 400° for 12-15 minutes or until golden brown. Remove from pans to wire racks. Combine glaze ingredients; drizzle over warm rolls.

YIELD: 2-1/2 dozen.

dorothea ladd

BALLSTON LAKE, NEW YORK

This recipe is a cinch because you can prepare the dough the night before and bake the rolls fresh in the morning.

SPICED GINGER COFFEE

PREP/TOTAL TIME: 5 min.

1/2 cup molasses
1/4 cup packed brown sugar
1 teaspoon ground ginger
3/4 teaspoon ground cinnamon

EACH SERVING:
1 cup hot brewed coffee
Milk, whipped cream and additional ground cinnamon, optional

In a small bowl, combine the molasses, brown sugar, ginger and cinnamon.

For each serving, place 2 teaspoons molasses mixture in a mug. Add 1 cup hot coffee; stir until combined. Serve with milk, whipped cream and cinnamon if desired.

Cover and store remaining molasses mixture in the refrigerator for up to 2 weeks.

YIELD: 15 servings (2/3 cup molasses mixture).

taste of home test kitchen

Treat your open-house guests to the flavor of gingerbread with this unique coffee recipe. Dressed up with whipped cream and cinnamon, it is a drink to savor!

SOUR CREAM COFFEE CAKE

PREP: 15 min. | **BAKE:** 40 min.

1/2 cup butter, softened
1 cup sugar
2 eggs
1 cup (8 ounces) sour cream
1 teaspoon vanilla extract
2 cups all-purpose flour
1 teaspoon baking powder
1 teaspoon baking soda
1/4 teaspoon salt

TOPPING:
1/4 cup sugar
1/3 cup packed brown sugar
2 teaspoons ground cinnamon
1/2 cup chopped pecans

In a large bowl, cream butter and sugar until light and fluffy. Beat in the eggs, sour cream and vanilla. Combine the flour, baking powder, baking soda and salt; add to creamed mixture and beat until combined. Pour half the batter into a greased 13-in. x 9-in. baking pan.

In a small bowl, combine the topping ingredients; sprinkle half of topping over batter. Add remaining batter and topping. Bake at 325° for 40 minutes or until a knife inserted near the center comes out clean. Cool on a wire rack.

YIELD: 12-15 servings.

sandra munyon
WATERTOWN, WISCONSIN

I'm from the dairyland state so I use sour cream made right here in Wisconsin in this delicious recipe. This coffee cake tastes like a dream and feeds a crowd, so it's perfect for a morning meeting or brunch buffet.

OVERNIGHT RAISIN FRENCH TOAST

PREP: 15 min. + chilling | **BAKE:** 45 min.

1 loaf (1 pound) cinnamon-raisin bread, cubed

1 package (8 ounces) cream cheese, cubed

8 eggs

1-1/2 cups half-and-half cream

1/2 cup sugar

1/2 cup maple syrup

2 tablespoons vanilla extract

1 tablespoon ground cinnamon

1/8 teaspoon ground nutmeg

Place half of the bread cubes in a greased 13-in. x 9-in. baking dish. Top with cream cheese and remaining bread.

In a large bowl, combine the remaining ingredients. Pour over the top. Cover and refrigerate overnight.

Remove from the refrigerator 30 minutes before baking. Cover and bake at 350° for 30 minutes. Uncover; bake 15-20 minutes longer or until a knife inserted near the center comes out clean.

YIELD: 12 servings.

stephanie weaver
SLIGO, PENNSYLVANIA

A colleague passed along this convenient make-ahead recipe that has become a morning family favorite! I sprinkle the pan with a cinnamon-sugar blend when it's fresh out of the oven.

SPICY HASH BROWNS

PREP: 1 hour 25 min. + chilling | **COOK:** 20 min.

    25 pounds potatoes, peeled
2-1/2 pounds fully cooked ham, diced
   1/4 cup sliced green onions
2-1/2 pounds green peppers, chopped
   1/2 pound fresh jalapeno peppers, chopped
     1 cup butter, *divided*
     2 jars (4 ounces *each*) pimientos, drained
         and chopped
    10 teaspoons salt
     5 teaspoons pepper
2-1/2 teaspoons cayenne pepper
2-1/2 teaspoons paprika
     8 cups (32 ounces) shredded cheddar
         cheese

Place potatoes in several large stockpots and cover with water. Bring to a boil. Reduce heat; cover and cook for 15-20 minutes or until tender. Drain. Chill for several hours or overnight.

Grate potatoes into several large bowls; set aside. In a several large skillets, saute the ham, onions and peppers in 1/4 cup butter until tender. Cool 10 minutes; add to the potatoes. Add pimientos and seasonings.

On a large griddle, cook potatoes in remaining butter until browned; turn over and cook the second side until browned. Place half of the potatoes on a platter; top with cheese and remaining potatoes.

YIELD: 90-100 servings.

mike marratzo
FLORENCE, ALABAMA

Forget plain hash browns. These zippy spuds are guaranteed to rise to the occasion at your next breakfast gathering!

MINI SAUSAGE QUICHES

PREP: 25 min. | **BAKE:** 20 min.

1/2 pound bulk hot Italian sausage
   2 tablespoons dried minced onion
   2 tablespoons minced chives
   1 tube (8 ounces) refrigerated crescent rolls
   4 eggs, lightly beaten
   2 cups (8 ounces) shredded Swiss cheese
   1 cup (8 ounces) 4% cottage cheese
1/3 cup grated Parmesan cheese
Paprika

In a large skillet, brown the sausage and onion over medium heat for 4-5 minutes or until the meat is no longer pink; drain. Stir in the chives.

On a lightly floured surface, unroll crescent dough into one long rectangle; seal seams and perforations. Cut into 48 pieces. Press onto the bottom and up the sides of greased miniature muffin cups.

Fill each with about 2 teaspoons of the sausage mixture. In a large bowl, combine the eggs and cheeses. Spoon 2 teaspoonfuls over the sausage mixture. Sprinkle mixture with the paprika.

Bake at 375° for 20-25 minutes or until a knife inserted in the center comes out clean. Cool for 5 minutes before removing from pans to wire racks. Serve warm. Refrigerate any leftovers.

YIELD: 4 dozen.

jan mead
MILFORD, CONNECTICUT

These bite-size quiches are loaded with sausage and cheese, plus their crescent roll bases make prep a snap. Serve these cute muffinettes at any brunch or potluck.

MINCING made easy

To mince an ingredient, hold the handle of a chef's knife with one hand, and rest the finger of your other hand on the top of the blade near the tip. Using the handle to guide and apply pressure, move the knife in an arc across the food with a rocking motion until pieces of food are the desired size.

p. 84

p. 75

p. 81

salads &
side dishes

MASHED POTATOES SUPREME

PREP: 40 min. | **BAKE:** 20 min.

3 pounds medium red potatoes, quartered
2 packages (3 ounces *each*) cream cheese, cubed
1/2 cup butter, cubed
1/2 cup half-and-half cream *or* milk
1 medium green pepper, chopped
4 green onions, thinly sliced
1 jar (2 ounces) sliced pimientos, drained
1/2 teaspoon salt
1/4 teaspoon pepper
1/2 cup shredded cheddar cheese, *divided*
1/2 cup grated Parmesan cheese, *divided*

Place potatoes in a large saucepan; cover with water. Bring to a boil. Reduce heat; cover and cook for 10-15 minutes or until tender. Drain.

In a large bowl, mash the potatoes. Add the cream cheese, butter and cream; beat until blended. Stir in the green pepper, onions, pimientos, salt and pepper. Stir in 1/3 cup cheddar cheese and 1/3 cup Parmesan cheese.

Transfer to a greased 11-in. x 7-in. baking dish. Sprinkle with remaining cheeses. Bake, uncovered, at 350° for 20-25 minutes or until heated through.

YIELD: 8 servings.

julia daubresse
SUN CITY CENTER, FLORIDA

I received this recipe from my sister some 60 years ago, and so many people have requested it since then! The potatoes are rich and creamy, and they taste like twice-baked spuds. This dish offers such nice make-ahead convenience, it's great for potlucks.

CLASSIC POTATO SALAD FOR 50

PREP: 1-1/4 hours | **COOK:** 30 min. + chilling

15 pounds potatoes, peeled and cubed
4 cups mayonnaise
1 cup sweet pickle relish
1/4 cup prepared mustard
1 jar (4 ounces) diced pimientos, drained
2 tablespoons salt
1 tablespoon sugar
2 teaspoons pepper
6 celery ribs, chopped
8 hard-cooked eggs, chopped
1 small onion, chopped
Paprika and green pepper rings, optional

Place potatoes in two large stockpots and cover with water. Bring to a boil. Reduce heat; cover and simmer for 10-15 minutes or until tender. Drain the potatoes and cool to room temperature.

In a large bowl, combine the mayonnaise, relish, mustard, pimientos, salt, sugar and pepper. Divide the potatoes, celery, eggs and onion between two very large bowls; add mayonnaise mixture. Stir to combine.

Cover and refrigerate for at least 1 hour. Garnish with paprika and green pepper rings if desired.

YIELD: 50 servings (3/4 cup each).

dixie terry
GOREVILLE, ILLINOIS

With creamy chunks of potato and crunchy bits of veggies, this treasured potato salad will gain rave reviews from your gang. It's perfect for large family reunions, church suppers and outdoor picnics.

SPEEDY potato salad

The day before making an extra-large batch of potato salad for a potluck, peel, dice and boil the potatoes. Drain and refrigerate overnight. The next day, prep goes quickly because the potatoes are chilled and ready to go.

HARVEST POTATO CASSEROLE

PREP: 40 min. + chilling | **BAKE:** 45 min.

8 large potatoes

2 bay leaves

1/4 cup butter, melted

1/2 teaspoon salt

1/4 teaspoon pepper

2 cups (16 ounces) sour cream

1 can (10-3/4 ounces) condensed cream of chicken soup, undiluted

2 cups (8 ounces) shredded cheddar cheese, *divided*

1 jar (2 ounces) diced pimientos, drained

4 green onions, chopped

1/2 cup crushed cornflakes

Place potatoes and bay leaves in a Dutch oven or large kettle; cover with water. Bring to a boil. Reduce heat; cover and simmer for 15-20 minutes or until tender. Remove from the heat; cool to room temperature. Place in the freezer (still covered by the cooking water) for 1 hour.

Drain potatoes; peel and grate. Place in a greased 13-in. x 9-in. baking dish. Drizzle with butter. Sprinkle with salt and pepper; toss to coat.

In a large bowl, combine the sour cream, soup, 1 cup cheese, pimientos and onions; spread over potatoes. Sprinkle with the remaining cheese; top with cornflakes (dish will be full).

Bake, uncovered, at 350° for 45-50 minutes or until bubbly.

YIELD: 12-15 servings.

robert cody
DALLAS, TEXAS

Sour cream and cream of chicken soup lend to the heavenly texture of this tried-and-true casserole. My large clan prefers this recipe to traditional mashed potatoes.

SPECIAL HERB DRESSING

PREP: 30 min. | **BAKE:** 35 min.

1 pound ground beef
1 pound bulk pork sausage
1 pound sliced fresh mushrooms
1 can (8 ounces) water chestnuts, drained and chopped
2 cups diced peeled apples
1 cup chopped onion
1/4 cup minced fresh parsley
1/4 cup chopped fresh celery leaves
1 cup chopped fresh *or* frozen cranberries
2 garlic cloves, minced
1-1/2 teaspoons salt
1 teaspoon dried savory
1 teaspoon dried thyme
1 teaspoon rubbed sage
3/4 teaspoon pepper
Pinch nutmeg
12 cups day-old bread cubes
1 cup chicken broth

In a large skillet, cook the beef and sausage over medium heat until meat is no longer pink; drain. Add the mushrooms, water chestnuts, apples, onion, parsley and celery leaves; cook for 6-8 minutes or until the mushrooms and apples are tender. Add the cranberries, garlic and seasonings; cook 2 minutes longer.

Place bread cubes in large bowl. Add meat mixture; stir in broth. Spoon into a greased 13-in. x 9-in. baking dish. Cover and bake at 350° for 35-45 minutes.

YIELD: 14-16 servings.

trudy williams
SHANNONVILLE, ONTARIO

Our budget was tight when our children were small, so I cooked with inexpensive ingredients such as ground beef. Now I make this creative casserole simply because we love it!

GREEN BEANS SUPREME

PREP/TOTAL TIME: 25 min.

- 4 packages (16 ounces *each*) frozen cut green beans
- 1/4 cup finely chopped onion
- 1/4 cup butter, cubed
- 2 tablespoons all-purpose flour
- 1 teaspoon salt
- 1 teaspoon paprika
- 1 teaspoon Worcestershire sauce
- 1/2 teaspoon ground mustard
- 2 cups evaporated milk
- 8 ounces process cheese (Velveeta), shredded

TOPPING:
- 1/4 cup dry bread crumbs
- 2 teaspoons butter, melted

Cook green beans according to package directions. Meanwhile, in a Dutch oven, saute onion in butter until tender. Remove from the heat; whisk in the flour, salt, paprika, Worcestershire sauce and mustard until blended.

Gradually stir in the milk. Bring to a boil; cook and stir for 2 minutes or until thickened and bubbly. Remove the mixture from the heat; stir in cheese.

Drain the beans; gently fold into cheese sauce. Transfer to a large serving bowl. Toss the bread crumbs and butter; sprinkle over the beans.

YIELD: 12-16 servings.

heather campbell
LAWRENCE, KANSAS

Here's a nice alternative to plain green bean casserole. I prepare a well-seasoned cheese sauce that lends a little zip to the familiar side dish.

CRUNCHY APPLE SALAD

PREP/TOTAL TIME: 10 min.

- 4 large apples, diced
- 1 cup chopped celery
- 1 cup raisins
- 1 cup chopped walnuts
- 1/2 cup mayonnaise

In a large bowl, combine the apples, celery, raisins and walnuts. Add mayonnaise; toss to coat. Cover and refrigerate until serving.

YIELD: 16 servings.

julie pearsall
UNION SPRINGS, NEW YORK

This old-fashioned fruit salad was one of my favorite dishes growing up. Crunchy apples, celery and walnuts blend well with the creamy mayonnaise.

CORE like a pro

Use an apple corer to core a whole apple. Push the corer into the center of a washed apple. Twist and remove the center seeds and membranes and then dice the fruit with a cutting knife.

TWO-BREAD DRESSING

PREP: 30 min. | **BAKE:** 45 min.

- 2 cups water
- 2 large onions, chopped
- 1-1/2 cups chopped celery
- 1-1/2 cups minced fresh parsley
- 1 cup butter, cubed
- 1 teaspoon ground nutmeg
- 2 loaves (1-1/2 pounds *each*) bread, toasted and cubed
- 12 cups cubed corn bread, toasted
- 10 eggs, lightly beaten
- 10 hard-cooked eggs, chopped
- 5 cups cubed cooked chicken
- 2 cans (14-1/2 ounces *each*) chicken broth

In a Dutch oven, combine the water, onions, celery, parsley, butter and nutmeg. Bring to a boil; cook and stir until vegetables are tender. In several large bowls, combine the bread, corn bread, eggs, hard-cooked eggs, chicken, broth and onion mixture.

Divide among four greased 3-qt. baking dishes. Bake, uncovered, at 350° for 45-50 minutes or until a thermometer reads 160°.
YIELD: 36-40 servings.

patty kierce
WEIR, TEXAS

It took 10 cooks to make this old-fashioned dressing to feed over 1,500 people at our church's fall festival. Your crowd may not be as large, but I guarantee everyone will love it!

MEXICORN GRITS

PREP: 20 min. | **BAKE:** 35 min.

- 4 cups milk
- 1/2 cup plus 1/3 cup butter, *divided*
- 1 cup quick-cooking grits
- 2 eggs
- 1 can (11 ounces) Mexicorn, drained
- 1 can (4 ounces) chopped green chilies
- 1 cup (4 ounces) shredded Mexican cheese blend
- 1 teaspoon salt
- 1/4 teaspoon white pepper
- 1 cup shredded Parmesan cheese

In a large saucepan, bring milk and 1/2 cup butter to a boil. Slowly stir in grits. Reduce heat; cook and stir for 5-7 minutes.

In a small bowl, whisk the eggs. Stir a small amount of hot grits into eggs; return all to the pan, stirring constantly. Melt remaining butter; stir into the grits. Add the corn, chilies, cheese, salt and pepper.

Transfer the mixture to a greased 2-qt. baking dish. Sprinkle with the Parmesan cheese. Bake, uncovered, at 350° for 35-40 minutes or until a knife inserted near the center comes out clean.
YIELD: 10 servings.

barbara moorhead
GAFFNEY, SOUTH CAROLINA

I grew up on grits and have fixed them in various ways. I decided to put a new twist on them with this recipe, and my husband says it's a keeper. Even the leftovers are good.

GOTTA love grits

Grits are a time-honored tradition in the South. The key to a successful baked dish calling for grits is to stir them frequently while cooking to prevent scorching.

DUO TATER BAKE

PREP: 40 min. | **BAKE:** 20 min. + chilling

- 4 pounds russet *or* Yukon Gold potatoes, peeled and cubed
- 3 pounds sweet potatoes, peeled and cubed
- 2 cartons (8 ounces *each*) spreadable chive and onion cream cheese
- 1 cup (8 ounces) sour cream
- 1/4 cup shredded Colby-Monterey Jack cheese
- 1/3 cup milk
- 1/4 cup shredded Parmesan cheese
- 1/2 teaspoon salt
- 1/2 teaspoon pepper

TOPPING:
- 1 cup (4 ounces) shredded Colby-Monterey Jack cheese
- 1/2 cup chopped green onions
- 1/4 cup shredded Parmesan cheese

Place russet potatoes in a Dutch oven and cover with water. Bring to a boil. Reduce heat; cover and cook for 10-15 minutes or until tender.

Meanwhile, place sweet potatoes in a large saucepan; cover with water. Bring to a boil. Reduce heat; cover and cook for 10-15 minutes or until tender. Drain; mash with half of the cream cheese and sour cream and all of Colby cheese.

Drain the russet potatoes; mash with the remaining cream cheese and sour cream. Stir in the milk, Parmesan cheese, salt and pepper.

Spread 2-2/3 cups russet potato mixture into each of two greased 11-in. x 7-in. baking dishes. Layer with 4 cups sweet potato mixture. Repeat the layers. Spread with the remaining russet potato mixture.

Bake, uncovered, at 350° for 15 minutes or until heated through. Combine topping ingredients; sprinkle over casseroles. Bake casseroles 2-3 minutes longer or until the cheese is melted.

YIELD: 2 casseroles (10 servings each).

joan mcculloch
ABBOTSFORD, BRITISH COLUMBIA

Cut down on holiday prep time with this creamy and comforting potato dish that combines sweet potatoes with regular spuds. I served this for Thanksgiving, and it was a winner with my family.

ROASTED VEGGIE PASTA

PREP: 40 min. | **BAKE:** 25 min.

4 small zucchini, halved lengthwise and cut into 1-inch slices

2 large onions, cut into wedges

2 medium yellow summer squash, halved lengthwise and cut into 1-inch slices

2 large sweet yellow peppers, cut into 1-inch pieces

1 cup fresh baby carrots, halved lengthwise

2 tablespoons olive oil

3-1/2 cups uncooked fusilli pasta

2 cups (8 ounces) shredded fontina cheese

1-1/2 cups heavy whipping cream

1/2 cup canned diced tomatoes in sauce

1/2 cup grated Parmesan cheese, *divided*

2 garlic cloves, minced

1/2 teaspoon salt

1/4 teaspoon pepper

In a large bowl, combine the first six ingredients. Transfer to two greased 15-in. x 10-in. x 1-in. baking pans. Bake at 450° for 20-25 minutes or until crisp-tender; set aside. Reduce heat to 350°.

Cook the pasta according to the package directions; drain. Add the fontina cheese, cream, tomatoes, 1/4 cup Parmesan cheese, garlic, salt and pepper. Stir in the vegetable mixture.

Transfer to a greased 13-in. x 9-in. baking dish. (Dish will be full). Sprinkle with the remaining Parmesan cheese. Bake pasta, uncovered, for 25-30 minutes or until hot and bubbly.

YIELD: 16 servings (3/4 cup each).

robyn baney
LEXINGTON PARK, MARYLAND

My sister gave me this recipe years ago, and it has become a make-ahead favorite when I host company. For a hearty meal, pair it with ham and dinner rolls.

ELEGANT VEGETABLE CASSEROLE

PREP: 1 hour | **BAKE:** 50 min.

PARSNIP POTATOES:
- 2 pounds potatoes, peeled and cubed (about 4 medium)
- 4 medium parsnips, peeled and cubed
- 1 carton (8 ounces) reduced-fat sour cream
- 3 tablespoons fat-free milk
- 1 teaspoon salt

SQUASH:
- 1 medium butternut squash (about 3 pounds), peeled and cubed
- 1/2 teaspoon salt
- 1/4 teaspoon ground nutmeg

SPINACH:
- 2 eggs
- 1 tablespoon fat-free milk
- 1/4 teaspoon salt
- 2 packages (10 ounces *each*) frozen chopped spinach, thawed and squeezed dry
- 1-1/2 cups (6 ounces) shredded reduced-fat Swiss cheese
- 3/4 cup soft bread crumbs
- 1 small onion, grated

Place the potatoes and parsnips in a large saucepan; cover with water and bring to a boil. Reduce the heat; cover and simmer for 15-20 minutes or until tender. Drain. Mash with sour cream, milk and salt; set aside.

Place squash in another large saucepan and cover with water. Bring to a boil. Reduce heat; cover and simmer for 15-20 minutes or until tender. Drain. Mash with salt and nutmeg; set aside.

In a small bowl, whisk the eggs, milk and salt. Stir in the spinach, cheese, bread crumbs and onion.

Place half of parsnip potatoes at one end of a 13-in. x 9-in. baking dish coated with cooking spray. Add squash to dish, forming a stripe. Repeat with the spinach. Place remaining parsnip potatoes at opposite end of dish. (Dish will be full.)

Cover and bake at 350° for 45-55 minutes or until a meat thermometer inserted in the spinach reads 160°.

YIELD: 14 servings (1 cup each).

virginia anthony
JACKSONVILLE, FLORIDA

Please everyone at the table with this innovative and space-saving dish. Three traditional sides line up to create a tasty, eye-appealing medley.

COVERED dishes

To keep your dish's cover on while driving to a potluck, simply set a rubber band around the lid's knob and over one of the dish's handles. Pull another rubber band around the knob and over the other handle.

DELIGHTFUL FRUIT SALAD

PREP: 35 min. + chilling

- 1 cup sugar
- 2 tablespoons all-purpose flour
- 1/2 teaspoon salt
- 1-3/4 cups unsweetened pineapple juice
- 2 eggs, lightly beaten
- 1 tablespoon lemon juice
- 1 package (16 ounces) acini di pepe pasta
- 3 cans (11 ounces *each*) mandarin oranges, drained
- 2 cans (20 ounces *each*) pineapple chunks, drained
- 1 can (20 ounces) crushed pineapple, drained
- 1 cup miniature marshmallows
- 1 cup flaked coconut
- 1 carton (12 ounces) frozen whipped topping, thawed

In a small saucepan, combine the sugar, flour and salt. Gradually stir in pineapple juice. Bring to a boil, stirring constantly. Stir a small amount of hot mixture into eggs; return all to the pan, stirring constantly. Bring to a gentle boil; cook and stir 2 minutes longer. Remove from the heat. Gently stir in lemon juice.

Transfer to a large bowl. Cool to room temperature without stirring. Cover surface of dressing with waxed paper; refrigerate until cooled.

Cook the pasta according to package directions; drain and rinse in cold water. Place in a very large bowl; stir in the oranges, pineapple, marshmallows, coconut and dressing. Fold in whipped topping. Cover and refrigerate until chilled.

YIELD: 24 servings (3/4 cup each).

elaine bailey
BLOOMFIELD, INDIANA

Add as much or as little whipped topping to this recipe as you like. I always add a few maraschino cherries to the top for a special touch. I use this recipe as a salad, but it's good enough to be dessert!

CRAB CAKES WITH RED PEPPER SAUCE

PREP: 30 min. + chilling | **COOK:** 20 min.

1/4 cup mayonnaise
1/4 cup minced chives
  2 tablespoons minced fresh parsley
  1 tablespoon lemon juice
1/2 teaspoon seafood seasoning
1/8 teaspoon cayenne pepper
Dash pepper
  1 pound lump crabmeat, cartilage removed
  4 to 5 slices French bread (1 inch thick),
    crust removed

RED PEPPER SAUCE:
1/4 cup mayonnaise
1/4 cup Dijon mustard
  2 tablespoons honey
  1 tablespoon lemon juice
1/2 cup chopped sweet red pepper
1/4 cup chopped green onions
  2 tablespoons minced shallots
  2 tablespoons minced fresh parsley
Salt and pepper to taste
  2 tablespoons butter
  1 tablespoon olive oil
Lemon wedges

In a large bowl, combine the first seven ingredients; stir in crab. In a food processor, process bread slices, a few at a time, until fine crumbs form (total volume should be 2-1/2 cups). Add 1 cup to the crab mixture.

Shape 1/4 cupfuls of crab mixture into patties. Coat both sides of patties with remaining bread crumbs, pressing to adhere. Place on a baking sheet; cover and refrigerate for up to 6 hours.

Meanwhile, for sauce, in a blender, combine the mayonnaise, mustard, honey, lemon juice, red pepper, onions, shallots, parsley, salt and pepper; cover and process until finely chopped. Refrigerate mixture until serving.

In a large skillet, melt half of the butter and half of the oil. Place half of the crab cakes in skillet. Cook over medium heat for 5 minutes on each side or until lightly browned (carefully turn the delicate cakes over). Repeat with remaining butter, oil and crab cakes. Serve crab cakes with the sauce and lemon wedges.
YIELD: 10 servings.

joylyn trickel
HELENDALE, CALIFORNIA

Don't forget to have lemons on hand so you and your guests can squeeze a little fresh lemon juice over these succulent crab cakes.

PEAS IN CHEESE SAUCE

PREP/TOTAL TIME: 20 min.

4-1/2 teaspoons butter
4-1/2 teaspoons all-purpose flour
1/4 teaspoon salt
1/8 teaspoon white pepper
1-1/2 cups milk
3/4 cup cubed process cheese (Velveeta)
  2 packages (10 ounces *each*) frozen peas, thawed

In a large saucepan, melt the butter over low heat. Stir in the flour, salt and pepper until smooth. Gradually add milk. Bring to a boil; cook and stir for 2 minutes or until thickened. Add the cheese; stir until melted. Stir in peas; cook 1-2 minutes longer or until mixture is heated through.
YIELD: 8 servings.

june blomquist
EUGENE, OREGON

Dress up convenient frozen peas with a quick-to-fix cheese sauce. This is a comforting side that goes well with any meat entree.

RAINBOW PASTA SALAD

PREP: 1 hour + chilling

- 2 packages (12 ounces *each*) tricolor spiral pasta
- 2 packages (16 ounces *each*) frozen California-blend vegetables, thawed
- 2 pints grape tomatoes
- 1 large zucchini, halved and thinly sliced
- 1 large yellow summer squash, quartered and thinly sliced
- 1 large red onion, finely chopped
- 1 block (8 ounces) cheddar cheese, cubed
- 1 block (8 ounces) Monterey Jack cheese, cubed
- 2 packages (4 ounces *each*) crumbled tomato and basil feta cheese
- 1 bottle (16 ounces) Italian salad dressing
- 3 tablespoons minced fresh parsley
- 1 tablespoon minced fresh basil
- 1 teaspoon Italian seasoning
- 1 teaspoon seasoned salt
- 1/2 teaspoon pepper
- 1 can (3.8 ounces) sliced ripe olives, drained

Grated Romano cheese, optional

Cook pasta according to package directions. Rinse with cold water; drain well. In two large bowls, combine the California vegetables, tomatoes, zucchini, yellow squash, onion, cheeses and pasta.

In a small bowl, combine the salad dressing, parsley, basil, Italian seasoning, seasoned salt and pepper. Pour over pasta mixture; toss to coat. Stir in olives. Cover and refrigerate for 8 hours or overnight.

Toss before serving. Serve with Romano cheese if desired.

YIELD: 36 servings.

benjamin &
sue ellen clark
WARSAW, NEW YORK

This colorful salad is hearty enough to be a light meal by itself. It's a great make-ahead dish, since the full flavors of the herbs and vegetables need a little time to blend.

FRESH veggies

If you want to use fresh veggies from your garden in place of the packaged frozen blend, cut to approximately one-half inch thick and blanch for the same duration as what it takes to cook the pasta.

VEGETABLE-STUFFED BAKED ONIONS

PREP: 25 min. | **BAKE:** 45 min.

    8 to 10 medium onions, peeled
    4 bacon strips, diced
    3/4 cup finely chopped carrots
    1/2 cup finely chopped sweet red pepper
    1-1/2 cups soft bread crumbs
    1/3 cup minced fresh parsley
    3 tablespoons butter, melted
    1-1/2 teaspoons salt
    1/2 teaspoon pepper
    3/4 cup beef broth

Cut 1/2 in. off the top of each onion; trim bottom so onion sits flat. Scoop out center, leaving a 1/2-in. shell. Chop the remaining onion; set aside 1/2 cup (discarding remaining onion or save for another use). Place onion shells in a Dutch oven and cover with water. Bring to a boil; reduce heat and cook for 8-10 minutes.

Meanwhile, in a large skillet, cook bacon over medium heat until crisp. Remove to paper towels; drain, reserving 1 teaspoon drippings. In same skillet, saute the chopped onions, carrots and red pepper in drippings for 8 minutes or until tender. Remove from the heat; stir in the bread crumbs, parsley, butter, salt, pepper and reserved bacon.

Drain onion shells; fill each with about 1/3 cup vegetable mixture. Place in an ungreased shallow 3-qt. baking dish. Pour broth over onions. Cover and bake at 350° for 45-50 minutes or until heated through.
YIELD: 8-10 servings.

ruth andrewson
LEAVENWORTH, WASHINGTON

Stuffed with carrots, red pepper, diced bacon and bread crumbs, these elegantly baked onions will dress up any special-occasion meal. My mother often pulled out this recipe when we hosted company.

MACARONI SALAD FOR 100

PREP: 20 min. + chilling

- 5 to 6 pounds fully cooked ham, cubed
- 5 to 6 pounds macaroni, cooked and drained
- 3 pounds shredded cheddar cheese
- 2 bags (20 ounces *each*) frozen peas, thawed
- 2 bunches celery, chopped (about 12 cups)
- 2 large onions, chopped (2 to 2-1/2 cups)
- 2 cans (5-3/4 ounces *each*) pitted ripe olives, drained and sliced

DRESSING:
- 8 cups mayonnaise
- 1 bottle (8 ounces) Western *or* French salad dressing
- 1/4 cup white vinegar
- 1/4 cup sugar
- 1 cup half-and-half cream
- 1-1/2 teaspoons onion salt
- 1-1/2 teaspoons garlic salt
- 1 teaspoon salt
- 1 teaspoon pepper

In several large bowls, combine the first seven ingredients. In a large bowl, combine all the dressing ingredients; pour over the ham mixture and toss to coat. Cover and refrigerate until serving.

YIELD: 100 servings.

PASTA pointer

Macaroni noodles are very absorbent, so to keep your salad from becoming too moist, add only two-thirds of the dressing. Allow the flavors to blend by chilling the salad and dressing for a few hours or overnight. Add the remainder of the dressing just before serving.

marna dunn
BULLHEAD CITY, ARIZONA

This classic pasta salad is sure to please appetites of all ages. This is my go-to recipe whenever I'm called upon to bring a dish to pass at large potlucks and church suppers.

BAKED POTATO CASSEROLE

PREP: 15 min. | BAKE: 50 min.

- 5 pounds red potatoes, cooked and cubed
- 1 pound sliced bacon, cooked and crumbled
- 1 pound cheddar cheese, cubed
- 4 cups (16 ounces) shredded cheddar cheese
- 1 large onion, finely chopped
- 1 cup mayonnaise
- 1 cup (8 ounces) sour cream
- 1 tablespoon minced chives
- 1 teaspoon salt
- 1/2 teaspoon pepper

In a very large bowl, combine potatoes and bacon. In another large bowl, combine the remaining ingredients; add to the potato mixture and gently toss to coat.

Transfer to a greased 4-1/2-qt. baking dish. Bake, uncovered, at 325° for 50-60 minutes or until casserole is bubbly and lightly browned.

YIELD: 20-24 servings.

karen berlekamp
MAINEVILLE, OHIO

I created this baked potato casserole with input from friends and neighbors who love cooking as much as I do. It makes a great all-around side dish for any party or gathering.

HAWAIIAN BAKED BEANS

PREP: 10 min. | **BAKE:** 1 hour 50 min.

4 jars (48 ounces *each*) great northern beans, rinsed and drained

4 cups chopped onions

1 package (2 pounds) dark brown sugar

2 pounds cubed fully cooked ham

1 bottle (28 ounces) ketchup

1 can (20 ounces) crushed pineapple, drained

1/2 cup prepared mustard

1/3 cup vinegar

In several large bowls, combine all the ingredients. Divide the mixture among four greased 13-in. x 9-in. baking pans.

Cover tightly; bake at 350° for 1-1/2 hours. Uncover and bake 20-30 minutes more or until bubbly.

YIELD: 80-100 servings.

charlene laper
LAKEVIEW, MICHIGAN

This twist on classic baked beans is perfect for a family reunion or any casual get-together. It's fast and easy to prepare, and you won't ever have to worry about bringing leftovers home...because there won't be any!

GLAZED CARROTS FOR A CROWD

PREP: 20 min. | **BAKE:** 30 min.

3 cups sugar

1 cup light corn syrup

1/2 cup butter, cubed

1/4 cup thawed orange juice concentrate

1 teaspoon salt

2 cans (no. 10 size *each*) baby carrots, drained *or* 12 pounds medium carrots, sliced and cooked

In a large saucepan, combine the first five ingredients; bring to a boil over medium heat. Boil mixture for 5 minutes, stirring occasionally. Place the carrots in two 13-in. x 9-in. baking pans.

Pour sugar mixture over carrots. Bake, uncovered, at 350° for 30-40 minutes or until heated through.

YIELD: 45 servings.

bonnie milner
DERIDDER, LOUISIANA

Whenever our church group plans a gathering, I'm undoubtedly asked to bring these sweet glazed carrots. I never complain because I enjoy them as much as everyone else!

SWEET POTATO SALAD

PREP: 25 min. + chilling

3 pounds sweet potatoes, cooked, peeled and cubed

1 cup chopped green pepper

1/2 cup finely chopped onion

1-1/2 teaspoons salt, optional

1/4 teaspoon pepper

1-1/2 cups light *or* regular mayonnaise

Dash hot pepper sauce

In a large bowl, combine the first five ingredients. Stir in mayonnaise and pepper sauce. Cover and refrigerate salad for at least 1 hour before serving.

YIELD: 10 servings.

lettie baker
PENNSBORO, WEST VIRGINIA

When I took this salad to a potluck dinner, several people asked me for the recipe. The sweet potatoes make it unique, and it really is delicious. I think you'll agree, it's a nice change of pace from traditional potato salads.

ANTIPASTO PASTA SALAD

PREP/TOTAL TIME: 30 min.

- 1 package (16 ounces) penne pasta
- 1 can (15 ounces) garbanzo beans *or* chickpeas, rinsed and drained
- 1 medium sweet red *or* green pepper, julienned
- 2 plum tomatoes, halved lengthwise and sliced
- 1 bunch green onions, sliced
- 4 ounces Monterey Jack cheese, julienned
- 4 ounces part-skim mozzarella cheese, julienned
- 4 ounces brick *or* provolone cheese, julienned
- 4 ounces thinly sliced hard salami, julienned
- 3 ounces thinly sliced pepperoni
- 1 can (2-1/4 ounces) sliced ripe olives, drained
- 1 to 2 tablespoons minced chives

BASIL VINAIGRETTE:
- 2/3 cup canola oil
- 1/3 cup red wine vinegar
- 3 tablespoons minced fresh basil *or* 1 tablespoon dried basil
- 1 garlic clove, minced
- 1/4 teaspoon salt

Cook pasta according to package directions; rinse with cold water and drain. In a large bowl, combine the pasta, beans, vegetables, cheeses, meats, olives and chives.

In a small bowl, whisk the vinaigrette ingredients. Pour over salad; toss to coat. Cover and refrigerate. Toss before serving.

YIELD: 18 servings.

JULIENNED defined

When a recipe calls for an ingredient to be julienned, it's indicating that the food be cut into long, thin matchstick shapes about 2 inches long and 1/8 inch thick.

bernadette nelson

ARCADIA, CALIFORNIA

This combination of beans, sausage, cheese and pasta is a hearty complement to any meal. It's also great to take to a picnic.

VEGGIE MAC 'N' CHEESE

PREP: 30 min. | **BAKE:** 15 min.

1-1/2 cups uncooked elbow macaroni
3 cups fresh broccoli florets
2 cups fresh cauliflowerets
3 large carrots, halved and thinly sliced
2 celery ribs, sliced
1 medium onion, chopped
1 tablespoon butter
1/4 cup all-purpose flour
1 cup milk
1 cup chicken broth
3 cups (12 ounces) shredded sharp cheddar cheese
1 tablespoon Dijon mustard
1/4 teaspoon salt
1/8 teaspoon pepper
1/4 teaspoon paprika

Cook the macaroni according to package directions, adding the broccoli, cauliflowerets, carrots and celery during the last 6 minutes. Drain; transfer to a greased 13-in. x 9-in. baking dish.

Meanwhile, in a Dutch oven, saute onion in butter until tender. Sprinkle with flour; stir until blended. Gradually stir in the milk and broth. Bring to a boil; cook and stir for 2 minutes or until thickened. Stir in the cheese, mustard, salt and pepper. Pour sauce over macaroni mixture; stir to coat. Sprinkle with the paprika.

Bake, uncovered, at 350° for 15-20 minutes or until heated through.
YIELD: 12 servings.

marsha morrill
BROWNSVILLE, OREGON

This creamy mac 'n' cheese definitely doesn't come from a box! Fresh veggies add crunch and color and will leave everyone saying, "More, please!"

LAYERED VEGGIE TORTELLINI SALAD

PREP/TOTAL TIME: 30 min.

- 1 package (16 ounces) frozen cheese tortellini
- 2 cups fresh broccoli florets
- 2 cups cherry tomatoes, quartered
- 2 celery ribs, finely chopped
- 1 can (2-1/4 ounces) sliced ripe olives, drained
- 1 cup (4 ounces) shredded cheddar cheese

PARMESAN DRESSING:
- 3/4 cup mayonnaise
- 3 tablespoons grated Parmesan cheese
- 2 tablespoons lemon juice
- 2 tablespoons heavy whipping cream
- 1 teaspoon dried thyme

Cook the tortellini according to package directions; drain and rinse in cold water. In a large 2-1/2-qt. glass salad bowl, layer the tortellini, broccoli, tomatoes, celery, olives and cheese.

In a small bowl, combine the dressing ingredients; spoon over salad. Cover and refrigerate until serving.

YIELD: 10 servings.

dennis vitale
NEW PRESTON, CONNECTICUT

With cheese tortellini and a creamy Parmesan dressing, this layered pasta salad is the perfect accompaniment to almost any entree.

BEANS WITH PARSLEY SAUCE

PREP/TOTAL TIME: 30 min.

- 2 pounds fresh green beans, trimmed
- 2 tablespoons butter
- 2 tablespoons all-purpose flour
- 1 teaspoon salt
- 1/8 teaspoon pepper
- 1-1/2 cups chicken broth
- 2 egg yolks
- 1/2 cup milk
- 1 cup minced fresh parsley

Place the beans in a large saucepan and cover with water; bring to a boil. Cook, uncovered, for 8-10 minutes or until crisp tender. Meanwhile, in a large skillet, melt butter over medium heat. Stir in the flour, salt and pepper until smooth. Gradually whisk in the broth. Bring to a boil; cook and stir for 1-2 minutes or until thickened. Remove from the heat.

In a small bowl, combine egg yolks and milk. Stir a small amount of hot broth mixture into egg mixture. Return all to the pan, stirring constantly. Bring to a gentle boil; cook and stir for 2 minutes or until thickened and coats the back of a metal spoon. Stir in parsley. Drain beans; serve with sauce.

YIELD: 8 servings.

veronica teipel
MANCHESTER, MISSOURI

You'll likely find the main ingredient for this side dish right in your garden! For extra pizzazz, try mixing wax beans with the green beans. The flavor is definitely worth the preparation time.

TRIMMED beans

To trim a big batch of fresh green beans quickly, simply line up the ends of the beans; then, using a chef's knife, slice several at a time.

FRUITY GELATIN SALAD

PREP: 15 min. + chilling

- 2 packages (6 ounces *each*) cherry gelatin
- 2 cups boiling water
- 2 packages (10 ounces *each*) frozen sweetened sliced strawberries
- 2 cans (20 ounces *each*) crushed pineapple, undrained
- 2 cans (16 ounces *each*) whole-berry cranberry sauce

In two large bowls, dissolve the gelatin in boiling water. Stir in the strawberries until the berries are separated. Stir in the pineapple and cranberry sauce until blended. Transfer the mixtures to two 13-in. x 9-in. dishes. Refrigerate until firm.

YIELD: 36-40 servings.

sarah baumann
SAGINAW, TEXAS

This pretty side dish is ideal for big holiday dinners. It's refreshing, sweet and has just the right amount of tang.

ELEGANT GREEN BEANS

PREP: 20 min. BAKE: 50 min.

- 1 can (8 ounces) sliced water chestnuts, drained
- 1 small onion, chopped
- 1 jar (4-1/2 ounces) sliced mushrooms, drained
- 6 tablespoons butter, *divided*
- 1/4 cup all-purpose flour
- 1 cup milk
- 1/2 cup chicken broth
- 1 teaspoon soy sauce
- 1/8 teaspoon hot pepper sauce
- Dash salt
- 1 package (16 ounces) frozen French-style green beans, thawed
- 1/2 cup shredded cheddar cheese
- 1 cup crushed french-fried onions

In a small skillet, saute the water chestnuts, onion and mushrooms in 2 tablespoons butter for 4-5 minutes or until crisp-tender; set aside.

In large skillet, melt the remaining butter; stir in flour until smooth. Stir in the milk, broth, soy sauce, pepper sauce and salt. Bring to a boil; cook and stir for 2 minutes or until thickened. Remove from the heat; stir in green beans and cheese.

Spoon half of the bean mixture into a greased 1-1/2-qt. baking dish. Layer with water chestnut mixture and remaining bean mixture. Bake, uncovered, at 350° for 45 minutes. Top with french-fried onions. Bake 5 minutes longer or until heated through.

YIELD: 8 servings.

taste of home
test kitchen
Mushrooms and water chestnuts give new life to ordinary green bean casserole. Every time I make it for friends, I'm asked to share the recipe.

TACO SALAD

PREP: 25 min. | **COOK:** 10 min.

1-1/2 pounds ground beef

   2 envelopes taco seasoning, *divided*

   1 medium head iceberg lettuce

   1 package (12-1/2 ounces) nacho tortilla chips, coarsely crushed

   2 pints grape tomatoes, halved

   2 cans (16 ounces *each*) kidney beans, rinsed and drained

   3 cans (2-1/4 ounces *each*) sliced ripe olives, drained

1-1/2 cups (6 ounces) shredded cheddar cheese

   1 large sweet onion, chopped

   2 cans (4 ounces *each*) chopped green chilies

1-1/2 cups Thousand Island salad dressing

1-1/3 cups salsa

  1/3 cup sugar

In a Dutch oven over medium heat, cook beef with 1 envelope plus 2 tablespoons taco seasoning until no longer pink; drain.

In a very large serving bowl, combine the lettuce, chips, tomatoes, beans, olives, cheese, onion, chilies and beef mixture.

In a small bowl, combine the salad dressing, salsa, sugar and remaining taco seasoning; pour over salad and toss to coat. Serve immediately.

YIELD: 26 servings (1-1/3 cups each).

lisa homer

AVON, NEW YORK

When I took this salad to a party, people were scrambling to figure out who made it. Needless to say, I only brought home an empty bowl and each guest went home with a full stomach!

ANTIPASTO POTATO BAKE

PREP: 15 min. | **BAKE:** 20 min.

2 cans (14-1/2 ounces *each*) sliced potatoes, drained

2 cans (14 ounces *each*) water-packed artichoke hearts, rinsed and drained

2 jars (7 ounces *each*) roasted sweet red peppers, drained

1 can (3.8 ounces) sliced ripe olives, drained

1/4 cup grated Parmesan cheese

1-1/2 teaspoons minced garlic

1/3 cup olive oil

1/2 cup seasoned bread crumbs

1 tablespoon butter, melted

In a large bowl, combine the potatoes, artichokes, peppers, olives, cheese and garlic. Drizzle with oil; toss gently to coat. Transfer to a greased 3-qt. baking dish. Toss bread crumbs and butter; sprinkle over the top.

Bake, uncovered, at 375° for 20-25 minutes or until lightly browned.
YIELD: 10 servings.

kelley butler-ludington
EAST HAVEN, CONNECTICUT

This hearty side dish has a surprising Mediterranean flavor. Red peppers and black olives give a pop of color, making this casserole a pretty addition to any buffet table.

TRADITIONAL MASHED POTATOES

PREP: 20 min. | **COOK:** 20 min.

  12 medium potatoes, peeled and cubed
1-1/4 to 1-1/2 cups half-and-half cream
  1/3 cup sour cream
  1/2 cup butter, cubed
    1 teaspoon salt
  1/2 teaspoon pepper
    1 tablespoon minced chives, optional

Place potatoes in a Dutch oven and cover with water. Bring to a boil. Reduce heat; cover and cook for 10-15 minutes or until tender. Drain.

Transfer to a large bowl. Add the cream, sour cream, butter, salt and pepper; beat potatoes until light and fluffy. Sprinkle with chives if desired.

YIELD: 16-18 servings.

taste of home test kitchen

It's just not Thanksgiving without these traditional spuds! In this version, our home economists stir in half-and-half, sour cream and chives.

APPLE 'N' CARROT SLAW

PREP/TOTAL TIME: 30 min.

  4 large heads cabbage, shredded
  1 pound carrots, shredded
  6 medium red apples, finely chopped
  3 cups mayonnaise
1/2 cup sugar
1/4 cup white vinegar
  3 teaspoons salt
  2 teaspoons pepper

In a very large bowl, combine the cabbage, carrots and apples. In a large bowl, combine the mayonnaise, sugar, vinegar, salt and pepper. Pour over the cabbage mixture and toss to coat. Cover and refrigerate mixture until serving.

YIELD: 42 (3/4-cup) servings.

julia livingston
FROSTPROOF, FLORIDA

This crispy, colorful slaw is a true crowd-pleaser at any picnic or church supper. The apples add a touch of sweetness.

BACON RANCH POTATOES

PREP: 10 min. | **BAKE:** 35 min.

  6 cups mashed potatoes (prepared with milk and butter)
  1 cup (8 ounces) 4% cottage cheese
1/2 cup milk
  1 medium onion, finely chopped
  2 tablespoons ranch salad dressing mix
  1 pound sliced bacon, cooked and crumbled
  2 cups (8 ounces) shredded Monterey Jack cheese
  1 cup crushed butter-flavored crackers (about 25 crackers)
1/4 cup butter, melted

In a large bowl, combine the potatoes, cottage cheese, milk, onion and dressing mix. Spread in a greased 3-qt. baking dish. Top with bacon and cheese. Combine cracker crumbs and butter; sprinkle over top.

Bake, uncovered, at 350° for 35-40 minutes or until bubbly.

YIELD: 8-10 servings.

kathryn hostetler
WEST FARMINGTON, OHIO

When I prepare mashed potatoes, I often make extras, just so we can have this scrumptious side the next day.

UNPEELED potatoes

The secret to rich, creamy potatoes is to boil them whole and unpeeled. This will decrease the amount of water absorbed while cooking. Wear an oven mitt to hold the warm potatoes to peel off the skins before chopping and mashing.

WILD RICE DRESSING

PREP: 25 min. | **BAKE:** 1 hour

2-1/2 cups chopped celery
2-1/2 cups chopped onion
   2 tablespoons poultry seasoning
1/2 cup butter, cubed
   1 pound bulk pork sausage, cooked and crumbled
 10 cups cubed crustless day-old white bread
  6 cups cooked wild rice
  4 cups chopped apples
  1 cup chopped walnuts
  1 cup chopped fresh parsley
  1 cup chopped fresh *or* frozen cranberries
  2 cups chicken broth
1/2 cup orange juice
  2 tablespoons brown sugar

In a large skillet, saute the celery, onion and poultry seasoning in butter until vegetables are tender.

Transfer to several large bowls. Add all the remaining ingredients. Place in two greased 6-qt. Dutch ovens. Cover and bake at 350° for 50 minutes or until apples are tender ; uncover and bake 10 minutes longer or until browned.

YIELD: 35 (3/4-cup) servings.

shirley werner
TWIN FALLS, IDAHO

This colorful dish makes a filling addition to any buffet table. Everyone comments on the tasty combination of bread, sausage, rice and fruit.

SCRUMPTIOUS SCRAMBLED SALAD

PREP: 45 min. + chilling

  2 large bunches romaine, torn
 12 green onions, thinly sliced
1-1/2 cups sliced water chestnuts, coarsely chopped
  1 package (16 ounces) frozen peas, thawed
2-1/4 cups mayonnaise
1/2 cup plus 1 tablespoon evaporated milk
1/4 cup plus 1-1/2 teaspoons cider vinegar
3/4 teaspoon garlic powder
  2 cups (8 ounces) shredded cheddar cheese
  3 medium tomatoes, chopped
  1 pound sliced bacon, cooked, crumbled and drained
  3 hard-cooked eggs, sliced

In a very large salad bowl, layer the romaine, onions, water chestnuts and peas. Combine the mayonnaise, milk, vinegar and garlic powder; spread over the peas. Sprinkle with the cheese. Cover the salad and refrigerate for 8 hours or overnight.

Just before serving, add the tomatoes, bacon and eggs; toss gently.

YIELD: 24 servings.

becky muldrow
HIGHLANDS, TEXAS

This recipe makes a large and absolutely delicious green salad that always disappears as fast as I make it!

COOL greens

When taking a tossed salad to a potluck, add an extra cup of frozen peas to the top and cover tightly. When it's time to serve, the peas will be mostly thawed and the salad greens will be cool and crisp.

DOUBLE-STUFFED POTATOES

PREP: 1-1/4 hours | BAKE: 20 min.

4 medium baking potatoes

3 medium sweet potatoes

2 medium pears, peeled and cubed

5 tablespoons butter, cubed

1/2 cup fat-free milk

1 egg, lightly beaten

1 teaspoon salt

1/4 teaspoon pepper

1/4 teaspoon ground cinnamon

1/2 cup packed brown sugar

Scrub and pierce the baking and sweet potatoes. Bake at 400° for 50-55 minutes or until tender. Meanwhile, place pears in a large saucepan and cover with water. Bring to a boil. Reduce heat; cover and cook for 15-20 minutes or until tender. Drain pears and set aside.

Cool potatoes slightly; cut each in half lengthwise. Scoop out the pulp, leaving thin shells. In a large bowl, mash the pulp with butter. Stir in the milk, egg, salt, pepper, cinnamon and reserved pears.

Spoon mixture into potato shells. Sprinkle with brown sugar. Place on a baking sheet. Bake, uncovered, at 400° for 20-25 minutes or until a thermometer reads 160°.

YIELD: 14 servings.

taste of home test kitchen

These special spuds come alive with the addition of creamy sweet potatoes, cinnamon and brown sugar. Fresh pears lend an unexpected touch.

CALICO CORN BREAD DRESSING

PREP: 45 min. + cooling | **BAKE:** 35 min.

- 4 cups all-purpose flour
- 4 cups yellow cornmeal
- 2 tablespoons plus 2 teaspoons baking powder
- 2 teaspoons salt
- 4 eggs
- 4 cups milk
- 1 cup canola oil

DRESSING:
- 4 pounds bulk pork sausage
- 5 cups water
- 8 cups sliced celery (about 1-1/2 bunches)
- 2 medium green peppers, chopped
- 2 tablespoons plus 1-1/2 teaspoons dried minced garlic
- 2 teaspoons pepper
- 1/4 teaspoon cayenne pepper
- 24 slices white bread, cubed
- 6 cans (14-1/2 ounces *each*) chicken broth
- 2 bunches green onions, sliced
- 1/4 cup minced fresh parsley

In a large bowl, combine the flour, cornmeal, baking powder and salt. In another large bowl, whisk the eggs, milk and oil; stir into dry ingredients just until moistened.

Pour into two greased 13-in. x 9-in. baking dishes. Bake at 425° for 15-20 minutes or until a toothpick inserted near the center comes out clean. Cool dishes on wire racks.

In two Dutch ovens, cook sausage over medium heat until no longer pink; drain. Stir in the water, celery, green peppers, garlic, pepper and cayenne. Bring to a boil. Reduce heat; cover and simmer for 5-7 minutes or until vegetables are crisp-tender.

In several large bowls, crumble corn bread into 1/2-in. pieces. Stir in the white bread, broth, onions and parsley. Add the sausage mixture. Divide among four greased 13-in. x 9-in. baking dishes.

Cover and bake at 350° for 25 minutes. Uncover; bake 10-15 minutes longer or until lightly browned.

YIELD: 58 servings (3/4 cup each).

colleen ruple
BEAUMONT, TEXAS

My mother first made this recipe after tasting her mother-in-law's corn bread dressing. It's now a family tradition for us to make it every Thanksgiving.

MARINATED VEGETABLE BEAN SALAD

PREP: 10 min. + chilling

2 cans (16 ounces *each*) kidney beans, rinsed and drained

2 cans (14-1/2 ounces *each*) cut green beans, drained

2 cans (14-1/2 ounces *each*) wax beans, drained

1 jar (10 ounces) small pimiento-stuffed olives

6 cups fresh broccoli florets, finely chopped (about 2 pounds)

2 medium green peppers, chopped

2 medium sweet red peppers, chopped

1 medium red onion, chopped

1 teaspoon dried basil

1/2 teaspoon garlic salt

1 bottle (16 ounces) Italian salad dressing

In a large salad bowl, combine the first 10 ingredients. Pour dressing over salad; toss to coat. Cover and refrigerate overnight. Stir before serving.

YIELD: about 20 servings.

kendra waterbury
E. THETFORD, VERMONT

Canned beans make this colorful salad hearty, and bottled Italian dressing is an easy and tasty topper.

SMOKY BEANS

PREP: 20 min. | **BAKE:** 45 min.

3 pounds sliced bacon, diced

3 medium sweet onions, chopped

6 cans (28 ounces *each*) baked beans, undrained

6 cans (16 ounces *each*) kidney beans, rinsed and drained

6 cans (16 ounces *each*) butter beans, rinsed and drained

4 packages (12 ounces *each*) miniature smoked sausages, cut in thirds

3 cups packed brown sugar

1-1/2 cups ketchup

1-1/2 cups cider vinegar

1 tablespoon garlic powder

1 tablespoon ground mustard

In a Dutch oven, cook the bacon over medium heat until crisp. Using a slotted spoon, remove to paper towels; drain, reserving 3 tablespoons drippings. Saute onions in reserved drippings until tender.

In a very large bowl, combine the beans, sausage, bacon and onions. Combine the remaining ingredients; stir into the bean mixture.

Pour into four greased 13-in. x 9-in. baking dishes. Bake, uncovered, at 350° for 45-55 minutes or until heated through.

YIELD: 90-95 servings.

pat turner
SENECA, SOUTH CAROLINA

These beans are a perfect side dish to almost any meal. We love them served alongside grilled chicken breasts or burgers.

> **TASTY** topper
>
> To add a little extra spark to baked beans, sprinkle a dash of cinnamon or finely crushed gingersnaps over the top of the dish after the beans are heated through.

STUFFED BAKED POTATOES

PREP: 15 min. | **BAKE:** 1-1/4 hours

        5 medium baking potatoes
    1/4 cup butter, softened
        2 cups (8 ounces) shredded cheddar
          cheese, *divided*
    3/4 cup sour cream
        1 envelope ranch salad dressing mix
        1 tablespoon minced chives
        1 garlic clove, minced
Crumbled cooked bacon and chopped green
    onions

Scrub and pierce potatoes. Bake at 375° for 1 hour or until tender. When cool enough to handle, cut a thin slice off the top of each potato and discard. Cut each potato in half lengthwise. Scoop out the pulp, leaving the thin shells.

In a large bowl, beat the pulp with butter. Stir in 1 cup of cheese, sour cream, salad dressing mix, chives and garlic. Spoon the mixture into the potato shells. Sprinkle with the remaining cheese.

Place on a baking sheet. Bake at 375 ° for 15-20 minutes or until heated through. Top with bacon and green onions.

YIELD: 10 servings.

kristyn drews
OMAHA, NEBRASKA

My mom gave me the recipe for these twice-baked potatoes, and I altered them by adding garlic, bacon and green onions. They're perfect for a potluck or any special meal. My kids absolutely love them!

SWIFT scoops

When preparing twice-baked potatoes, use a melon baller to scoop the cooked potato out of the shells. It will come out quickly and neatly without tearing the potato skins.

SPOON BREAD CORN CASSEROLE

PREP: 15 min. | **BAKE:** 55 min.

        2 cups (16 ounces) sour cream
        1 cup butter, melted and cooled
        2 packages (8-1/2 ounces *each*) corn bread/
          muffin mix
        2 cans (15-1/4 ounces *each*) whole kernel
          corn, drained
        2 cans (14-3/4 ounces *each*) cream-style
          corn
    1/4 cup diced pimientos
    1/8 teaspoon salt
    1/8 teaspoon pepper
    1/8 teaspoon cayenne pepper

In a large bowl, combine the sour cream and butter; stir in the muffin mixes. Fold in the remaining ingredients.

Transfer to two greased 8-in. square baking dishes. Bake, uncovered, at 350° for 55-60 minutes or until a knife inserted near the center comes out clean. Serve warm.

YIELD: about 32 servings.

linda fabian
WHEATLAND, WYOMING

To keep our nuptials simple and fun, my husband and I asked our guests to bring their favorite covered dish along with a copy of the recipe to include in a wedding cookbook. We ended up with an outstanding buffet, including this delightful down-home casserole.

BROCCOLI BEAN BAKE

PREP: 15 min. | **BAKE:** 20 min.

  6 cups fresh broccoli florets
1/3 cup chopped onion
  1 teaspoon minced garlic
  3 tablespoons butter, *divided*
  1 can (15-1/2 ounces) great northern beans,
    rinsed and drained
  1 jar (4 ounces) diced pimientos, drained
  1 teaspoon dried oregano
1/2 teaspoon salt
1/8 teaspoon pepper
  2 cups (8 ounces) shredded cheddar
    cheese
  3 tablespoons dry bread crumbs

Place broccoli in a saucepan; add 1 in. of water. Bring to a boil. Reduce heat; cover and simmer for 5-8 minutes or until crisp-tender. Meanwhile, in a skillet, saute the onion and garlic in 1 tablespoon butter. Spread mixture into a greased 11-in. x 7-in. baking dish.

Drain broccoli; place over onion mixture. Top with beans and pimientos. Sprinkle with oregano, salt, pepper, cheese and bread crumbs. Melt remaining butter; pour over the top. Bake, uncovered, at 375° for 20-25 minutes or until heated through.

YIELD: 8 servings.

valerie mcinroy
WATERLOO, IOWA

Broccoli and beans may sound like an unusual combination, but one bite and you'll agree it tastes delicious. This side is a tasty way to get my family to eat these good-for-you ingredients.

CREAMED POTATO CASSEROLES

PREP: 1-1/4 hours | **BAKE:** 40 min.

10 pounds medium potatoes (about 30)
2/3 cup plus 3 tablespoons butter, *divided*
2/3 cup all-purpose flour
5 cups chicken broth
5 cups half-and-half cream
8 egg yolks, lightly beaten
1-1/2 cups minced fresh parsley
3 teaspoons salt
3/4 teaspoon pepper
1/4 teaspoon cayenne pepper
1 cup seasoned bread crumbs

Place potatoes in a large stockpot; cover with water. Bring to a boil. Reduce heat; cover and simmer for 15-20 minutes or until crisp-tender. Drain and rinse in cold water. When cool enough to handle, peel potatoes and cut into 1/4-in. slices; set aside.

In a large saucepan, melt 2/3 cup butter. Stir in flour until smooth; gradually add broth and cream. Bring to a boil; cook and stir for 2 minutes or until thickened. Remove from the heat. Stir 1 cup hot cream mixture into egg yolks; return all to the pan, stirring constantly. Add the parsley, salt, pepper and cayenne. Bring to a gentle boil; cook and stir 2 minutes longer. Remove from the heat.

Spread 1 cup sauce into each of two 3-qt. baking dishes. Top with a third of the potato slices. Repeat the layers twice. Spread with remaining sauce. Melt the remaining butter; toss with the bread crumbs. Sprinkle over casseroles. Bake, uncovered, at 375° for 40-45 minutes or until bubbly.
YIELD: 2 casseroles (12 servings each).

norma harder
SASKATOON, SASKATCHEWAN

This classic potato side makes enough for 24 hungry people. It's great alongside ham and other entrees. Guests always remark on the rich, creamy sauce and the buttery crumb topping.

FIESTA RICE

PREP: 15 min. | **BAKE:** 1 hour 35 min.

2 cups chopped onion

1/4 cup butter, cubed

4 cups uncooked long grain rice

2 cans (6 ounces *each*) small pitted ripe olives, drained

2 cans (28 ounces *each*) tomatoes with liquid, cut up

1 cup chopped green pepper

1 tablespoon salt

1 to 2 teaspoons chili powder

1 teaspoon dried oregano

1/2 teaspoon pepper

4 cups water

3 cups (12 ounces) shredded cheddar cheese

In a small skillet over medium heat, saute the onion in butter until the onion is tender. Transfer to a large bowl. Stir in the next eight ingredients.

Divide between two ungreased 13-in. x 9-in. baking pans. Stir 2 cups of water into each pan. Cover and bake at 350° for 1-1/2 hours. Uncover; sprinkle with cheese. Return to the oven for 5-10 minutes or until the cheese melts.

YIELD: 30-36 servings.

rita wilken
BLOOMFIELD, NEBRASKA

This delicious dish is filled with eye-appealing colors and tastes that makes even a large batch disappear fast. It's easy to assemble and pop in the oven.

GRILLED GARDEN VEGGIES

PREP/TOTAL TIME: 30 min.

2 tablespoons olive oil, *divided*

1 small onion, chopped

2 garlic cloves, minced

1 teaspoon dried rosemary, crushed, *divided*

2 small zucchini, sliced

2 small yellow summer squash, sliced

1/2 pound medium fresh mushrooms, quartered

1 large tomato, diced

3/4 teaspoon salt

1/4 teaspoon pepper

Drizzle 1 tablespoon oil over a double thickness of heavy-duty foil (about 24 in. x 12 in.). Combine the onion, garlic and 1/2 teaspoon rosemary; spoon over foil. Top with the zucchini, yellow squash, mushrooms and tomato; drizzle with the remaining oil. Sprinkle vegetables with the salt, pepper and remaining rosemary.

Fold the foil around vegetables and seal tightly. Grill, covered, over medium heat for 15-20 minutes or until tender. Open foil carefully to allow steam to escape.

YIELD: 8 servings.

holly wilhelm
SIOUX FALLS, SOUTH DAKOTA

This is a versatile recipe because you can use whatever veggies you have on hand. The good-for-you salad tastes great with just about any combination!

SNACKABLE squash

Turn leftover zucchini or squash into yummy party nibblers. Beat an egg with milk, salt and pepper, then add enough flour to make a batter. Dip slices of fresh squash into the batter and deep-fry until crisp-tender.

p. 112

p. 104

p. 117

soups &
sandwiches

BROCCOLI-CAULIFLOWER CHEESE SOUP

PREP: 15 min. | **COOK:** 50 min.

- 3 quarts water
- 8 teaspoons chicken bouillon granules
- 2-1/2 cups diced peeled potatoes
- 1 cup chopped celery
- 1/2 cup chopped onion
- 2 packages (10 ounces *each*) frozen chopped broccoli
- 1 package (16 ounces) frozen cauliflowerets
- 2 cans (10-3/4 ounces *each*) condensed cream of chicken soup, undiluted
- 1 pound process American cheese (Velveeta), cubed
- 1/2 teaspoon dried thyme
- 1/4 teaspoon pepper

In a Dutch oven, combine the first five ingredients. Bring to a boil. Reduce heat, cover and simmer for about 20 minutes or until the vegetables are tender. Add broccoli and cauliflower; cook over medium heat for 10 minutes.

Stir in the soup, cheese, thyme and pepper; simmer for 20 minutes or until heated through, stirring occasionally.

YIELD: 18-20 servings (about 5-1/2 quarts).

janet hall
PLEASANT VALLEY, IOWA

Even those who aren't particularly fond of broccoli and cauliflower won't be able to resist this tempting cream soup.

ITALIAN SUBS

PREP: 15 min. + chilling

- 1/3 cup olive oil
- 4-1/2 teaspoons white wine vinegar
- 1 tablespoon dried parsley flakes
- 2 to 3 garlic cloves, minced
- 1 can (2-1/4 ounces) sliced ripe olives, drained
- 1/2 cup chopped pimiento-stuffed olives
- 1 loaf (1 pound, 20 inches) French bread, unsliced
- 24 thin slices hard salami
- 24 slices provolone *or* part-skim mozzarella cheese
- 24 slices fully cooked ham

Lettuce leaves, optional

In a small bowl, combine the oil, vinegar, parsley and garlic. Stir in olives. Cover and refrigerate for 8 hours or overnight.

Cut bread in half lengthwise. Spread olive mixture on the bottom of the bread. Top with salami, cheese and ham; add lettuce if desired. Replace top. Cut into 2-in. slices. Insert a toothpick in each slice.

YIELD: 10 servings.

delores christner
SPOONER, WISCONSIN

Olive lovers are sure to rejoice over this stacked sandwich! Stuffed and ripe olives are marinated in white wine vinegar and garlic before using them to flavor these speedy salami, ham and provolone subs.

TASTE of Italy

To give these subs a truly authentic Italian flair, replace the sliced ham with prosciutto and the provolone or mozzarella with caciocavallo or scamorza cheese.

GRANDMOTHER'S CHOWDER

PREP: 20 min. | **COOK:** 30 min.

1 pound ground beef
1 medium onion, chopped
12 medium potatoes, peeled and cubed
3 cups water
Salt and pepper to taste
2 cups whole milk
1 can (15-1/4 ounces) whole kernel corn,
  drained
2 teaspoons dried parsley flakes
1 cup (8 ounces) sour cream

In a Dutch oven, cook beef and onion over medium heat until meat is no longer pink; drain. Add the potatoes, water, salt and pepper; bring to a boil. Reduce heat; cover and simmer for 15-20 minutes or until potatoes are tender.

Stir in the milk, corn and parsley; cook for 5 minutes or until heated through. Add a small amount of hot soup to sour cream. Gradually return all to pan, stirring constantly. Heat through but do not boil.
YIELD: 14 servings (3-1/2 quarts).

dulyse molnar
OSWEGO, NEW YORK

Nothing can compare to homemade soup, especially when this is the delicious result! Winter days seem a little warmer when I serve this savory chowder.

CHICKEN BURRITOS

PREP: 20 min. + freezing | **BAKE:** 55 min.

- 1 large onion, chopped
- 1/4 cup chopped green pepper
- 6 tablespoons butter
- 1/2 cup all-purpose flour
- 3 cups chicken broth
- 1 can (10 ounces) diced tomatoes and green chilies
- 2 tablespoons chopped jalapeno pepper, optional
- 1 teaspoon ground cumin
- 1 teaspoon chili powder
- 1/2 teaspoon garlic powder
- 1/2 teaspoon salt
- 1 can (15 ounces) chili with beans
- 1 package (8 ounces) cream cheese, cubed
- 8 cups cubed cooked chicken
- 24 flour tortillas (6 inches), warmed
- 6 cups (24 ounces) shredded Colby-Monterey Jack cheese

Salsa, optional

In a large skillet, saute onion and green pepper in butter until tender. Stir in flour until blended. Gradually stir in broth.

Bring to a boil; cook and stir for 2 minutes. Reduce heat; add the tomatoes, jalapeno pepper if desired and seasonings. Cook for 5 minutes or until heated through. Stir in chili and cream cheese until cheese is melted. Stir in chicken.

Spoon about 1/2 cup down the center of each tortilla; sprinkle each with 1/4 cup Colby-Monterey Jack cheese. Fold ends and sides over filling. Place in two greased 13-in. x 9-in. baking dishes.

Cover and freeze one casserole for up to 3 months. Cover and bake the remaining casserole at 350° for 35-40 minutes or until heated through. Serve with salsa if desired.

TO USE FROZEN BURRITOS: Thaw burritos in the refrigerator overnight. Bake at 350° for 50-55 minutes or until heated through.

YIELD: 2 casseroles (1 dozen burritos each).

sonya nightingale
BURLEY, IDAHO

This mouthwatering Southwestern recipe makes enough burritos to fill two baking pans, so you can enjoy some today and freeze the remaining for a another time. They're super to have on hand when you need a dish to pass at a Mexican-themed party.

CHURCH SUPPER CHILI

PREP: 15 min. | **COOK:** 50 min.

2-1/2 pounds ground beef
1/2 cup chopped green pepper
1 cup chopped celery
2 cups chopped onion
1 garlic clove, minced
3 tablespoons chili powder
2 teaspoons salt
1/2 teaspoon pepper
1 can (14-1/2 ounces) diced tomatoes, undrained
1 can (46 ounces) tomato juice
4 cups V8 juice
2 cans (16 ounces *each*) kidney beans, rinsed and drained
2 cans (16 ounces *each*) hot chili beans, undrained

In a large Dutch oven, cook the beef over medium heat until no longer pink; drain. Add the green pepper, celery and onion; cook until tender. Add the garlic; cook 1 minute longer.

Stir in the spices, tomatoes and juices. Bring to a boil. Reduce heat; simmer, uncovered, for 20 minutes. Add the beans and simmer 20 minutes longer or until heated through.

YIELD: 20-24 servings.

dorothy smith
NAPOLEON, OHIO

We grow tomatoes and vegetables for local canneries—and for use in this original recipe of mine, which won first place in a "Best Chili" contest! It's great for church suppers or any large gathering.

BRUNSWICK STEW

PREP: 1-1/2 hours + chilling | **COOK:** 1 hour

1 pound bone-in pork loin chops
2 bone-in chicken breast halves, skin removed
1 pound beef top round steak, cut into bite-size pieces
6 cups water
2 cans (14-1/2 ounces *each*) diced tomatoes, undrained
2 cups chopped onion
1 can (8 ounces) tomato sauce
1/2 cup cider vinegar
1/4 cup sugar
4 to 5 garlic cloves, minced
2 teaspoons hot pepper sauce
2 cans (15-1/4 ounces *each*) whole kernel corn, drained
2 cans (14-3/4 ounces *each*) cream-style corn
1 cup dry bread crumbs, toasted
Salt and pepper to taste

Place the pork chops, chicken and round steak in a large Dutch oven; cover with water. Cover and cook for 1-1/2 hours or until meat is tender.

Strain stock into another large kettle; refrigerate overnight. Remove bones from meat; dice and place in a separate bowl. Cover and refrigerate overnight.

The next day, skim fat from stock. Add the tomatoes, onion, tomato sauce, vinegar, sugar, garlic and pepper sauce. Simmer, uncovered, for 45 minutes.

Add the kernel corn, cream-style corn and reserved meat; heat through. Stir in bread crumbs; season with salt and pepper.

YIELD: 6 quarts.

alyce ray
FOREST PARK, GEORGIA

Brunswick Stew dates back to the 1860s when it was considered a complete meal. It's delicious picnic fare when served with country ribs, coleslaw or potato salad. When I make this stew, I double the recipe and freeze small portions so we can enjoy it at several meals.

STEW defined

A stew is any dish prepared by stewing— simmering food in liquid for a long period of time in a covered pot. Stew most often refers to a main dish that contains meat, vegetables and a thick broth made from the stewing juices.

BIG-BATCH BEAN SOUP

PREP: 10 min. | **COOK:** 2 hours 40 min.

- 6 cans (15 ounces *each*) white kidney *or* cannellini beans, rinsed and drained
- 8 meaty ham bones
- 7 gallons ham *or* chicken stock
- 4-1/2 cups finely chopped onions (about 2 pounds)
- 2-3/4 cups shredded carrots (about 1 pound)
- 2 teaspoons pepper
- 2 cups all-purpose flour
- 3 cups cold water

Place the beans and ham bones in a large stockpot; add ham stock. Bring to a boil. Reduce heat; cover and simmer for 1 to 1-1/2 hours or until the beans are tender.

Stir in the onions, carrots and pepper; cover and simmer for 30 minutes or until vegetables are tender. Combine flour and water until smooth; gradually stir into soup. Cook for 10 minutes or until thickened, stirring occasionally. If too thick, add additional water.

YIELD: 100 servings (6-1/4 gallons).

jene cain
NORTHRIDGE, CALIFORNIA

When I was a cook in the service, I learned all I could from the cooks in the gallery. This soup was a favorite and yields enough to serve a large crowd.

HEARTY MEATBALL SOUP

PREP: 20 min. | **COOK:** 45 min.

- 2 eggs
- 1 cup soft bread crumbs
- 1 teaspoon salt
- 1/2 teaspoon pepper
- 1 pound lean ground beef (90% lean)
- 1 pound ground pork
- 1/2 pound ground turkey
- 4 cups beef broth
- 1 can (46 ounces) tomato juice
- 2 cans (14-1/2 ounces *each*) stewed tomatoes
- 8 cups shredded cabbage
- 1 cup thinly sliced celery
- 1 cup thinly sliced carrots
- 8 green onions, sliced
- 3/4 cup uncooked long grain rice
- 2 teaspoons dried basil
- 3 tablespoons minced fresh parsley
- 2 tablespoons soy sauce

In a large bowl, combine the eggs, bread crumbs, salt and pepper. Crumble the meat over the mixture and mix well. Shape into 1-in. balls.

In a stockpot, bring broth to a boil. Carefully add the meatballs. Add the tomato juice, tomatoes, vegetables, rice and basil. Bring to a boil. Reduce heat; cover and simmer for 30 minutes.

Add the parsley and soy sauce. Simmer, uncovered, for 10 minutes or until the meatballs are no longer pink and the vegetables are tender.

YIELD: 22 servings (5-3/4 quarts).

janice thompson
LANSING, MICHIGAN

A little bit of this thick and robust soup goes a long way, so it's terrific to take to potlucks. Be sure to bring copies of the recipe!

HAM 'N' SAUSAGE STROMBOLI

PREP: 25 min. | **BAKE:** 35 min. + cooling

1 package (16 ounces) hot roll mix
1-1/4 cups warm water (120° to 130°)
3 tablespoons olive oil, *divided*
1/3 pound sliced deli ham
1/3 pound sliced salami
4 slices process American cheese, cut into thin strips
1 cup (4 ounces) shredded part-skim mozzarella *or* provolone cheese
1/4 pound bulk Italian sausage, cooked and crumbled
2 tablespoons grated Parmesan cheese
1 teaspoon dried oregano
1/2 teaspoon garlic powder
1/4 teaspoon coarsely ground pepper

In a large bowl, combine the contents of the roll mix and yeast packets. Stir in warm water and 2 tablespoons oil until dough pulls away from sides of bowl.

Turn onto a floured surface; knead until smooth and elastic, about 5 minutes. Cover and let rest for 5 minutes. Press into a lightly greased 15-in. x 10-in. x 1-in. baking pan.

Layer the ham, salami, American cheese, mozzarella cheese and Italian sausage over dough. Roll up jelly-roll style, starting with a long side; pinch seam to seal. Place diagonally in pan. Brush dough with remaining oil; sprinkle with Parmesan cheese, oregano, garlic powder and pepper.

Bake at 375° for 35-40 minutes or until golden brown. Let stand for 10 minutes before slicing.

YIELD: 18 servings.

lee gregory
ASHLAND, OHIO

This hearty stromboli isn't difficult to make and is great for serving a group.

MIX it up

Bringing a few loaves of stromboli to a potluck? Experiment with a variety of ingredients in each to suit everyone's tastes. A few flavor combos include pizza sauce, pepperoni and mozzarella or chicken, mushrooms and Swiss cheese.

CHEESEBURGER PARADISE SOUP

PREP: 30 min. | **COOK:** 25 min.

- 6 medium potatoes, peeled and cubed
- 1 small carrot, grated
- 1 small onion, chopped
- 1/2 cup chopped green pepper
- 2 tablespoons chopped seeded jalapeno pepper
- 3 cups water
- 2 tablespoons plus 2 teaspoons beef bouillon granules
- 2 garlic cloves, minced
- 1/8 teaspoon pepper
- 2 pounds ground beef
- 1/2 pound sliced fresh mushrooms
- 2 tablespoons butter
- 5 cups milk, *divided*
- 6 tablespoons all-purpose flour
- 1 package (16 ounces) process cheese (Velveeta), cubed
- Crumbled cooked bacon

In a Dutch oven, combine the first nine ingredients; bring to a boil. Reduce heat; cover and simmer for 10-15 minutes or until potatoes are tender.

Meanwhile, in a large skillet, cook beef and mushrooms in butter over medium heat until meat is no longer pink; drain. Add to soup. Stir in 4 cups milk; heat through.

In a small bowl, combine the flour and remaining milk until smooth; gradually stir into soup. Bring to a boil; cook and stir for 2 minutes or until thickened. Reduce heat; stir in cheese until melted. Garnish with bacon.
YIELD: 14 servings (about 3-1/2 quarts).

nadina ladimarco
BURTON, OHIO

I've never met a person who didn't enjoy this creamy soup. It's hearty enough to serve as a main course with your favorite bread or rolls.

PEA SOUP FOR A CROWD

PREP: 30 min. | **BAKE:** 5 hours

- 1 pound dried navy beans *or* yellow split peas
- 3 cups (1-1/2 pounds) dried yellow split peas
- 2 pounds smoked pork shoulder *or* picnic ham
- 3-1/2 quarts water
- 4 celery ribs, chopped
- 3 large carrots, shredded
- 2 cups chopped onion
- 1-1/4 teaspoons salt
- 1 teaspoon pepper

Rinse and sort beans. Place in a large Dutch oven; cover with water. Bring to a boil; boil for 2 minutes. Remove from the heat; let stand for 1-4 hours or until beans are softened. Drain beans and discard liquid. Rinse and sort split peas. Place beans in an 8-qt. roaster. Add remaining ingredients.

Cover and bake at 350° for 5-7 hours or until peas are tender and soup is thick, stirring occasionally. Remove pork; allow to cool. Remove meat from bones and cut into bite-size pieces. Discard bones. Return meat to pan; heat through.

YIELD: 20-26 servings (6-1/2 quarts).

maria bosma
COBOURG, ONTARIO

This soup is perfect for busy days because it bakes in the oven for hours with little fuss. I've served it several times with great success to various church groups I belong to.

STEAK SAUCE SLOPPY JOES

PREP: 15 min. | **COOK:** 30 min.

- 3 pounds ground beef
- 4 medium onions, chopped
- 2 celery ribs, chopped
- 1 garlic clove, minced
- 1 can (28 ounces) diced tomatoes, undrained
- 1/4 cup Worcestershire sauce
- 1/4 cup A.1. steak sauce
- 2 tablespoons chili powder
- 2 tablespoons paprika
- 1/4 teaspoon pepper
- 15 hamburger buns, split

In a Dutch oven, cook the beef, onions and celery over medium heat until meat is no longer pink. Add garlic; cook 1 minute longer. Drain.

Stir in the tomatoes, Worcestershire sauce, steak sauce, chili powder, paprika and pepper. Bring to a boil. Reduce heat; simmer, uncovered, for 20 minutes or until thickened and heated through. Serve on buns.

YIELD: 15 servings.

patti basten
DEPERE, WISCONSIN

Everyone in our family loves these flavorful barbecue sandwiches. The recipe makes a big batch, and it freezes nicely, too.

ELIMINATE grease

When making sloppy joes, eliminate the greasy appearance by thoroughly draining the ground beef after it's cooked. After draining, blot the meat with paper towels or rinse with hot water to eliminate any additional fat. When using shredded meat for barbecued beef, discard any visible fat before shredding.

HOT ITALIAN ROAST BEEF SANDWICHES

PREP: 10 min. | **COOK:** 3-1/2 hours

1 tablespoon butter
1 beef sirloin tip roast (5 pounds)
1 can (28 ounces) tomatoes with juice, cut up
1/3 cup water
1 tablespoon ground thyme
1 to 3 teaspoons crushed dried red pepper
Bread *or* rolls of your choice

In a Dutch oven, melt butter over medium heat. Brown roast on all sides. Add remaining ingredients except rolls; cover and simmer until the roast is tender, about 3-1/2 to 4 hours. Add additional water, if necessary, to keep roast simmering in broth.

Remove meat from the broth and reserve broth. Let the meat stand 20 minutes. Trim any fat and thinly slice meat. When ready to serve, reheat sliced beef in the broth. Serve on rolls.

YIELD: about 20 sandwiches.

betty claycomb
ALVERTON, PENNSYLVANIA

There's nothing better than warm, tender roast beef on a chilly night. These sandwiches always make a big hit at potlucks and church suppers.

CHUNKY TURKEY CHILI

PREP: 30 min. | **COOK:** 2 hours

5 pounds ground turkey
6 cups chopped celery
2 medium green peppers, chopped
2 large onions, chopped
2 cans (28 ounces *each*) crushed tomatoes
2 cups water
2 envelopes (1-3/4 ounces *each*) chili seasoning
1 to 2 tablespoons chili powder
2 cans (16 ounces *each*) kidney beans, rinsed and drained

In a Dutch oven over medium heat, brown turkey; drain. Add the celery, peppers and onions; cook and stir for 5 minutes. Add the next four ingredients; bring to a boil. Reduce heat; cover and simmer for 2 hours. Add beans; heat through.

YIELD: 24 servings (6 quarts).

judith southcombe
AURORA, COLORADO

I made this hearty chili when I needed a dish for a benefit cook-off at work, but to keep things light, I substituted ground turkey for the beef. Everyone raved about the delicious flavor, and many people requested the recipe.

CABBAGE SOUP

PREP: 15 min. | **COOK:** 25 min.

1 cup chopped celery
1 cup chopped onion
1 medium head cabbage, chopped
8 cups water
1 teaspoon beef bouillon granules
1 tablespoon salt
2 teaspoons pepper
1-1/2 pounds ground beef, browned and drained
2 cans (15 ounces *each*) tomato sauce
1 tablespoon brown sugar
1/4 cup ketchup

In a large Dutch oven, cook the celery, onion and cabbage in water until tender. Add the bouillon, salt, pepper, beef and tomato sauce. Bring to a boil; reduce heat and simmer 10 minutes. Stir in brown sugar and ketchup; simmer another 10 minutes or until heated through.

YIELD: 16-20 servings (5 quarts).

nancy stevens
MORRISON, ILLINOIS

My husband was never too fond of cabbage—until the first time he tried this soup recipe from my aunt. Now it's a favorite at our house.

DELI SANDWICH PARTY PLATTER

PREP/TOTAL TIME: 30 min.

1 bunch green leaf lettuce
2 pounds sliced deli turkey
2 pounds sliced deli roast beef
1 pound sliced deli ham
1 pound thinly sliced hard salami
2 cartons (7 ounces *each*) roasted red pepper hummus
2 cartons (6-1/2 ounces *each*) garden vegetable cheese spread
Assorted breads and mini bagels

Arrange lettuce leaves on a serving platter; top with deli meats, rolled up if desired. Serve with hummus, cheese spread, breads and bagels.
YIELD: 24 servings.

taste of home test kitchen

Four kinds of meat, two different spreads and an assortment of breads add up to dozens of delicious sandwiches guests can assemble themselves.

OPEN-FACED MEATBALL SANDWICHES

PREP: 30 min. | **COOK:** 10 min.

1/4 cup egg substitute
1/2 cup soft bread crumbs
1/4 cup finely chopped onion
2 garlic cloves, minced
1/2 teaspoon onion powder
1/2 teaspoon dried oregano
1/2 teaspoon dried basil
1/4 teaspoon pepper
Dash salt
1-1/4 pounds lean ground beef (90% lean)
2 cups garden-style pasta sauce
4 hoagie buns, split
2 tablespoons shredded part-skim
    mozzarella cheese
Shredded Parmesan cheese, optional

In a large bowl, combine the first nine ingredients. Crumble beef over mixture and mix well. Shape into 40 meatballs. In a large skillet coated with cooking spray, brown meatballs in batches; drain.

Place the meatballs in a large saucepan. Add the pasta sauce; bring to a boil. Reduce the heat; cover and simmer for 10-15 minutes or until the meat is no longer pink. Spoon the meatballs and sauce onto bun halves; sprinkle with mozzarella and Parmesan cheeses if desired.

YIELD: 8 servings.

karen barthel
NORTH CANTON, OHIO

My husband and I love classic meatball subs. You can easily transport the meatballs in a slow cooker to keep them warm, and slice the bread to make sandwiches when you arrive at the potluck. Freeze any leftovers for a quick and easy meal on a busy weeknight.

GROUND BEEF TURNOVERS

PREP: 30 min. + chilling | **BAKE:** 35 min.

4 cups all-purpose flour
1 tablespoon sugar
2 teaspoons salt
1-3/4 cups shortening
1/2 cup ice water
1 egg, lightly beaten
1 tablespoon white vinegar

FILLING:

2 pounds lean ground beef (90% lean)
1 cup diced carrots
2 medium potatoes, peeled and cut into 1/4-inch cubes
1 medium onion, chopped
1 to 2 teaspoons salt
1/4 teaspoon pepper
Half-and-half cream

In a large bowl, combine the flour, sugar and salt; cut in the shortening until the mixture resembles coarse crumbs. In a small bowl, combine the water, egg and vinegar. Add to the shortening mixture, 1 tablespoon at a time, tossing lightly with a fork until the mixture forms a ball. Cover and chill for 30 minutes.

Meanwhile, combine the first six filling ingredients. Divide pastry into 15 equal portions. On a lightly floured surface, roll out one portion into a 6-1/2-in. circle.

Mound a heaping 1/3 cup filling on half of circle. Moisten the edges with water; fold the dough over the filling and press edges with a fork to seal. Transfer to a greased baking sheet. Repeat with the remaining pastry and filling.

Cut three slits in the top of each turnover; brush with cream. Bake at 375° for 35-40 minutes or until vegetables are tender and crust is golden brown.

YIELD: 15 turnovers.

wendy tomlinson
ECHO BAY, ONTARIO

My husband likes these handheld meat pies so much that he'll even eat leftovers cold! They're easily portable so I take them to shared dinners.

FOCACCIA SANDWICH

PREP/TOTAL TIME: 15 min.

1/3 cup mayonnaise
1 can (4-1/4 ounces) chopped ripe olives, drained
1 focaccia bread (about 12 ounces), halved lengthwise
4 romaine leaves
1/4 pound shaved deli ham
1 medium sweet red pepper, thinly sliced into rings
1/4 pound shaved deli turkey
1 large tomato, thinly sliced
1/4 pound thinly sliced hard salami
1 jar (7 ounces) roasted sweet red peppers, drained
4 to 6 slices provolone cheese

In a small bowl, combine mayonnaise and olives; spread over the bottom half of bread. Layer with remaining ingredients; replace bread top. Cut focaccia into wedges; secure with toothpicks.

YIELD: 24 servings.

peggy woodward
EAST TROY, WISCONSIN

Slices of this pretty sandwich are great for any casual get-together. Add or change the ingredients to suit your taste.

VEGETABLE BEEF SOUP FOR 50

PREP: 40 min. | **COOK:** 2-1/2 hours

- 8 pounds boneless beef chuck, cut into 1/2-inch cubes
- 1 cup all-purpose flour
- 1 tablespoon salt
- 2 teaspoons pepper
- 1/2 cup canola oil
- 4 garlic cloves, minced
- 2 bay leaves
- 2 teaspoons dried thyme
- 6 quarts water
- 4 cans (15 ounces *each*) tomato sauce
- 1 can (46 ounces) tomato juice
- 1/4 cup beef bouillon granules
- 2 cups medium pearl barley
- 2 pounds potatoes, peeled and cubed
- 1-1/2 pounds carrots, sliced
- 1 pound chopped cabbage
- 1 pound onions, chopped
- 1 package (16 ounces) frozen green beans
- 1 package (16 ounces) frozen peas

In a large resealable plastic bag, combine the flour, salt and pepper. Add beef, a few pieces at a time, and shake to coat.

In a large Dutch oven, brown the meat in oil in batches; drain. Transfer to a large stockpot; add the garlic, bay leaves, thyme, water, tomato sauce and juice, beef bouillon and barley.

Bring to a boil. Reduce heat; cover and simmer for 1 hour. Add vegetables; bring to a boil. Reduce heat; cover and simmer for 1-1/2 to 2 hours or until vegetables and meat are tender. Remove bay leaves.

YIELD: 50 servings.

elsie schimmer
GRAND ISLAND, NEBRASKA

Do you cringe at the thought of making soup for a large crowd? This wonderfully seasoned recipe with a rich broth is so easy to make...and oh-so delicious to eat!

TRANSPORT soup

Whenever you're bringing a stew, soup or chili to a potluck, you'll find it can be easily transported in a 5-quart slow cooker.

BAKED HAM SANDWICHES

PREP: 10 min. + freezing | **BAKE:** 10 min.

- 1/3 cup butter, softened
- 1/2 cup dried minced onion
- 1/3 to 1/2 cup prepared mustard
- 2 tablespoons poppy seeds
- 8 hamburger buns, split
- 16 slices deli ham
- 8 slices Swiss cheese

In a small bowl, combine the butter, onion, mustard and poppy seeds; spread about 2 tablespoons on each bun. Layer with ham and cheese; replace the tops. Wrap each sandwich in foil.

Bake at 350° for 6-10 minutes or until the cheese is melted, or freeze for up to 2 months.

TO USE FROZEN SANDWICHES: Bake at 350° for 30-35 minutes or until cheese is melted.

YIELD: 8 servings.

charlotte rowe
ALTO, NEW MEXICO

Minced onion and prepared mustard put a flavorful spin on these ham and cheese sandwiches. I simply take a few foil-wrapped favorites from the freezer and warm them in the oven for effortless lunches.

SWEET POTATO PORK STEW

PREP: 10 min. | **COOK:** 1 hour 5 min.

- 3 tablespoons Dijon mustard
- 2 pounds boneless pork, trimmed and cut into 1-inch cubes
- 1/2 cup all-purpose flour
- 3 tablespoons brown sugar
- 3 tablespoons canola oil
- 2 garlic cloves, minced
- 2-1/3 cups chicken broth
- 4 to 5 small onions, quartered
- 2 medium sweet potatoes, peeled and cubed
- 1/2 teaspoon salt
- 1/4 teaspoon pepper
- 1/4 cup minced fresh parsley

Rub mustard over pork. In a large resealable plastic bag, combine flour and brown sugar; add pork and shake to coat.

In a large skillet, over medium-high heat, brown pork in oil. Add garlic; cook 1 minute longer. Add broth; bring to a boil. Scrape bottom of skillet to loosen any browned bits. Reduce the heat; cover and simmer for 30 minutes or until pork is no longer pink.

Add the onions, sweet potatoes, salt and pepper; cover and simmer 30 minutes more or until the pork and potatoes are tender. Stir in the parsley.

YIELD: 6-8 servings (2 quarts).

susan schlenvogt
WAUKESHA, WISCONSIN

I'm an avid recipe collector and have fun trying new dishes. Fortunately, my family doesn't mind experimenting with new tastes. Everyone loves the blend of flavors in my hearty stew.

STROMBOLI SANDWICHES

PREP: 30 min. | **BAKE:** 25 min.

2 pounds ground beef

1/4 cup finely chopped onion

1 cup ketchup

1 cup tomato sauce

1/4 cup grated Parmesan cheese

2 teaspoons garlic powder, *divided*

1 teaspoon dried oregano

1/2 teaspoon fennel seed

1/2 teaspoon Italian seasoning

1/2 cup butter, softened

2 loaves (1 pound *each*) Italian bread, halved lengthwise

2 cups (8 ounces) shredded part-skim mozzarella cheese

In a Dutch oven, cook beef and onion over medium heat until meat is no longer pink; drain. Stir in the ketchup, tomato sauce, Parmesan cheese, 1/2 teaspoon garlic powder, oregano, fennel seed and Italian seasoning. Bring to a boil. Reduce heat; simmer, uncovered, for 15 minutes or until thickened, stirring occasionally.

Meanwhile, in a small bowl, combine butter and remaining garlic powder; spread over top halves of bread. Sprinkle 1/2 cup mozzarella cheese over each bottom bread half. Spoon meat mixture over top; sprinkle with remaining mozzarella cheese.

Replace bread tops; wrap each sandwich loaf in foil. Bake at 350° for 25-30 minutes or until cheese is melted.

YIELD: 2 sandwich loaves (8 servings each).

darlis wilfer
WEST BEND, WISCONSIN

Like a sloppy joe with Italian seasonings, these hearty sandwich slices fill the bill at card parties, potlucks, reunions and more. I've made them dozens of times and always get compliments.

HARVEST CHICKEN RICE SOUP

PREP: 20 min. | **COOK:** 2-1/4 hours

2 celery ribs with leaves
2 medium carrots
1 pound white potatoes, peeled
1 pound sweet potatoes, peeled
3 quarts water
2 pounds broiler/fryer chicken pieces, skin removed
2 large onions, halved
3 reduced-sodium chicken bouillon cubes
3 cups cooked rice (prepared without added salt)
Pepper to taste

Cut vegetables into 2-in. pieces; place in a 5-qt. Dutch oven. Add the water, chicken, onions and bouillon. Bring to a boil; skim the fat. Reduce the heat; cover and simmer for 2 hours.

Strain the broth and skim fat. Remove chicken; cool. Remove meat from bones and cut into bite-size pieces; set meat aside. Discard bones.

Puree the vegetables and broth in a blender; strain. Return chicken and broth to Dutch oven. Stir in the rice. Cook over medium heat until bubbly, stirring occasionally. Season with pepper.

YIELD: 20 servings (5 quarts).

diane winningham
UNIONTOWN, MISSOURI

The produce in this soup is pureed, so it's a cinch to get the little ones to eat their veggies! Kids of all ages will surely savor this all-time classic.

STROGANOFF IN A BUN

PREP/TOTAL TIME: 25 min.

2 pounds ground beef
1 large onion, chopped
1 can (10-3/4 ounces) condensed cream of mushroom soup, undiluted
1 cup mayonnaise
3/4 cup finely chopped celery
2/3 cup condensed cheddar cheese soup, undiluted
18 hamburger buns, split

In a large skillet, cook the beef and onion over medium heat until meat is no longer pink; drain.

Stir in the mushroom soup, mayonnaise, celery and cheese soup. Bring to a boil. Reduce the heat; simmer, uncovered, for 10 minutes or until heated through. Serve on hamburger buns.

YIELD: 18 servings.

corrine lingberg
BERESFORD, SOUTH DAKOTA

I fixed these rich-tasting sandwiches for a volunteer fighfighters' lunch. After just one taste, the members of the unit couldn't get enough of them. The bites are great with deviled eggs and baked beans.

POTLUCK PASTA SOUP

PREP: 15 min. | **COOK:** 1 hour 25 min.

1-1/2 pounds ground beef
8 cups water
2 cans (14-1/2 ounces *each*) Italian stewed tomatoes
2 cups diced carrots
1-1/2 cups diced celery
1 cup chopped onion
1 can (8 ounces) tomato sauce
1 envelope onion soup mix
1 tablespoon sugar
1 teaspoon Italian seasoning
2 garlic cloves, minced
2 bay leaves
1/2 teaspoon pepper
3 cups cooked elbow macaroni
1 can (15 ounces) garbanzo beans *or* chickpeas, rinsed and drained
1/2 cup chopped green pepper

In a stockpot, cook beef over medium heat until no longer pink; drain. Add the water, vegetables, tomato sauce, soup mix, sugar and seasonings; bring to a boil. Reduce heat; simmer, uncovered, for 1 hour.

Stir in the macaroni, beans and green pepper; heat through. Discard bay leaves.

YIELD: 20 servings (5 quarts).

marilyn foss
BEAVERTOWN, OHIO

I came up with this recipe in an attempt to duplicate a soup I tried at an Italian restaurant. Friends and family are willing dinner guests when it's on the menu at our house.

ITALIAN seasoning

You can mix up your own Italian seasoning by blending 1/4 teaspoon each of basil, thyme, rosemary and oregano for each teaspoon of Italian seasoning called for in a recipe.

KRAUTBURGERS

PREP: 35 min. + rising | BAKE: 25 min.

1 package (1/4 ounce) active dry yeast
1-1/4 cups warm water (110° to 115°)
1 cup warm milk (110° to 115°)
1/4 cup sugar
2 tablespoons shortening
2 teaspoons salt
5-3/4 to 6-1/4 cups all-purpose flour
1-1/2 pounds ground beef
1 medium cabbage, shredded
1 medium onion, chopped
Salt, pepper and seasoned salt to taste
Melted butter

In a large bowl, dissolve yeast in warm water. Add the milk, sugar, shortening and salt. Stir in enough flour to form a soft dough. Turn onto a floured surface; knead the dough until smooth and elastic, about 6-8 minutes.

Place in a greased bowl, turning once to grease top. Cover and let rise in a warm place until doubled, about 1 hour.

Meanwhile, in a large skillet, cook beef over medium heat until no longer pink; drain. In a large saucepan, cook cabbage and onion until tender.

In a large bowl, combine the meat, cabbage mixture, salt, pepper and seasoned salt. Punch dough down. Turn onto a lightly floured surface; divide in half. Roll each into a 16-in. square. Cut into 4-in. squares. Place 1/4 cup filling in the center of each. Bring corners over filling; pinch to seal.

Place, seam side down, on greased baking sheets. Do not let rise. Bake at 425° for 10 minutes. Reduce heat to 350°; bake 15-20 minutes longer or until golden brown. Remove from pans to wire racks. Brush with the melted butter. Serve burgers warm. Refrigerate the leftovers.

YIELD: 32 buns.

naomi dyer
EATON, COLORADO

I love to bake and cook for family and friends. The recipe for these homemade yeast bundles stuffed with cabbage, beef and onion has been in my personal collection for years.

SNIPPED parsley

Here's a simple way to trim parsley that doesn't require a cutting board or knife. Simply place parsley in a small glass container and snip sprigs with kitchen shears until minced.

HAM SALAD CROISSANTS

PREP/TOTAL TIME: 30 min.

3 cups ground fully cooked ham
2 cups (8 ounces) shredded cheddar cheese
2 celery ribs, finely chopped
8 green onions, chopped
1/3 cup unsalted sunflower kernels
1/3 cup finely chopped green pepper
1/3 cup chopped dill pickle
1/3 cup mayonnaise
1/3 cup sour cream
1 jar (4 ounces) diced pimientos, drained
1 teaspoon ranch salad dressing mix
1 teaspoon coarsely ground pepper
1 teaspoon minced fresh parsley
8 lettuce leaves
8 croissants, split

In a large bowl, combine the first seven ingredients. In a small bowl, combine the mayonnaise, sour cream, pimientos, salad dressing mix, pepper and parsley. Pour over ham mixture; toss to coat. Serve on lettuce-lined croissants.

YIELD: 8 servings.

jo riley
HART, TEXAS

This crunchy, full-flavored ham salad is always a favorite at church picnics and luncheons. It's great as a filling on a sandwich or can be scooped onto fresh cantaloupe wedges.

ROOT VEGETABLE SOUP WITH SAUSAGE

PREP: 30 min. | **COOK:** 45 min.

1/4 pound bulk Italian sausage
1 medium butternut squash (about 3 pounds), peeled and cubed
4 large potatoes, peeled and cubed
3 large sweet potatoes, peeled and cubed
1 large rutabaga, peeled and cubed
1 pound fresh baby carrots
1 medium turnip, peeled and diced
10 cups water
2 cans (14-1/2 ounces *each*) vegetable broth
2 tablespoons sugar
1-1/2 teaspoons salt
1 teaspoon ground ginger
1/8 teaspoon pepper
1/4 cup heavy whipping cream

Crumble sausage into a stockpot. Cook over medium heat until no longer pink; drain.

Stir in the vegetables, water, broth, sugar and seasonings; bring to a boil. Reduce heat; cover and simmer for 35-40 minutes or until vegetables are tender. Cool slightly.

In a blender, process soup in batches until smooth. Return to the pan; whisk in cream. Heat through (do not boil).

YIELD: 20 servings (1 cup each).

donna class
KEYSER, WEST VIRGINIA

I tasted a similar soup at a restaurant and re-created it at home. To my surprise, it came out even better than the original! This soup actually won top honors in our town's annual cook-off.

MEATBALL SUB SANDWICHES

PREP/TOTAL TIME: 30 min.

2 eggs, lightly beaten
1 cup dry bread crumbs
2 tablespoons grated Parmesan cheese
2 tablespoons finely chopped onion
1 teaspoon salt
1/2 teaspoon pepper
1/2 teaspoon garlic powder
1/4 teaspoon Italian seasoning
2 pounds ground beef
1 jar (28 ounces) spaghetti sauce
Additional Parmesan cheese, and sliced onion and green peppers, optional
12 sandwich rolls, split

In a large bowl, combine the first eight ingredients. Crumble beef over mixture and mix well. Shape into 1-in. balls. Place in a single layer in a 3-qt. microwave-safe dish.

Cover and microwave on high for 3-4 minutes. Turn meatballs; cook 3-4 minutes longer or until no longer pink. Drain. Add spaghetti sauce.

Cover and microwave on high for 2-4 minutes or until heated through. Top with additional cheese, onion and green peppers if desired. Serve on rolls.

YIELD: 12 servings.

deena hubler
JASPER, INDIANA

Making these saucy meatballs in advance and reheating them saves me precious time when expecting company. These sandwiches are great fare for any casual get-together.

SHREDDED BEEF 'N' SLAW SANDWICHES

PREP: 20 min. | **COOK:** 2-3/4 hours

- 4 pounds beef stew meat, cut into 1-inch cubes
- 2 cups water
- 2 cups ketchup
- 1/2 to 3/4 cup Worcestershire sauce
- 2 tablespoons lemon juice
- 2 tablespoons prepared horseradish
- 1 tablespoon prepared mustard
- 2 teaspoons salt
- 8 cups shredded cabbage
- 30 sandwich buns, split

In a Dutch oven, bring the beef and water to a boil. Reduce the heat; cover and simmer for 2 hours or until tender.

Remove beef with a slotted spoon; shred with two forks and set aside. Skim the fat from cooking liquid. Stir in the ketchup, Worcestershire sauce, lemon juice, horseradish, mustard and salt. Add the shredded beef and cabbage. Bring to a boil. Reduce the heat; cover and simmer for 45 minutes or until cabbage is tender.

Spoon 1/3 cup onto each sandwich bun.

YIELD: 30 sandwiches.

mary johnson
WHITEHOUSE, OHIO

I have served these tangy, hearty sandwiches for family gatherings and office potlucks. They have always gone over quite well with everyone.

SPEEDY SEAFOOD GUMBO

PREP/TOTAL TIME: 15 min.

- 3 cups water, *divided*
- 1 tablespoon butter
- 1/4 teaspoon salt
- 1 cup uncooked instant rice
- 4 cans (10-3/4 ounces *each*) condensed chicken gumbo soup, undiluted
- 1 pound frozen cooked shrimp, peeled and deveined
- 1 package (10 ounces) frozen cut okra
- 1 package (8 ounces) imitation crabmeat, flaked
- 1 tablespoon dried minced onion
- 1 teaspoon Cajun seasoning
- 1/2 teaspoon garlic powder

In a small saucepan, bring 1 cup of water, butter and salt to a boil. Stir in the rice; cover and remove from the heat. Let mixture stand for 5 minutes.

Meanwhile, in a Dutch oven, combine the soup, shrimp, okra, crab, onion, Cajun seasoning, garlic power and remaining water. Bring to a boil. Reduce heat; cover and cook over medium heat until heated through. Stir in cooked rice.

YIELD: 12 servings (3 quarts).

lori costo
SPRING, TEXAS

I needed a quick meal one night when my husband was coming home late with the kids. So I put together this tasty gumbo with ingredients I had on hand, and we really liked it.

IMITATION crab

Imitation crabmeat, also called surimi, is fish that is shaped, flavored and colored to resemble crab. It is typically made from Alaskan pollock, a lean, firm fish with a delicate flavor. Both natural and artificial flavors are used as well as artificial coloring.

HOT TURKEY SANDWICHES

PREP: 15 min. | **BAKE:** 2 hours + standing

- 3 bone-in turkey breasts (6 to 7 pounds each)
- 3 cups sliced fresh mushrooms
- 3 cups thinly sliced green onions
- 1-1/2 cups butter, cubed
- 3/4 cup all-purpose flour
- 3 to 4 tablespoons dried basil
- 3 teaspoons salt
- 1 teaspoon pepper
- 6 cups chicken broth
- 3 cups heavy whipping cream
- 50 sandwich rolls, split

Place turkey on racks in roasting pans. Bake, uncovered, at 325° for 2 hours or until a meat thermometer reads 170°, basting several times with pan drippings. Cover and let stand for 10 minutes. Shred turkey.

In several Dutch ovens or large pans, saute mushrooms and onions in butter until tender. Stir in flour, basil, salt and pepper until blended. Gradually stir in broth. Bring to a boil; cook and stir for 2 minutes or until thickened and bubbly. Add the turkey and heat through. Stir in the cream; cook until heated through. Spoon 1/2 cup of filling onto each roll.

YIELD: 50 servings.

janice bilek
HOLLAND, MICHIGAN

If you're looking for a deliciously different entree, try these comforting sandwiches. I set tender shredded turkey in a basil cream sauce. It's a nice change of pace from turkey in traditional gravy.

BARBECUED BEEF SANDWICHES

PREP: 15 min. | **COOK:** 2-1/2 hours

- 2 pounds beef stew meat
- 2 cups water
- 4 cups shredded cabbage
- 1/2 cup barbecue sauce
- 1/2 cup ketchup
- 1/3 cup Worcestershire sauce
- 1 tablespoon prepared horseradish
- 1 tablespoon prepared mustard
- 10 hamburger *or* other sandwich buns, split

In a Dutch oven, combine the beef and water. Bring to a boil. Reduce heat; cover and simmer for 1-1/2 hours or until tender. Drain cooking liquid, reserving 3/4 cup.

Cool beef; shred and return to the Dutch oven. Add the cabbage, barbecue sauce, ketchup, Worcestershire sauce, horseradish, mustard and reserved cooking liquid. Cover and simmer for 1 hour. Spoon onto buns.

YIELD: 10 servings.

denise marshall
BAGLEY, WISCONSIN

The great thing about this recipe—especially for non-cabbage lovers—is that you can't taste the cabbage in the meat. Yet, at the same time, the vegetable adds heartiness and moistness to the sandwiches.

CHILI FOR A CROWD

PREP: 20 min. | **COOK:** 1-1/4 hours

- 5 pounds ground beef
- 3 large onions, chopped
- 5 celery ribs, chopped
- 2 cans (28 ounces *each*) diced tomatoes, undrained
- 2 cans (16 ounces *each*) kidney beans, rinsed and drained
- 1 can (28 ounces) pork and beans
- 2 cans (10-3/4 ounces *each*) condensed tomato soup, undiluted
- 2-2/3 cups water
- 1/4 cup chili powder
- 3 teaspoons salt
- 2 teaspoons garlic powder
- 2 teaspoons seasoned salt
- 2 teaspoons pepper
- 1 teaspoon ground cumin
- 1 teaspoon *each* dried thyme, oregano and rosemary, crushed
- 1/2 teaspoon cayenne pepper

In a large stockpot, cook the beef, onions and celery over medium heat until meat is no longer pink; drain. Stir in the remaining ingredients. Bring to a boil. Reduce heat; simmer, uncovered, for 1 hour.

YIELD: 24 servings (1 cup each).

LEFTOVER chili

Freeze leftover chili in small portions in muffin cups. Later, you can serve chili dogs by heating the muffin cups in the oven and serving the portions over cooked hot dogs. Leftover chili can also be used as a tasty filling for meat pies.

linda boehme
FAIRMONT, MINNESOTA

A coworker made this robust and well-seasoned chili for a potluck at work, and I just had to have the recipe. Sometimes I'll make a big batch for my family and freeze any leftovers for a quick-to-fix meal.

HAWAIIAN HAM SANDWICHES

PREP/TOTAL TIME: 25 min.

- 8 submarine *or* hoagie buns (8 inches)
- 8 slices Swiss cheese, halved
- 1/2 medium sweet red pepper, julienned
- 1/2 medium green pepper, julienned
- 6 to 8 green onions, sliced
- 2 teaspoons canola oil
- 1 pound sliced fully cooked ham, julienned
- 1 can (20 ounces) pineapple tidbits, drained
- 1 cup (4 ounces) shredded part-skim mozzarella cheese

Cut thin slices off tops of rolls. Hollow out bread in the center, leaving 1/4-in. shells; set aside tops and discard hollowed-out bread (or save for another use). Place rolls on a baking sheet; line the inside of each with Swiss cheese.

In a large skillet, saute the peppers and onions in oil for 3 minutes. Add ham; cook for 3 minutes. Add pineapple. Remove from the heat; drain.

Spoon the filling into rolls. Bake at 450° for 5 minutes. Sprinkle with mozzarella cheese; return to the oven until cheese is melted, about 1 minute. Replace the roll tops. Serve sandwiches immediately.

YIELD: 8 servings.

alice lewis
RED OAK, IOWA

Fans of pizza topped with pineapple and Canadian bacon are sure to savor these baked ham sandwiches. I've made them many times for parties, and I often get asked for the recipe.

WALDORF SANDWICHES

PREP: 20 min. + chilling

1 can (20 ounces) unsweetened crushed pineapple
3 cups cubed cooked turkey breast
1 medium red apple, chopped
1 medium green apple, chopped
1/2 cup chopped walnuts
1 cup sliced celery
1 cup fat-free mayonnaise
1 tablespoon poppy seeds
1 teaspoon grated lemon peel
1/2 teaspoon vanilla extract
1/2 teaspoon salt-free seasoning blend
16 hard rolls, split

Drain pineapple, pressing out excess juice; discard all but 1/4 cup juice. In a large bowl, combine the pineapple, turkey, apples, walnuts and celery.

In a small bowl, combine the mayonnaise, poppy seeds, lemon peel, vanilla, seasoning blend and reserved pineapple juice. Pour over turkey mixture and toss well. Chill. Serve on rolls.

YIELD: 16 servings.

darlene sutton
ARVADA, COLORADO

The fresh fruity filling for this sandwich is a nice variation on the classic Waldorf salad. My clan loves the cool and creamy combination, so I serve these often for lunch or a light dinner.

CLAM CHOWDER FOR 60

PREP: 40 min. | **COOK:** 45 min.

30 cans (6-1/2 ounces *each*) minced clams
8 cups diced onions
1-1/2 pounds butter, cubed
2 cups all-purpose flour
3 quarts milk
3 bunches celery, sliced
3 cups minced fresh parsley
12 pounds potatoes, peeled and cubed
3 pounds shredded sharp cheddar cheese
Salt and pepper to taste

Drain and rinse clams, reserving juice; set aside. In two stockpots, saute the onions in butter until tender. Add flour; stir to form a smooth paste. Gradually add the milk, stirring constantly until slightly thickened (do not boil). Add the celery, parsley and potatoes; cook until the vegetables are tender, about 45 minutes.

Add clams and cheese; cook until cheese is melted and soup is heated through. Add the reserved clam juice, salt and pepper.

YIELD: 60 servings.

gretchen draeger
SANTA CRUZ, CALIFORNIA

I made this recipe when my neighborhood put on a "Soup Day" potluck. Everyone agreed it tasted as good—if not better— than the version so popular in New England.

OPEN-FACED PIZZA BURGERS

PREP/TOTAL TIME: 30 min.

1-1/2 pounds ground beef
1/4 cup chopped onion
1 can (15 ounces) pizza sauce
1 can (4 ounces) mushroom stems and pieces, drained
1 tablespoon sugar
1/2 teaspoon dried oregano
6 hamburger buns, split and toasted
1-1/2 cups (6 ounces) shredded part-skim mozzarella cheese

In a large skillet, cook beef and onion over medium heat until the meat is no longer pink; drain. Stir in the pizza sauce, mushrooms, sugar and oregano; mix well. Spoon onto the buns; sprinkle with the mozzarella cheese.

Place on ungreased baking sheets. Broil 4 in. from the heat for 2 minutes or until cheese is melted.

To freeze for quick lunches later, place the split and toasted buns on a baking sheet. Spoon the meat mixture onto buns; freeze for 1 hour. Transfer to heavy-duty resealable plastic bags or airtight containers.

TO USE FROZEN PIZZA BURGERS: Thaw pizza burgers in the refrigerator; sprinkle with cheese. Broil 4 in. from heat for 2 minutes or until cheese is melted.

YIELD: 12 servings.

sharon schwartz
BURLINGTON, WISCONSIN

My family requests these hearty sandwiches whenever they have a hankering for pizza or burgers. A dash of oregano livens up the convenient canned sauce.

CHICKEN GUMBO

PREP: 40 min. | **COOK:** 35 min.

- 6 celery ribs, chopped
- 3 medium green peppers, chopped
- 3 medium onions, chopped
- 3/4 cup butter, cubed
- 10 quarts chicken broth
- 7 cans (14-1/2 ounces *each*) diced tomatoes, undrained
- 3 bay leaves
- 2 tablespoons minced fresh parsley
- 1 tablespoon pepper
- 2 to 3 tablespoons garlic powder
- 2 teaspoons salt
- 2 cups uncooked long grain rice
- 10 cups cubed cooked chicken
- 6 cups cubed fully cooked ham
- 1 package (16 ounces) frozen chopped okra
- 2 pounds cooked small shrimp, peeled and deveined, optional

In several large stockpots, saute the celery, green peppers and onions in butter until tender. Add the next seven ingredients; bring to a boil. Stir in the rice. Reduce heat; cover and simmer for 15-20 minutes or until the rice is tender.

Stir in the chicken, ham, okra and shrimp. Simmer for 8-10 minutes or until the shrimp turn pink and the okra is tender. Discard the bay leaves.

YIELD: 48 servings (1 cup each).

GUMBO defined

Gumbo is a hearty, stew-like soup usually served with rice that starts with a dark roux of flour and oil or butter. It may contain shellfish, chicken, sausage, ham, tomatoes, onions, garlic, sweet peppers and celery. In addition to the roux, okra is used as a thickening agent.

willa govoro
ST. CLAIR, MISSOURI

Chicken, ham, shrimp, rice and a host of good-for-you veggies make this gumbo a surefire people-pleaser.

MINI CHICKEN SALAD CROISSANTS

PREP: 20 min. + chilling

- 1/3 cup sour cream
- 1/3 cup mayonnaise
- 4 teaspoons lemon juice
- 1 teaspoon salt
- 1/4 teaspoon pepper
- 3 cups cubed cooked chicken
- 4 celery ribs, thinly sliced
- 1 cup chopped fresh mushrooms
- 1/4 cup chopped green pepper
- 1/4 cup chopped sweet red pepper
- 4 bacon strips, cooked and crumbled
- 1/2 cup chopped pecans, toasted
- 20 lettuce leaves
- 20 miniature croissants, split

In a small bowl, combine the sour cream, mayonnaise, lemon juice, salt and pepper. In a large bowl, combine the chicken, celery, mushrooms and peppers; stir in the sour cream mixture until combined. Cover and refrigerate for at least 4 hours.

Just before serving, stir in the bacon and pecans. Spoon 1/4 cup chicken salad onto each lettuce-lined croissant.

YIELD: 20 sandwiches.

patricia tjugum
TOMAHAWK, WISCONSIN

Fresh-tasting and great for a get-together, this popular chicken salad could also be served on lettuce or a slice of cantaloupe or honeydew. When there will be kids in the crowd, I will often substitute halved red seedless grapes for the green and red peppers.

HAM AND CORN CHOWDER

PREP: 20 min. | **COOK:** 25 min.

8 bacon strips, cut into 1-inch pieces
1 medium onion, finely chopped
1 cup sliced celery
1/2 cup diced green pepper
3 cups cubed peeled potatoes
  (about 3 medium)
3 cups chicken broth
4 cups whole milk, *divided*
4 cups fresh *or* frozen whole kernel corn,
  divided
2 cups cubed fully cooked ham
2 tablespoons butter
3 tablespoons minced fresh parsley
1 teaspoon salt
1/8 teaspoon pepper
1/8 teaspoon hot pepper sauce, optional

In a large saucepan, cook bacon until crisp. Remove the bacon to paper towels to drain, reserving 1/4 cup drippings in pan. Saute the onion, celery and green pepper in drippings for 5 minutes. Add the potatoes and broth. Reduce the heat; cover and simmer for 10 minutes.

Place 1/2 cup milk and 2 cups corn in a blender; cover and process until pureed. Pour into the saucepan. Add the ham and remaining corn; simmer for 10 minutes or until the vegetables are tender. Stir in the butter, parsley, salt, pepper, hot pepper sauce if desired and remaining milk; heat through. Garnish with bacon.

YIELD: 10-12 servings (3 quarts).

sharon rose brand
STAYTON, OREGON

I like to experiment with recipes to shake up the flavors. I sometimes omit the bacon and butter in this soup, and I have used canned corn and creamed corn with good results. We like to eat this chowder with big soft hot pretzels instead of crackers.

GRILLED ITALIAN SAUSAGE SANDWICHES

PREP: 30 min. | **GRILL:** 10 min.

4 large green peppers, thinly sliced
1/2 cup chopped onion
2 tablespoons olive oil
4 garlic cloves, minced
1 can (15 ounces) tomato sauce
1 can (12 ounces) tomato paste
1 cup water
1 tablespoon sugar
2 teaspoons dried basil
1 teaspoon salt
1 teaspoon dried oregano
20 uncooked Italian sausage links
20 sandwich buns
Shredded part-skim mozzarella cheese, optional

In a large saucepan, saute peppers and onion in oil until crisp-tender. Add garlic; cook 1 minute longer. Drain. Stir in the tomato sauce, tomato paste, water, sugar, basil, salt and oregano. Bring to a boil. Reduce the heat; cover and simmer for 30 minutes or until heated through.

Meanwhile, grill sausages, covered, over medium heat for 10-16 minutes or until no longer pink, turning occasionally. Serve on buns with sauce and cheese if desired.

YIELD: 20 servings.

mike yaeger
BROOKINGS, SOUTH DAKOTA

Whether you bring these to a picnic, backyard barbecue or for tailgating at the ballpark, folks won't be able to get enough! The zippy peppers make the perfect condiment to these grilled favorites!

BEEF BRISKET ON BUNS

PREP: 25 min. + standing | **BAKE:** 5 hours

1/2 teaspoon ground ginger
1/2 teaspoon ground mustard
1 fresh beef brisket (4 to 5 pounds)
2 cups water
1 cup ketchup
1/2 cup Worcestershire sauce
2 tablespoons brown sugar
2 teaspoons Liquid Smoke, optional
1 teaspoon chili powder
16 to 20 sandwich buns, split, optional

Combine the ginger and mustard; rub over brisket. Place on a rack in a shallow roasting pan. Bake, uncovered, at 325° for 2 hours.

Let stand for 20 minutes. Thinly slice meat across the grain. Place in a foil-lined 13-in. x 9-in. baking dish. In a bowl, combine the water, ketchup, Worcestershire sauce, brown sugar, Liquid Smoke if desired and chili powder; pour over meat. Cover tightly with foil; bake 3 hours longer or until tender. Serve on buns if desired.

YIELD: 16 servings.

deb waggoner
GRAND ISLAND, NEBRASKA

These fork-tender brisket sandwiches turns out delicious every time! The recipe is quick to prep, and the mouthwatering aroma will linger for hours.

RICH CLAM CHOWDER

PREP: 45 min. | **COOK:** 25 min.

6 cups diced peeled red potatoes
3 large onions, finely chopped
6 celery ribs, finely chopped
3 cups water
6 cans (6-1/2 ounces *each*) minced clams
1-1/2 cups butter, cubed
1-1/2 cups all-purpose flour
8 cups half-and-half cream
1/4 cup red wine vinegar
2 tablespoons minced fresh parsley
3 teaspoons salt
1/4 teaspoon pepper

In a stockpot, combine the potatoes, onions, celery and water. Drain clams, reserving juice; set clams aside. Add juice to potato mixture. Bring to a boil. Reduce heat; cover and simmer for 10 minutes or until potatoes are tender.

Meanwhile, in a large saucepan, melt the butter over medium heat. Whisk in the flour. Cook and stir for 5 minutes or until lightly browned. Gradually stir in the cream. Bring to a boil; cook and stir for 2 minutes or until thickened. Gradually stir into the potato mixture.

Add the vinegar, parsley, salt, pepper and clams. Cook 5-10 minutes longer or until heated through.

YIELD: 22 servings (1 cup each).

teresa dastrup
MERIDIAN, IDAHO

I came across a chowder recipe I liked and made just enough changes to give it a unique flavor...and feed a pretty large crowd. People always go back for a second serving, and then they ask me for the recipe.

CHOWDER defined

A chowder is a chunky, thick, rich soup frequently made with seafood or vegetables (such as corn), but it can be made with other meat. Chowders have a milk or cream base and may be thickened with flour.

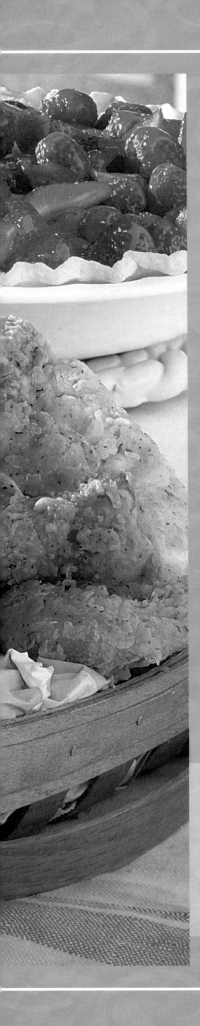

p. 129

p. 145

hearty
main dishes

BEEF BISCUITS

PREP: 25 min. | **COOK:** 25 min.

2 tubes (16.3 ounces *each*) large
    refrigerated buttermilk biscuits
1 pound ground beef
1 small onion, chopped
1/4 cup chopped green pepper
1 can (8 ounces) tomato sauce
1 teaspoon salt
1/2 teaspoon pepper
1/2 teaspoon dried oregano
Canola oil

On a floured surface, roll each biscuit into a 6-in. circle; set aside.

In a large skillet, cook the beef, onion and green pepper over medium heat until meat is no longer pink; drain. Stir in the tomato sauce, salt, pepper and oregano. Place 2 rounded tablespoonfuls of meat mixture onto each biscuit. Fold in half and press firmly with the tines of a fork to seal edges.

Heat about 3 in. of oil to 375° in a deep fryer. Fry each biscuit until golden brown; drain on paper towels. Serve warm.
YIELD: 12 biscuits.

carolyn pauling
PAULINA, IOWA

My granddaughter introduced me to these tasty beef-filled biscuits that she made in her home economics class. It's easy to transport a large batch to a party or potluck.

OLD-FASHIONED BAKED HAM

PREP: 10 min. | **BAKE:** 70 min.

1 can (8 ounces) sliced pineapple
1 can (5 pounds) boneless fully cooked
    ham
1/2 cup packed brown sugar
1 teaspoon ground mustard
1/4 teaspoon ground cloves
1 tablespoon cider vinegar
Maraschino cherries

Drain pineapple, reserving 2 tablespoons juice; set aside pineapple and reserved juice. Save remaining juice for another use. Place the ham in a baking dish. Bake at 350° for 30 minutes.

In a small bowl, combine the brown sugar, mustard, cloves, vinegar and reserved pineapple juice. Score ham; place pineapple slices and cherries over ham. Spoon glaze over top.

Bake the ham for another 40-45 minutes or until a meat thermometer reads 140°, basting occasionally.
YIELD: 8-10 servings.

rosemary pryor
PASADENA, MARYLAND

I can still see the table meticulously set for a country meal at our 150-year-old farm. My mother often made this ham for our large family, and now I'm happy to share the tradition with my own clan.

TANGY TURKEY MEATBALLS

PREP: 15 min. | **COOK:** 20 min.

2 tablespoons dry bread crumbs
2 tablespoons chopped green pepper
1 egg white
1 garlic clove, minced
2 drops Louisiana-style hot sauce
1/3 pound lean ground turkey
1 teaspoon canola oil

SAUCE:
1/4 cup ketchup
2 tablespoons water
4 teaspoons lemon juice
4 teaspoons red wine vinegar
2 teaspoons brown sugar
2 teaspoons molasses
1/2 teaspoon ground mustard
1/4 to 1/2 teaspoon chili powder
1/8 to 1/4 teaspoon cayenne pepper
1/8 teaspoon pepper

In a large bowl, combine the bread crumbs, green pepper, egg white, garlic and hot sauce. Crumble the ground turkey over the mixture and mix well. Shape into 1-in. balls. In a small nonstick skillet, brown meatballs in oil; drain.

Combine the sauce ingredients; pour over meatballs. Bring to a boil. Reduce heat; cover and simmer for 10 minutes or until heated through.

YIELD: 8 servings.

taste of home
test kitchen
Serve these juicy meatballs as an appetizer or double the recipe and serve as an entree on buns or over rice.

NO-STICK molasses

When a recipe calls for molasses and oil, measure the oil first and pour it out. Then measure the molasses in the same cup. It will flow out without sticking because the inside of the cup is still slightly "oiled."

BAKED RIGATONI

PREP: 35 min. | **BAKE:** 30 min.

1 medium onion, chopped
1 small green pepper, diced
2 tablespoons canola oil
1 can (28 ounces) diced tomatoes, drained
1 can (8 ounces) tomato sauce
1 can (6 ounces) tomato paste
3/4 cup water
1 jar (4-1/2 ounces) sliced mushrooms, drained
1/4 cup minced fresh parsley
3 garlic cloves, minced
1 bay leaf
2 teaspoons sugar
1-1/2 teaspoons salt
1 teaspoon oregano
1/4 teaspoon pepper
1 package (16 ounces) rigatoni
2 tablespoons butter
2 eggs, lightly beaten
1 carton (15 ounces) ricotta cheese
1/2 cup grated Parmesan cheese
Additional Parmesan cheese

In a large skillet, saute onion and green pepper in oil until tender. Add the tomatoes, sauce, paste, water, mushrooms, parsley, garlic and seasonings. Simmer, uncovered, for 30 minutes. Discard bay leaf.

Meanwhile, cook the pasta according to package directions; drain and toss with butter. In a small bowl, combine the eggs, ricotta and Parmesan cheese. Stir into rigatoni mixture. Transfer to a 3-qt. baking dish; top with tomato mixture.

Bake dish, uncovered, at 350° for 30-40 minutes or until heated through. Sprinkle with additional Parmesan cheese.

YIELD: 8-10 servings.

esther perea
VAN NUYS, CALIFORNIA

You can bet the pasta was homemade when my aunt made this dish. You don't have to make your own pasta, of course, especially if you want the preparation to go a lot quicker. The recipe calls for rigatoni, but you can substitute any noodle of your choice.

CONEY DOGS FOR A CROWD

PREP/TOTAL TIME: 30 min.

2 pounds ground beef
2 celery ribs, chopped
1 medium onion, chopped
1/4 cup packed brown sugar
1/4 cup cornstarch
1 teaspoon salt
1/4 teaspoon pepper
1 bottle (32 ounces) ketchup
2 cups tomato juice
4 packages (1 pound *each*) hot dogs
32 to 40 hot dog buns, split

In a large saucepan, cook the beef, celery and onion until meat is no longer pink; drain. Combine the brown sugar, cornstarch, salt and pepper; stir into beef mixture. Add ketchup and tomato juice. Bring to a boil; cook and stir for 2 minutes or until thickened. Reduce heat; simmer, uncovered, for 15-20 minutes or until heated through.

Cook hot dogs according to package directions; place on buns. Top each with about 1/4 cup beef mixture.

YIELD: 32-40 servings.

betty ann miller
HOLMESVILLE, OHIO

Jazz up plain hot dogs by topping them with this slightly sweet meat sauce. They're a lot more filling than plain dogs, and everyone will devour them in a hurry.

HERBED RUBBED TURKEY

PREP: 10 min. | BAKE: 4 hours

2 tablespoons rubbed sage
1 tablespoon salt
2 teaspoons garlic powder
2 teaspoons celery seed
2 teaspoons dried parsley flakes
2 teaspoons curry powder
2 to 3 teaspoons pepper
1 teaspoon paprika
1/2 teaspoon ground mustard
1/4 teaspoon ground allspice
3 bay leaves
1 turkey (14 to 16 pounds)

In a small bowl, combine the first 10 ingredients. Rub half the seasoning mixture in the cavity of the turkey; add the bay leaves. Rub the remaining mixture over the turkey skin.

Tie the drumsticks together and place turkey in a roasting pan. Roast turkey using your favorite cooking method until a meat thermometer reads 180°. Cover turkey and let stand for 15 minutes before slicing.

YIELD: 12-14 servings.

twila burkholder
MIDDLEBURG, PENNSYLVANIA

Rubs really have a way of locking in flavor. Here a wonderful blend of seasonings makes this turkey extraordinary.

JUICIER turkey

After baking your whole turkey until a meat thermometer reads 180°, remove from the oven and cover with foil. Let stand for 15 to 20 minutes before carving and you'll have a moister, juicier turkey.

BEEF ENCHILADAS

PREP: 25 min. | **BAKE:** 30 min.

2-1/2 pounds ground beef
2/3 cup chopped onion
2 cans (15 ounces *each*) enchilada sauce
1 can (10-3/4 ounces) condensed cream of mushroom soup, undiluted
1 can (10-3/4 ounces) condensed tomato soup, undiluted
20 flour tortillas (8 inches), warmed
2-1/2 cups (10 ounces) shredded cheddar cheese
Additional shredded cheddar cheese

In a large skillet, cook the beef and onion over medium heat until meat is no longer pink; drain. Combine enchilada sauce and soups; pour 1 cup into each of two ungreased 13-in. x 9-in. baking dishes. Stir 1-1/2 cups of sauce into beef mixture; set remaining sauce aside.

Spoon 1/4 cup beef mixture down the center of each tortilla; top with 2 tablespoons cheese. Roll up tightly; place 10 enchiladas seam side down in each prepared dish. Top with remaining sauce. Cover and freeze one pan for up to 3 months.

Cover and bake the remaining pan at 350° for 25-30 minutes. Uncover; sprinkle with additional cheese. Bake 5-10 minutes longer or until cheese is melted.

TO USE FROZEN ENCHILADAS: Thaw in the refrigerator overnight. Bake as directed.

YIELD: 20 servings.

rosemary gonser
CLAY CENTER, KANSAS

This spicy entree is a good dish to feed a large group. You'll really appreciate the make-ahead convenience.

CHICKEN CORDON BLEU

PREP: 20 min. | **BAKE:** 40 min.

8 boneless skinless chicken breast halves (8 ounces *each*)
8 thin slices deli ham
8 slices Swiss cheese
2 eggs
1 cup 2% milk
2 cups crushed cornflakes
1/2 teaspoon garlic powder
1/2 teaspoon salt
1/2 teaspoon pepper

Flatten chicken to 1/4-in. thickness. Top each with a slice of ham and cheese. Roll up and tuck in ends; secure with toothpicks.

In a shallow bowl, whisk eggs and milk. In another shallow bowl, combine cornflakes and seasonings. Dip chicken in egg mixture, then roll in crumbs.

Place on a greased baking sheet. Bake at 350° for 40-45 minutes or until chicken is no longer pink. Discard toothpicks.

YIELD: 8 servings.

merle dyck
ELKFORD, BRITISH COLUMBIA

These attractive chicken rolls are a nice choice for Christmas dinner or any special occasion. A ham and Swiss cheese filling dresses them up, and everyone will enjoy the golden-brown coating.

CRISPY FRIED CHICKEN

PREP: 10 min. | **COOK:** 10 min./batch

4 cups all-purpose flour, *divided*
2 tablespoons garlic salt
1 tablespoon paprika
3 teaspoons pepper, *divided*
2-1/2 teaspoons poultry seasoning
2 eggs
1-1/2 cups water
1 teaspoon salt
2 broiler/fryer chickens (3-1/2 to 4 pounds each), cut up
Oil for deep-fat frying

In a large resealable plastic bag, combine 2-2/3 cups flour, garlic salt, paprika, 2-1/2 teaspoons pepper and poultry seasoning. In a shallow bowl, beat eggs and water; add salt and remaining flour and pepper. Dip the chicken in the egg mixture, then place in the bag, a few pieces at a time, and shake until coated.

In a deep-fat fryer, heat oil to 375°. Fry chicken, several pieces at a time, for 5-6 minutes on each side or until golden brown and crispy and juices run clear. Drain on paper towels.

YIELD: 8 servings.

jeanne schnitzler
LIMA, MONTANA

Always a picnic favorite, this crispy chicken is delicious hot or cold.

ABOUT chicken

A broiler/fryer chicken is about 7 weeks old and weighs 2-1/2 to 4-1/2 pounds. It will yield two breast halves, two thighs, two drumsticks and two wings.

CREAMY SEAFOOD-STUFFED SHELLS

PREP: 40 min. | **BAKE:** 30 min.

- 24 uncooked jumbo pasta shells
- 1 tablespoon finely chopped green pepper
- 1 tablespoon chopped red onion
- 1 teaspoon plus 1/4 cup butter, *divided*
- 2 cans (6 ounces *each*) lump crabmeat, drained
- 1 package (5 ounces) frozen cooked salad shrimp, thawed
- 1 egg, lightly beaten
- 1/2 cup shredded part-skim mozzarella cheese
- 1/4 cup mayonnaise
- 2 tablespoons plus 4 cups milk, *divided*
- 1-1/2 teaspoons seafood seasoning, *divided*
- 1/4 teaspoon pepper
- 1/4 cup all-purpose flour
- 1/4 teaspoon coarsely ground pepper
- 1-1/2 cups grated Parmesan cheese

Cook pasta according to package directions. Meanwhile, in a small skillet, saute green pepper and onion in 1 teaspoon butter until tender; set aside.

In a large bowl, combine the crab, shrimp, egg, mozzarella cheese, mayonnaise, 2 tablespoons milk, 1 teaspoon seafood seasoning, pepper and green pepper mixture.

Drain and rinse pasta; stuff each shell with 1 rounded tablespoon of the seafood mixture. Place in a greased 13-in. x 9-in. baking dish.

In a small saucepan, melt remaining butter over medium heat. Whisk in flour and coarsely ground pepper; gradually whisk in remaining milk. Bring to a boil; cook and stir for 2 minutes or until thickened. Stir in Parmesan cheese.

Pour the sauce over the stuffed shells. Sprinkle with remaining seafood seasoning. Bake, uncovered, at 350° for 30-35 minutes or until bubbly.

YIELD: 8 servings.

katie sloan
CHARLOTTE, NORTH CAROLINA

Inspired by my love of lasagna, pasta shells and seafood, I created this recipe that's easy to make but special enough for company. I serve it with garlic bread and a salad for a complete meal.

SPAGHETTI 'N' MEATBALLS

PREP: 30 min. | **COOK:** 1 hour 40 min.

2 eggs
1 cup dry bread crumbs
1/2 cup grated Parmesan cheese
1/2 cup tomato juice, milk *or* beef broth
1/4 cup finely chopped green pepper
1/4 cup finely chopped onion
1 teaspoon Italian seasoning
1/2 teaspoon *each* salt, poultry seasoning and garlic powder
2 pounds bulk pork sausage

SAUCE:

4 cups water
2 cans (11-1/2 ounces *each*) tomato juice
3 cans (6 ounces *each*) tomato paste
1 jar (1/2 ounce) dried celery flakes
1 bay leaf
1 teaspoon Italian seasoning
1 teaspoon salt
1/2 teaspoon pepper
1/2 cup finely chopped green pepper
1/2 cup finely chopped onion
2 garlic cloves, minced
Hot cooked spaghetti

In a large bowl, combine eggs, bread crumbs, cheese, tomato juice, green pepper, onion and the seasonings. Crumble sausage over mixture and mix well. Shape into 1-in. balls. In a skillet, brown meatballs over medium heat; drain.

In a large saucepan, combine the first eight sauce ingredients. Add green pepper, onion and garlic. Bring to a boil. Reduce heat; simmer, uncovered, for 30-45 minutes or until thickened, stirring occasionally. Discard bay leaf.

Add meatballs to sauce; simmer for 1 hour or until meat is no longer pink. Serve with spaghetti.

YIELD: 10 servings.

marilou krumm
STANHOPE, IOWA

My mom's Italian friend taught her the secret to this saucy spaghetti dish loaded with tender meatballs. My mom passed the recipe to me, and it's now a stand-by for any time I need a dish to pass.

SLOPPY JOE PIZZA

PREP/TOTAL TIME: 25 min.

2 tubes (13.8 ounces *each*) refrigerated pizza crust
1 pound ground beef
1 can (15-1/2 ounces) sloppy joe sauce
2 cups (8 ounces) shredded part-skim mozzarella cheese
1 cup (4 ounces) shredded cheddar cheese
1/2 cup grated Parmesan cheese

Unroll pizza dough; place on two greased 12-in. pizza pans. Bake at 425° for 6-7 minutes or until golden brown.

In a large skillet, cook beef over medium heat until no longer pink; drain. Add sloppy joe sauce. Spread over crusts. Sprinkle with cheeses. Bake at 425° for 6-8 minutes or until cheese is melted.

YIELD: 2 pizzas (8 slices each).

brenda rohlman
KINGMAN, KANSAS

If your children like sloppy joes, they're sure to like this change-of-pace pizza. The six-ingredient recipe has kid-pleasing flavor and goes together in a flash.

CHICKEN PIZZAS

PREP: 20 min. + rising | **BAKE:** 20 min.

CRUST:
- 1 package (1/4 ounce) active dry yeast
- 1 cup warm water (110° to 115°)
- 2-3/4 to 3 cups all-purpose flour
- 1 tablespoon canola oil
- 1 tablespoon sugar
- 1/2 teaspoon salt

TOPPING:
- 1 can (10-3/4 ounces) condensed cream of mushroom soup, undiluted
- 1 teaspoon paprika
- 1 teaspoon dried oregano
- 1/2 teaspoon garlic powder
- 1/2 teaspoon salt
- 1/4 teaspoon pepper
- 1 medium green pepper, chopped
- 1 small onion, chopped
- 1/2 pound fresh mushrooms, sliced
- 1 cup diced cooked chicken
- 1-1/2 cups (6 ounces) shredded cheddar cheese
- 2-1/2 cups (10 ounces) shredded mozzarella cheese

In a large bowl, dissolve yeast in water. Add 1-1/2 cups flour, oil, sugar and salt; beat until smooth. Add enough remaining flour to form a soft dough.

Turn onto a floured surface; knead until smooth and elastic, about 6-8 minutes. Place in a greased bowl, turning once to grease top. Cover and let rise in a warm place until doubled, about 1 hour.

Punch dough down. Divide in half and roll each half into a 13-in. circle. Place each dough circle on a lightly greased 12- to 13-in. pizza pan.

In a small bowl, combine the soup, paprika, oregano, garlic powder, salt and pepper; spread over each pizza. Layer with the green pepper, onion, mushrooms and chicken. Combine the cheeses; sprinkle over the pizzas.

Bake at 425° for 20-25 minutes or until crust is browned and cheese is melted.
YIELD: 12-16 servings (2 pizzas).

dorothy near
COWANSVILLE, QUEBEC

A homemade crust is topped with tender chicken, a creamy seasoned mushroom sauce, fresh veggies and lots of cheese in this crowd-pleasing pie. Prepare the vegetables and other toppings in advance so you can easily assemble this pizza for a fast, delicious dinner.

SUMMER STUFFED PEPPERS

PREP: 20 min. | **COOK:** 30 min.

- 8 medium yellow, green *or* sweet red peppers
- 1-1/2 pounds lean ground beef (90% lean)
- 1 medium onion, minced
- 1/2 cup finely chopped cabbage
- 1 medium carrot, shredded
- 1/2 cup shredded zucchini
- 1/2 garlic clove, minced
- 1 can (28 ounces) diced tomatoes, undrained
- 1/2 cup uncooked long-grain rice
- 1 tablespoon brown sugar
- 1/4 teaspoon dried basil
- Pepper to taste

Cut the tops off each pepper and reserve. Cook peppers in boiling water until crisp-tender, about 2-3 minutes. Remove from pan and rinse with cold water. Remove stems from pepper tops and chop enough of the tops to make 1/3 cup.

In a large skillet, brown ground beef over medium heat; drain if necessary. Add the onion, cabbage, carrot, zucchini and the reserved chopped peppers. Saute until vegetables are tender. Add garlic; cook 1 minute longer. Stir in the tomatoes, rice, sugar, basil and pepper. Reduce heat; simmer about 20 minutes or until rice is tender.

Stuff hot meat mixture into peppers. Serve immediately.
YIELD: 8 servings.

pat whitaker
ALSEA, OREGON

These colorful stuffed peppers call for garden-fresh ingredients and make a satisfying meal for hungry guests. Omit the ground beef if you prefer a meatless version.

JAMBALAYA

PREP: 25 min. | **BAKE:** 1 hour

12 small pork sausage links, cut into 1-inch pieces
1 cup finely chopped onion
1 cup finely chopped green pepper
4 garlic cloves, minced
2 tablespoons canola oil
1-1/2 cups cooked cubed chicken
1-1/2 cups cooked cubed ham
1 can (28 ounces) diced tomatoes, undrained
1 cup uncooked long grain rice
1 can (14-1/2 ounces) chicken broth
3 tablespoons minced fresh parsley
1 teaspoon salt
1/2 to 1 teaspoon pepper
1/2 to 3/4 teaspoon dried thyme

In large heavy skillet, saute the sausage, onion, green pepper and garlic in oil until the vegetables are tender. Add the chicken and ham; cook for 5 minutes. Stir in the remaining ingredients.

Transfer to a 2-qt. baking dish. Cover and bake at 350° for 1 hour or until rice is tender and liquid absorbed.

YIELD: 8 servings.

lizzie whitten
OAK GROVE, LOUISIANA

Break away from standard meat and potatoes with this colorful, zippy main dish. We're from Louisiana, so we serve this traditional Cajun sensation at all our family get-togethers.

SEAFOOD MEDLEY WITH LINGUINE

PREP: 35 min. | **COOK:** 5 min.

    1 large onion, chopped
    2 tablespoons butter
    1 tablespoon olive oil
    3 garlic cloves, minced
    1 cup white wine *or* chicken broth
    1 can (28 ounces) diced fire-roasted
      tomatoes
    1 tablespoon minced fresh rosemary *or*
      1 teaspoon dried rosemary, crushed
    1 teaspoon sugar
    1 teaspoon minced fresh oregano *or*
      1/4 teaspoon dried oregano
  1/4 teaspoon salt
  1/4 teaspoon pepper
    1 package (16 ounces) linguine
    1 pound sea scallops
    9 ounces uncooked large shrimp, peeled
      and deveined
    2 tablespoons minced fresh parsley
Shredded Parmesan cheese, optional

In a large skillet, saute onion in butter and oil until tender. Add garlic; cook 1 minute longer. Add wine. Bring to a boil; cook until the liquid is reduced to 1/2 cup. Add the tomatoes, rosemary, sugar, oregano, salt and pepper. Bring to a boil over medium heat. Reduce heat; simmer, uncovered, for 15 minutes.

Meanwhile, cook linguine according to package directions. Add scallops and shrimp to tomato mixture; cook for 4-5 minutes or until shrimp turn pink and scallops are opaque. Stir in parsley.

Drain the linguine. Serve seafood mixture over the linguine; garnish with the Parmesan cheese if desired.

YIELD: 8 servings.

charlene chambers
ORMOND BEACH, FLORIDA

Who can resist a savory blend of seafood and pasta? This dish of steaming scallops and shrimp with linguine and tomatoes is nutritious and rich in flavor.

BRISKET WITH GINGERSNAP GRAVY

PREP: 2-1/2 hours + chilling | **BAKE:** 30 min.

1 beef brisket (about 5 pounds)
1 cup water
3/4 cup chili sauce
1 envelope onion soup mix
5 to 6 gingersnaps, crushed

Place the brisket in a roasting pan. In a small bowl, combine the water, chili sauce and soup mix; pour over the meat. Cover and bake at 325° for 2-1/2 to 3 hours or until the meat is tender. Cool; cover and refrigerate brisket overnight.

Remove meat and cut into 1/4-in.-thick slices; return to the pan. Sprinkle with the gingersnap crumbs. Cover and bake at 350° for 30-45 minutes or until heated through.
YIELD: 16-18 servings.

teri lindquist
GURNEE, ILLINOIS

This is the first and only recipe I've ever used to prepare a fresh beef brisket. It's delicious served on a platter as an entree or as a filling for sandwiches.

FISH TACOS

PREP: 30 min. | **COOK:** 20 min.

3/4 cup fat-free sour cream
1 can (4 ounces) chopped green chilies
1 tablespoon fresh cilantro leaves
1 tablespoon lime juice
4 tilapia fillets (4 ounces *each*)
1/2 cup all-purpose flour
1 egg white, beaten
1/2 cup panko (Japanese) bread crumbs
1 tablespoon canola oil
1/2 teaspoon salt
1/2 teaspoon *each* white pepper, cayenne pepper and paprika
8 corn tortillas (6 inches), warmed
1 large tomato, finely chopped

Place the sour cream, chilies, cilantro and lime juice in a food processor; cover and process until blended. Set aside.

Cut each tilapia fillet lengthwise into two portions. Place the flour, egg white and bread crumbs in separate shallow bowls. Dip the tilapia in flour, then in the egg white, then in the crumbs.

In a large skillet over medium heat, cook tilapia in oil in batches for 4-5 minutes on each side or until fish flakes easily with a fork. Combine the seasonings; sprinkle over the fish.

Place a portion of fish on each tortilla; top with about 2 tablespoons of sour cream mixture. Sprinkle with tomato.
YIELD: 8 servings.

lena lim
SEATTLE, WASHINGTON

A cool sauce with just a bit of zing tops these crispy, spicy fish tacos. It's guilt-free and doesn't break the bank, which is always a good thing when you have a crowd to feed!

TERRIFIC tilapia

Tilapia has a mild flavor, so it's a great choice if you're looking for a fish that doesn't taste too "fishy." If you want to make this dish ligher, skip the bread crumb coating and grill the fish instead of frying.

CORNY TACOS

PREP: 15 min. | **BAKE:** 30 min.

2 pounds ground beef
1 can (8-3/4 ounces) cream-style corn
1 can (8 ounces) tomato sauce
1 cup milk
1 can (6 ounces) ripe olives, drained and chopped
1/3 cup cornmeal
1/4 teaspoon salt
Chili powder to taste
20 taco shells
Toppings: shredded cheddar cheese, shredded lettuce, chopped tomatoes

In a large skillet, cook beef over medium heat until no longer pink; drain. Add the corn, tomato sauce, milk, olives, cornmeal, salt and chili powder. Transfer to a greased 11-in. x 7-in. baking dish.

Bake, uncovered, at 350° for 30 minutes or until heated through. Spoon about 1/4 cupful of mixture into each taco shell. Serve with toppings of your choice.

YIELD: 20 tacos.

mary lannen
MILAN, ILLINOIS

My mother received this recipe from a friend in Texas. Unlike ordinary taco fillings, this one-of-a-kind version is baked and includes corn and olives.

GARLIC-HERB ROASTED CHICKEN

PREP: 10 min. | **BAKE:** 1-1/2 hours

1 roasting chicken (4 to 5 pounds)
2 teaspoons *each* minced fresh parsley, rosemary, sage and thyme
3/4 teaspoon salt
1/4 teaspoon pepper
20 garlic cloves, peeled and sliced
1 medium lemon, halved
1 large whole garlic bulb
1 sprig *each* fresh parsley, rosemary, sage and thyme

MAKING an herb rub

It's easy to create a flavorful herb rub for poultry or pork. Crush any large herbs. Combine all herbs. Sprinkle the mixture over the entire roast and rub into the surface of the meat. Roast as the recipe directs.

With fingers, carefully loosen skin around the chicken breast, leg and thigh. Combine minced parsley, rosemary, sage, thyme, salt and pepper; rub half under skin. Place sliced garlic cloves under skin. Squeeze half of the lemon into the cavity and place the squeezed half in the cavity.

Remove papery outer skin from whole garlic bulb (do not peel or separate cloves). Cut top off garlic bulb. Place garlic bulb and herb sprigs in the cavity. Skewer chicken openings; tie the drumsticks together with kitchen string.

Place the chicken breast side up on a rack in a roasting pan. Squeeze the remaining lemon half over chicken; rub the remaining herb mixture over chicken.

Bake, uncovered, at 350° for 1-1/2 to 1-3/4 hours or until chicken juices run clear and a meat thermometer reads 180° (cover loosely with foil if browning too quickly). Baste with pan drippings if desired.

Cover and let stand for 15 minutes. Remove and discard skin, garlic, lemon and herbs from cavity before carving.

YIELD: 8 servings.

cindy steffen
CEDARBURG, WISCONSIN

Garlic and herbs roasting in and on the bird make this roasted chicken so flavorful you can even eliminate the salt from the recipe if you like. The aroma from the oven while it's baking is tantalizing.

HALIBUT ENCHILADAS

PREP: 45 min. | **BAKE:** 40 min.

3 pounds halibut fillets
1/2 teaspoon salt
1/8 teaspoon pepper
1/8 teaspoon cayenne pepper
1 medium onion, finely chopped
1 medium green pepper, finely chopped
1 tablespoon canola oil
2 garlic cloves, minced
1 can (10 ounces) hot enchilada sauce
1 can (10 ounces) green enchilada sauce
1 cup (8 ounces) sour cream
1 cup mayonnaise
2 cans (4 ounces *each*) chopped green
   chilies
2 cans (10 ounces *each*) mild enchilada
   sauce
4 cups (16 ounces) shredded
   Colby-Monterey Jack cheese
24 flour tortillas (6 inches), warmed
1 bunch green onions, thinly sliced
2 tablespoons chopped ripe olives

Place the fillets on a greased baking sheet. Sprinkle with salt, pepper and cayenne. Bake, uncovered, at 350° for 15-20 minutes or until fish flakes easily with a fork.

Meanwhile, in a large skillet, saute onion and green pepper in oil until tender. Add garlic; cook 1 minute longer.

Flake fish with two forks; set aside. In a large bowl, combine the hot enchilada sauce, green enchilada sauce, sour cream, mayonnaise, chilies, onion mixture and fish. Spread 1/2 cup mild enchilada sauce into each of two greased 13-in. x 9-in. baking dishes. Sprinkle each with 1 cup cheese.

Place a heaping 1/3 cup halibut mixture down the center of each tortilla. Roll up each and place seam side down over cheese. Pour remaining sauce over top.

Cover and bake at 350° for 30 minutes. Sprinkle with the green onions, olives and remaining cheese. Bake, uncovered, for 10-15 minutes longer or until cheese is melted.

YIELD: 12 servings.

carole lynn derifield
VALDEZ, ALASKA

I roll our local Alaskan halibut into tortillas to create a dish where the far north meets south-of-the-border. It's one of my most requested recipes and a mainstay for potlucks.

HERBED LAMB KABOBS

PREP: 15 min. + marinating | GRILL: 20 min.

1 cup canola oil
1 medium onion, chopped
1/2 cup lemon juice
1/2 cup minced fresh parsley
3 to 4 garlic cloves, minced
2 teaspoons salt
2 teaspoons dried marjoram
2 teaspoons dried thyme
1/2 teaspoon pepper
2 pounds boneless lamb
1 medium red onion, cut into wedges
1 large green pepper, cut into 1-inch pieces
1 large sweet red pepper, cut into 1-inch pieces

In a small bowl, combine the first nine ingredients. Pour 1 cup into a large resealable plastic bag; add the lamb. Seal the bag and turn to coat; refrigerate for 6-8 hours. Cover and refrigerate the remaining marinade for basting.

Drain and discard marinade. On eight metal or soaked wooden skewers, alternately thread the lamb, onion and peppers. Grill, uncovered, over medium-hot heat for 8-10 minutes on each side or until meat reaches desired doneness (for medium-rare, a meat thermometer should read 145°; medium, 160°; well-done, 170°), basting frequently with reserved marinade.

YIELD: 8 servings.

janet dingler
CEDARTOWN, GEORGIA

This colorful kabob wouldn't be the same without its delicious herb marinade and tender-crisp vegetables. Together, they add delicious flavor and texture to the lamb pieces.

PEPPERED RIBEYE ROAST

PREP: 15 min. + marinating | **BAKE:** 2 hours

- 1/3 to 1/2 cup coarsely ground pepper
- 1 teaspoon ground cardamom
- 2 beef ribeye roasts (5 to 6 pounds *each*)
- 2 cups soy sauce
- 1-1/2 cups cider vinegar
- 2 tablespoons tomato paste
- 2 teaspoons garlic powder
- 2 teaspoons paprika

Combine the pepper and cardamom; rub over roasts. In a large bowl, combine the soy sauce, vinegar, tomato paste, garlic powder and paprika. Pour half into each of two large resealable plastic bags; place each roast in one of the bags. Seal bags and turn to coat; refrigerate overnight.

Drain and discard marinade. Place each roast in a roasting pan. Bake, uncovered, at 350° for 2 hours or until the meat reaches desired doneness (for medium-rare, a meat thermometer should read 145°; medium, 160°; well-done, 170°).

YIELD: 24-30 servings.

ruth andrewson
LEAVENWORTH, WASHINGTON

Roasts are fuss-free entrees to serve when entertaining. After marinating the meat overnight, simply pop in the oven and bake for a couple of hours. It turns out terrific every time.

MEXICAN-STYLE SPAGHETTI

PREP: 15 min. | **COOK:** 2 hours

- 2 pounds ground beef (90% lean)
- 2 medium onions, chopped
- 1 medium green pepper, chopped
- 3 garlic cloves, minced
- 1 can (29 ounces) tomato puree
- 1 can (16 ounces) kidney beans, rinsed and drained
- 1 cup water
- 1/4 cup minced fresh parsley
- 2 tablespoons chili powder
- 1 teaspoon ground cumin
- 1 teaspoon dried marjoram
- 1 teaspoon dried oregano
- 1 teaspoon salt, optional
- 1/4 to 1/2 teaspoon cayenne pepper
- 1 package (12 ounces) spaghetti, cooked and drained

In a Dutch oven, cook the beef, onions and green pepper over medium heat until meat is no longer pink. Add garlic; cook 1 minute longer. Drain. Add the next 10 ingredients. Cover and simmer for 2 hours, stirring occasionally. Serve with spaghetti.

YIELD: 8 servings.

mary detweiler
MIDDLEFIELD, OHIO

When my clan gets tired of the "same old spaghetti," I spice things up with this south-of-the-border version. Cumin, chili powder and cayenne give it a twist.

EASY lasagna

Layer any leftover spaghetti noodles and meat sauce along with shredded Monterey Jack cheese between the layers and on top for a quick and easy lasagna. Bake in a 13-in. x 9-in. dish at 350° until hot and bubbly.

GLAZED MEAT LOAF

PREP: 20 min. | **BAKE:** 1-1/2 hours

10-1/2 cups rolled oats
1/4 cup plus 3 tablespoons salt
1-1/2 tablespoons pepper
3-1/2 cups chopped onion
14 eggs
10-1/2 cups milk *or* tomato juice
21 pounds ground beef

GLAZE:
1-1/4 cups ketchup
3/4 cup packed brown sugar
3/4 cup prepared mustard

In several large bowls, combine the oats, salt, pepper, onion, eggs and milk or tomato juice. Sprinkle the beef over mixture and mix well.

Shape mixture into loaves of desired size and place in shallow baking pans. Bake at 350° for 30 minutes.

In a large bowl, combine all of the glaze ingredients; spread evenly over tops of loaves. Bake for about 1 hour more or until no pink remains and a meat thermometer reads 160°. (Two-pound loaves will need to bake for 1-1/2 hours or until no pink remains and a meat thermometer reads 160°.)

YIELD: 100 servings.

dorothy hoffmann
WHEATLAND, NORTH DAKOTA

The brown sugar glaze on this meat loaf is what makes it special at any big gathering. Serve this entree alongside baked potatoes, coleslaw, green beans, hot rolls, and cake and coffee for dessert.

PICNIC CHICKEN

PREP: 20 min. | **BAKE:** 1 hour + chilling

3 eggs
3 tablespoons water
1-1/2 cups dry bread crumbs
2 teaspoons paprika
1 teaspoon salt
1/2 teaspoon *each* dried marjoram, thyme and rosemary, crushed
1/2 teaspoon pepper
1 cup butter, melted
12 chicken drumsticks
12 bone-in chicken thighs

CREAMY LEEK DIP:
1 cup heavy whipping cream
1-1/2 cups plain yogurt
1 envelope leek soup mix
1 cup (4 ounces) shredded Colby cheese

In a shallow bowl, whisk eggs and water. In another shallow bowl, combine the bread crumbs and seasonings. Divide the butter between two 13-in. x 9-in. baking dishes.

Dip chicken pieces in egg mixture, then coat with crumb mixture. Place in prepared pans. Bake, uncovered, at 375° for 1 hour or until juices run clear, turning once. Cool for 30 minutes; refrigerate until chilled.

For dip, in a small bowl, beat cream until stiff peaks form. In another bowl, combine yogurt, soup mix and cheese; fold in whipped cream. Cover and refrigerate until serving. Serve with cold chicken.

YIELD: 24 servings (4 cups dip).

ami okasinski
MEMPHIS, TENNESSEE

I made this well-seasoned chicken one evening for dinner and served it hot from the oven. While raiding the fridge the next day, I discovered how delicious it was cold and created the yogurt dip to go with it.

PAELLA

PREP: 55 min. | **COOK:** 35 min.

jane montgomery
HILLIARD, OHIO

  3 pounds uncooked skinless turkey breast, cubed
  4 pounds uncooked chorizo, cut into 1-1/2-inch pieces *or* bulk spicy pork sausage
  3 tablespoons olive oil
  2 medium onions, chopped
  1 medium sweet red pepper, chopped
  4 garlic cloves, minced
  1/2 teaspoon cayenne pepper
  2 cups tomato puree
  1 cup white wine *or* chicken broth
  5 cups water
  4 cups uncooked long grain rice
  3-1/2 cups chicken broth
  2 teaspoons salt
  1 teaspoon dried thyme
  3/4 teaspoon saffron threads *or* 2 teaspoons ground turmeric
  1 bay leaf
  2 pounds uncooked medium shrimp, peeled and deveined
  3/4 cup pitted Greek olives
  1/2 cup minced fresh parsley

In a large skillet, cook turkey and chorizo in oil in batches until browned. Remove with a slotted spoon and keep warm.

In the same skillet, saute onions and red pepper until tender. Add garlic and cayenne; cook 1 minute longer. Stir in tomato puree and wine. Bring to a boil; cook and stir for 2 minutes or until thickened.

Transfer to a stock pot. Stir in the water, rice, broth, salt, thyme, saffron, bay leaf, turkey and chorizo. Bring to a boil. Reduce heat; cover and simmer for 20 minutes or until rice is tender.

Add shrimp; cook for 2-3 minutes or until shrimp turn pink. Remove from the heat; discard bay leaf. Stir in olives and parsley.

YIELD: 24 servings (1 cup each).

A big pan of paella is the perfect choice when cooking for a crowd. Round out the meal with fresh bread and a green salad.

CHORIZO defined

Chorizo is a coarsely ground fresh or smoked pork sausage that has Mexican, Spanish and Portuguese origins. Traditionally flavored with paprika or chili powder, which gives it its reddish color, chorizo is often used in egg dishes, soups, casseroles and a variety of Mexican dishes.

GRILLED BREADED CHICKEN

PREP: 15 min. + marinating | **GRILL:** 10 min.

1 cup (8 ounces) reduced-fat sour cream
1/4 cup lemon juice
4 teaspoons Worcestershire sauce
2 teaspoons paprika
1 teaspoon celery salt
1/8 teaspoon garlic powder
8 boneless skinless chicken breast halves
    (4 ounces *each*)
2 cups crushed seasoned stuffing
Refrigerated butter-flavored spray

In a large resealable plastic bag, combine the first six ingredients; add the chicken. Seal the bag and turn to coat; refrigerate for up to 4 hours.

Using long-handled tongs, moisten a paper towel with cooking oil and lightly coat the grill rack. Drain and discard marinade. Coat both sides of chicken with stuffing crumbs; spritz with butter-flavored spray.

Grill chicken, covered, over medium heat or broil 4 in. from the heat for 4-7 minutes on each side or until a meat thermometer reads 170°.

YIELD: 8 servings.

kristy mcclellan
MORGAN, UTAH

This recipe will please folks who love the flavor and crispiness of fried chicken, but don't want all the fat and calories that go with it. The sizzling grilled entree is a great addition to any backyard barbecue.

CHUNKY BEEF STEW

PREP: 15 min. | **COOK:** 70 min.

2 quarts water
3 medium potatoes, peeled and cubed
3 medium carrots, sliced
1 medium onion, chopped
2 celery ribs, chopped
1 teaspoon salt
1 pound lean ground beef (90% lean), cooked and drained
1 can (15-1/4 ounces) whole kernel corn, drained
1 can (14-1/2 ounces) diced tomatoes, undrained
1 can (8-1/4 ounces) peas, drained
1 can (8 ounces) tomato sauce
3/4 cup ketchup
2 tablespoons prepared mustard
1 tablespoon chili powder
1 garlic clove, minced
1 teaspoon garlic salt
1 teaspoon dried thyme
Dash hot pepper sauce
Dash pepper
1 cup elbow macaroni, cooked and drained

In a Dutch oven, combine the first six ingredients; bring to a boil. Reduce heat; cover and simmer for 20 minutes or until vegetables are tender.

Add beef, corn, tomatoes, peas, tomato sauce, ketchup, mustard and seasonings. Cover and simmer for 30 minutes. Add macaroni; simmer 10 minutes longer or until heated through.

YIELD: 20 servings.

miriam wages
ARNOLDSVILLE, GEORGIA

I'm fortunate to have a husband who loves to cook, and this comfort-food classic is one of his specialties. This recipe yields a big batch, so it's perfect for a large group.

LEFTOVER beef stew

You can make a whole new meal out of any leftover beef stew you bring home from a potluck. Add some beef broth to the stew and process it in a blender to make a thick soup. Or bake it with a pastry crust on top for a mouthwatering potpie.

TURKEY CLUB PIZZA

PREP/TOTAL TIME: 20 min.

1 prebaked 12-inch pizza crust
1/2 cup mayonnaise
1-1/2 cups (6 ounces) shredded Monterey Jack cheese, *divided*
1 cup diced cooked turkey
1/2 cup real bacon bits
2 plum tomatoes, sliced

Place pizza crust on a baking sheet; spread with mayonnaise. Top with 1 cup cheese, turkey, bacon and tomatoes. Sprinkle with remaining cheese. Bake at 450° for 10-12 minutes or until cheese is melted.

YIELD: 8 servings.

pippa milburn
DOVER, OHIO

This extremely easy pizza will be a hit with your family and will keep you out of the kitchen! It's terrific on busy school nights, hectic weekends or any time you just don't want to wait on dinner.

CORN DOGS

PREP/TOTAL TIME: 25 min.

- 3/4 cup yellow cornmeal
- 3/4 cup self-rising flour
- 1 egg, lightly beaten
- 2/3 cup milk
- 10 Popsicle sticks
- 10 hot dogs
- Oil for deep-fat frying

In a large bowl, combine cornmeal, flour and egg. Stir in milk to make a thick batter; let stand 4 minutes. Insert sticks into hot dogs; dip in batter.

In an electric skillet or deep-fat fryer, heat the oil to 375°. Fry corn dogs, a few at a time, about 6-8 minutes or until golden brown, turning occasionally. Drain the corn dogs on paper towels.

YIELD: 10 servings.

ruby williams
BOGALUSA, LOUISIANA

You can prepare corn dogs at home that taste just like those sold at the fair. Kids and grown-ups alike will enjoy this summer favorite.

LEFTOVER pork roast

Add leftover pork loin roast to fried rice for a quick and easy supper. In a skillet, fry leftover diced pork in canola oil. Stir in a beaten egg until it's cooked. Add rice, chopped green onions and soy sauce. Cover and simmer for 5 minutes before serving.

SEASONED PORK LOIN ROAST

PREP: 20 min. | **BAKE:** 1-1/2 hours + standing

- 2 teaspoons garlic salt
- 2 teaspoons garlic-pepper blend
- 2 teaspoons lemon-pepper seasoning
- 1 boneless rolled pork loin roast (about 5 pounds)

BASTING SAUCE:
- 3 cups water
- 2 tablespoons lemon juice
- 1-1/2 teaspoons dried minced onion
- 1/2 teaspoon garlic salt
- 1/2 teaspoon garlic-pepper blend
- 1/2 teaspoon lemon-pepper seasoning
- 1/2 teaspoon crushed red pepper flakes
- 1/2 teaspoon grated lemon peel

Combine the garlic salt, garlic-pepper and lemon-pepper; rub over roast. Place roast on a rack in a shallow roasting pan. Bake, uncovered, at 325° for 1-1/2 to 2 hours or until a meat thermometer reads 160°.

Meanwhile, in a large saucepan, combine the basting sauce ingredients. Bring to a boil; reduce heat. Simmer, uncovered, for 10 minutes. Brush over roast occasionally while baking. Let the roast stand for 10 minutes before slicing.

YIELD: 15-18 servings.

elaine seip
MEDICINE HAT, ALBERTA

This is a guaranteed crowd-pleaser and perfect any time of year. I like to barbecue the pork during the hot-weather months and roast it during the cold-weather months.

HEARTY BURRITOS

PREP: 20 min. | BAKE: 25 min.

1/2 pound ground beef

1 large green pepper, chopped

1 medium onion, chopped

1 package (16 ounces) frozen cubed hash brown potatoes, thawed

1 can (15 ounces) black beans, rinsed and drained

1 can (14-1/2 ounces) Mexican diced tomatoes, undrained

1 cup frozen corn, thawed

1/2 cup salsa

1/2 cup cooked rice

2 teaspoons chili powder

1/2 teaspoon salt

2 cups (8 ounces) shredded cheddar cheese

8 flour tortillas (10 inches), warmed

Sour cream, chopped tomatoes, guacamole, additional shredded cheddar cheese and salsa, optional

In a large skillet, cook the beef, green pepper and onion over medium heat until meat is no longer pink; drain. Add the potatoes, beans, tomatoes, corn, salsa, rice, chili powder and salt. Sprinkle 1/4 cup cheese off-center on each tortilla; top with about 1 cup of the beef mixture. Fold the sides and ends over filling.

Wrap burritos individually in foil and freeze for up to 3 months. Or place burritos seam side down on a baking sheet.

Bake burritos at 350° for 25 minutes or until heated through. Serve with the sour cream, tomatoes, guacamole, additional cheese and salsa if desired.

TO USE FROZEN BURRITOS: Thaw the burritos in refrigerator overnight. Then bake and serve as directed.

YIELD: 8 burritos.

janelle mceachern
RIVERSIDE, CALIFORNIA

These beyond-compare burritos are chock-full of tasty ingredients and frozen individually, so you can bake only as many as you need for your next party or potluck and save the rest for a quick weeknight dinner.

MINIATURE MEAT PIES

PREP: 30 min. + freezing | **BAKE:** 15 min.

- 1 pound ground beef
- 1/2 cup chili sauce
- 2 tablespoons onion soup mix

DOUGH:

- 3 cups all-purpose flour
- 1 to 2 tablespoons sesame seeds, optional
- 1 teaspoon salt
- 1 cup shortening
- 3/4 cup shredded cheddar cheese
- 3/4 cup evaporated milk
- 1 tablespoon cider vinegar

EASY as pie

Triple the amount of filling for your favorite meat pie and freeze small portions separately. On busy days, simply thaw the filling and bake in mini crusts cut from a refrigerated pie crust.

In a large skillet, cook beef over medium heat until no longer pink; drain. Stir in chili sauce and soup mix; set aside.

In a large bowl, combine the flour, sesame seeds if desired and salt. Cut in shortening and cheese until crumbly. Combine the milk and vinegar; gradually add to the flour mixture, tossing with a fork until the dough forms a ball.

Divide dough in half; roll out to 1/8-in. thickness. Cut with a lightly floured 2-1/2-in. round cutter. Place half of the circles 2 in. apart on ungreased baking sheets. Top each with a rounded tablespoonful of beef mixture; top with remaining circles. Moisten edges with water and press with a fork to seal. Cut a slit in the top of each.

Bake at 425° for 12-16 minutes or until golden brown. Serve immediately. Or cool, then wrap individually in plastic wrap and place in a freezer bag; seal and freeze for up to 3 months.

TO USE FROZEN MEAT PIES: Unwrap and place on an ungreased baking sheet. Bake at 425° for 14-16 minutes or until heated through.

YIELD: about 1-1/2 dozen.

gayle lewis
YUCAIPA, CALIFORNIA

These cute little bites of flaky dough stuffed with an easy-to-season ground beef mixture are filling and oh-so-good served with ketchup. They're a fun pop-in-your-mouth treat for any celebration or get-together.

APPLE COUNTRY RIBS

PREP: 10 min. + marinating | **GRILL:** 40 min.

3/4 cup unsweetened apple juice
1/2 cup beer *or* nonalcoholic beer
1/2 cup canola oil
1/4 cup packed brown sugar
1 tablespoon Worcestershire sauce
1 tablespoon minced garlic
1 teaspoon salt
1 teaspoon dried thyme
1 teaspoon pepper
1/2 teaspoon cayenne pepper
3 pounds boneless country-style pork ribs

In a small bowl, combine the first 10 ingredients. Pour 1-1/2 cups marinade into a large resealable plastic bag; add the ribs. Seal the bag and turn to coat; refrigerate for 5 hours or overnight, turning once. Cover ribs and refrigerate the remaining marinade for basting.

Prepare grill for indirect heat. Drain and discard marinade. Grill ribs, covered, over indirect medium heat for 10 minutes on each side. Baste with some of the reserved marinade. Grill 20-25 minutes longer or until the ribs are tender, turning and basting occasionally.

YIELD: 12 servings.

taste of home
test kitchen

For a melt-in-your-mouth delicious main course at your next event, try these super-tender boneless ribs. They're marinated in an apple juice, brown sugar and herb combination that's sure to have folks asking for seconds.

CHICKEN NUGGETS

PREP/TOTAL TIME: 30 min.

1 cup all-purpose flour
4 teaspoons seasoned salt
1 teaspoon poultry seasoning
1 teaspoon ground mustard
1 teaspoon paprika
1/2 teaspoon pepper
2 pounds boneless skinless chicken breasts
1/4 cup canola oil

In a large resealable bag, combine the first six ingredients. Flatten chicken to 1/2-in. thickness, then cut into 1-1/2-in. pieces. Add chicken, a few pieces at a time, to bag and shake to coat.

In a large skillet, cook chicken in oil in batches for 6-8 minutes or until meat is no longer pink.

YIELD: 8 servings.

annette ellyson
CAROLINA, WEST VIRGINIA

I like to make these golden chicken nuggets because they're so quick and easy. They're great for kids' birthday parties because they get gobbled up fast! The seasoning is also tasty on baked chicken breasts.

SOUTHWESTERN DEEP-DISH PIZZA

PREP: 20 min. | **BAKE:** 20 min.

2-1/2 cups biscuit/baking mix
1/2 cup cornmeal
3/4 cup water
1 pound ground beef
1 medium onion, finely chopped
1 can (8 ounces) tomato sauce
2 teaspoons chili powder
1 teaspoon ground cinnamon
1 can (16 ounces) refried beans
Hot pepper sauce to taste
2 cups (8 ounces) shredded Monterey Jack *or* cheddar cheese
Salsa and sliced ripe olives, optional

In a large bowl, combine biscuit mix and cornmeal. Stir in water until mixture forms a soft dough. Press onto the bottom and up the sides of a lightly greased 15-in. x 10-in. x 1-in. baking pan. Bake at 425° for 10 minutes or until lightly browned.

Meanwhile, in a large skillet, cook beef and onion over medium heat until meat is no longer pink; drain. Add the tomato sauce, chili powder and cinnamon. Bring to a boil. Reduce the heat; simmer mixture, uncovered, for 5 minutes. Remove from the heat.

Combine refried beans and hot pepper sauce; spread over crust. Top with meat mixture; sprinkle with cheese. Bake at 425° for 10 minutes or until cheese is melted. Let stand 10 minutes before cutting. Serve with salsa and olives if desired.

YIELD: 16 servings.

diane halferty
TUCSON, ARIZONA

With a rich, hearty beef and bean filling, a slice of this slightly spicy pizza goes a long way. The Southwestern zip is a nice change of pace from typical pepperoni or sausage pizzas.

PECAN-CRUSTED CHICKEN

PREP: 25 min. | **BAKE:** 15 min.

1/4 cup milk
1/2 cup all-purpose flour
1/2 cup finely chopped pecans
2 tablespoons sesame seeds
1-1/2 teaspoons paprika
1-1/2 teaspoons pepper
1 teaspoon salt
8 boneless skinless chicken breast halves (4 ounces *each*), partially flattened
2 tablespoons canola oil

Place the milk in a shallow bowl. In another shallow bowl, combine the flour, pecans, sesame seeds, paprika, pepper and salt. Dip chicken in milk, then coat in flour mixture.

In a large nonstick skillet, brown chicken in oil on both sides. Transfer the chicken to a 15-in. x 10-in. x 1-in. baking pan coated with cooking spray. Bake, uncovered, at 350° for 15-20 minutes or until no longer pink.

YIELD: 8 servings.

molly lloyd
BOURNEVILLE, OHIO

These moist, tender chicken breasts have a crunchy coating of pecans and sesame seeds. They're good served alone or with chicken gravy.

MOCK MANICOTTI

PREP: 25 min. | **BAKE:** 45 min.

3 cups (24 ounces) fat-free cottage cheese, drained

1 package (10 ounces) frozen chopped spinach, thawed and squeezed dry

1 package (8 ounces) reduced-fat cream cheese

1/2 cup reduced-fat sour cream

1 teaspoon garlic powder

1/8 teaspoon salt

1/8 teaspoon pepper

8 lasagna noodles, cooked, rinsed and drained

1 cup (4 ounces) shredded part-skim mozzarella cheese

1 cup meatless spaghetti sauce, optional

In a large bowl, combine the first seven ingredients. Spread 1/2 cup over each noodle; roll up jelly-roll style. Place seam side down in an 11-in. x 7-in. baking dish coated with cooking spray. Sprinkle with mozzarella cheese.

Cover and bake at 350° for 35 minutes. Uncover; drizzle with spaghetti sauce if desired. Bake 10 minutes longer or until heated through.

YIELD: 8 servings.

deanne schwarting
NORTH ENGLISH, IOWA

Getting the little ones to eat their veggies is not always easy. When my son tried manicotti at a restaurant and liked it, I came up with this version that calls for spinach. This dish is also great for pasta bar parties with friends.

p. 162

p. 182

p. 184

casseroles &
one-dish wonders

CHICKEN SUPREME WITH GRAVY

PREP: 1 hour | **BAKE:** 1 hour 20 min.

1-1/2 bunches celery, diced (about 6 cups)

  6 medium onions, diced (about 4 cups)

  2 cups butter, cubed

  3 loaves day-old white bread (1-1/2 pounds *each*), cut into 1-inch cubes

  3 tablespoons salt

  3 tablespoons rubbed sage

  1 tablespoon baking powder

  2 teaspoons pepper

 12 eggs

  9 cups milk

 24 cups diced cooked chicken (about 6 whole chickens)

  3 cans (14-1/2 ounces *each*) chicken broth

GRAVY:

  8 cans (10-3/4 ounces *each*) condensed cream of chicken and mushroom soup, undiluted

  9 to 10 cups water

In several Dutch ovens, saute celery and onions in butter. Meanwhile, in several large bowls, combine the bread, salt, sage, baking powder and pepper; toss to coat. Stir in celery mixture. Beat the eggs and milk; add to the bread mixture.

Divide half of the chicken among four greased 13-in. x 9-in. baking dishes. Cover with half of the bread mixture. Repeat layers. Pour broth into each dish.

Cover and bake at 325° for 70 minutes or until hot and bubbly; uncover and bake 10-15 minutes longer.

For gravy, in a stockpot, combine soup and water. Bring to a boil. Reduce heat; simmer, uncovered, for 10 minutes. Serve with chicken.

YIELD: 70-80 servings.

bernice hartje
CAVALIER, NORTH DAKOTA

A group of friends and I have met often throughout the years to swap recipes. This tried-and-true dish has always garnered me lots of compliments.

CORDON BLEU CASSEROLE

PREP: 10 min. | **BAKE:** 50 min.

  6 slices whole wheat bread

  6 boneless skinless chicken breast halves, cooked and sliced

  1 package (8 ounces) cream cheese, thinly sliced

 1/2 pound sliced fully cooked ham

1-1/2 cups (6 ounces) shredded Swiss cheese, *divided*

  2 packages (10 ounces *each*) frozen broccoli spears, thawed and drained

  2 cans (10-3/4 ounces *each*) condensed cream of chicken soup, undiluted

 1/4 teaspoon pepper

Place bread in a greased 13-in. x 9-in. baking dish. Layer with chicken, cream cheese slices and ham. Sprinkle with 1 cup Swiss cheese. Top with broccoli.

Combine soup and pepper; spoon over broccoli. Sprinkle with remaining Swiss cheese. Bake, uncovered, at 350° for 50-55 minutes or until bubbly.

YIELD: 8-10 servings.

colleen baker
WONEWOC, WISCONSIN

Featuring all four food groups, this spirit-warming casserole is destined to become one of your favorite one-dish meals. Everyone will rave over its rich, savory goodness.

EASY substitution

Time-pressed cooks can ease the preparation of Cordon Bleu Casserole by using sliced ham from the deli counter and poultry cut from a precooked rotisserie chicken.

CHICKEN POTPIES

PREP: 20 min. | **BAKE:** 35 min.

4 cups cubed cooked chicken

4 cups frozen cubed hash brown potatoes, thawed

1 package (16 ounces) frozen mixed vegetables, thawed and drained

1 can (10-3/4 ounces) condensed cream of chicken soup, undiluted

1 can (10-3/4 ounces) condensed cream of onion soup, undiluted

1 cup milk

1 cup (8 ounces) sour cream

2 tablespoons all-purpose flour

1/2 teaspoon salt

1/2 teaspoon pepper

1/4 teaspoon garlic powder

1 package (15 ounces) refrigerated pie pastry

In a large bowl, combine the first 11 ingredients. Divide between two 9-in. deep-dish pie plates. Roll out pastry to fit the top of each pie. Place over filling; trim, seal and flute edges. Cut slits in top or make decorative cutouts in pastry.

Cover and freeze one potpie for up to 3 months. Bake the remaining potpie at 400° for 35-40 minutes or until golden brown.

TO USE FROZEN POTPIE: Remove from the freezer 30 minutes before baking. Cover edges loosely with foil; place on a baking sheet. Bake at 425° for 30 minutes. Reduce heat to 350°; remove foil and bake 50-55 minutes longer or until golden brown.

YIELD: 2 potpies (6 servings each).

taste of home test kitchen

The golden crust and creamy sauce make this comforting pie a sure hit. Canned soup and frozen veggies keep prep simple, and you'll love having that extra frozen pie waiting for you the next time you're called upon to bring something to a potluck.

POTLUCK LASAGNA

PREP: 30 min. | **BAKE:** 55 min. + standing

- 1 pound ground beef
- 1 can (14-1/2 ounces) Italian stewed tomatoes, cut up
- 1 can (6 ounces) tomato paste
- 1 tablespoon minced fresh parsley
- 1/2 teaspoon minced garlic
- 2 eggs
- 1-1/2 cups (12 ounces) 4% cottage cheese
- 1-1/2 cups ricotta cheese
- 1 cup grated Parmesan cheese
- 1 teaspoon salt
- 1 teaspoon pepper
- 6 lasagna noodles, cooked and drained
- 2 cups (8 ounces) shredded part-skim mozzarella cheese

In a large skillet, cook beef over medium heat until no longer pink; drain. Stir in the tomatoes, tomato paste, parsley and garlic; remove from the heat.

In a large bowl, combine the eggs, cottage cheese, ricotta cheese, Parmesan cheese, salt and pepper. In a greased 13-in. x 9-in. baking dish, layer three noodles, half of the cottage cheese mixture, 1 cup mozzarella cheese and half of the meat sauce. Repeat the layers.

Cover and freeze for up to 3 months. Or, cover and bake at 375° for 30 minutes. Uncover; bake 25-30 minutes longer or until a meat thermometer reads 160°. Let stand for 10 minutes before cutting.

TO USE FROZEN LASAGNA: Thaw in refrigerator overnight. Remove from the refrigerator 30 minutes before baking. Bake as directed.

YIELD: 12-15 servings.

colleen wolfisberg
EVERSON, WASHINGTON

This is a variation on a lasagna dish a coworker made for a company potluck. When I was expecting our third son, I often prepared meals and froze them. It was so nice to have a substantial entree like this one on hand to simply pop in the oven for dinner.

PHYLLO CHICKEN

PREP: 15 min. | **BAKE:** 35 min.

- 1/2 cup butter, melted, *divided*
- 12 sheets phyllo dough (14 inches x 9 inches)
- 3 cups diced cooked chicken
- 1/2 pound sliced bacon, cooked and crumbled
- 3 cups frozen chopped broccoli, thawed and drained
- 2 cups (8 ounces) shredded cheddar *or* Swiss cheese
- 6 eggs
- 1 cup half-and-half cream *or* evaporated milk
- 1/2 cup milk
- 1 teaspoon salt
- 1/2 teaspoon pepper

Brush sides and bottom of a 13-in. x 9-in. baking dish with some of the melted butter. Place one sheet of phyllo in bottom of dish; lightly brush with butter; repeat with five more sheets of phyllo. Keep remaining phyllo covered with plastic wrap and a damp towel to prevent it from drying out.

In a large bowl, combine the chicken, bacon, broccoli and cheese; spread evenly over phyllo in baking dish. In a small bowl, whisk the eggs, cream, milk, salt and pepper; pour over chicken mixture. Cover filling with one sheet of phyllo; brush with butter. Repeat with remaining phyllo dough. Brush top with remaining butter.

Bake, uncovered, at 375° for 35-40 minutes or until a thermometer reaches 160°. Let stand for 5-10 minutes before cutting.
YIELD: 12 servings.

joyce mummau
MT. AIRY, MARYLAND

Phyllo dough is fun to work with. Its flakiness turns everyday ingredients into a special entree that is just perfect for a large gathering of friends.

HASH BROWN PORK BAKE

PREP: 15 min. | **BAKE:** 1 hour

- 2 cups (16 ounces) sour cream
- 1 can (10-3/4 ounces) condensed cream of chicken soup, undiluted
- 1 package (32 ounces) frozen cubed hash brown potatoes, thawed
- 2 cups cubed cooked pork
- 1 pound process cheese (Velveeta), cubed
- 1/4 cup chopped onion
- 2 cups crushed cornflakes
- 1/2 cup butter, melted
- 1 cup (4 ounces) shredded part-skim mozzarella cheese

In a large bowl, combine sour cream and soup. Stir in the hash browns, pork, process cheese and onion. Transfer to a greased 3-qt. baking dish.

Toss cornflake crumbs and butter; sprinkle over the top. Bake, uncovered, at 350° for 50 minutes. Sprinkle with mozzarella cheese. Bake 10 minutes longer or until bubbly.
YIELD: 8 servings.

darlis wilfer
WEST BEND, WISCONSIN

Everyone adores this comforting family-style casserole. I love that it calls for convenient frozen hash brown potatoes.

TRY poultry

You can replace the pork called for in Hash Brown Pork Bake with cubed cooked chicken or turkey, or omit the meat altogether and serve as a side dish.

BEEF POTPIE

PREP: 30 min. | **BAKE:** 45 min. + standing

- 1/4 cup *each* chopped onion, green pepper and sweet red pepper
- 1 tablespoon canola oil
- 2 garlic cloves, minced
- 3 cups cubed cooked roast beef
- 2 cups frozen cubed hash brown potatoes
- 1 can (10-3/4 ounces) condensed cream of mushroom soup, undiluted
- 1 package (10 ounces) frozen corn
- 1 jar (4-1/2 ounces) sliced mushrooms, drained
- 1 teaspoon Worcestershire sauce
- 1/8 teaspoon salt
- Dash pepper

ONION PASTRY:
- 2-1/2 cups all-purpose flour
- 1-1/4 teaspoons salt
- 1 cup butter-flavored shortening
- 4 teaspoons grated onion
- 4 to 5 tablespoons cold water

In a large skillet, saute onion and peppers in oil for 3 minutes. Add garlic; cook 1 minute longer. Stir in the beef, potatoes, soup, corn, mushrooms, Worcestershire sauce, salt and pepper. Bring to a boil. Reduce heat; cover and simmer for 10 minutes.

For the pastry, combine the flour and salt in a large bowl. Cut in the shortening until crumbly; sprinkle with the onion. Gradually add the water, tossing with a fork until the dough forms a ball.

Divide dough in half so that one ball is slightly larger than the other. On a lightly floured surface, roll out larger ball to fit a 9-in. deep-dish pie plate.

Transfer pastry to plate; trim even with edge. Add filling. Roll out remaining pastry to fit top of pie; place over filling. Trim, seal and flute edges. Cut slits in top.

Bake at 375° for 45-50 minutes or until filling is bubbly and crust is golden brown. Let stand for 15 minutes before cutting.

YIELD: 8 servings.

lucile cline
WICHITA, KANSAS

This comforting meat pie is a delicious way to put leftover roast beef to use. Grated onion adds a nice flavor to the pie crust.

CHEESY CHICKEN CASSEROLE

PREP: 20 min. | **BAKE:** 20 min.

- 10 cups diced cooked chicken
- 10 cups chopped celery
- 2 cups slivered almonds
- 2 bunches green onions with tops, sliced
- 2 cans (4 ounces *each*) chopped green chilies
- 2 cans (2-1/4 ounces *each*) sliced ripe olives, drained
- 5 cups (20 ounces) shredded cheddar cheese, *divided*
- 2 cups mayonnaise
- 2 cups (16 ounces) sour cream
- 5 cups crushed potato chips

In a very large bowl, combine the first six ingredients; add 2 cups cheese. In a small bowl, combine mayonnaise and sour cream; add to chicken mixture and toss to coat.

Transfer to two greased 3-qt. baking dishes. Sprinkle with chips and remaining cheese. Bake, uncovered, at 350° for 20-25 minutes or until heated through.

YIELD: 2 casseroles (12 servings each).

marna dunn
BULLHEAD CITY, ARIZONA

If you're looking to feed a big group, here's your recipe! It's full of ooey-gooey goodness that will hit the spot on a cool fall day. The potato chips add a kid-friendly crunch, too.

CASEROLE FOR A CROWD

PREP: 25 min. | **BAKE:** 30 min.

 2 pounds ground beef
 1 large onion, chopped
 8 ounces wide egg noodles, cooked and
   drained
 1 can (15-1/4 ounces) whole kernel corn,
   drained
 1 can (15-1/4 ounces) peas, drained
 1 can (8 ounces) mushroom stems and
   pieces, drained
 4 cups (16 ounces) shredded cheddar
   cheese, *divided*
 1 can (10-3/4 ounces) condensed cream
   of celery soup, undiluted
1-1/4 cups milk
 1 tablespoon chili powder
 1 tablespoon Worcestershire sauce
 2 teaspoons salt
1/4 teaspoon pepper
1/4 teaspoon garlic powder

In a large skillet, cook the beef and onion over medium heat until the meat is no longer pink; drain. Transfer to a greased roasting pan. Stir in the noodles, corn, peas and mushrooms.

In a large saucepan, combine 2-1/2 cups cheese with the remaining ingredients. Cook and stir over low heat until cheese is melted. Pour over noodle mixture and mix well. Sprinkle with remaining cheese.

Bake, uncovered, at 350° for 30 minutes or until heated through.

YIELD: 12-14 servings.

fran huettner
BEAVER DAM, WISCONSIN

All five of my grown children and all of my grandchildren expect me to serve this casserole when they visit. It makes just the right amount for our large family get-togethers.

MEXICAN LASAGNA

PREP: 20 min. | **BAKE:** 65 min. + standing

2 pounds ground beef

1 can (16 ounces) refried beans

1 can (4 ounces) chopped green chilies

1 envelope taco seasoning

2 tablespoons hot salsa

12 ounces uncooked lasagna noodles

4 cups (16 ounces) shredded Colby-Monterey Jack cheese, *divided*

1 jar (16 ounces) mild salsa

2 cups water

2 cups (16 ounces) sour cream

1 can (2-1/4 ounces) sliced ripe olives, drained

3 green onions, chopped

1 medium tomato, chopped, optional

In a large skillet, cook beef over medium heat until no longer pink; drain. Stir in the beans, green chilies, taco seasoning and hot salsa.

In a greased 13-in. x 9-in. baking dish, layer a third of the noodles and meat mixture. Sprinkle with 1 cup of cheese. Repeat layers twice.

Combine mild salsa and water; pour over top. Cover and bake at 350° for 1 hour or until heated through.

Top with the sour cream, olives, onions, tomato if desired and remaining cheese. Bake, uncovered, 5 minutes longer. Let stand for 10-15 minutes before cutting.

YIELD: 12 servings.

rose ann buhle
MINOOKA, ILLINOIS

I collect recipes, and my husband teases me that I won't live long enough to try half of the ones in my files. But rest assured I've made this fiesta-style lasagna for gatherings of all kinds...and I've never come home with leftovers!

ITALIAN MEATBALL TORTES

PREP: 1-1/4 hours + rising | **BAKE:** 30 min.

    1 package (1/4 ounce) active dry yeast
1/4 cup warm water (110° to 115°)
3/4 cup warm milk (110° to 115°)
1/4 cup sugar
1/4 cup shortening
    1 egg
    1 teaspoon salt
3-1/2 to 3-3/4 cups all-purpose flour

MEATBALLS:

    1 can (5 ounces) evaporated milk
    2 eggs, lightly beaten
    1 cup quick-cooking oats
    1 cup crushed saltines
1/2 cup chopped onion
1/2 cup chopped celery
    2 teaspoons salt
    2 teaspoons chili powder
1/2 teaspoon garlic powder
1/2 teaspoon pepper
    3 pounds ground beef

FILLING:

    1 can (15 ounces) crushed tomatoes
1/2 cup chopped onion
1/3 cup grated Parmesan cheese
1-1/2 teaspoons dried basil
1-1/2 teaspoons dried oregano
    1 teaspoon minced fresh parsley
    1 teaspoon salt
1-1/2 cups (6 ounces) shredded part-skim
    mozzarella cheese

In a large bowl, dissolve the yeast in warm water. Add the milk, sugar, shortening, egg, salt and 2 cups flour. Beat until smooth. Stir in enough of the remaining flour to form a soft dough.

Turn onto a floured surface; knead until smooth and elastic, about 6-8 minutes. Place in a greased bowl, turning once to grease the top. Cover and let rise in a warm place until doubled, 1 to 1-1/2 hours.

In a large bowl, combine the milk, eggs, oats, saltines, onion, celery and seasonings. Crumble beef over mixture and mix well. Shape into 1-1/2-in. balls. In a large skillet over medium heat, cook meatballs in batches until no longer pink.

Meanwhile, place tomatoes and onion in a small saucepan. Bring to a boil. Reduce heat; simmer, uncovered, for 10 minutes or until slightly thickened. Stir in the Parmesan cheese, herbs and salt.

Punch dough down. Divide into three portions. Roll two portions into 11-in. circles; line the bottoms and press partially up the sides of two greased 9-in. springform pans. Roll third portion into a 12-in. x 10-in. rectangle; cut the dough into twelve 10-in. x 1-in. strips.

Place meatballs in prepared crusts; top with tomato mixture and mozzarella cheese. Make lattice crusts with strips of dough; trim and seal edges. Cover and let rise for 30 minutes. Bake at 350° for 30-35 minutes or until golden brown. Cut into wedges.

YIELD: 2 tortes (6 servings each).

sandy blessing
OCEAN SHORES, WASHINGTON

With classic Italian flavor, everyone will love this hearty pie filled with tomatoes, mozzarella and moist, homemade meatballs. Preparation takes some time, but it's well worth it.

LAZY HAM BAKE

PREP: 10 min. | **BAKE:** 30 min.

1-1/2 pounds fully cooked ham, cubed
    1 package (16 ounces) frozen cut broccoli,
    thawed and drained
2-1/2 cups milk, *divided*
    1 can (10-3/4 ounces) condensed cream of
    mushroom soup, undiluted
    1 can (10-3/4 ounces) condensed cheddar
    cheese soup, undiluted
1/2 teaspoon onion powder
1/4 teaspoon garlic powder
    2 cups biscuit/baking mix
Minced fresh parsley, optional

In a large bowl, combine the ham, broccoli, 1 cup milk, soups, onion powder and garlic powder. Spoon into an ungreased 13-in. x 9-in. baking dish. Combine biscuit mix and remaining milk. Pour over ham mixture.

Bake, uncovered, at 450° for 30 minutes or until hot and bubbly. Garnish with parsley if desired.

YIELD: 8-10 servings.

elaine green
MECHANICSVILLE, MARYLAND

Canned soups create a quick-to-fix creamy sauce for this biscuit-topped ham casserole. It's an all-in-one meal everyone enjoys.

FIVE-CHEESE LASAGNA

PREP: 1 hour | **BAKE:** 40 min. + cooling

- 6 packages (16 ounces *each*) lasagna noodles
- 10 pounds bulk Italian sausage
- 10 medium onions, chopped
- 30 garlic cloves, minced
- 11 cans (29 ounces *each*) tomato sauce
- 2/3 cup dried basil
- 3 tablespoons ground nutmeg
- 2 tablespoons fennel seed, crushed
- 1 tablespoon salt
- 1 tablespoon pepper
- 6 cartons (32 ounces *each*) ricotta cheese
- 10 pounds shredded part-skim mozzarella cheese
- 4 cartons (8 ounces *each*) grated Parmesan cheese
- 5 blocks (5 ounces *each*) Romano cheese, grated
- 10 packages (6 ounces *each*) sliced provolone cheese, cut into strips
- 1 cup minced fresh parsley

In a stockpot, cook the noodles in boiling water for 5 minutes; rinse noodles in cold water and drain.

In several large skillets, cook sausage and onions until meat is no longer pink. Add garlic; cook 1 minute longer. Drain. Add tomato sauce and seasonings; bring to a boil. Reduce heat; simmer, uncovered, for 50-60 minutes.

Grease ten 13-in. x 9-in. baking dishes. In each dish, layer with about 1-1/2 cups tomato sauce, four noodles, about 1-1/4 cups ricotta, 1-1/2 cups mozzarella cheese, about 1/3 cup Parmesan cheese, 1/4 cup Romano and three slices provolone. Repeat layers. Top with four noodles, about 1-1/2 cups of tomato sauce, 1 cup mozzarella cheese and about 1 tablespoon parsley.

Bake, uncovered, at 375° for 40-50 minutes or until browned and bubbly. Let stand 10-15 minutes before serving.

YIELD: 120-150 servings.

todd newman
LA PORTE, TEXAS

I prepared this cheesy classic for a Cub Scout banquet. It was easy since there was nothing to do at the last minute but cut and serve. It was a big success!

LAYERED BEEF CASSEROLE

PREP: 25 min. | **BAKE:** 2 hours + standing

- 6 medium potatoes, peeled and thinly sliced
- 1 can (15-1/4 ounces) whole kernel corn, drained
- 1/2 cup chopped green pepper
- 1 cup chopped onion
- 2 cups sliced fresh carrots
- 1-1/2 pounds lean ground beef (90% lean)
- 1 can (8 ounces) tomato sauce
- Salt and pepper to taste
- 1 cup (4 ounces) shredded process cheese (Velveeta)

In a greased 13-in. x 9-in. baking dish, layer the potatoes, corn, green pepper, onion and carrots. Crumble beef over vegetables. Pour tomato sauce over top. Sprinkle with salt and pepper.

Cover and bake at 350° for 2 hours or until meat is no longer pink and a meat thermometer reads 160°. Sprinkle with cheese. Let casserole stand for 10 minutes before serving.

YIELD: 8 servings.

dorothy wiedeman
EATON, COLORADO

With my busy days, I treasure meal-in-one recipes like this. Toss together a salad, and dinner is ready in no time.

FIREFIGHTER'S CHICKEN SPAGHETTI

PREP: 20 min. | **BAKE:** 45 min.

- 12 ounces uncooked spaghetti, broken in half
- 1 can (10-3/4 ounces) condensed cream of chicken soup, undiluted
- 1 can (10-3/4 ounces) condensed cream of mushroom soup, undiluted
- 1 cup (8 ounces) sour cream
- 1/2 cup milk
- 1/4 cup butter, melted, *divided*
- 2 tablespoons dried parsley flakes
- 1/2 teaspoon garlic powder
- 1/2 teaspoon salt
- 1/4 teaspoon pepper
- 2 cups (8 ounces) shredded part-skim mozzarella cheese
- 1 cup grated Parmesan cheese
- 2 to 3 celery ribs, chopped
- 1 medium onion, chopped
- 1 can (4 ounces) mushroom stems and pieces, drained
- 5 cups cubed cooked chicken
- 1-1/2 cups crushed cornflakes

Cook spaghetti according to the package directions; drain. In a large bowl, combine the soups, sour cream, milk, 2 tablespoons butter and seasonings. Add the cheeses, celery, onion and mushrooms. Stir in the chicken and spaghetti.

Transfer to a greased 3-qt. baking dish (dish will be full). Combine cornflakes and remaining butter; sprinkle over the top.

Bake, uncovered, at 350° for 45-50 minutes or until bubbly.

YIELD: 12-14 servings.

krista davis-keith
NEW CASTLE, INDIANA

I enjoy treating folks to my casserole creations. My husband is a firefighter, and the members of his unit count this dish among their favorites.

GRATED parmesan

To keep prep simple when making a recipe that calls for grated Parmesan, use the finely grated kind sold in the containers with the shaker/pourer tops.

HEARTY CHICKEN LASAGNA

PREP: 50 min. | **BAKE:** 40 min. + standing

  12 lasagna noodles
   2 cans (14-1/2 ounces *each*) diced
     tomatoes, drained
   3 cans (6 ounces *each*) tomato paste
   2 cups sliced fresh mushrooms
 1/3 cup chopped onion
4-1/2 teaspoons dried basil
1-3/4 teaspoons salt, *divided*
 1/8 teaspoon garlic powder
   4 cups shredded cooked chicken
   2 eggs, lightly beaten
   4 cups (32 ounces) 2% cottage cheese
 3/4 cup grated Parmesan cheese
 1/2 cup minced fresh parsley
 3/4 teaspoon pepper
   3 cups (12 ounces) shredded part-skim
     mozzarella cheese

Cook the noodles according to the package directions. Meanwhile, in a large saucepan, combine the tomatoes, tomato paste, mushrooms, onion, basil, 3/4 teaspoon salt and garlic powder. Bring to a boil. Reduce heat; cover and simmer for 25 minutes to allow the flavors to blend. Add the chicken; heat through.

In a large bowl, combine the eggs, cottage cheese, Parmesan cheese, parsley, pepper and remaining salt.

Drain noodles. Place four noodles in a 13-in. x 9-in. baking dish coated with cooking spray. Layer with a third of the cheese mixture, chicken mixture and mozzarella cheese. Repeat layers twice.

Cover and bake at 375° for 30 minutes. Uncover; bake 10-15 minutes longer or until bubbly and top is lightly browned. Let stand for 15 minutes before cutting.
YIELD: 12 servings.

sharon skildum
MAPLE GROVE, MINNESOTA

Give this good-for-you lasagna a try. The lean chicken is a nice change of pace from traditional lasagnas calling for Italian sausage or ground beef.

ITALIAN SPAGHETTI BAKE

PREP: 20 min. | **BAKE:** 20 min.

- 2 packages (one 16 ounces, one 8 ounces) spaghetti
- 1-1/2 pounds ground beef
- 1 large green pepper, chopped
- 1 medium onion, chopped
- 2 cans (15 ounces *each*) tomato sauce
- 1 package (8 ounces) sliced pepperoni
- 1 can (8 ounces) mushroom stems and pieces, drained
- 1 can (3.8 ounces) sliced ripe olives, drained
- 1/2 teaspoon dried basil
- 1/2 teaspoon dried oregano
- 1/4 teaspoon garlic salt
- 1/4 teaspoon pepper
- 4 cups (16 ounces) shredded part-skim mozzarella cheese
- 1/2 cup grated Parmesan cheese

Cook spaghetti according to package directions. Meanwhile, in a Dutch oven, cook the beef, green pepper and onion over medium heat until meat is no longer pink; drain. Stir in the tomato sauce, pepperoni, mushrooms, olives and seasonings. Drain the spaghetti.

Spoon 1 cup meat mixture into each of two greased 13-in. x 9-in. baking dishes. Layer with spaghetti and remaining meat mixture. Sprinkle with cheeses.

Cover and freeze one casserole for up to 3 months. Bake the remaining casserole, uncovered, at 350° for 20-25 minutes or until heated through.

TO USE FROZEN CASSEROLE: Thaw in the refrigerator overnight. Remove from the refrigerator 30 minutes before baking. Cover and bake at 350° for 40 minutes. Uncover; bake 5-10 minutes longer or until the cheese is melted.

YIELD: 2 casseroles (8 servings each).

janice fredrickson
ELGIN, TEXAS

This recipe yields two large casseroles. The tasty layers of meat sauce, spaghetti and gooey cheese are sure to appeal to pizza lovers!

SCALLOPED POTATOES AND HAM

PREP: 30 min. | **BAKE:** 1 hour 20 min.

- 2 cans (10-3/4 ounces *each*) condensed cream of mushroom soup, undiluted
- 2 cans (10-3/4 ounces *each*) condensed cream of celery soup, undiluted
- 1 can (10-3/4 ounces) condensed cheddar cheese soup, undiluted
- 1 can (12 ounces) evaporated milk
- 10 pounds medium potatoes, peeled and thinly sliced
- 5 pounds fully cooked ham, cubed
- 4 cups (16 ounces) shredded cheddar cheese

In two large bowls, combine soups and milk. Add potatoes and ham; toss to coat. Divide the mixture among four greased 13-in. x 9-in. baking dishes.

Cover and bake at 325° for 1-1/4 hours or until potatoes are tender. Uncover; sprinkle with cheese. Bake 5-10 minutes longer or until cheese is melted.

YIELD: 4 casseroles (10 servings each).

ruth ann stelfox
RAYMOND, ALBERTA

A friend served this scrumptious dish at her wedding, and I liked it so much, I asked for the recipe. The potatoes and ham taste great covered in the creamy cheese sauce.

HOT dishes

To keep potluck favorites hot, cover each dish with plastic wrap, then place a lid on top. Then wrap the dishes in warm towels for added insulation.

DELICIOUS TOMATO PIE

PREP: 15 min. | **BAKE:** 30 min.

1-1/4 pounds plum tomatoes (about 5 large), cut into 1/2-inch slices
1 pastry shell (9 inches), baked
1/2 cup thinly sliced green onions
2 tablespoons minced fresh basil
1/4 teaspoon salt
1/4 teaspoon pepper
1/2 cup reduced-fat mayonnaise
1/2 cup shredded reduced-fat cheddar cheese
2 bacon strips, cooked and crumbled
2 tablespoons shredded Parmesan cheese

Place half of the tomatoes in pastry shell. Top with onions and remaining tomatoes. Sprinkle with the basil, salt and pepper. Combine mayonnaise and cheddar cheese; spread over tomatoes, leaving 1-1/2 in. around the edge. Sprinkle with bacon and Parmesan cheese.

Bake at 350° for 30-35 minutes or until tomatoes are tender.

YIELD: 8 servings.

edie despain
LOGAN, UTAH

How about pie for dinner? This savory staple is a wonderful way to accentuate summer's abundance of tomatoes from the garden or farmer's market.

THE FIREHOUSE SPECIAL

PREP: 45 min. | **BAKE:** 55 min.

2 cans (14-1/2 ounces *each*) chicken broth
3 cups uncooked instant rice
4 tablespoons butter, *divided*
2 pounds ground beef
2 packages (12 ounces *each*) bulk spicy pork sausage
1 pound sliced fresh mushrooms
3 garlic cloves, minced
2 packages (10 ounces *each*) frozen chopped spinach, thawed and squeezed dry
2 cups (16 ounces) 4% cottage cheese
8 eggs, lightly beaten
1 envelope onion soup mix
1 envelope leek soup mix
2 teaspoons garlic powder
1 teaspoon Creole seasoning
1/4 cup grated Parmesan cheese

In a large saucepan, bring broth to a boil. Stir in rice; cover and remove from the heat. Let stand for 5 minutes. Stir in 2 tablespoons butter; set aside.

Meanwhile, in a large skillet, cook beef and sausage over medium heat until no longer pink; drain. Transfer to a large bowl.

In the same skillet, saute mushrooms in remaining butter until tender. Add garlic; cook 1 minute longer. Add to meat mixture. Stir in the spinach, cottage cheese, eggs, soup mixes, garlic powder, Creole seasoning and reserved rice mixture.

Divide between two greased 13-in. x 9-in. baking dishes; sprinkle with cheese. Cover and bake at 350° for 45 minutes. Uncover; bake casseroles for 10-15 minutes longer or until heated through.

YIELD: 2 casseroles (10 servings each).

darrell alvord
BOISE, IDAHO

This versatile dish can be eaten for breakfast, lunch or dinner. It's great hot or cold, and it tastes even better the second day. Top it with salsa or sour cream.

WORTH IT LASAGNA

PREP: 1 hour | BAKE: 55 min. + standing

2 jars (26 ounces *each*) meatless spaghetti sauce

1 can (14-1/2 ounces) diced tomatoes, drained

1/2 cup Burgundy wine

2 tablespoons brown sugar

3 garlic cloves, minced

2 pounds Italian turkey sausage links, casings removed

3/4 cup raisins

2 teaspoons Italian seasoning

1-1/2 pounds sliced fresh mushrooms

1 medium onion, chopped

2 eggs, lightly beaten

2 cartons (15 ounces *each*) ricotta cheese

1 package (10 ounces) frozen chopped spinach, thawed and squeezed dry

1 cup grated Parmesan cheese

2 packages (24 ounces *each*) frozen cheese ravioli, thawed

1 cup shredded Parmesan cheese

18 slices provolone cheese, cut in half

6 cups (24 ounces) shredded Monterey Jack cheese

5 large tomatoes, sliced

In a Dutch oven, bring first five ingredients to a boil. Reduce heat; simmer, uncovered, for 20 minutes, stirring often.

In a large skillet, cook sausage over medium heat until no longer pink; drain. Stir in raisins and Italian seasoning; add to sauce. In the same skillet, saute mushrooms and onion until moisture has evaporated. Stir into sauce. In a large bowl, combine the eggs, ricotta, spinach and grated Parmesan cheese; set aside.

In each of two greased 13-in. x 9-in. baking dishes, layer with 1-1/3 cups sauce, half of a package of ravioli, 1-1/3 cups sauce, 1/4 cup shredded Parmesan cheese, six half slices of provolone cheese, 1 cup Monterey Jack cheese and 2-1/2 cups of the ricotta-spinach mixture.

Top each with six half slices of provolone cheese, 1 cup Monterey Jack cheese, 1-1/3 cups sauce, remaining ravioli and sauce, 1/4 cup shredded Parmesan cheese, six half slices of provolone cheese, sliced tomatoes and remaining Monterey Jack cheese (dishes will be full).

Cover and bake at 375° for 45 minutes. Uncover; bake 10-15 minutes longer or until bubbly. Let stand for 15 minutes before serving.

YIELD: 2 casseroles (12 servings each).

joan broxholme
BOULDER CITY, NEVADA

I break out this lasagna recipe whenever I need to feed a crowd. People love that it's made with ravioli instead of traditional lasagna noodles.

RICOTTA cheese

If a lasagna recipe calls for a ricotta cheese mixture, place the mixture in a large resealable plastic bag with one corner snipped off. Then squeeze the mixture out evenly onto the layers of ingredients. It's easy, and there's no mess or big clumps of cheese.

POTLUCK HAM AND PASTA

PREP: 40 min. | **BAKE:** 25 min.

- 1 package (16 ounces) elbow macaroni
- 4 cups fresh broccoli florets
- 1/2 cup finely chopped onion
- 1/2 cup butter, cubed
- 1/2 cup all-purpose flour
- 1 teaspoon ground mustard
- 1 teaspoon salt
- 1/4 teaspoon pepper
- 6 cups milk
- 1 jar (15 ounces) process cheese sauce
- 2 cups (8 ounces) shredded cheddar cheese, *divided*
- 4 cups cubed fully cooked ham

Cook the macaroni according to package directions, adding broccoli during the last 3-4 minutes; drain.

In a Dutch oven, saute onion in butter for 2 minutes. Stir in the flour, mustard, salt and pepper until blended. Gradually stir in milk. Bring to a boil; cook and stir for 2 minutes or until thickened. Stir in cheese sauce and 1 cup cheddar cheese until blended.

Remove from the heat; stir in the ham, macaroni and broccoli. Divide between a greased 13-in. x 9-in. baking dish and a greased 8-in. square baking dish. Sprinkle with remaining cheese.

Bake, uncovered, at 350° for 25-35 minutes or until casserole is bubbly and heated through.

YIELD: 12 servings.

nancy foust
STONEBORO, PENNSYLVANIA

This easy meal-in-one dish is a real crowd-pleaser on chilly nights. Because it bakes in two pans, you can take one to a potluck, and freeze the other one for a future dinner at home. It's creamy and filling and has a wonderful ham-and-cheese flavor.

TURKEY RICE CASSEROLE

PREP: 50 min. | **BAKE:** 25 min.

- 4 cups chicken broth
- 1/4 cup uncooked wild rice
- 1-3/4 cups uncooked long grain rice
- 2 cups sliced fresh mushrooms
- 1/2 cup fresh broccoli florets
- 1 small onion, chopped
- 1/4 cup grated carrot
- 1/4 cup sliced celery
- 2 tablespoons olive oil
- 5 cups cubed cooked turkey
- 1 jar (2 ounces) diced pimientos, drained
- 1 teaspoon salt
- 1/2 teaspoon dried marjoram
- 1/2 teaspoon dried oregano
- 5 tablespoons all-purpose flour
- 3 cups milk
- 1/4 cup white wine *or* chicken broth
- 2 cups (8 ounces) shredded Swiss cheese
- 2 cups (8 ounces) shredded cheddar cheese, *divided*

In a large saucepan, bring broth to a boil; add the wild rice. Cover and simmer for 25 minutes. Add the long grain rice; simmer 25 minutes longer or until tender.

In a large skillet, saute the mushrooms, broccoli, onion, carrot and celery in oil until tender. Add the turkey, pimientos, salt, marjoram and oregano. Stir in the rice.

In a large saucepan, combine the flour, milk and wine until smooth. Bring to a boil; cook and stir for 2 minutes or until thickened. Stir in the Swiss cheese and 1 cup cheddar cheese until melted. Add to turkey mixture.

Transfer to a greased 13-in. x 9-in. baking dish. Sprinkle with the remaining cheddar cheese. Bake, uncovered, at 350° for 25-30 minutes or until heated through.

YIELD: 12 servings.

ferne carter chapman
TACOMA, WASHINGTON

This rich casserole is always one of the first to go in a buffet line. When I want to indicate serving size, I use sliced cheese squares on the top rather than shredded cheese.

CALIFORNIA CASSEROLE

PREP: 20 min. | **BAKE:** 1 hour

- 2 pounds ground beef
- 1 medium green pepper, chopped
- 3/4 cup chopped onion
- 1 can (14-3/4 ounces) cream-style corn
- 1 can (10-3/4 ounces) condensed tomato soup, undiluted
- 1 can (10 ounces) tomatoes with green chilies, undrained
- 1 can (8 ounces) tomato sauce
- 1 jar (4-1/2 ounces) whole mushrooms, drained
- 1 jar (4 ounces) chopped pimientos, drained
- 1 can (2-1/4 ounces) sliced ripe olives, drained
- 1-1/2 teaspoons celery salt
- 1/2 teaspoon ground mustard
- 1/2 teaspoon chili powder
- 1/4 teaspoon pepper
- 8 ounces wide egg noodles, cooked and drained
- 2 cups (8 ounces) shredded cheddar cheese

In a large skillet, cook the beef, green pepper and onion over medium heat until meat is no longer pink and vegetables are tender; drain. Stir in the next 11 ingredients. Add the noodles.

Pour into a greased 13-in. x 9-in. baking dish. Cover and bake at 350° for 50 minutes. Sprinkle with cheese; bake 10 minutes longer or until the cheese is melted.

YIELD: 12-16 servings.

PASTA pointer

Drain pasta thoroughly in a colander without rinsing when it is to be combined in a baked dish. Rinsing can wash away starch that may help to slightly thicken the casserole.

---

hope lashier
AMARILLO, TEXAS

This colorful casserole is named after the West Coast, but it always brings appreciative oohs and aahs when I serve it to fellow Texans. It complements a variety of side dishes.

CHICKEN CORDON BLEU BAKE

PREP: 20 min. | **BAKE:** 40 min.

- 2 packages (6 ounces *each*) reduced-sodium stuffing mix
- 1 can (10-3/4 ounces) condensed cream of chicken soup, undiluted
- 1 cup milk
- 8 cups cubed cooked chicken
- 1/2 teaspoon pepper
- 3/4 pound sliced deli ham, cut into 1-inch strips
- 1 cup (4 ounces) shredded Swiss cheese
- 3 cups (12 ounces) shredded cheddar cheese

Prepare stuffing mixes according to package directions. Meanwhile, in a large bowl, combine soup and milk; set aside.

Divide chicken between two greased 13-in. x 9-in. baking dishes. Sprinkle with pepper. Layer with ham, Swiss cheese, 1 cup cheddar cheese, soup mixture and stuffing. Sprinkle with remaining cheddar cheese.

Cover and freeze one casserole for up to 3 months. Cover and bake the remaining casserole at 350° for 30 minutes. Uncover; bake 10-15 minutes longer or until cheese is melted.

TO USE FROZEN CASSEROLE: Thaw in the refrigerator overnight. Remove from the refrigerator 30 minutes before baking. Cover and bake at 350° for 45 minutes. Uncover; bake 10-15 minutes longer or until heated through and cheese is melted.

YIELD: 2 casseroles (6 servings each).

rea newell
DECATUR, ILLINOIS

This recipe yields a big batch so I freeze several half portions in disposable pans to share at potlucks and to pull out for supper on busy weeknights.

FOIL pans

Use foil pans and lids for potluck casseroles. Wrap each pan in a thick layer of newspaper, like a gift package, sealing it with tape. This makes for easy transporting and keeps the food insulated. When the get-together is over, you can simply toss the pan and lid.

HEARTY TURKEY CASSEROLE

PREP: 20 min. | **BAKE:** 35 min.

- 2 cups uncooked elbow macaroni
- 2 cups cubed cooked turkey breast
- 2 cups 2% milk
- 1 can (10-3/4 ounces) condensed cream of mushroom soup, undiluted
- 1 can (10-3/4 ounces) condensed cream of celery soup, undiluted
- 1 can (8 ounces) sliced water chestnuts, drained
- 1/2 pound process cheese (Velveeta), cubed
- 3 hard-cooked eggs, chopped
- 1 jar (2 ounces) diced pimientos, drained
- 1 teaspoon grated onion

Cook macaroni according to the package directions; drain and place in a large bowl. Add the remaining ingredients.

Transfer to a greased 13-in. x 9-in. baking dish. Bake, uncovered, at 350° for 35-40 minutes or until bubbly.

YIELD: 9 servings.

eunice holmberg
WILLMAR, MINNESOTA

This creamy, cheesy delight is a great way to use up leftover Thanksgiving turkey. It's guaranteed to please guests of all ages.

MOSTACCIOLI CASSEROLE

PREP: 25 min. | **BAKE:** 25 min.

1 package (16 ounces) mostaccioli
1-1/2 pounds ground beef
1-1/4 cups chopped green pepper
1 cup chopped onion
1 jar (26 ounces) spaghetti sauce
1 can (10-3/4 ounces) condensed cheddar cheese soup, undiluted
1-1/2 teaspoons Italian seasoning
3/4 teaspoon pepper
2 cups (8 ounces) shredded part-skim mozzarella cheese, *divided*

Cook mostaccioli according to package directions. Meanwhile, in a large skillet, cook the beef, green pepper and onion over medium heat until meat is no longer pink; drain. Stir in the spaghetti sauce, soup, Italian seasoning and pepper.

Drain mostaccioli. Add mostaccioli and 1-1/2 cups cheese to beef mixture. Transfer to two greased 11-in. x 7-in. baking dishes. Sprinkle with remaining cheese.

Cover and freeze one casserole for up to 3 months. Cover and bake the remaining casserole at 350° for 20 minutes. Uncover; bake 5-10 minutes longer or until bubbly and cheese is melted.

TO USE FROZEN CASSEROLE: Thaw in the refrigerator overnight. Remove from the refrigerator 30 minutes before baking. Cover and bake at 350° for 50-60 minutes or until heated through and cheese is melted.

YIELD: 2 casseroles (6 servings each).

margaret mcneil
GERMANTOWN, TENNESSEE

This rich and hearty casserole is comfort food at its best. It freezes and rebakes so well that no one will ever guess you made it ahead of time!

REUNION CASSEROLE

PREP: 15 min. | **BAKE:** 45 min.

- 1 pound ground beef
- 1/2 pound bulk spicy pork sausage
- 1 cup chopped onion
- 2 cups (8 ounces) shredded cheddar cheese, *divided*
- 1 medium green pepper, chopped
- 1 can (11 ounces) whole kernel corn, drained
- 1 can (10-3/4 ounces) condensed tomato soup, undiluted
- 1 can (8 ounces) tomato sauce
- 1/3 cup sliced pimiento-stuffed olives
- 1 garlic clove, minced
- 1/2 teaspoon salt
- 8 ounces wide egg noodles, cooked and drained

In a large Dutch oven, cook the beef, sausage and onion over medium heat until meat is no longer pink; drain. Stir in 1 cup cheese, green pepper, corn, soup, tomato sauce, olives, garlic, salt and noodles.

Transfer to a greased 13-in. x 9-in. baking dish. Sprinkle with remaining cheese. Cover and bake at 350° for 35 minutes. Uncover; bake 10 minutes longer.

YIELD: 8-10 servings.

bernice morris
MARSHFIELD, MISSOURI

This is a noodle casserole just like Mom used to make! Its down-home taste has great appeal at family gatherings. It is also fast to prepare and can be made ahead of time. You won't have leftovers!

SPINACH TUNA CASSEROLE

PREP: 25 min. | **BAKE:** 50 min.

5 cups uncooked egg noodles
2 cups (16 ounces) sour cream
1-1/2 cups mayonnaise
2 to 3 teaspoons lemon juice
2 to 3 teaspoons whole milk
1/4 teaspoon salt
1 package (10 ounces) frozen chopped spinach, thawed and squeezed dry
1 package (6 ounces) chicken stuffing mix
1/3 cup seasoned bread crumbs
1 can (6 ounces) tuna, drained and flaked
3 tablespoons grated Parmesan cheese

Cook the noodles according to the package directions. Meanwhile, in a large bowl, combine the sour cream, mayonnaise, lemon juice, milk and salt. Stir in the spinach, stuffing mix, bread crumbs and tuna until well combined.

Drain the noodles and place in a greased 13-in. x 9-in. baking dish. Top with tuna mixture; sprinkle with cheese. Cover and bake at 350° for 45 minutes. Uncover; bake 5-10 minutes longer or until lightly browned and heated through.

YIELD: 8 servings.

karla hamrick
WAPAKONETA, OHIO

Everyone will love this thick, comforting take on the classic tuna bake. The frozen spinach adds a boost of nutrition.

DEEP-DISH BEEF BAKE

PREP: 15 min. | **BAKE:** 35 min.

1 pound ground beef
2 cups biscuit/baking mix
1/2 cup cold water
3 medium tomatoes, thinly sliced
1 medium green pepper, chopped
2 large onions, chopped
1 cup (4 ounces) shredded cheddar cheese, *divided*
1 cup (8 ounces) sour cream
2/3 cup mayonnaise

In a large skillet, cook beef over medium heat until no longer pink; drain.

Meanwhile, in a large bowl, combine biscuit mix and water until a soft dough forms. Spread into a greased 13-in. x 9-in. baking dish. Layer with the beef, tomatoes and green pepper.

In a large bowl, combine the onions, 1/2 cup cheese, sour cream and mayonnaise; spread over top.

Bake, uncovered, at 375° for 30-35 minutes or until edges are browned. Sprinkle with the remaining cheese. Bake 5 minutes longer or until the cheese is melted.

YIELD: 12 servings.

karen owen
RISING SUN, INDIANA

This easy recipe requires just 15 minutes of assembly before you pop it in the oven and forget it. The golden crust is topped with beef, tomatoes and a creamy cheese layer.

CRUNCH TOP HAM AND POTATO CASSEROLE

PREP: 10 min. | **BAKE:** 1 hour

1 package (32 ounces) frozen cubed hash brown potatoes, thawed
2 cups cubed cooked ham
2 cups (16 ounces) sour cream
1-1/2 cups (6 ounces) shredded cheddar cheese
1 can (10-3/4 ounces) condensed cream of chicken soup, undiluted
1/2 cup butter, melted
1/3 cup chopped green onions
1/2 teaspoon pepper

TOPPING:
2 cups crushed cornflakes
1/4 cup butter, melted

In a large bowl, combine the first eight ingredients. Transfer to a greased 13-in. x 9-in. baking dish. Combine the topping ingredients; sprinkle over the top. Bake, uncovered, at 350° for 1 hour or until heated through.

YIELD: 10 servings.

nancy schmidt
DELHI, CALIFORNIA

Hash browns, ham and cheese combine for a meal that's sure to satisfy. Serve this casserole as part of your brunch buffet or for dinner alongside your favorite vegetable.

BEANS AND FRANKS BAKE

PREP: 20 min. | **BAKE:** 40 min.

- 2 packages (8-1/2 ounces *each*) corn bread/muffin mix
- 1 can (28 ounces) baked beans
- 4 hot dogs, halved lengthwise and sliced
- 1/2 pound sliced bacon, cooked and crumbled
- 1 cup ketchup
- 1/2 cup packed brown sugar
- 1/2 cup chopped onion
- 2 cups (8 ounces) shredded part-skim mozzarella cheese

Prepare corn bread batter according to the package directions; set aside. In a large bowl, combine the beans, hot dogs, bacon, ketchup, brown sugar and onion. Transfer to two greased 8-in. square baking dishes. Sprinkle with the cheese; top with the corn bread batter.

Cover and freeze one casserole for up to 3 months. Bake the second casserole, uncovered, at 350° for 40-45 minutes or until a toothpick inserted near the center comes out clean.

TO USE FROZEN CASSEROLE: Remove from the freezer 30 minutes before baking. Cover and bake at 350° for 40 minutes. Uncover; bake 15-20 minutes longer or until casserole is heated through.

YIELD: 2 casseroles (4 servings each).

roxanne vangelder
ROCHESTER, NEW HAMPSHIRE

I've made this casserole several times, and it's always a hit. The kid-pleasing combo has a sweet flavor from the baked beans and the corn bread topping.

MAC 'N' CHEESE FOR A BUNCH

PREP: 30 min. | **BAKE:** 35 min.

- 3 packages (two 16 ounces, one 7 ounces) elbow macaroni
- 1-1/4 cups butter, *divided*
- 3/4 cup all-purpose flour
- 2 teaspoons salt
- 3 quarts milk
- 3 pounds sharp cheddar cheese, shredded
- 1-1/2 cups dry bread crumbs

Cook macaroni according to package directions until almost tender. Meanwhile, in a large stockpot, melt 1 cup butter. Stir in flour and salt until smooth. Gradually stir in milk. Bring to a boil; cook and stir for 2 minutes or until thickened. Reduce heat. Add cheese, stirring until melted. Drain macaroni; stir into sauce.

Transfer to three greased 13-in. x 9-in. baking dishes. Melt remaining butter; toss with the bread crumbs. Sprinkle the crumbs over the casseroles.

Bake, uncovered, at 350° for 35-40 minutes or until golden brown.

YIELD: 36 servings (1 cup each).

dixie terry
GOREVILLE, ILLINOIS

You'll delight many taste buds with this rich and comforting dish. Tender macaroni is covered in a creamy, homemade cheese sauce and then topped with golden bread crumbs for a classic meal.

SUPREME PIZZA CASSEROLE

PREP: 20 min. | BAKE: 30 min.

8 ounces uncooked fettuccine

2 pounds ground beef

1 medium onion, chopped

2 cans (8 ounces *each*) mushroom stems and pieces, drained

1 can (15 ounces) tomato sauce

1 jar (14 ounces) pizza sauce

1 can (6 ounces) tomato paste

1/2 teaspoon sugar

1/2 teaspoon garlic powder

1/2 teaspoon onion powder

1/2 teaspoon dried oregano

4 cups (16 ounces) shredded part-skim mozzarella cheese, *divided*

1 package (3-1/2 ounces) sliced pepperoni

1/2 cup grated Parmesan cheese

Cook fettuccine according to package directions. Meanwhile, in a Dutch oven, cook beef and onion over medium heat until meat is no longer pink; drain. Stir in the mushrooms, tomato sauce, pizza sauce, tomato paste, sugar and seasonings. Drain pasta; stir into meat sauce.

Divide half of the mixture between two greased 2-qt. baking dishes; sprinkle each with 1 cup mozzarella cheese. Repeat the layers. Top each dish with the pepperoni and Parmesan cheese.

Cover and bake at 350° for 20 minutes. Uncover; bake 10-15 minutes longer or until heated through.

YIELD: 2 casseroles (8 servings each).

nancy foust
STONEBORO, PENNSYLVANIA

You can guarantee the pan will come home empty when you bring this ooey-gooey, pepperoni-topped casserole to an event or potluck. It tastes like pizza in a dish—and who wouldn't love that?

MONTEREY SAUSAGE PIE

PREP: 15 min. | **BAKE:** 25 min. + standing

1 pound bulk pork sausage

1 cup chopped onion

1 cup chopped sweet red pepper

1/2 cup chopped fresh mushrooms

3 teaspoons minced garlic

2-1/2 cups (10 ounces) shredded Monterey Jack cheese, *divided*

1-1/3 cups milk

3 eggs

3/4 cup biscuit/baking mix

3/4 teaspoon rubbed sage

1/4 teaspoon pepper

In a large skillet, cook the sausage, onion, red pepper and mushrooms over medium heat until meat is no longer pink. Add garlic; cook 1 minute longer. Drain. Stir in 2 cups cheese. Transfer to a greased 9-in. deep-dish pie plate.

In a small bowl, combine the milk, eggs, biscuit mix, sage and pepper. Pour over sausage mixture.

Bake at 400° for 20-25 minutes or until a knife inserted near the center comes out clean. Sprinkle with remaining cheese; bake 1-2 minutes longer or until cheese is melted. Let stand for 10 minutes before cutting.

YIELD: 8 servings.

bonnie marlow
OTTOVILLE, OHIO

Baking mix makes this pie a snap to assemble. I got the idea from a similar recipe calling for ground beef and cheddar cheese. That version was too bland for my family's tastes, but I made a few changes, and this was the result.

SHEPHERD'S PIE

PREP: 20 min. | **BAKE:** 30 min.

2-1/2 pounds potatoes, peeled and cooked
1 to 1-1/2 cups (8 to 12 ounces) sour cream
Salt and pepper to taste
2 pounds ground beef
1/2 cup chopped onion
1 medium sweet red pepper, chopped
1 teaspoon garlic salt
1 can (10-3/4 ounces) condensed cream of mushroom soup, undiluted
1 can (16 ounces) whole kernel corn, drained
1/2 cup milk
2 tablespoons butter, melted
Chopped fresh parsley, optional

In a large bowl, mash the potatoes with sour cream. Add the salt and pepper; set aside. In a large skillet, cook the beef with onion and red pepper until the meat is no longer pink and vegetables are tender; drain. Stir garlic salt into meat mixture. Stir in the soup, corn and milk.

Spread meat mixture into a greased 13-in. x 9-in. baking dish. Top with mashed potatoes; drizzle with butter.

Bake, uncovered, at 350° for 30-35 minutes or until heated through. For additional browning, place pan under broiler for a few minutes. Sprinkle with the parsley if desired.

YIELD: 8-10 servings.

valerie merrill
TOPEKA, KANSAS

I received the recipe for this economical dish from a friend who was a whiz at pinching pennies without sacrificing hearty flavor.

CAVATINI PASTA

PREP: 30 min. + simmering | **BAKE:** 35 min.

2 pounds ground beef
2 medium onions, chopped
1 medium green pepper, chopped
6 garlic cloves, minced
4 cups water
1 can (12 ounces) tomato paste
1 can (4 ounces) mushroom stems and pieces, drained
1 package (3-1/2 ounces) sliced pepperoni
2 envelopes spaghetti sauce mix
1 teaspoon Italian seasoning

PASTA:
8 cups water
1 cup *each* uncooked elbow macaroni, bow tie pasta and medium pasta shells
2 cups (8 ounces) shredded part-skim mozzarella cheese

In a Dutch oven, cook the beef, onions and pepper over medium heat until meat is no longer pink; drain. Add garlic; cook 1 minute longer. Stir in the water, tomato paste, mushrooms, pepperoni, sauce mix and Italian seasoning. Bring to a boil. Reduce heat; simmer, uncovered, for 1 hour.

Meanwhile, for pasta, bring water to a boil in a large saucepan. Add macaroni and pastas. Return to a boil, stirring occasionally. Cook, uncovered, for 10-12 minutes or until tender; drain. Stir into tomato sauce. Transfer mixture to a greased 13-in. x 9-in. baking dish (dish will be full).

Bake at 350° for 30 minutes. Sprinkle with the cheese. Bake 5-10 minutes longer or until the cheese is melted.

YIELD: 14 servings.

russ palmer
SARANAC, MICHIGAN

This recipe has been in my family as long as I can remember, and it is still a favorite. I make it whenever we host guests, and it never fails to please!

TAMALE CASSEROLE

PREP: 35 min. | **BAKE:** 55 min.

7 pounds ground beef

6 medium onions, chopped

2 celery ribs, chopped

3 garlic cloves, minced

2 cans (14-1/2 ounces *each*) diced tomatoes, undrained

2 cans (12 ounces *each*) tomato paste

2 cans (15-1/4 ounces *each*) whole kernel corn, drained

2 cans (4-1/2 ounces *each*) mushroom stems and pieces, drained

3 cans (2-1/4 ounces *each*) sliced ripe olives, drained

2-1/4 to 2-3/4 cups water

2 to 3 tablespoons chili powder

1 tablespoon seasoned salt

1/2 to 1 teaspoon crushed red pepper flakes

1 teaspoon pepper

3 jars (13-1/2 ounces *each*) tamales, papers removed and halved

2 cups (8 ounces) shredded cheddar cheese

In several Dutch ovens, cook the beef, onions and celery until meat is no longer pink. Add garlic; cook 1 minute longer. Drain. Stir in the tomatoes and tomato paste. Add the corn, mushrooms and olives. Stir in the water and seasonings. Bring to a boil; remove from the heat.

Spoon into three greased 13-in. x 9-in. baking dishes. Top with tamales. Cover and bake at 350° for 50-60 minutes. Sprinkle with cheese. Bake 5-10 minutes longer or until cheese is melted.

YIELD: 3 casseroles (8-10 servings each).

elaine daniels
SANTA ANA, CALIFORNIA

I served this casserole at a large Mexican-themed party I hosted. It was a big hit with its zippy tomato and ground beef sauce.

TUNA MAC AND CHEESE BAKE

PREP: 15 min. | **BAKE:** 30 min.

1 package (7-1/4 ounces) macaroni and cheese dinner mix

1 can (12 ounces) light water-packed tuna, drained and flaked

1 can (10-3/4 ounces) condensed cream of mushroom soup, undiluted

1-1/3 cups 2% milk

2 packages (9 ounces *each*) frozen peas and pearl onions

1 can (4 ounces) mushroom stems and pieces, drained

1 can (2.8 ounces) French-fried onions, *divided*

Prepare macaroni and cheese according to the package directions. Stir in the tuna, soup, milk, peas, mushrooms and half of the fried onions.

Place in a greased 11-in. x 7-in. baking dish. Bake, uncovered, at 325° for 25 minutes. Sprinkle with remaining fried onions; bake 5 minutes longer or until heated through.

YIELD: 8 servings.

bonnie hord
LEE'S SUMMIT, MISSOURI

Tuna lovers will gobble up this flavorful twist on mac and cheese. The recipe calls for everyday ingredients you likely already have in stock.

LITTLE tummies

Kids often don't like casserole-type foods that are served at potlucks. To make sure the little ones will eat, bring hot dogs, chicken nuggets or a big pan of plain mac 'n' cheese.

CHEESY SPAGHETTI BAKE

PREP: 45 min. | **BAKE:** 40 min.

- 1 pound uncooked spaghetti, broken into 3-inch pieces
- 4 pounds ground beef
- 2 large onions, chopped
- 1 large green pepper, chopped
- 4 cups milk
- 4 cans (10-3/4 ounces *each*) condensed tomato soup, undiluted
- 2 cans (10-3/4 ounces *each*) condensed cream of mushroom soup, undiluted
- 4 cups (16 ounces) shredded sharp cheddar cheese, *divided*

Cook the spaghetti according to package directions. Drain and place in two greased 13-in. x 9-in. baking dishes; set aside.

In two Dutch ovens or stockpots, cook the beef, onions and green pepper over medium heat until meat is no longer pink; drain. To each pot, add 2 cups of milk, two cans of tomato soup, one can of mushroom soup and 1 cup of cheese. Bring to a boil.

Spoon over the spaghetti (spaghetti will absorb liquid during baking). Sprinkle with remaining cheese. Bake, uncovered, at 350° for 40-45 minutes or until bubbly and top is lightly browned.

YIELD: 2 casseroles (12 servings each).

sue braunschweig
DELAFIELD, WISCONSIN

Featuring all the classic ingredients of spaghetti and meat sauce, this recipe makes two hearty family-style casseroles. It's a great standby for those times you're called upon to bring a dish to pass.

GROUND BEEF SPIRAL BAKE

PREP: 40 min. | **BAKE:** 25 min.

- 1 package (16 ounces) spiral pasta
- 2 pounds ground beef
- 2/3 cup chopped onion
- 1 teaspoon minced garlic
- 2 jars (28 ounces *each*) spaghetti sauce
- 2 tablespoons tomato paste
- 1 teaspoon dried basil
- 1 teaspoon dried oregano
- 4 cups (16 ounces) shredded part-skim mozzarella cheese

Cook pasta according to package directions; drain. Meanwhile, in a Dutch oven, cook beef and onion over medium heat until meat is no longer pink. Add garlic; cook 1 minute longer. Drain. Stir in the spaghetti sauce, tomato paste, basil and oregano. Bring to a boil. Reduce the heat; simmer, uncovered, for 5-10 minutes.

Stir pasta into meat mixture. Transfer to two greased 13-in. x 9-in. baking dishes. Sprinkle each with 2 cups cheese.

Cover and freeze one casserole for up to 3 months. Bake the second casserole, uncovered, at 350° for 25-30 minutes or until heated through.

TO USE FROZEN CASSEROLE: Thaw in the refrigerator overnight. Bake, uncovered, at 350° for 35-40 minutes or until heated through.

YIELD: 2 casseroles (8-10 servings each).

monika rahn
DILLSBURG, PENNSYLVANIA

I received this recipe many years ago from my mother-in-law's neighbor who happened to be a chef. It's easy to make and freezes well. You can try large shell macaroni or ziti noodles if you prefer.

MOM'S GROUND BEEF CASSEROLE

PREP: 15 min. | **BAKE:** 45 min.

2 pounds ground beef
1 medium green pepper, chopped
1 medium onion, chopped
9 cups cooked wide egg noodles
1 pound process cheese (Velveeta)
1 can (15-1/4 ounces) whole kernel corn, drained
1 can (11-1/2 ounces) condensed chicken with rice soup, undiluted
1 can (10-3/4 ounces) condensed cream of mushroom soup, undiluted
1/2 cup milk
1 teaspoon salt
1/4 teaspoon pepper

In a Dutch oven, cook beef, green pepper and onion until meat is no longer pink; drain. Remove from the heat; stir in the remaining ingredients.

Transfer to two greased 2-1/2-qt. baking dishes. Cover and bake at 350° for 45-50 minutes or until bubbly.

YIELD: 2 casseroles (8-9 servings each).

julie gillespie
KIRKLIN, INDIANA

This family-favorite recipe was passed down from my mom. It yields two casseroles, so it's perfect for a crowd. Just add a green vegetable for a complete meal.

CHEESY HAM MACARONI

PREP: 25 min. | **BAKE:** 25 min.

1 package (8 ounces) elbow macaroni
6 tablespoons butter, *divided*
1/4 cup all-purpose flour
1/2 teaspoon salt
Dash pepper
2 cups milk
2 cups (8 ounces) shredded sharp cheddar cheese
2 cups cubed fully cooked ham
1 can (4 ounces) mushroom stems and pieces, drained
1 jar (2 ounces) diced pimientos, drained
1/2 cup crushed butter-flavored crackers (about 11 crackers)
Minced fresh parsley, optional

Cook the macaroni according to package directions. Meanwhile in large saucepan, melt 4 tablespoons butter. Stir in the flour, salt and pepper until smooth; gradually whisk in milk. Bring to a boil; cook and stir for 1 minute or until thickened. Reduce heat. Add the cheese; cook and stir until melted. Stir in the ham, mushrooms and pimientos. Drain macaroni; stir into ham mixture.

Transfer to a greased shallow 2-1/2-qt. baking dish. Sprinkle with cracker crumbs; dot with remaining butter. Bake, uncovered, at 350° for 25-30 minutes or until heated through and bubbly. Sprinkle casserole with parsley if desired.

YIELD: 8 servings.

molly seidel
EDGEWOOD, NEW MEXICO

I'm often asked to bring this comforting casserole to potluck dinners, and it's a great weeknight meal, too. The rich and creamy dish is a smart way to make use of leftover baked ham.

HOSTESS gift

Watch rummage sales and thrift stores for pretty dishes priced inexpensively. Use the dishes to take casseroles to potlucks and parties, and let your host keep the dish. Then you don't have to worry about losing a cherished serving piece.

BISCUIT-TOPPED LEMON CHICKEN

PREP: 40 min. | **BAKE:** 35 min.

2 large onions, finely chopped

4 celery ribs, finely chopped

1 cup butter, cubed

2 garlic cloves, minced

8 green onions, thinly sliced

2/3 cup all-purpose flour

8 cups 2% milk

12 cups cubed cooked chicken

2 cans (10-3/4 ounces *each*) condensed cream of chicken soup, undiluted

1/2 cup lemon juice

2 tablespoons grated lemon peel

2 teaspoons pepper

1 teaspoon salt

CHEDDAR BISCUITS:

5 cups self-rising flour

2 cups 2% milk

2 cups (8 ounces) shredded cheddar cheese

1/4 cup butter, melted

In a Dutch oven, saute onions and celery in butter. Add garlic; cook 1 minute longer. Add green onions. Stir in flour until blended; gradually add milk. Bring to a boil; cook and stir for 2 minutes or until thickened.

Stir in the chicken, soup, lemon juice and peel, pepper and salt; heat through. Pour into two greased 13-in. x 9-in. baking dishes; set aside.

In a large bowl, combine the biscuit ingredients just until moistened. Turn onto a lightly floured surface; knead 8-10 times. Pat or roll out dough to 3/4-in. thickness. With a floured 2-1/2-in. biscuit cutter, cut out 30 biscuits.

Place biscuits over chicken mixture. Bake, uncovered, at 350° for 35-40 minutes or until golden brown.

YIELD: 15 servings (30 biscuits).

pattie ishee
STRINGER, MISSISSIPPI

This home-style recipe combines two of my favorite things—hot, crusty biscuits and a flavorful lemon-pepper sauce. It's also delicious with potatoes and carrots baked inside.

BAKED SPAGHETTI

PREP: 25 min. | **BAKE:** 25 min.

2 pounds ground beef

2 medium onions, chopped

2 cans (one 15 ounces, one 8 ounces) tomato sauce

1 can (8 ounces) sliced mushrooms, drained

1 teaspoon garlic powder

1 teaspoon dried oregano

2 packages (7 ounces *each*) uncooked spaghetti

1 package (8 ounces) cream cheese, softened

2 cups (16 ounces) 4% cottage cheese

1/2 cup sour cream

2 tablespoons minced chives

1/4 cup dry bread crumbs

1-1/2 teaspoons butter, melted

In a large skillet, cook beef and onions over medium heat until meat is no longer pink; drain. Add the tomato sauce, mushrooms, garlic powder and oregano. Bring to a boil. Reduce heat; simmer, uncovered, for 15 minutes, stirring occasionally.

Meanwhile, cook the spaghetti according to package directions; drain. In a small bowl, combine the cream cheese, cottage cheese, sour cream and chives; beat well. Place half of spaghetti in a greased 4-qt. baking dish. Spoon cream cheese mixture evenly over top. Layer with remaining spaghetti and all of the beef mixture.

Toss bread crumbs and butter; sprinkle over the top. Cover and bake at 350° for 20 minutes. Uncover; bake 5-10 minutes longer until heated through.

YIELD: 12 servings.

doris heath
FRANKLIN, NORTH CAROLINA

This casserole is a standby for church suppers and other potluck functions. Add a tossed green salad and breadsticks to round out a memorable meal.

SWEET POTATO SAUSAGE CASSEROLE

PREP: 20 min. | **BAKE:** 25 min.

8 ounces uncooked spiral pasta

8 ounces smoked sausage, cut into 1/4-inch slices

2 medium sweet potatoes, peeled and cut into 1/2-inch cubes

1 cup chopped green pepper

1/2 cup chopped onion

2 tablespoons olive oil

1 teaspoon minced garlic

1 can (14-1/2 ounces) diced tomatoes, undrained

1 cup heavy whipping cream

1/4 teaspoon salt

1/4 teaspoon pepper

1 cup (4 ounces) shredded cheddar cheese

Cook pasta according to package directions. Meanwhile, in a large skillet, cook the sausage, sweet potatoes, green pepper and onion in oil over medium heat for 5 minutes or until vegetables are tender. Add garlic; cook 1 minute longer. Drain.

Add the tomatoes, cream, salt and pepper. Bring to a boil; remove from the heat. Drain pasta; stir into sausage mixture. Transfer to a greased 13-in. x 9-in. baking dish. Sprinkle with cheese.

Bake, uncovered, at 350° for 25-30 minutes or until bubbly. Let stand for 5 minutes before serving.

YIELD: 8 servings.

rickey madden
CLINTON, SOUTH CAROLINA

You may have never considered combining sweet potatoes with pasta and sausage, but I promise you'll love this recipe I adapted from several others. You can add more cheese or sausage to suit your taste.

p. 216

p. 190

p. 202

slow cooker
sensations

SLOW-COOKED RIBS

PREP: 15 min. | **COOK:** 6 hours

4 pounds boneless country-style pork ribs
1 cup barbecue sauce
1 cup Catalina salad dressing
1/2 teaspoon minced garlic
2 tablespoons all-purpose flour
1/4 cup cold water

Cut ribs into serving-size pieces. Place in a 5-qt. slow cooker. Combine barbecue sauce and salad dressing; pour over ribs. Sprinkle with garlic. Cover and cook on low for 6-7 hours or until meat is tender.

Remove meat to a serving platter; keep warm. Skim fat from cooking juices; transfer to a small saucepan. Bring liquid to a boil. Combine flour and water until smooth. Gradually stir into the pan. Bring to a boil; cook and stir for 2 minutes or until thickened. Serve with meat.

YIELD: 8 servings.

sharon crider
JUNCTION CITY, KANSAS

Nothing says comfort like a plate full of mouthwatering ribs coated in tangy barbecue sauce. Use of the slow cooker makes them delicious and fall-off-the-bone tender.

TURKEY CHILI

PREP: 20 min. | **COOK:** 6-1/2 hours

1 pound lean ground turkey
3/4 cup *each* chopped onion, celery and green pepper
1 can (28 ounces) diced tomatoes, undrained
1 jar (26 ounces) meatless spaghetti sauce
1 can (16 ounces) hot chili beans, undrained
1-1/2 cups water
1/2 cup frozen corn
2 tablespoons chili powder
1 teaspoon ground cumin
1/4 teaspoon pepper
1/8 to 1/4 teaspoon cayenne pepper
1 can (16 ounces) kidney beans, rinsed and drained
1 can (15 ounces) pinto beans, rinsed and drained
Sour cream, optional

In a large nonstick skillet, cook the turkey, onion, celery and green pepper over medium heat until the meat is no longer pink and the vegetables are tender; drain.

Transfer to a 5-qt. slow cooker. Add the next nine ingredients. Cover and cook on high for 1 hour.

Reduce heat to low; cook for 5-6 hours. Add kidney and pinto beans; cook 30 minutes longer. Garnish with sour cream if desired.

YIELD: 13 servings.

celesta zanger
BLOOMFIELD HILLS, MICHIGAN

I took my mother's recipe for chili and altered it a bit to make it thicker and more robust. It's a crowd-pleaser, especially in fall and winter.

GROUND turkey

Shake up the flavor of Turkey Chili by adding about 1 teaspoon of fennel seed to 1 pound of ground turkey as you brown it. This will yield a flavor similar to sausage.

GONE-ALL DAY STEW

PREP: 25 min. | **BAKE:** 4 hours

1/4 cup all-purpose flour
1 boneless beef chuck roast (2 pounds), cut into 1-inch cubes
2 tablespoons canola oil
1 can (10-3/4 ounces) condensed tomato soup, undiluted
1 cup water *or* red wine
2 teaspoons beef bouillon granules
3 teaspoons Italian seasoning
1 bay leaf
1/2 teaspoon coarsely ground pepper
6 medium onions, quartered
4 medium potatoes, cut into 1-1/2-inch chunks
3 medium carrots, cut into 1-inch slices
12 large fresh mushrooms
1/2 cup celery, cut into 1-inch slices
Hot cooked egg noodles, optional

Place flour in a large resealable plastic bag. Add the beef, a few pieces at a time and shake to coat.

In a large skillet, brown meat in oil in batches; drain. Transfer to a 5-qt. slow cooker. In a small bowl, combine the tomato soup, water, bouillon and seasonings; pour over beef. Add the onions, potatoes, carrots, mushrooms and celery.

Cover and cook on low for 4-5 hours or until meat is tender. Discard bay leaf. Serve with egg noodles if desired.

YIELD: 8 servings.

patricia kile
ELIZABETHTOWN, PENNSYLVANIA

This healthy stew is one of my husband's favorite meals. I always use fresh mushrooms, and I toss low-sodium bouillon cubes right into the roaster. No additional salt is necessary.

BAKED POTATO SOUP

PREP: 35 min. | **COOK:** 6 hours

- 2 large onions, chopped
- 3 tablespoons butter
- 2 tablespoons all-purpose flour
- 2 cups water, *divided*
- 4 cups chicken broth
- 2 medium potatoes, peeled and diced
- 1-1/2 cups mashed potato flakes
- 1/2 pound sliced bacon, cooked and crumbled
- 3/4 teaspoon pepper
- 1/2 teaspoon salt
- 1/2 teaspoon dried basil
- 1/8 teaspoon dried thyme
- 1 cup half-and-half cream
- 1/2 cup shredded cheddar cheese
- 2 green onions, sliced

In a large skillet, saute onions in butter until tender. Stir in flour. Gradually stir in 1 cup water. Bring to a boil; cook and stir for 2 minutes or until thickened. Transfer to a 5-qt. slow cooker.

Add the broth, potatoes, potato flakes, bacon, pepper, salt, basil, thyme and remaining water. Cover and cook on low for 6-8 hours or until potatoes are tender. Stir in cream; heat through. Garnish with cheese and green onions.

YIELD: 10 servings.

barbara bleigh
COLONIAL HEIGHTS, VIRGINIA

The only thing that beats the comforting flavor of this thick and hearty potato soup is possibly the idea that it simmers on its own all day.

SPICY MEATBALLS WITH SAUCE

PREP: 30 min. | **COOK:** 5 hours

1 egg, lightly beaten
3/4 cup crushed seasoned salad croutons
1/2 cup finely chopped onion
1/4 cup finely chopped green pepper
1 teaspoon garlic powder
1 teaspoon ground cumin
1 teaspoon dried oregano
1 teaspoon pepper
1 pound ground turkey
1 pound bulk Italian sausage

SAUCE:

3 tablespoons cornstarch
1 tablespoon sugar
3/4 cup beef broth
2 cans (28 ounces *each*) crushed tomatoes
3 medium carrots, diced
1 can (6 ounces) tomato paste
1 envelope onion soup mix
3 garlic cloves, minced
1 teaspoon dried basil
1/2 teaspoon crushed red pepper flakes
Hot cooked pasta

In a large bowl, combine the egg, croutons, onion, green pepper, garlic powder, cumin, oregano and pepper. Crumble turkey and sausage over mixture and mix well. Shape into 1-in. balls. Place in a 5-qt. slow cooker.

In a large bowl, combine the cornstarch, sugar and broth until smooth; stir in the tomatoes, carrots, tomato paste, soup mix, garlic, basil and pepper flakes. Pour over meatballs. Cover and cook on low for 5-6 hours or until meat is no longer pink. Serve with the pasta.

YIELD: 8 servings (1 cup sauce with 5 meatballs).

rosanne bergman
ALTA LOMA, CALIFORNIA

I rely on Italian sausage to make these delicious meatballs. They cook to perfection in the slow cooker along with a homemade sauce.

PULLED PORK SUBS

PREP: 15 min. | **COOK:** 5 hours

1 small onion, finely chopped
1 boneless pork shoulder butt roast (2-1/2 pounds)
1 bottle (18 ounces) barbecue sauce
1/2 cup water
1/4 cup honey
6 garlic cloves, minced
1 teaspoon seasoned salt
1 teaspoon ground ginger
8 submarine buns, split

Place onion and roast in a 5-qt. slow cooker. In a small bowl, combine the barbecue sauce, water, honey, garlic, seasoned salt and ginger; pour over the meat. Cover and cook on high for 5-6 hours or until the meat is tender.

Remove meat; cool slightly. Shred meat with two forks and return to the slow cooker; heat through. Serve on buns. Cut sandwiches in half.

YIELD: 16 servings.

denise davis
PORTER, MAINE

Honey and ground ginger are the flavor boosters behind my no-stress sandwiches. A bottle of barbecue sauce ties it all together in a pinch.

SHREDDING meat

Remove cooked meat from pan with a slotted spoon if necessary. Reserve cooking liquid if called for. Place meat in a shallow pan. With two forks, pull meat into thin shreds. Return shredded meat to the pan to warm or use as recipe directs.

SHREDDED VENISON SANDWICHES

PREP: 5 min. | **COOK:** 4-1/2 hours

1 boneless venison roast (4 pounds)
1-1/2 cups ketchup
3 tablespoons brown sugar
1 tablespoon ground mustard
1 tablespoon lemon juice
1 tablespoon soy sauce
1 tablespoon Liquid Smoke, optional
2 teaspoons celery salt
2 teaspoons pepper
2 teaspoons Worcestershire sauce
1 teaspoon onion powder
1 teaspoon garlic powder
1/8 teaspoon ground nutmeg
3 drops hot pepper sauce
14 to 18 hamburger buns, split

Cut venison roast in half; place in a 5-qt. slow cooker. In a large bowl, combine the ketchup, brown sugar, mustard, lemon juice, soy sauce, Liquid Smoke if desired and seasonings. Pour over venison. Cover and cook on high for 4-1/2 to 5 hours or until meat is tender.

Remove the roast; set aside to cool. Strain sauce and return to slow cooker. Shred meat with two forks; return to the slow cooker and heat through. Using a slotted spoon, spoon meat mixture onto each bun.

YIELD: 14-18 servings.

ruth setterlund
FREYBURG, MAINE

My husband hunts for deer every November, so I'm always looking for new recipes for venison. The whole family loves these sandwiches, seasoned with soy sauce, brown sugar, ketchup and hot pepper sauce.

SOUTHWESTERN CHICKEN SOUP

PREP: 10 min. | **COOK:** 7 hours

1-1/4 pounds boneless skinless chicken breasts, cut into thin strips
1 to 2 tablespoons canola oil
2 cans (14-1/2 ounces *each*) chicken broth
1 package (16 ounces) frozen corn, thawed
1 can (14-1/2 ounces) diced tomatoes, undrained
1 medium onion, chopped
1 medium green pepper, chopped
1 medium sweet red pepper, chopped
1 can (4 ounces) chopped green chilies
1-1/2 teaspoons seasoned salt, optional
1 teaspoon ground cumin
1/2 teaspoon garlic powder

In a large skillet, saute the chicken in oil until lightly browned. Transfer to a 5-qt. slow cooker with a slotted spoon. Stir in the remaining ingredients. Cover and cook on low for 7-8 hours. Stir before serving.

YIELD: 10 servings.

harold tartar
WEST PALM BEACH, FLORIDA

This satisfying recipe brings people back for seconds. Chock-full of chicken, corn, tomatoes, peppers and chilies, the savory soup is sure to put a little zip in mealtime.

BAVARIAN MEATBALLS

PREP: 15 min. | **COOK:** 3-1/2 hours

1 package (32 ounces) frozen fully cooked
   Italian meatballs
1/2 cup chopped onion
1/4 cup packed brown sugar
1 envelope onion soup mix
1 can (12 ounces) beer *or* nonalcoholic beer
12 hoagie buns, split
3 cups (12 ounces) shredded Swiss cheese

In a 3-qt. slow cooker, combine the meatballs, onion, brown sugar, soup mix and beer.

Cover and cook on low for 3-1/2 to 4-1/2 hours or until heated through.

Serve with toothpicks for an appetizer. Or for sandwiches, place six meatballs on each bun bottom. Sprinkle each sandwich with 1/4 cup cheese. Place on baking sheets.

Broil 4-6 in. from the heat for 2-3 minutes or until cheese is melted. Replace bun tops.

YIELD: 12 servings.

peggy rios
MECHANICSVILLE, VIRGINIA

These mouthwatering meatballs are just one of the reasons I love my slow cooker so much. They're a guaranteed crowd-pleaser when I serve them as a party appetizer or as a yummy sandwich filling spooned over crusty rolls and topped with cheese.

SLOW-COOKED BEEF SANDWICHES

PREP: 20 min. | **COOK:** 8-1/4 hours

    1 boneless beef chuck roast (3 pounds)
1-1/2 cups ketchup
    1/4 cup packed brown sugar
    1/4 cup barbecue sauce
    2 tablespoons Worcestershire sauce
    2 tablespoons Dijon mustard
    1 teaspoon Liquid Smoke, optional
1/2 teaspoon salt
1/4 teaspoon garlic powder
1/4 teaspoon pepper
    12 sandwich buns, split
Sliced onions, dill pickles and pickled jalapenos,
    optional

Cut roast in half and place in a 3- or 4-qt. slow cooker. In a small bowl, combine the ketchup, brown sugar, barbecue sauce, Worcestershire sauce, mustard, Liquid Smoke if desired and seasonings. Pour over the beef.

Cover and cook on low for 8-10 hours or until meat is tender. Remove meat; cool slightly. Skim fat from cooking liquid.

Shred the beef with two forks; return to the slow cooker. Cover and cook for 15 minutes or until heated through. Using a slotted spoon, place 1/2 cup on each bun. Serve sandwiches with onions, pickles and jalapenos if desired.

YIELD: 12 servings.

tatina smith
SAN ANGELO, TEXAS

Chuck roast makes delicious shredded beef sandwiches after simmering in a rich, homemade sauce all day. The meat is moist, juicy and hard to resist.

SLOW-COOKED PORK AND BEANS

PREP: 15 min. | **COOK:** 6 hours

- 1 boneless whole pork loin roast (3 pounds)
- 1 medium onion, sliced
- 3 cans (15 ounces *each*) pork and beans
- 1-1/2 cups barbecue sauce
- 1/4 cup packed brown sugar
- 1 teaspoon garlic powder

Cut the roast in half; place in a 5-qt. slow cooker. Top with the onion. In a large bowl, combine the beans, barbecue sauce, brown sugar and garlic powder; pour over the meat. Cover and cook on low for 6 hours or until the meat is tender.

Remove roast; shred with two forks. Return meat to slow cooker; heat through.

YIELD: 12 servings.

patricia hager
NICHOLASVILLE, KENTUCKY

I like to get this dish started before leaving for work in the morning. When I get home, my supper's ready! It's a hearty slow cooker meal that is also good for a potluck. A generous helping of tender pork and beans is perfect alongside a slice of warm corn bread.

SAVORY CHICKEN SANDWICHES

PREP: 25 min. | **COOK:** 8 hours

- 4 bone-in chicken breast halves
- 4 bone-in chicken thighs (about 1-1/2 pounds)
- 1 envelope onion soup mix
- 1/4 teaspoon garlic salt
- 1/4 cup prepared Italian salad dressing
- 1/4 cup water
- 14 to 16 hamburger buns, split

Remove skin from chicken if desired. Place chicken in a 5-qt. slow cooker. Sprinkle with soup mix and garlic salt. Pour dressing and water over chicken. Cover and cook on low for 8-9 hours or until meat is tender.

Remove the chicken; cool slightly. Skim the fat from cooking juices. Remove chicken from the bones; cut into bite-size pieces and return to the slow cooker. Serve with a slotted spoon on buns.

YIELD: 14-16 servings.

joan parker
GASTONIA, NORTH CAROLINA

As a mom of eight, I know how to whip up a meal everyone will love. This succulent chicken tastes like you fussed, but requires few ingredients. You can also thicken the juices and serve it over rice.

WARM SPICED CIDER PUNCH

PREP: 5 min. | **COOK:** 4 hours

- 4 cups apple cider *or* unsweetened apple juice
- 2-1/4 cups water
- 3/4 cup orange juice concentrate
- 3/4 teaspoon ground nutmeg
- 3/4 teaspoon ground ginger
- 3 whole cloves
- 2 cinnamon sticks

Orange slices and additional cinnamon sticks, optional

In a 3-qt. slow cooker, combine the apple cider, water, orange juice concentrate, nutmeg and ginger. Place cloves and cinnamon sticks on a double thickness of cheesecloth; bring up corners of cloth and tie with string to form a bag. Place bag in slow cooker.

Cover and cook on low for 4-5 hours or until heated through. Remove and discard spice bag. Garnish with orange slices and additional cinnamon sticks if desired.

YIELD: 8 servings.

susan smith
FOREST, VIRGINIA

This beverage will warm folks on chilly days. You'll love the aroma emanating from the slow cooker as the punch simmers.

SLOW cooker tips

Choose the correct size slow cooker for your recipe. A slow cooker should be half to two-thirds full. In general, set your slow cooker at 200° for the "low" setting and 300° for the "high" setting.

CHIPOTLE HAM 'N' CHEESE DIP

PREP: 15 min. | **COOK:** 1 hour

- 2 packages (8 ounces *each*) cream cheese, cubed
- 1 can (12 ounces) evaporated milk
- 8 ounces Gouda cheese, shredded
- 1 cup (4 ounces) shredded cheddar cheese
- 2 tablespoons chopped chipotle pepper in adobo sauce
- 1 teaspoon ground cumin
- 2 cups diced fully cooked ham

Fresh vegetables *or* tortilla chips

In a 3-qt. slow cooker, combine the first six ingredients. Cover and cook on low for 40 minutes.

Stir in ham; cook 20 minutes longer or until heated through. Serve warm with vegetables or tortilla chips.

YIELD: 7 cups.

lisa renshaw
KANSAS CITY, MISSOURI

When time is tight, and you need a quick appetizer, you can't beat slow cooker recipes like this one. Best of all, it lets you visit with your guests instead of working in the kitchen.

GREEN CHILI BEEF BURRITOS

PREP: 20 min. | **COOK:** 8 hours + cooling

- 2 beef sirloin tip roasts (3 pounds *each*)
- 4 cans (4 ounces *each*) chopped green chilies
- 1 medium onion, chopped
- 3 medium jalapeno peppers, seeded and chopped
- 3 garlic cloves, sliced
- 3 teaspoons chili powder
- 1-1/2 teaspoons ground cumin
- 1 teaspoon salt-free seasoning blend, optional
- 1 cup reduced-sodium beef broth
- 24 fat-free flour tortillas (8 inches), warmed

Chopped tomatoes, shredded lettuce and shredded reduced-fat cheddar cheese, optional

Trim fat from roasts; cut meat into large chunks. Place in a 5-qt. slow cooker. Top with chilies, onion, jalapenos, garlic, chili powder, cumin and seasoning blend if desired. Pour broth over all. Cover and cook on low for 8-9 hours.

Remove beef; cool slightly. Shred with two forks. Cool cooking liquid slightly; skim fat. In a blender, cover and process cooking liquid in small batches until smooth.

Return liquid and beef to slow cooker; heat through. Place 1/3 cup beef mixture on each tortilla. Top with tomatoes, lettuce and cheese if desired. Fold in ends and sides.

YIELD: 2 dozen.

shirley davidson
THORNTON, COLORADO

We enjoy all sorts of foods with Southwestern flair, especially these tender beef-stuffed tortillas. These are quick and easy for potlucks, and folks can assemble their own burritos with their choice of garnishes.

BEER-BRAISED BEEF

PREP: 20 min. | **COOK:** 6 hours

3 bacon strips, diced

2 pounds beef stew meat, cut into
1-inch cubes

1/2 teaspoon pepper

1/4 teaspoon salt

1 teaspoon canola oil

1 medium onion, cut into wedges

1 teaspoon minced garlic

1 bay leaf

1 can (12 ounces) beer *or* nonalcoholic beer

1 tablespoon soy sauce

1 tablespoon Worcestershire sauce

1 teaspoon dried thyme

2 tablespoons all-purpose flour

1/4 cup water

Hot cooked noodles

In a large skillet, cook bacon over medium heat until crisp. Remove to paper towels; drain, discarding drippings. Sprinkle beef with pepper and salt. In the same skillet, brown beef on all sides in oil; drain.

Transfer mixture to a 5-qt. slow cooker. Add the bacon, onion, garlic and bay leaf. In a small bowl, combine the beer, soy sauce, Worcestershire sauce and thyme. Pour over beef mixture.

Cover and cook on low for 5-1/2 to 6 hours or until meat is tender.

In a small bowl, combine flour and water until smooth. Gradually stir into slow cooker. Replace the cover and cook on high for 30 minutes longer or until thickened. Discard bay leaf. Serve beef with noodles.

YIELD: 8 servings.

geri faustich
APPLETON, WISCONSIN

I modified the ingredients in this main dish to suit my family's tastes. It's quick to put together in the morning, and at the end of the day, all that's left to do is cook the noodles and eat! This recipe can easily be doubled or tripled to serve large crowds.

SLOPPY JOE SUPPER

PREP: 15 min. | **COOK:** 4 hours

1 package (32 ounces) frozen shredded hash brown potatoes, thawed

1 can (10-3/4 ounces) condensed cheddar cheese soup, undiluted

1/4 cup egg substitute

1 teaspoon salt

1/2 teaspoon pepper

2 pounds ground beef

2 tablespoons finely chopped onion

1 can (15-1/2 ounces) sloppy joe sauce

In a large bowl, combine the potatoes, soup, egg substitute, salt and pepper. Spread into a lightly greased 5-qt. slow cooker. In a large skillet, cook the beef and onion over medium heat until the meat is no longer pink; drain. Stir in the sloppy joe sauce. Spoon over the potato mixture.

Cover and cook on low for 4 to 4-1/2 hours or until heated through.

YIELD: 8 servings.

karla wiederholt
CUBA CITY, WISCONSIN

Here's an easy way to serve up the flavor of sloppy joes in a one-dish dinner. It's great to come home to the aroma of this tasty entree simmering in the slow cooker.

CHILI SANDWICHES

PREP: 30 min. + standing | **COOK:** 3 hours

- 1 pound dried navy beans
- 2 pounds beef stew meat
- 2 cups water
- 1 pound sliced bacon, diced
- 1 cup chopped onion
- 1 cup shredded carrots
- 1 cup chopped celery
- 1/3 cup chopped green pepper
- 1/3 cup chopped sweet red pepper
- 4 garlic cloves, minced
- 3 cans (14-1/2 ounces *each*) diced tomatoes, undrained
- 1 cup barbecue sauce
- 1 cup chili sauce
- 1/2 cup honey
- 1/4 cup hot pepper sauce
- 1 tablespoon chili powder
- 1 tablespoon baking cocoa
- 1 tablespoon Dijon mustard
- 1 tablespoon Worcestershire sauce
- 1 bay leaf
- 4 teaspoons beef bouillon granules
- 30 hamburger buns, split

Place beans in a large saucepan; add water to cover by 2 in. Bring to a boil; boil for 2 minutes. Remove from the heat; cover and let stand for 1 to 4 hours or until beans are softened. Drain and rinse beans, discarding liquid. In a large kettle or Dutch oven, simmer beans and beef in water for 2 hours or until very tender; drain. Shred beef and place beef and beans in a 5-qt. slow cooker.

In a large skillet, cook the bacon over medium heat until crisp. Using a slotted spoon, remove bacon to slow cooker. Discard all but 3 tablespoons drippings.

Saute onion, carrots, celery and peppers in drippings until tender. Add garlic; cook 1 minute longer. Transfer to the slow cooker. Add all the remaining ingredients except buns. Cover and cook on high for 3-4 hours, stirring often. Discard bay leaf. Spoon 1/2 cup onto each bun.

YIELD: 30 servings.

kerry haglund
WYOMING, MINNESOTA

No one will be able to resist these special sandwiches stuffed with spicy chili. The chili is also fantastic served in a bowl alongside corn bread.

EASY MINESTRONE

PREP: 20 min. | **COOK:** 6 hours

- 4 medium tomatoes, chopped
- 2 medium carrots, chopped
- 2 celery ribs, chopped
- 1 medium zucchini, halved and sliced
- 1-1/2 cups shredded cabbage
- 1 can (16 ounces) kidney beans, rinsed and drained
- 1 can (15 ounces) garbanzo beans *or* chickpeas, rinsed and drained
- 6 cups reduced-sodium chicken broth *or* vegetable broth
- 1-1/4 teaspoons Italian seasoning
- 1 teaspoon salt
- 1/4 teaspoon pepper
- 2 cups cooked elbow macaroni
- 5 tablespoons shredded Parmesan cheese

In a 5-qt. slow cooker, combine the first 11 ingredients. Cover and cook on low for 6-8 hours or until vegetables are tender.

Just before serving, stir in macaroni and heat through. Serve with cheese.

YIELD: 10 servings (about 3-1/4 quarts).

yvonne andrus
HIGHLAND, UTAH

This is a wonderful recipe to put together in the morning and forget about the rest of the day. I have three small boys who are not big fans of vegetables, but they especially enjoy this hearty soup.

REVIVING celery

To give limp celery a second chance, cut the ends from the stalks. Place in a glass of cold water and refrigerate for several hours or overnight.

FRENCH DIP SANDWICHES

PREP: 15 min. | **COOK:** 10 hours

- 1 beef sirloin tip roast (3 to 4 pounds)
- 1/2 cup light soy sauce
- 1 teaspoon reduced-sodium beef bouillon granules
- 1 bay leaf
- 3 to 4 whole peppercorns
- 1 teaspoon dried crushed rosemary
- 1 teaspoon dried thyme
- 1 teaspoon garlic powder
- Hard rolls *or* French bread

Remove and discard all visible fat from roast; cut roast in half. Place in a 5-qt. slow cooker. In a small bowl, combine the soy sauce, bouillon and spices; pour over roast. Add water to almost cover roast. Cover and cook over low heat 10-12 hours or until meat is very tender.

Remove meat from broth; reserve broth. Shred meat with two forks. Serve on hard rolls or French bread slices with broth.

YIELD: 12 sandwiches.

dianne joy richardson
COLORADO SPRINGS, COLORADO

This recipe is great for an easy meal, since the meat cooks all day without any attention. Kids of all ages are fond of these super sandwiches whenever I serve them.

SLOW COOKER VEGETABLE SOUP

PREP: 10 min. | **COOK:** 8 hours

- 1 pound beef top round steak, cut into 1/2-inch cubes
- 1 can (14-1/2 ounces) no-salt-added whole tomatoes, undrained
- 3 cups water
- 2 medium potatoes, peeled and cubed
- 2 medium onions, diced
- 3 celery ribs, sliced
- 2 carrots, sliced
- 3 reduced-sodium beef bouillon cubes
- 1/2 teaspoon dried basil
- 1/2 teaspoon dried oregano
- 1/2 teaspoon salt-free seasoning blend
- 1/4 teaspoon pepper
- 1-1/2 cups frozen mixed vegetables

In a 5-qt. slow cooker, combine the first 12 ingredients. Cover and cook on high for 6 hours. Add vegetables; cover and cook on high 2 hours longer or until the meat and vegetables are tender.

YIELD: 8-10 servings (about 2-1/2 quarts).

heather thurmeier
PENSE, SASKATCHEWAN

What a treat to come home from work and have this savory soup ready to eat. It's a nice traditional beef soup with old-fashioned goodness.

MEXICAN FONDUE

PREP: 15 min. | **COOK:** 1-1/2 hours

- 1 can (14-3/4 ounces) cream-style corn
- 1 can (14-1/2 ounces) diced tomatoes, drained
- 3 tablespoons chopped green chilies
- 1 teaspoon chili powder
- 1 package (16 ounces) process cheese (Velveeta), cubed
- French bread cubes

In a small bowl, combine the corn, tomatoes, green chilies and chili powder. Stir in cheese. Pour mixture into a 1-1/2-qt. slow cooker coated with cooking spray.

Cover and cook on high for 1-1/2 hours, stirring every 30 minutes or until cheese is melted. Serve warm with bread cubes.

YIELD: 4-1/2 cups.

nella parker
HERSEY, MICHIGAN

A handful of items and a few moments of prep work are all you'll need for this festive fondue. Not only does it take advantage of canned goods and other convenience items, but the slow cooker does all the work so you can relax before the party!

ZIPPY SPAGHETTI SAUCE

PREP: 20 min. | **COOK:** 6 hours

2 pounds ground beef

1 cup chopped onion

1/2 cup chopped green pepper

2 cans (15 ounces *each*) tomato sauce

1 can (28 ounces) diced tomatoes, undrained

1 can (12 ounces) tomato paste

1/2 pound sliced fresh mushrooms

1 cup grated Parmesan cheese

1/2 to 3/4 cup dry red wine *or* beef broth

1/2 cup sliced pimiento-stuffed olives

1/4 cup dried parsley flakes

1 to 2 tablespoons dried oregano

2 teaspoons Italian seasoning

2 teaspoons minced garlic

1 teaspoon salt

1 teaspoon pepper

Hot cooked spaghetti

In a large skillet, cook the beef, onion and green pepper over medium heat until meat is no longer pink; drain.

Transfer to a 5-qt. slow cooker. Stir in the tomato sauce, tomatoes, tomato paste, mushrooms, cheese, wine, olives, parsley, oregano, Italian seasoning, garlic, salt and pepper. Cover and cook on low for 6-8 hours. Serve with spaghetti.

YIELD: about 3 quarts.

elaine priest
DOVER, PENNSYLVANIA

This thick and hearty sauce goes a long way to fill a hungry crowd! Any leftovers can be enjoyed another day ladled over thick slices of garlic bread. I keep a bag of chopped green pepper in my freezer and minced garlic in my fridge so I can whip this up on a moment's notice.

SWEET 'N' TANGY CHICKEN WINGS

PREP: 20 min. | **COOK:** 3-1/4 hours

3 pounds chicken wingettes (about 30)
1/2 teaspoon salt, *divided*
Dash pepper
1-1/2 cups ketchup
1/4 cup packed brown sugar
1/4 cup red wine vinegar
2 tablespoons Worcestershire sauce
1 tablespoon Dijon mustard
1 teaspoon minced garlic
1 teaspoon Liquid Smoke, optional
Sesame seeds, optional

Sprinkle chicken wings with a dash of salt and pepper. Broil 4-6 in. from the heat for 5-10 minutes on each side or until golden brown. Transfer the wings to a greased 5-qt. slow cooker.

Combine ketchup, brown sugar, vinegar, Worcestershire sauce, mustard, garlic, Liquid Smoke if desired and remaining salt; pour over wings. Toss to coat.

Cover and cook on low for 3-1/4 to 3-3/4 hours or until the chicken juices run clear. Sprinkle with sesame seeds if desired.
YIELD: about 2-1/2 dozen.

ida tuey
SOUTH LYON, MICHIGAN

Put the wings in before you prepare for a party, and in a few hours, you'll have wonderful appetizers ready for guests!

SAUSAGE SAUERKRAUT SUPPER

PREP: 25 min. | **COOK:** 8 hours

4 cups carrot chunks (2-inch pieces)

4 cups red potato chunks

2 cans (14 ounces *each*) sauerkraut, rinsed and drained

2-1/2 pounds fresh Polish sausage links, cut into 3-inch pieces

1 medium onion, thinly sliced

3 garlic cloves, minced

1-1/2 cups dry white wine *or* chicken broth

1 teaspoon pepper

1/2 teaspoon caraway seeds

In a 5-qt. slow cooker, layer the carrots, potatoes and sauerkraut. In a large skillet, brown sausages; transfer to the slow cooker (slow cooker will be full). Reserve 1 tablespoon drippings; saute onion and garlic in reserved drippings until tender.

Gradually add wine. Bring to a boil; stir to loosen browned bits. Stir in pepper and caraway. Pour over sausage. Cover and cook on low for 8-9 hours or until vegetables are tender and sausage is no longer pink.

YIELD: 10-12 servings.

joalyce graham
ST. PETERSBURG, FLORIDA

With big, tender chunks of sausage, potatoes and carrots, this meal-in-one has old-world flavor that will satisfy even the heartiest of appetites. Whether I serve it at a large family gathering or at an office potluck, it always disappears in a hurry!

FORGOTTEN JAMBALAYA

PREP: 35 min. | **COOK:** 4-1/4 hours

1 can (14-1/2 ounces) diced tomatoes, undrained

1 can (14-1/2 ounces) beef *or* chicken broth

1 can (6 ounces) tomato paste

2 medium green peppers, chopped

1 medium onion, chopped

3 celery ribs, chopped

5 garlic cloves, minced

3 teaspoons dried parsley flakes

2 teaspoons dried basil

1-1/2 teaspoons dried oregano

1-1/4 teaspoons salt

1/2 teaspoon cayenne pepper

1/2 teaspoon hot pepper sauce

1 pound boneless skinless chicken breasts, cut into 1-inch cubes

1 pound smoked sausage, halved and cut into 1/4-inch slices

1/2 pound uncooked medium shrimp, peeled and deveined

Hot cooked rice

In a 5-qt. slow cooker, combine the tomatoes, broth and tomato paste. Stir in the green peppers, onion, celery, garlic and seasonings. Stir in chicken and sausage.

Cover and cook on low for 4 hours or until chicken is tender. Stir in shrimp. Cover and cook 15-30 minutes longer or until shrimp turn pink. Serve with rice.

YIELD: 11 servings.

cindi coss
COPPELL, TEXAS

During chilly weather, I fix this jambalaya at least once a month. It's so easy...just chop the vegetables, dump everything in the slow cooker and forget it! Even my sons, who are picky about spicy things, like this dish.

WHEN to stir

Some foods have a tendency to stick and cook unevenly in slow cookers since the heat comes from below the pan and cycles on and off. You may need to stir occasionally to prevent this. Since heat escapes every time the lid is lifted, you should add 15 to 20 minutes to the overall cooking time each time you remove the lid to stir.

HOT GERMAN POTATO SALAD

PREP: 15 min. | **COOK:** 4 hours

- 8 medium potatoes, peeled and cut into 1/4-inch slices
- 2 celery ribs, chopped
- 1 large onion, chopped
- 1 cup water
- 2/3 cup cider vinegar
- 1/3 cup sugar
- 2 tablespoons quick-cooking tapioca
- 1 teaspoon salt
- 3/4 teaspoon celery seed
- 1/4 teaspoon pepper
- 6 bacon strips, cooked and crumbled
- 1/4 cup minced fresh parsley

In a 3-qt. slow cooker, combine the potatoes, celery and onion. In a small bowl, combine water, vinegar, sugar, tapioca, salt, celery seed and pepper. Pour over potatoes; stir gently to coat.

Cover and cook on high for 4-5 hours or until potatoes are tender. Just before serving, sprinkle with bacon and parsley.

YIELD: 8-10 servings.

marlene muckenhirn
DELANO, MINNESOTA

I make this zesty salad with potatoes, celery and onion. It's a terrific side dish when served warm with crumbled bacon and fresh parsley sprinkled on top.

LABEL potluck dishes

Label the dishes you bring to a potluck so guests know what it is before sampling. It's also important to list any ingredients that are common food allergies or foods that contain dairy or gluten.

CREAMY ARTICHOKE DIP

PREP: 20 min. | **COOK:** 1 hour

- 2 cans (14 ounces *each*) water-packed artichoke hearts, rinsed, drained and coarsely chopped
- 2 cups (8 ounces) shredded part-skim mozzarella cheese
- 1 package (8 ounces) cream cheese, cubed
- 1 cup shredded Parmesan cheese
- 1/2 cup mayonnaise
- 1/2 cup shredded Swiss cheese
- 2 tablespoons lemon juice
- 2 tablespoons plain yogurt
- 1 tablespoon seasoned salt
- 1 tablespoon chopped seeded jalapeno pepper
- 1 teaspoon garlic powder

Tortilla chips

In a 3-qt. slow cooker, combine the first 11 ingredients. Cover and cook on low for 1 hour or until heated through. Serve with tortilla chips.

YIELD: 5 cups.

mary spencer
WAUKESHA, WISCONSIN

This creamy dip is a family favorite. It's loaded with cheese, artichokes and just the right amount of spice for a crowd-pleasing flavor.

SLOW-COOKED SAUSAGE DRESSING

PREP: 20 min. | **COOK:** 3 hours

- 1/2 pound reduced-fat bulk pork sausage
- 2 celery ribs, chopped
- 1 large onion, chopped
- 7 cups seasoned stuffing cubes
- 1 can (14-1/2 ounces) reduced-sodium chicken broth
- 1 medium tart apple, chopped
- 1/3 cup chopped pecans
- 2 tablespoons reduced-fat butter, melted
- 1-1/2 teaspoons rubbed sage
- 1/2 teaspoon pepper

In a large nonstick skillet, cook the sausage, celery and onion over medium heat until the meat is no longer pink; drain. Transfer to a large bowl; stir in the remaining ingredients.

Transfer to a 5-qt. slow cooker coated with cooking spray. Cover and cook on low for 3-4 hours or until heated through and apple is tender, stirring once.

YIELD: 8 cups.

raquel haggard
EDMOND, OKLAHOMA

This dressing is so delicious, no one will know it's lower in fat. And best of all, it cooks effortlessly in the slow cooker, so the stove and oven are freed up for other dishes!

PIZZA IN A POT

PREP: 15 min. | **COOK:** 3 hours

1-1/2 pounds ground beef
1 medium green pepper, chopped
1 medium onion, chopped
1 can (15 ounces) tomato sauce
1 jar (14 ounces) pizza sauce
2 tablespoons tomato paste
3 cups spiral pasta, cooked and drained
2 packages (3-1/2 ounces *each*) sliced pepperoni
2 cups (8 ounces) shredded part-skim mozzarella cheese

In a large skillet, cook the beef, green pepper and onion over medium heat until meat is no longer pink; drain. Stir in the tomato sauce, pizza sauce and tomato paste.

In a 5-qt. slow cooker, layer the pasta, beef mixture, pepperoni and cheese. Cover and cook on low for 3-4 hours or until mixture is heated through.

YIELD: 8 servings.

dianna cline
PHILIPPI, WEST VIRGINIA

With warm breadsticks or garlic toast on the side, this is one dinner I know my family will always eagerly eat.

GONE-ALL-DAY CASSEROLE

PREP: 15 min. | **COOK:** 6 hours

- 1 cup uncooked wild rice, rinsed and drained
- 1 cup chopped celery
- 2 tablespoons canola oil
- 2 cans (4 ounces *each*) mushroom stems and pieces, drained
- 1 large onion, chopped
- 1 garlic clove, minced
- 1/2 cup slivered almonds
- 3 beef bouillon cubes
- 2-1/2 teaspoons seasoned salt
- 2 pounds boneless round steak, cut into 1-inch cubes
- 3 cups water

Place ingredients in order listed in a 3-qt. slow cooker (do not stir). Cover and cook on low for 6-8 hours or until rice is tender. Stir before serving.

YIELD: 12 servings.

janet haak aarness
PELICAN RAPIDS, MINNESOTA

Even less expensive cuts of meat become deliciously tender when cooked slowly in this savory casserole-like dish. Wild rice and almonds give this meal a special look and taste.

SLOW-COOKED BEAN MEDLEY

PREP: 25 min. | **COOK:** 5 hours

- 1-1/2 cups ketchup
- 2 celery ribs, chopped
- 1 medium onion, chopped
- 1 medium green pepper, chopped
- 1 medium sweet red pepper, chopped
- 1/2 cup packed brown sugar
- 1/2 cup water
- 1/2 cup Italian salad dressing
- 2 bay leaves
- 1 tablespoon cider vinegar
- 1 teaspoon ground mustard
- 1/8 teaspoon pepper
- 1 can (16 ounces) kidney beans, rinsed and drained
- 1 can (15-1/2 ounces) black-eyed peas, rinsed and drained
- 1 can (15-1/2 ounces) great northern beans, rinsed and drained
- 1 can (15-1/4 ounces) whole kernel corn, drained
- 1 can (15-1/4 ounces) lima beans, rinsed and drained
- 1 can (15 ounces) black beans, rinsed and drained

In a 5-qt. slow cooker, combine the first 12 ingredients. Stir in the remaining ingredients. Cover and cook on low for 5-7 hours or until onion and peppers are tender. Discard the bay leaves.

YIELD: 12 servings.

peggy gwillim
STRASBOURG, SASKATCHEWAN

I often change the variety of beans in this recipe, using whatever I have on hand to total five 15- to 16-ounce cans. The sauce makes any combination scrumptious! This is a nice dish for any gathering as many people are following gluten-free diets.

GLUTEN-FREE recipes

Read all ingredient labels for possible gluten content prior to use. Ingredient formulas can change, and production facilities vary among brands. Contact the manufacturer if you're not sure if the item contains gluten.

TANGY PORK MEATBALLS

PREP/TOTAL TIME: 30 min.

　　2 eggs, lightly beaten
　2/3 cup dry bread crumbs
　　2 tablespoons dried minced onion
　　2 teaspoons seasoned salt
　　2 pounds ground pork
SAUCE:
1-1/2 cups ketchup
　　1 can (8 ounces) tomato sauce
　　3 tablespoons Worcestershire sauce
　　2 to 3 tablespoons cider vinegar
　　2 teaspoons Liquid Smoke, optional

In a large bowl, combine the eggs, bread crumbs, onion and salt. Crumble the pork over the mixture and mix well. Shape into 3/4-in. balls.

Place the meatballs on a greased rack in a shallow baking pan. Bake at 400° for 15 minutes or until the meat is no longer pink; drain.

Meanwhile, in a large saucepan, combine sauce ingredients. Simmer, uncovered, for 10 minutes, stirring occasionally. Add the meatballs. Serve in a 5-qt. slow cooker or chafing dish.

YIELD: 7-1/2 dozen.

katie koziolek
HARTLAND, MINNESOTA

Yuletide buffet grazers stampede for these meatballs! The mouthwatering morsels go so fast, I often make several batches at once. Barbecue sauce adds a nice bite to the mildly seasoned ground pork.

SPICED CHILI

PREP: 20 min. | **COOK:** 4 hours

1-1/2 pounds ground beef
　1/2 cup chopped onion
　　4 garlic cloves, minced
　　2 cans (16 ounces *each*) kidney beans, rinsed and drained
　　2 cans (15 ounces *each*) tomato sauce
　　2 cans (14-1/2 ounces *each*) stewed tomatoes, cut up
　　1 cup water
　　2 bay leaves
　1/4 cup chili powder
　　1 tablespoon salt
　　1 tablespoon brown sugar
　　1 tablespoon dried basil
　　1 tablespoon Italian seasoning
　　1 tablespoon dried thyme
　　1 tablespoon pepper
　　1 teaspoon dried oregano
　　1 teaspoon dried marjoram
Shredded cheddar cheese, optional

In a large skillet, cook beef and onion over medium heat until meat is no longer pink. Add garlic; cook 1 minute longer. Drain.

Transfer to a 5-qt. slow cooker. Stir in the beans, tomato sauce, tomatoes, water and seasonings. Cover and cook on low for 4-5 hours. Discard bay leaves. Garnish with cheese if desired.

YIELD: 12 servings (about 3 quarts).

julie brendt
GOLD RIVER, CALIFORNIA

My father was a cook in the Army and taught me the basics in the kitchen. My childhood baby-sitter inspired my love of cooking, too...in fact, she gave me this recipe.

LEFTOVER chili

There are so many fun options for putting leftover chili to good use. One is to reheat the chili, then stir in plain yogurt and process American cheese to make a hearty dip for tortilla chips. Or use the chili to jazz up plain baked potatoes.

NO-FUSS SWISS STEAK

PREP: 10 min. | COOK: 6 hours

- 3 pounds beef top round steak, cut into serving-size pieces
- 2 tablespoons canola oil
- 2 medium carrots, cut into 1/2-inch slices
- 2 celery ribs, cut into 1/2-inch slices
- 1-3/4 cups water
- 1 can (11 ounces) condensed tomato rice soup, undiluted
- 1 can (10-1/2 ounces) condensed French onion soup, undiluted
- 1/2 teaspoon pepper
- 1 bay leaf

In a large skillet, brown beef in oil over medium-high heat; drain. Transfer to a 5-qt. slow cooker. Add carrots and celery. Combine the remaining ingredients; pour over meat and vegetables.

Cover and cook on low for 6-8 hours or until meat is tender. Discard the bay leaf. Thicken cooking juices if desired.

YIELD: 8-10 servings.

sharon morrell
PARKER, SOUTH DAKOTA

I received the recipe for this dish from my cousin. I make it regularly because our children love the savory steak, tangy gravy and fork-tender veggies.

SLOW-COOKED SHREDDED PORK

PREP: 15 min. | **COOK:** 6 hours

1 boneless whole pork loin roast
  (2 to 3 pounds)
1 large onion, thinly sliced
1 cup beer *or* nonalcoholic beer
1 cup chili sauce
2 tablespoons brown sugar
1 tablespoon prepared horseradish
8 sandwich rolls, split

Place the roast in a 3-qt. slow cooker. Top with onion. Combine the beer, chili sauce, brown sugar and horseradish; pour over pork and onion. Cover and cook on low for 6 to 6-1/2 hours or until meat is tender.

Remove pork; shred with two forks. Return meat to cooking juices; heat through. Use a slotted spoon to serve on rolls.

YIELD: 8 servings.

shirleymae haefner
O'FALLON, MISSOURI

The tasty pork filling for these sandwiches requires very little work because it's prepared in the slow cooker. The mild, sweet sauce is appealing.

SLOW-COOKED PORK BARBECUE

PREP: 15 min. | **COOK:** 5 hours

        1 boneless pork loin roast (3 to 4 pounds)
1-1/2 teaspoons seasoned salt
        1 teaspoon garlic powder
        1 cup barbecue sauce
        1 cup cola
      10 sandwich buns, split

Cut roast in half; place in a 5-qt. slow cooker. Sprinkle with the seasoned salt and garlic powder. Cover and cook on low for 4 hours or until meat is tender.

Remove meat; skim fat from cooking juices. Shred meat with two forks and return to the slow cooker. Combine barbecue sauce and cola; pour over meat. Cover and cook on high for 1-2 hours or until the sauce is thickened. Serve on rolls.

YIELD: 10 servings.

connie johnson
SPRINGFIELD, MISSOURI

I need only five ingredients to fix this sweet and tender pork for sandwiches. I think it's perfect just the way it is, but feel free to adjust the sauce ingredients to suit your family's tastes.

WASSAIL BOWL PUNCH

PREP: 10 min. | **COOK:** 1 hour

      4 cups hot brewed tea
      4 cups cranberry juice
      4 cups unsweetened apple juice
      2 cups orange juice
      1 cup sugar
  3/4 cup lemon juice
      3 cinnamon sticks (3 inches)
    12 whole cloves

In a 5-qt. slow cooker, combine the first six ingredients. Place the cinnamon sticks and cloves on a double thickness of cheesecloth; bring up corners of cloth and tie with string to form a bag. Add to the slow cooker. Cover and cook on high for 1 hour or until the punch begins to boil. Discard the spice bag. Serve punch warm.

YIELD: 3-1/2 quarts.

margaret harms
JENKINS, KENTUCKY

All ages will enjoy this warming punch. The blend of spice, fruit and citrus flavors is scrumptious. You can assemble it before heading out for a winter activity and sip away the chill when you return. It's ready whenever you are.

SWEET POTATO STUFFING

PREP: 15 min. | **COOK:** 4 hours

  1/2 cup chopped celery
  1/2 cup chopped onion
  1/4 cup butter, cubed
      6 cups dry bread cubes
      1 large sweet potato, cooked, peeled and finely chopped
  1/2 cup chicken broth
  1/4 cup chopped pecans
  1/2 teaspoon poultry seasoning
  1/2 teaspoon rubbed sage
  1/2 teaspoon salt, optional
  1/2 teaspoon pepper

In a large skillet, saute celery and onion in butter until tender. Stir in the remaining ingredients. Transfer to a greased 3-qt. slow cooker. Cover and cook on low for 4 hours or until vegetables are tender.

YIELD: 10 servings.

kelly pollock
LONDON, ONTARIO

During the holidays, my mother treats our large clan to this sweet delight in addition to the traditional stuffing cooked inside the turkey.

SWEET potatoes

Select sweet potatoes that are firm with no cracks or bruises. If stored in a cool, dark, well-ventilated place, they'll remain fresh for about 2 weeks. Once cooked, sweet potatoes can be stored up to 1 week in the refrigerator.

SAVORY BEEF FAJITAS

PREP: 10 min. | **COOK:** 7 hours

- 1 beef flank steak (2 pounds), thinly sliced
- 1 cup tomato juice
- 2 garlic cloves, minced
- 1 tablespoon minced fresh cilantro
- 1 teaspoon chili powder
- 1 teaspoon ground cumin
- 1/2 teaspoon salt
- 1/2 teaspoon ground coriander
- 1 medium onion, sliced
- 1 medium green pepper, julienned
- 1 medium sweet red pepper, julienned
- 1 medium jalapeno, cut into thin strips
- 12 flour tortillas (6 inches)

Sour cream, guacamole, salsa *or* shredded cheddar cheese, optional

Place beef in a 3-qt. slow cooker. Combine the next seven ingredients; pour over beef. Cover and cook on low for 6-7 hours.

Add onion, peppers and jalapeno. Cover and cook 1 hour longer or until meat and vegetables are tender.

Using a slotted spoon, place about 1/2 cup of meat-vegetable mixture on each tortilla. Add desired toppings. Roll up.

YIELD: 12 servings.

EDITOR'S NOTE: When cutting hot peppers, disposable gloves are recommended. Avoid touching your face.

twila burkholder
MIDDLEBURG, PENNSYLVANIA

My family loves beef, and I love to use the slow cooker, so this dish pleases everyone. The meat comes out nice and tender to create these wonderfully tempting fajitas.

EASY main dish

Add 1 to 1-1/2 cups cubed fully cooked ham, chicken or turkey to turn Creamy Hash Brown Potatoes into a comforting main dish. Serve with a tossed green salad and rolls to round out the meal.

CREAMY HASH BROWN POTATOES

PREP: 5 min. | **COOK:** 3-1/2 hours

- 1 package (32 ounces) frozen cubed hash brown potatoes
- 1 can (10-3/4 ounces) condensed cream of potato soup, undiluted
- 2 cups (8 ounces) shredded Colby-Monterey Jack cheese
- 1 cup (8 ounces) sour cream
- 1/4 teaspoon pepper
- 1/8 teaspoon salt
- 1 carton (8 ounces) spreadable chive and onion cream cheese

Place potatoes in a lightly greased 3-qt. slow cooker. In a large bowl, combine the soup, cheese, sour cream, pepper and salt. Pour over potatoes and mix well.

Cover and cook on low for 3-1/2 to 4 hours or until potatoes are tender. Stir in cream cheese.

YIELD: 12-14 servings.

julianne henson
STREAMWOOD, ILLINOIS

I like to fix a batch of these cheesy slow cooker potatoes for potlucks and big group gatherings. Convenient frozen hash browns, canned soup and flavored cream cheese make this side dish so quick to put together.

BEEF STROGANOFF

PREP: 25 min. | **COOK:** 7 hours

3 to 4 pounds beef top sirloin steak, cubed
2 cans (14-1/2 ounces *each*) chicken broth
1 pound sliced fresh mushrooms
1 can (12 ounces) regular cola
1/2 cup chopped onion
1 envelope onion soup mix
1 to 2 teaspoons garlic powder
2 teaspoons dried parsley flakes
1/2 teaspoon pepper
2 envelopes country gravy mix
2 cups (16 ounces) sour cream
Hot cooked noodles

In a 5-qt. slow cooker, combine the first nine ingredients. Cover and cook on low for 7-8 hours or until beef is tender.

With a slotted spoon, remove beef and mushrooms. Place gravy mix in a large saucepan; gradually whisk in cooking liquid. Bring to a boil; cook and stir for 2 minutes or until thickened. Remove from the heat; stir in sour cream. Add beef and mushrooms to the gravy. Serve with noodles.
YIELD: 12-16 servings.

lisa vanegmond
ANNAPOLIS, ILLINOIS

This slow cooker recipe makes a traditional dinner completely fuss-free. Tender sirloin steak in flavorful gravy is served over noodles for a home-style meal your whole family will request time and again.

TEXICAN CHILI

PREP: 25 min. | **COOK:** 9 hours

    8 bacon strips, diced

2-1/2 pounds beef stew meat, cut into
    1/2-inch cubes

    2 cans (one 28 ounces, one 14-1/2 ounces)
    stewed tomatoes, undrained

    2 cans (8 ounces *each*) tomato sauce

    1 can (16 ounces) kidney beans, rinsed and
    drained

    2 cups sliced carrots

    1 cup chopped celery

  3/4 cup chopped onion

  1/2 cup chopped green pepper

  1/4 cup minced fresh parsley

    1 tablespoon chili powder

    1 teaspoon salt, optional

  1/2 teaspoon ground cumin

  1/4 teaspoon pepper

In a large skillet, cook bacon until crisp. Remove to paper towels to drain. Brown beef in the drippings over medium heat; drain. Transfer to a 5-qt. slow cooker; add bacon and remaining ingredients. Cover and cook on low for 9-10 hours or until meat is tender, stirring occasionally.

YIELD: 16-18 servings.

stacy law
CORNISH, UTAH

This flavorful, meaty chili is a favorite...and it's so easy to prepare in the slow cooker. It's a fantastic way to serve a large crowd without worrying about last-minute preparations.

SOUTHWESTERN NACHOS

PREP: 40 min. | **COOK:** 7-1/4 hours

- 2 boneless whole pork loin roasts (3-1/2 pounds *each*)
- 1 cup unsweetened apple juice
- 6 garlic cloves, minced
- 1 teaspoon salt
- 1 teaspoon Liquid Smoke, optional
- 2-1/2 cups barbecue sauce, *divided*
- 1/3 cup packed brown sugar
- 2 tablespoons honey
- 1 package (10 ounces) tortilla chip scoops
- 1-1/2 cups frozen corn
- 1 can (15 ounces) black beans, rinsed and drained
- 1 medium tomato, seeded and chopped
- 1 medium red onion, chopped
- 1/3 cup minced fresh cilantro
- 1 jalapeno pepper, seeded and chopped
- 2 teaspoons lime juice
- 1 package (16 ounces) process cheese (Velveeta), cubed
- 2 tablespoons milk

Cut each roast in half; place in two 5-qt. slow cookers. Combine the apple juice, garlic, salt and Liquid Smoke if desired; pour over meat. Cover and cook on low for 7-8 hours or until tender.

Shred the pork with two forks; place in a very large bowl. Stir in 2 cups barbecue sauce, brown sugar and honey. Divide the tortilla chips between two greased 13-in. x 9-in. baking dishes; top with the pork mixture. Combine the corn, beans, tomato, onion, cilantro, jalapeno and lime juice; spoon over the pork mixture.

Bake, uncovered, at 375° for 15-20 minutes or until heated through. Meanwhile, in a small saucepan, melt cheese with milk. Drizzle the cheese sauce and remaining barbecue sauce over nachos.
YIELD: 30 servings.

kelly byler
GOSHEN, INDIANA

Guests will go crazy when you serve two heaping pans of this cheesy nacho casserole featuring tender chunks of pork. You don't need to worry about filling the chip bowl...the tortilla chips are conveniently baked right in the dish!

SLOW-COOKED PORK TACOS

PREP: 20 min. | **COOK:** 4 hours

- 1 boneless pork sirloin roast (2 pounds), cut into 1-inch pieces
- 1-1/2 cups salsa verde
- 1 medium sweet red pepper, chopped
- 1 medium onion, chopped
- 1/4 cup chopped dried apricots
- 2 tablespoons lime juice
- 2 garlic cloves, minced
- 1 teaspoon ground cumin
- 1/2 teaspoon salt
- 1/4 teaspoon white pepper
- Dash hot pepper sauce
- 10 flour tortillas (8 inches), warmed
- Reduced-fat sour cream, thinly sliced green onions, cubed avocado, shredded reduced-fat cheddar cheese and chopped tomato, optional

In a 3-qt. slow cooker, combine the first 11 ingredients. Cover and cook on high for 4-5 hours or until meat is very tender.

Shred pork with two forks. Place about 1/2 cup pork mixture down the center of each tortilla. Serve with toppings if desired.
YIELD: 10 tacos.

kathleen wolf
NAPERVILLE, ILLINOIS

These pork tacos make great party fare. Serve them alongside refried beans and Spanish rice for a zippy Southwestern meal.

TASTY twist

Pork-filled tacos are a nice change of pace from typical ground beef or chicken tacos. For a fun variation, try serving the pork filling and topping ingredients inside Bibb lettuce leaves, on sandwich buns or atop tortilla chips.

SHREDDED BEEF SANDWICHES

PREP: 10 min. | **COOK:** 10 hours

- 1 can (10-1/2 ounces) condensed beef broth, undiluted
- 1 cup ketchup
- 1/2 cup packed brown sugar
- 1/2 cup lemon juice
- 3 tablespoons steak sauce
- 2 garlic cloves, minced
- 1 teaspoon pepper
- 1 teaspoon Worcestershire sauce
- 1 beef eye round roast (3-1/2 pounds), cut in half
- 1 teaspoon salt
- 16 sandwich buns, split

Dill pickle slices, optional

In a small bowl, whisk the first eight ingredients. Pour half of mixture into a 5-qt. slow cooker. Sprinkle beef with salt; add to the slow cooker and top with the remaining broth mixture.

Cover and cook on low for 10-12 hours or until meat is tender. Shred meat with two forks and return to slow cooker. Using a slotted spoon, place 1/2 cup beef mixture on each bun. Top with pickles if desired.

YIELD: 16 servings.

bunny palmertree
CARROLLTON, MISSISSIPPI

I like to serve these mouthwatering sandwiches with a side of coleslaw. The homemade barbecue sauce is exceptional...and it's wonderful for dipping!

EXTENSION cords

It's a good idea to take an extension cord to the potluck with you. This way, you'll be able to plug in your slow cooker even if an outlet isn't directly behind the buffet table.

SLOW-COOKED PORK LOIN

PREP: 20 min. | **COOK:** 5 hours

- 1 boneless whole pork loin roast (3-1/2 to 4 pounds)
- 1 tablespoon canola oil
- 1 medium onion, chopped
- 1 celery rib, cut into 1-inch pieces
- 1 envelope brown gravy mix
- 1 cup water
- 1 cup unsweetened apple juice
- 1/2 cup unsweetened applesauce
- 2 teaspoons Worcestershire sauce
- 1/2 teaspoon seasoned salt
- 1/2 teaspoon pepper

Cut roast in half. In a large skillet, brown roast in oil on all sides. Transfer to a 5-qt. slow cooker. In the same skillet, saute onion and celery until tender; add to slow cooker.

In a small bowl, combine gravy mix and water. Stir in the remaining ingredients; pour over pork. Cover and cook on low for 5-6 hours or until meat is tender. Skim fat from cooking juices; thicken if desired. Serve with roast.

YIELD: 12 servings.

kathleen hendrick
ALEXANDRIA, KENTUCKY

Sweet apple undertones lend special flair to this low-calorie pork loin. I top it with gravy for down-home appeal, creating a slimmed-down dish that will keep 'em coming back for more.

HOT CHILI CHEESE DIP

PREP: 20 min. | **COOK:** 4 hours

1 medium onion, finely chopped

2 teaspoons canola oil

2 garlic cloves, minced

2 cans (15 ounces *each*) chili without beans

2 cups salsa

2 packages (3 ounces *each*) cream cheese, cubed

2 cans (2-1/4 ounces *each*) sliced ripe olives, drained

Tortilla chips

In a small skillet, saute onion in oil until tender. Add garlic; cook 1 minute longer.

Transfer to a 3-qt. slow cooker. Stir in the chili, salsa, cream cheese and olives. Cover and cook on low for 4 hours or until heated through, stirring occasionally. Stir before serving with tortilla chips.

YIELD: 6 cups.

jeanie carrigan

MADERA, CALIFORNIA

I simplify preparation by using my slow cooker to create this cheesy dip. This is a fantastic appetizer for birthday celebrations and game-day parties.

p. 235

p. 227

p. 236

breads,
rolls & muffins

CAPPUCCINO MUFFINS

PREP: 15 min. | **BAKE:** 20 min.

2-1/2 cups all-purpose flour
2/3 cup sugar
2-1/2 teaspoons baking powder
1-1/2 teaspoons ground cinnamon
3/4 teaspoon salt
1/2 teaspoon baking soda
1 egg
1-1/3 cups buttermilk
3 tablespoons canola oil
4-1/2 teaspoons instant coffee granules
2 teaspoons vanilla extract
12 chocolate kisses

TOPPING:
2 tablespoons sugar
1/2 teaspoon ground cinnamon

In a large bowl, combine the flour, sugar, baking powder, cinnamon, salt and baking soda. In another bowl, beat egg, buttermilk, oil, coffee granules and vanilla until coffee granules dissolve. Stir into dry ingredients just until moistened.

Spoon 2 tablespoons batter into greased muffin cups. Place a chocolate kiss in the center of each; top with remaining batter. Combine sugar and cinnamon; sprinkle over batter.

Bake at 425° for 16-20 minutes or until a toothpick inserted near the center comes out clean. Cool for 5 minutes before removing from pan to a wire rack. Serve warm.
YIELD: 1 dozen.

susan wagers
MINOT, NORTH DAKOTA

These airy muffins capture the wonderful flavor of coffee. Folks are pleasantly surprised to find a creamy chocolate center.

EASY lift-off

When making a quick bread, coat the loaf pan with nonstick cooking spray and line it with parchment paper that extends 2 inches beyond the sides. When the loaf is cool, pull on the parchment paper with both hands and the loaf will easily lift right out of the pan.

ALMOND APRICOT BREAD

PREP: 15 min. | **BAKE:** 55 min. + cooling

2-1/2 cups all-purpose flour
1/2 cup sugar
1/2 cup packed brown sugar
3 teaspoons baking powder
1 teaspoon salt
1 package (7 ounces) apricots with mixed fruit baby food, *divided*
1 egg
3/4 cup plus 1 teaspoon milk, *divided*
3 tablespoons canola oil
1-1/8 teaspoons almond extract, *divided*
2/3 cup sliced almonds, coarsely chopped
1/2 cup diced dried apricots
1/2 cup confectioners' sugar

In a large bowl, combine the flour, sugars, baking powder and the salt. Set aside 1 tablespoon baby food for glaze. In another bowl, beat egg, 3/4 cup milk, oil, 1 teaspoon almond extract and remaining baby food. Stir into dry ingredients just until moistened. Fold in almonds and apricots.

Pour into a greased 9-in. x 5-in. loaf pan. Bake at 350° for 55-65 minutes or until a toothpick inserted near the center comes out clean. Cool for 10 minutes before removing from pan to a wire rack to cool completely.

For glaze, combine the confectioners' sugar, reserved baby food, and remaining milk and extract until smooth. Drizzle over bread.
YIELD: 1 loaf (16 slices).

kathy cary
WILDWOOD, MISSOURI

My mother, who is a big apricot and almond fan, inspired me to create this recipe. I bake a batch of these sweet loaves to treat the teachers at my kids' school every Christmas.

APPLE CRUNCH MUFFINS

PREP: 15 min. | **BAKE:** 20 min.

1-1/2 cups all-purpose flour
3/4 cup sugar
2 teaspoons baking powder
1 teaspoon ground cinnamon
1/4 teaspoon baking soda
1/4 teaspoon salt
1/4 teaspoon ground allspice
1/8 teaspoon ground nutmeg
2 eggs
1-1/4 cups sour cream
1/2 cup butter, melted
1 cup chopped tart apple

TOPPING:
1/2 cup chopped walnuts
1/4 cup all-purpose flour
3 tablespoons sugar
1/4 teaspoon ground cinnamon
1/8 teaspoon ground nutmeg
2 tablespoons cold butter

In a large bowl, combine the first eight ingredients. In another bowl, beat the eggs, sour cream and butter. Stir into the dry ingredients just until moistened. Fold in apple. Fill greased or paper-lined muffin cups one-third full.

For topping, combine the walnuts, flour, sugar, cinnamon and nutmeg. Cut in butter until mixture resembles coarse crumbs. Sprinkle about two-thirds of the topping over batter. Top with remaining batter; sprinkle with remaining topping.

Bake at 375° for 20-25 minutes or until a toothpick inserted near the center comes out clean. Cool for 5 minutes before removing from pans to wire racks. Serve warm.
YIELD: 16 muffins.

brenda betz
OAKLAND, MARYLAND

These apple-filled muffins taste like little coffee cakes. I sometimes drizzle hot caramel over the muffins and serve them for dessert.

CRUSTY FRENCH BREAD

PREP: 20 min. + rising | **BAKE:** 25 min. + cooling

1 package (1/4 ounce) active dry yeast
1 cup warm water (110° to 115°)
2 tablespoons sugar
2 tablespoons canola oil
1-1/2 teaspoons salt
3 to 3-1/4 cups all-purpose flour
Cornmeal
1 egg white
1 teaspoon cold water

In a large bowl, dissolve the yeast in warm water. Add the sugar, oil, salt and 2 cups flour. Beat until blended. Stir in enough remaining flour to form a stiff dough.

Turn onto a floured surface; knead until smooth and elastic, about 6-8 minutes. Place in a greased bowl, turning once to grease top. Cover and let rise in a warm place until doubled, about 1 hour. Punch dough down; return to bowl. Cover dough and let rise for 30 minutes.

Punch dough down. Turn onto a lightly floured surface. Shape into a 16-in. x 2-1/2-in. loaf with tapered ends. Sprinkle a greased baking sheet with cornmeal; place loaf on the baking sheet. Cover and let rise until doubled, about 25 minutes.

Beat egg white and cold water; brush over dough. With a sharp knife, make diagonal slashes 2 in. apart across top of loaf. Bake at 375° for 25-30 minutes or until golden brown. Remove from pan to a wire rack to cool.
YIELD: 1 loaf (16 slices).

deanna naivar
TEMPLE, TEXAS

A delicate texture makes this bread absolutely wonderful. I sometimes use the dough to make breadsticks, which I brush with melted butter and sprinkle with garlic powder.

COCONUT-GLAZED ORANGE SCONES

PREP/TOTAL TIME: 30 min.

3-3/4 cups self-rising flour
1/4 cup sugar
2 teaspoons baking powder
1/2 cup cold butter
2 eggs
1 cup plus 1 to 2 tablespoons fat-free milk, *divided*
1 teaspoon grated orange peel
1/2 cup confectioners' sugar
1/4 teaspoon coconut extract

In a large bowl, combine the flour, sugar and baking powder. Cut in butter until mixture resembles coarse crumbs. In a small bowl, whisk eggs, 1 cup milk and orange peel; stir into crumb mixture just until moistened. Turn onto a floured surface; knead 10 times.

Roll into a 14-in. x 8-in. rectangle. Using a floured pizza cutter, cut widthwise into 2-in. strips, then cut diagonally into 2-in. strips, forming diamond shapes. Place 2 in. apart on baking sheets coated with cooking spray.

Bake at 400° for 8-10 minutes or until lightly browned. Remove to wire racks.

For glaze, in a small bowl, combine the confectioners' sugar, coconut extract and enough remaining milk to achieve desired consistency; drizzle over scones. Serve warm.
YIELD: 1-1/2 dozen.

taste of home
test kitchen

Guaranteed to brighten up gloomy winter afternoons, these treats offer refreshing tropical flair with the flavors of orange and coconut. An easy glaze completes the light scones with sweet results.

CARAWAY PUFFS

PREP: 15 min. + rising | BAKE: 15 min.

1 package (1/4 ounce) active dry yeast
1/4 cup warm water (110° to 115°)
1 cup (8 ounces) warm 4% cottage cheese (110° to 115°)
2 tablespoons sugar
1 tablespoon butter, softened
2 teaspoons caraway seeds
1 teaspoon salt
1/4 teaspoon baking soda
2-1/3 cups all-purpose flour, *divided*
1 egg

In a large bowl, dissolve the yeast in warm water. Add the cottage cheese, sugar, butter, caraway seeds, salt, baking soda and 1-1/3 cups flour. Beat on medium speed for 3 minutes. Add egg and 1/2 cup flour; beat 2 minutes longer. Stir in enough remaining flour to form a firm dough (batter will be stiff). Do not knead. Cover and let rise in a warm place until doubled, about 45 minutes. Stir dough down.

Spoon into greased muffin cups. Cover and let rise in a warm place until doubled, about 35 minutes.

Bake at 400° for 12-14 minutes. Cool in pan for 1 minute. Serve immediately.
YIELD: 1 dozen.

glennis endrud
BUXTON, NORTH DAKOTA

Our daughter took these light-as-a-feather rolls to a 4-H event and came home with a grand champion ribbon! We think they're especially delectable served straight from the oven.

NO-STICK muffins

If you use paper liners to bake muffins or cupcakes, spray the liners with nonstick cooking spray before filling. The liners peel off easily and leave no crumbs behind.

EASY CRESCENT ROLLS

PREP: 20 min. + rising | **BAKE:** 10 min.

1 package (1/4 ounce) active dry yeast
1 cup warm water (110° to 115°)
3 eggs
4 to 4-1/2 cups all-purpose flour
1/2 cup sugar
1 teaspoon salt
1/2 cup shortening

In a small bowl, dissolve yeast in warm water. In another small bowl, beat eggs until light lemon color. Add to yeast mixture; set aside.

In a large bowl, combine 1 cup flour, sugar and salt. Cut in shortening until mixture resembles coarse crumbs. Stir in yeast mixture. Stir in enough remaining flour until dough leaves the side of the bowl and is soft (dough will be sticky). Do not knead. Cover and refrigerate overnight.

Punch dough down. Turn onto a well-floured surface; divide into thirds. Roll each into a 12-in. circle; cut each circle into 12 wedges. Roll up wedges from wide end and place with pointed end down 2 in. apart on greased baking sheets. Curve ends to form a crescent shape. Cover and let rise in a warm place until doubled, about 45 minutes.

Bake at 375° for 10-12 minutes or until light golden brown. Remove from pans to wire racks.

YIELD: 3 dozen.

ruth sanford
WASILLA, ALASKA

I learned to cook and bake under my mother's fantastic guidance. She always treated the family to home-baked bread and I've learned to do the same.

SWEET POTATO ROLLS

PREP: 15 min. + rising | **BAKE:** 10 min./batch

1/2 cup water (70° to 80°)
1 egg
3 tablespoons butter, softened
3/4 cup mashed sweet potatoes (without added milk and butter)
4 to 4-1/2 cups all-purpose flour
3 tablespoons sugar
1-1/2 teaspoons salt
2 packages (1/4 ounce *each*) active dry yeast

In bread machine pan, place all ingredients in order suggested by manufacturer. Select dough setting (check dough after 5 minutes of mixing; add 1 to 2 tablespoons of water or flour if needed).

When cycle is completed, turn dough onto a lightly floured surface. Punch down. Divide into 30 portions; roll each into a ball. Place on greased baking sheets. Cover and let rise in a warm place until doubled, about 30 minutes.

Bake at 400° for 8-10 minutes or until golden brown. Serve warm.

YIELD: 2-1/2 dozen.

peggy burdick
BURLINGTON, MICHIGAN

This convenient recipe takes advantage of a bread machine to create a batch of home-style rolls. They're wonderful served warm with honey and butter.

VIRGINIA BOX BREAD

PREP: 20 min. + rising | **BAKE:** 20 min.

1 package (1/4 ounce) active dry yeast
2/3 cup warm water (110° to 115°)
2 eggs, lightly beaten
5 tablespoons butter, melted and cooled
2 tablespoons sugar
1 teaspoon salt
3-1/4 to 3-3/4 cups all-purpose flour

In a large bowl, dissolve the yeast in warm water. Add the eggs, butter, sugar, salt and 2 cups flour; beat until smooth. Add enough remaining flour to form a soft dough.

Turn onto a floured surface; knead until smooth and elastic, about 6-8 minutes. Place in a greased bowl, turning once to grease top. Cover and let rise in a warm place until doubled, about 1-1/2 hours.

Punch dough down. On a lightly floured surface, roll dough into a 13-in. x 9-in. rectangle. Transfer to a greased 13-in. x 9-in. baking pan. Using a sharp knife, cut dough into 16 squares. Cover and let rise until doubled, about 30 minutes.

Bake at 375° for 20 minutes or until golden brown. To serve, separate into rolls.
YIELD: 16 servings.

thelma richardson
LA CROSSE, WISCONSIN

This recipe for "melt in your mouth" rolls was given to me more than 40 years ago when we lived in the South. My family has been known to devour them as soon as they come out of the oven! Dividing the dough into rolls in the pan is a time-saver.

ITALIAN DINNER ROLLS

PREP: 20 min. + rising | **BAKE:** 20 min.

3-1/2 to 4 cups all-purpose flour
    2 tablespoons sugar
    1 package (1/4 ounce) active dry yeast
1-1/2 teaspoons garlic salt
    1 teaspoon onion powder
    1 teaspoon Italian seasoning
    1 teaspoon dried parsley flakes
    1 cup 2% milk
1/2 cup water
    4 tablespoons butter, *divided*
    1 egg
3/4 cup grated Parmesan cheese, *divided*

In a large bowl, combine 1-1/2 cups flour, sugar, yeast and seasonings. In a small saucepan, heat milk, water and 2 tablespoons butter to 120°-130°. Add to dry ingredients; beat until moistened. Add egg; beat on medium speed for 3 minutes. Stir in 1/2 cup cheese and enough remaining flour to form a soft dough.

Turn onto floured surface; knead until smooth and elastic, about 6-8 minutes. Place in a greased bowl, turning once to grease top. Cover and let rest for 15 minutes.

Punch dough down. Turn onto a lightly floured surface; divide into 15 pieces. Shape each into a ball. Melt the remaining butter; dip the tops of the balls in the butter and the remaining cheese.

Place in a greased 13-in. x 9-in. baking pan. Cover and let rest for 10 minutes.

Bake at 375° for 20-25 minutes or until golden brown. Remove from pans to wire racks to cool.

YIELD: 15 rolls.

marie elaine
basinger
CONNELLSVILLE, PENNSYLVANIA

Over the years, I've added a pinch of this and a dash of that to this recipe until my family agreed it was just right. These rolls are especially good served warm with your favorite Italian pasta dishes.

PEANUT BUTTER MINI MUFFINS

PREP/TOTAL TIME: 25 min.

1-3/4 cups all-purpose flour
2/3 cup packed brown sugar
2-1/2 teaspoons baking powder
1/4 teaspoon salt
1 egg
3/4 cup 2% milk
2/3 cup chunky peanut butter
1/4 cup canola oil
1-1/2 teaspoons vanilla extract
2/3 cup miniature semisweet chocolate chips

In a large bowl, combine the flour, brown sugar, baking powder and salt. In another bowl, whisk the egg, milk, peanut butter, oil and vanilla. Stir into dry ingredients just until moistened. Fold in chocolate chips.

Fill greased or paper-lined miniature muffin cups two-thirds full. Bake at 350° for 15-17 minutes or until a toothpick inserted near the center comes out clean. Cool for 5 minutes before removing from pans to wire racks. Serve warm.

YIELD: 4 dozen.

connie barz
SAN ANTONIO, TEXAS

These bite-size muffins are perfect to send in our kids' lunches for snacktime. I make regular-size muffins for church functions, and they always disappear fast.

CINNAMON RAISIN BREAD

PREP: 15 min. | BAKE: 55 min. + cooling

4 cups all-purpose flour
2 cups sugar, *divided*
2 teaspoons baking soda
1 teaspoon salt
2 eggs
2 cups buttermilk
1/2 cup canola oil
1/2 cup raisins
3 teaspoons ground cinnamon

In a large bowl, combine the flour, 1-1/2 cups sugar, baking soda and salt. In a small bowl, whisk the eggs, buttermilk and oil. Stir into dry ingredients just until moistened. Fold in raisins. Combine cinnamon and remaining sugar; set aside.

Spoon half of the batter into two greased 8-in. x 4-in. loaf pans. Sprinkle with half of the reserved cinnamon-sugar; repeat layers. Cut through batter with a knife to swirl.

Bake at 350° for 55-60 minutes or until a toothpick inserted near the center comes out clean. Cool for 10 minutes before removing from pans to wire racks.

YIELD: 2 loaves (12 slices each).

flo burtnett
GAGE, OKLAHOMA

I serve warm slices of this bread swirled with raisins and cinnamon to my holiday visitors. No one can resist the flavor of this heavenly treat.

QUICK breads

Serve quick breads a day after baking; that is when they slice and taste the best. Wrap cooled bread in foil or plastic wrap; leave at room temperature overnight. Store quick breads at room temperature for up to 3 days, but refrigerate quick breads made with cheese, cream cheese or other perishable foods.

ORANGE CHOCOLATE CHIP BREAD

PREP: 15 min. + standing | **BAKE:** 55 min. + cooling

- 4 teaspoons grated orange peel (about 1 medium orange)
- 1/3 cup orange juice
- Boiling water
- 2 cups all-purpose flour
- 1 cup sugar
- 1 teaspoon baking powder
- 1/2 teaspoon salt
- 1/2 teaspoon baking soda
- 1 egg
- 2 tablespoons butter, melted
- 1 teaspoon vanilla extract
- 1 cup (6 ounces) semisweet chocolate chips

Place orange peel in a small bowl. Pour juice in a measuring cup; add enough boiling water to measure 1 cup. Pour over orange peel; let stand for 10 minutes.

Meanwhile, in a large bowl, combine the flour, sugar, baking powder, salt and baking soda. In another bowl, whisk the egg, butter, vanilla and reserved orange mixture. Stir into dry ingredients just until moistened. Fold in chocolate chips.

Pour into a greased 8-in. x 4-in. loaf pan. Bake at 350° for 55-65 minutes or until a toothpick inserted near the center comes out clean. Cool for 10 minutes before removing from pan to a wire rack.

YIELD: 1 loaf (16 servings).

luene byers
ENOCH, UTAH

The classic combination of flavors in this recipe reminds me of the orange and chocolate candy my grandmother made for the holidays. We like to snack on this bread throughout the day.

BUTTERMILK BISCUITS

PREP: 25 min. | **BAKE:** 15 min.

- 2 cups all-purpose flour
- 1 tablespoon sugar
- 1 teaspoon baking powder
- 1/2 teaspoon salt
- 1/2 teaspoon baking soda
- 1/4 cup cold shortening
- 3/4 cup buttermilk

In a large bowl, combine the flour, sugar, baking powder, salt and baking soda. Cut in shortening until mixture resembles coarse crumbs. Add buttermilk; stir just until the dough clings together.

Turn onto a lightly floured surface; knead gently, about 10-12 times. Roll to 1/2-in. thickness; cut with a floured 2-in. round biscuit cutter. Place 1 in. apart on a greased baking sheet. Bake at 450° for 11-12 minutes or until lightly browned. Serve warm.

YIELD: about 1-1/2 dozen.

jean parsons
SARVER, PENNSYLVANIA

The recipe for these classic biscuits has been in our family for years. They're simple to make and smell so good while baking. Take them to your next outdoor picnic—they taste delicious served with fried chicken and coleslaw.

NORTHWOODS MUFFINS

PREP/TOTAL TIME: 30 min.

  2 cups all-purpose flour
1/2 cup sugar
  3 teaspoons baking powder
1/2 teaspoon salt
  2 eggs
3/4 cup buttermilk
1/4 cup butter, melted
  1 cup cooked wild rice
1/2 cup fresh *or* frozen blueberries
1/2 cup fresh *or* frozen cranberries

In a large bowl, combine the flour, sugar, baking powder and salt. In another bowl, whisk the eggs, buttermilk and butter. Stir in dry ingredients just until moistened. Fold in the rice, blueberries and cranberries.

Fill greased or paper-lined muffin cups two-thirds full. Bake at 375° for 20-25 minutes or until a toothpick inserted near the center comes out clean. Cool for 5 minutes before removing from pans to wire racks. Serve warm.

YIELD: 16 muffins.

kay englund

HAM LAKE, MINNESOTA

Even family and friends who aren't fond of wild rice rave about these golden muffins flecked with colorful blueberries and cranberries. They're a terrific take-along treat.

PERFECT DINNER ROLLS

PREP: 30 min. + rising | **BAKE:** 15 min.

1 tablespoon active dry yeast
2-1/4 cups warm water (110° to 115°)
1/3 cup sugar
1/3 cup shortening
1/4 cup powdered nondairy creamer
2-1/4 teaspoons salt
6 to 7 cups bread flour

In a large bowl, dissolve the yeast in warm water. Add the sugar, shortening, creamer, salt and 5 cups flour. Beat until smooth. Stir in enough remaining flour to form a soft dough (dough will be sticky).

Turn onto a floured surface; knead until smooth and elastic, about 6-8 minutes. Place in a bowl coated with cooking spray, turning once to coat the top. Cover and let rise in a warm place until doubled, about 1 hour.

Punch dough down. Turn onto a lightly floured surface; divide into 24 pieces. Shape each into a roll. Place 2 in. apart on baking sheets coated with cooking spray. Cover and let rise until doubled, about 30 minutes.

Bake at 350° for 12-15 minutes or until lightly browned. Remove rolls from pans to wire racks.

YIELD: 2 dozen.

gayleen grote
BATTLEVIEW, NORTH DAKOTA

These rolls melt in your mouth. I loved them as a child, and I'm happy to make them for my kids because I know I am making for them the same wonderful memories my mom made for me!

EASY BANANA BREAD

PREP: 15 min. | **BAKE:** 50 min. + standing

1/3 cup shortening
1/2 cup sugar
2 eggs
1-3/4 cups all-purpose flour
1 teaspoon baking powder
1/2 teaspoon baking soda
1/2 teaspoon salt
1 cup mashed ripe bananas

In a large bowl, cream shortening and sugar. Beat in eggs. Combine the flour, baking powder, baking soda and salt; add to the creamed mixture alternately with bananas, beating well after each addition. Pour into a greased 8-in. x 4-in. loaf pan.

Bake at 350° for 50-55 minutes or until a toothpick inserted near the center comes out clean. Let stand for 10 minutes before removing from pan; cool on a wire rack.
YIELD: 1 loaf (16 slices.).

sharon ward
KING FERRY, NEW YORK

I taught my kids to bake using guaranteed-to-be good recipes like this classic loaf. The moist slices are so scrumptious, they disappear as soon as they are served.

MINIATURE ORANGE MUFFINS

PREP: 30 min. | **BAKE:** 10 min./batch

1-1/2 cups plus 2 tablespoons all-purpose flour, *divided*
1/2 cup sugar
2 teaspoons baking powder
1/2 teaspoon salt
1 egg
1 cup 2% milk
9 tablespoons butter, melted, *divided*
3 tablespoons orange juice concentrate
2-1/2 teaspoons grated orange peel, *divided*
1/4 cup packed brown sugar
1/4 cup chopped pecans
ORANGE BUTTER:
1/2 cup butter, softened
1/4 cup sweet orange marmalade
1 teaspoon honey

In a large bowl, combine 1-1/2 cups flour, sugar, baking powder and salt. In another bowl, whisk the egg, milk, 8 tablespoons butter, orange juice concentrate and 2 teaspoons orange peel; stir into the dry ingredients just until moistened.

Fill greased miniature muffin cups half full. Combine the brown sugar, pecans and remaining flour, butter and orange peel; sprinkle over batter.

Bake at 400° for 10-12 minutes or until a toothpick inserted near the center comes out clean. Cool for 5 minutes before removing from pans to wire racks.

In a small bowl, beat the orange butter ingredients until blended. Serve butter with warm muffins.
YIELD: 4-1/2 dozen.

bonita kinney
FIRTH, NEBRASKA

Orange peel and orange juice flavor these fun streusel-topped muffins that are perfect for a buffet table. The accompanying orange marmalade butter really makes them special.

MUFFIN prep

When you want oven-fresh muffins in the morning, do some of the prep work the night before, like combining dry ingredients in a plastic bag and measuring any other ingredients that will hold. The following morning, you can quickly stir together the batter and pop the muffins in the oven.

EASY BLUEBERRY MUFFINS

PREP/TOTAL TIME: 30 min.

3 cups self-rising flour
1-1/2 cups sugar
1 cup buttermilk
1/2 cup canola oil
2 eggs, lightly beaten
2 cups fresh *or* frozen blueberries

In a large bowl, combine the flour and sugar. In another bowl, combine the buttermilk, oil and eggs. Stir into dry ingredients just until moistened. Stir in blueberries.

Fill greased or paper-lined muffin cups two-thirds full. Bake at 400° for 14-18 minutes or until golden brown and a toothpick inserted near the center comes out clean. Cool for 5 minutes before removing from pans to wire racks. Serve warm.
YIELD: 2 dozen.

janie ramming
DUNCAN, OKLAHOMA

Nothing welcomes the morning like fresh blueberry muffins. These sweet little bites are delicious and are ready in no time.

HONEY WHOLE WHEAT BRAIDS

PREP: 35 min. + rising | **BAKE:** 30 min. + cooling

1 package (1/4 ounce) active dry yeast
2-1/4 cups warm water (110° to 115°), *divided*
1 tablespoon sugar
1/3 cup honey
3 tablespoons canola oil
1/2 cup instant nonfat dry milk powder
1-1/2 teaspoons salt
6 to 6-1/2 cups whole wheat flour
All-purpose flour
Melted butter

In a large bowl, dissolve the yeast in 1/4 cup warm water. Add the sugar; let stand for 5 minutes. Add the honey, oil, milk powder, salt, 3 cups whole wheat flour and remaining water; beat for 3 minutes. Stir in enough of the remaining whole wheat flour to form a soft dough.

Turn onto a surface dusted with all-purpose flour; knead until smooth and elastic, about 8-10 minutes. Place in a greased bowl, turning once to grease top. Cover and let rise in a warm place until doubled, about 2 hours.

Punch dough down. Turn onto a lightly floured surface; divide into six portions. Shape each into a 15-in. rope. Braid three ropes; pinch ends to seal and tuck under. Repeat with remaining dough. Place in two greased 8-in. x 4-in. loaf pans. Cover and let rise until doubled, about 1 hour.

Bake at 350° for 30-35 minutes or until golden brown. Remove from pans to wire racks. Brush with melted butter. Cool.
YIELD: 2 loaves (16 slices each).

pat young
BACKUS, MINNESOTA

This hearty, wholesome bread has a slightly sweet honey flavor. It tastes divine with a little peanut butter and honey spread on top or as a sandwich filled with sliced honey-glazed ham or deli turkey.

LEMON BREAD

PREP: 10 min. | **BAKE:** 45 min. + cooling

1/2 cup butter, softened
1 cup sugar
2 eggs
2 tablespoons lemon juice
1 tablespoon grated lemon peel
1-1/2 cups all-purpose flour
1 teaspoon baking powder
1/8 teaspoon salt
1/2 cup 2% milk

GLAZE:
2 tablespoons lemon juice
1/2 cup confectioners' sugar

In a large bowl, cream butter and sugar until light and fluffy. Beat in the eggs, lemon juice and peel. Combine the flour, baking powder and salt; gradually stir into creamed mixture alternately with milk, beating well after each addition.

Pour batter into a greased 8-in. x 4-in. loaf pan. Bake at 350° for 45 minutes or until a toothpick inserted near the center comes out clean.

Combine glaze ingredients. Remove bread from pan; immediately drizzle with glaze. Cool on a wire rack. Serve warm. **YIELD:** 1 loaf (16 slices).

kathy scott
LINGLE, WYOMING

You'll often find me baking this sunshiny-sweet bread when company's due. It has a pound cake-like texture that everyone loves.

LEMON peel

The quickest and easiest way to make grated lemon peel for recipes is to slice off big pieces of peel and grind them in a food processor for just a few seconds.

BROWN SUGAR OAT MUFFINS

PREP/TOTAL TIME: 30 min.

1 cup old-fashioned oats
1 cup whole wheat flour
3/4 cup packed brown sugar
1/2 cup all-purpose flour
2 teaspoons baking powder
1/2 teaspoon salt
2 eggs
3/4 cup 2% milk
1/4 cup canola oil
1 teaspoon vanilla extract

In a small bowl, combine the first six ingredients. In another small bowl, beat the eggs, milk, oil and vanilla. Stir into the dry ingredients just until moistened.

Fill greased or paper-lined muffin cups two-thirds full. Bake at 400° for 15-17 minutes or until a toothpick inserted near the center comes out clean. Cool for 5 minutes before removing from pan to a wire rack. Serve warm.

YIELD: 1 dozen.

regina stock
TOPEKA, KANSAS

With Kansas being one of the top wheat-producing states, it seems only fitting to share a recipe containing whole wheat flour. These are great muffins to have for breakfast or as a late-night snack with a cup of hot cocoa.

TANGY LEMON CLOVERS

PREP: 30 min. + rising | **BAKE:** 15 min.

2 packages (1/4 ounce *each*) active dry yeast
1-1/2 cups warm water (110° to 115°)
1/2 cup sugar
1/2 cup nonfat dry milk powder
1/2 cup butter-flavored shortening
3 eggs
1 teaspoon salt
1 teaspoon lemon extract
1/2 teaspoon ground cinnamon
1/2 teaspoon ground nutmeg
1/4 teaspoon ground ginger
5 to 5-1/2 cups all-purpose flour

TOPPING:

1 cup sugar
1 teaspoon grated lemon peel
1/2 teaspoon ground nutmeg
1/4 cup butter, melted

In a large bowl, dissolve the yeast in warm water. Add the sugar, dry milk powder, shortening, eggs, salt, extract, spices and 2 cups flour. Beat until smooth. Stir in enough remaining flour to form a soft dough.

Turn onto a lightly floured surface; knead until smooth and elastic, about 6-8 minutes. Place in a greased bowl; turning once to grease top. Cover and let rise in a warm place until doubled, about 1 hour.

Punch dough down. Turn onto a floured surface; divide in half. Cover and let rest for 15 minutes. Shape each portion into a 16-in. log. Cut each log into 12 pieces; shape each piece into a ball.

In a shallow bowl, combine the sugar, peel and nutmeg. Dip tops of balls in butter, then in sugar mixture.

Place topping side up in well-greased muffin cups. Using greased kitchen scissors, cut rolls into quarters, almost to the bottom. Cover and let rise until doubled, about 45 minutes.

Brush with remaining butter; sprinkle with remaining sugar mixture. Bake at 375° for 15-20 minutes or until golden brown. Remove from pans to wire racks. Serve warm.
YIELD: 2 dozen.

judy jack
HOLT, MISSOURI

These rolls feature a refreshing lemon flavor. A sprinkling of sugar on top makes them impossible to resist.

STRAWBERRY RIBBON BREAD

PREP: 15 min. | **BAKE:** 70 min. + cooling

3 cups all-purpose flour
2 cups sugar
1 teaspoon baking soda
1 teaspoon salt
1 teaspoon ground cinnamon
4 eggs, lightly beaten
1/4 cup canola oil
2 packages (10 ounces *each*) frozen sliced strawberries, thawed
1 teaspoon red food coloring, optional

FILLING:

2 packages (3 ounces *each*) cream cheese, softened
1 egg
1/3 cup sugar
1 tablespoon all-purpose flour
1/2 teaspoon orange extract

In a large bowl, combine the flour, sugar, baking soda, salt and cinnamon. In another bowl, combine the eggs, oil, strawberries and food coloring if desired. Stir into dry ingredients just until moistened.

For filling, beat cream cheese in a small bowl. Add the egg, sugar, flour and extract; beat well.

Spoon a fourth of the batter into each of two greased 8-in. x 4-in. loaf pans. Spread half of the filling over each. Top with the remaining batter.

Bake at 350° for 70-80 minutes or until a toothpick inserted near the center comes out clean. Cover loosely with foil if top browns too quickly. Cool for 10 minutes before removing from pans to wire racks to cool completely. Store in the refrigerator.
YIELD: 2 loaves.

carol wilson
MISSOULA, MONTANA

This ribbon bread allows you to savor the classic combination of sweet strawberries and smooth cream cheese. The recipe makes two loaves so you can take one to a picnic or family reunion and save the other to enjoy later.

CORN BREAD FOR A CROWD

PREP/TOTAL TIME: 30 min.

3-1/2 cups cornmeal
2-1/2 cups all-purpose flour
   2 tablespoons baking powder
1-1/2 teaspoons baking soda
1-1/2 teaspoons salt
   4 eggs
   3 cups buttermilk
   1 cup canola oil

In a large bowl, combine the cornmeal, flour, baking powder, baking soda and salt. In a small bowl, combine the eggs, buttermilk and oil; stir into the dry ingredients just until moistened.

Pour into a greased 13-in. x 9-in. baking pan and a greased 9-in. square baking pan. Bake at 425° for 20-25 minutes or until a toothpick inserted near the center comes out clean. Serve warm.

YIELD: 30-36 servings.

samuel warnock
UNION, OHIO

These sunny squares are a terrific accompaniment to chili or any savory dish with gravy or sauce.

BIG-BATCH baked goods

If you like bringing baked goods to potlucks, but don't always have time the day before the event to do the prep work, devote 1 day a month to making large batches of rolls, muffins, pound cakes and quick breads. Place them in heavy-duty resealable plastic bags labeled with the date. Most items freeze for about 2 months. On the day of the party, set them out to thaw and then pop them in a microwave at the party to warm. Everyone will love the fresh-baked flavor.

OATMEAL MINI LOAVES

PREP: 25 min. + rising | **BAKE:** 30 min.

1-1/2 cups old-fashioned oats
   3/4 cup whole wheat flour
   1/2 cup packed brown sugar
   1/4 cup toasted wheat germ
   3 teaspoons salt
   1 package (1/4 ounce) active dry yeast
2-1/2 cups water
   2 tablespoons butter
5-1/2 to 6 cups all-purpose flour
Melted butter, optional
Additional old-fashioned oats, optional

In a large bowl, combine the oats, whole wheat flour, brown sugar, wheat germ, salt and yeast. In a small saucepan, heat water and butter to 120°-130°. Add to dry ingredients just until moistened. Add 3 cups all-purpose flour; beat until smooth. Stir in enough remaining all-purpose flour to form a soft dough.

Turn onto a floured surface; knead until smooth and elastic, about 6-8 minutes. Place in a greased bowl, turning once to grease top. Cover and let rise in a warm place until doubled, about 1 hour.

Punch dough down. Turn onto a lightly floured surface; divide into five portions. Shape each into a loaf. Place in five greased 5-in. x 3-in. x 2-in. loaf pans. Cover and let rise until doubled, about 30 minutes.

Bake at 350° for 30-35 minutes or until golden brown. Remove from pans to wire racks. Brush with melted butter; sprinkle with additional oats if desired. Cool.

YIELD: 5 mini loaves (5 slices each).

doris kosmicki
PINCKNEY, MICHIGAN

I first came across this recipe in an old cookbook. As I became more brave with baking bread, I decided to experiment by changing and adding ingredients to enhance flavor and nutrition. This crowd-pleasing loaf will work for any gathering.

FEATHER WHOLE WHEAT ROLLS

PREP: 30 min. + chilling | **BAKE:** 10 min.

- 4 tablespoons active dry yeast
- 2 tablespoons plus 2/3 cup sugar, *divided*
- 2 cups warm water (110° to 115°)
- 2 cups warm milk (110° to 115°)
- 4 eggs, lightly beaten
- 2/3 cup canola oil
- 2 teaspoons salt
- 4 cups whole wheat flour
- 4-1/2 to 5 cups all-purpose flour
- 1/4 cup butter, melted

In a large bowl, dissolve the yeast and 2 tablespoons sugar in warm water. Add the milk, eggs, oil, salt, remaining sugar and whole wheat flour. Beat until smooth. Stir in enough all-purpose flour to form a soft dough (dough will be sticky). Do not knead. Cover and refrigerate for 8 hours.

Punch dough down. Divide into thirds. Cover and refrigerate two portions. Turn the remaining portion onto a lightly floured surface; roll or pat to 1/2-in. thickness. Cut with a lightly floured 2-1/2-in. biscuit cutter. Repeat with remaining dough. Place rolls 2-1/2-in. apart on greased baking sheets. Cover and let rise in a warm place until doubled, about 2 hours.

Bake at 425° for 8-12 minutes or until golden brown. Brush with butter. Remove to wire racks.

YIELD: about 5 dozen.

leann sain
OREM, UTAH

My grandmother and mother have made this recipe famous in our family as well as our community. We never sit down to Thanksgiving or Christmas dinner without these melt-in-your-mouth rolls.

BEST CHEESE BREAD

PREP: 10 min. | **BAKE:** 55 min. + cooling

3-3/4 cups all-purpose flour
2-1/2 cups (10 ounces) shredded cheddar cheese
5 teaspoons baking powder
1/2 teaspoon garlic powder
1/2 teaspoon dill weed
2 eggs
1-1/2 cups milk
1/3 cup canola oil
3 tablespoons honey

In a large bowl, combine the flour, cheese, baking powder, garlic powder and dill. In another bowl, whisk the eggs, milk, oil and honey. Stir into the dry ingredients just until moistened.

Pour into a greased 9-in. x 5-in. loaf pan. Bake at 350° for 55-65 minutes or until a toothpick inserted near the center comes out clean (top will have an uneven appearance). Cool for 10 minutes before removing from pan to a wire rack. Serve warm. Refrigerate any leftovers.

YIELD: 1 loaf (16 slices each).

joanie elbourn
GARDNER, MASSACHUSETTS

My husband and I enjoy the garlic, dill and cheddar flavors in this savory loaf. We serve it fresh from the oven for a meal of bread and salad. It also makes a fantastic addition for potluck parties that serve up big plates of spaghetti or lasagna.

CHOCOLATE BRAIDS

PREP: 40 min. + rising | **BAKE:** 30 min. + cooling

- 2 packages (1/4 ounce *each*) active dry yeast
- 1/2 cup warm water (110° to 115°)
- 1/3 cup honey, *divided*
- 6 tablespoons butter, softened
- 1 egg
- 1/2 cup baking cocoa
- 1/2 teaspoon salt
- 2-1/2 to 3 cups bread flour

CREAM CHEESE FILLING:
- 4 ounces cream cheese, softened
- 1/4 cup sugar
- 1/4 cup all-purpose flour
- 1 teaspoon vanilla extract
- 1/4 teaspoon ground nutmeg

TOPPING:
- 1/4 cup all-purpose flour
- 1/4 cup sugar
- 1/2 teaspoon ground cinnamon
- 2 tablespoons cold butter
- 1/4 cup chopped macadamia nuts

ICING:
- 1-1/2 cups confectioners' sugar
- 1 tablespoon baking cocoa
- 1/4 teaspoon vanilla extract
- 3 to 4 tablespoons milk

In a large bowl, dissolve the yeast in warm water. Add 2 teaspoons honey; let stand for 5 minutes. Add the butter, egg, cocoa, salt, 1-1/2 cups bread flour and remaining honey. Beat for 2 minutes or until smooth. Stir in enough remaining bread flour to form a soft dough.

Turn onto a floured surface; knead until smooth and elastic, about 6-8 minutes. Place in a greased bowl, turning once to grease top. Cover and let rise in a warm place until doubled, about 1 hour.

Punch dough down; divide in half. On a lightly floured surface, roll one portion into a 12-in. x 7-in. rectangle.

In a small bowl, beat filling ingredients until smooth. Spread half of the filling over dough to within 1 in. of edges. Roll up jelly-roll style, starting with a long side; pinch seams to seal.

Place seam side down on a large greased baking sheet. With a sharp knife, cut roll in half lengthwise, leaving one end intact. Carefully turn cut sides up. Loosely twist strips around each other, keeping cut side up. Pinch ends to seal. Repeat with remaining dough and filling. Cover and let rise in a warm place for 30 minutes.

For topping, combine the flour, sugar and cinnamon in a small bowl; cut in the butter until crumbly. Add the nuts. Sprinkle topping over loaves.

Bake at 350° for 30-35 minutes or until golden brown. Remove from pans to wire racks to cool. Combine icing ingredients; drizzle over loaves.

YIELD: 2 loaves (8 slices each).

erika aylward
CLINTON, MICHIGAN

This bread is fantastic and gets rave reviews every time. The recipe is a little more complicated than some, but worth the extra effort.

PROSCIUTTO PARMESAN PINWHEELS

PREP: 20 min. | **BAKE:** 15 min.

- 1 package (17.3 ounces) frozen puff pastry, thawed
- 2 tablespoons Dijon mustard
- 6 ounces thinly sliced prosciutto *or* deli ham, chopped
- 1-1/4 cups shredded Parmesan cheese

Unfold puff pastry. Spread mustard over pastry to within 1/2 in. of edges. Sprinkle with prosciutto and cheese. Roll up each pastry sheet. Using a serrated knife, cut into 1 in. slices.

Place on greased baking sheets. Bake at 400° for 12-15 minutes or until puffed and golden brown. Serve warm.

YIELD: 20 appetizers.

virginia galloway
HOUSTON, TEXAS

Puff pastry from the freezer section makes these tasty appetizers a snap to assemble. The golden-brown pinwheels get their fabulous flavor from prosciutto, Dijon mustard and Parmesan cheese.

GLAZED LEMON MUFFINS

PREP: 25 min. | BAKE: 25 min.

1-1/2 cups all-purpose flour
1-1/2 cups sugar
1/4 cup cold butter, cubed

MUFFINS:
1-1/2 cups butter, softened
3 cups sugar
6 eggs
1-1/2 cups (12 ounces) sour cream
3 tablespoons lemon juice
2 tablespoons grated lemon peel
4-1/2 cups all-purpose flour
1/2 teaspoon baking soda
1/2 teaspoon salt

GLAZE:
3/4 cup confectioners' sugar
1/3 cup lemon juice

In a large bowl, combine flour and sugar. Cut in butter until crumbly; set aside.

In a large bowl, cream butter and sugar until light and fluffy. Beat in eggs. Beat in the sour cream, lemon juice and peel. Combine the flour, baking soda and salt; gradually add to creamed mixture just until moistened.

Fill greased or paper-lined muffin cups two-thirds full. Sprinkle with reserved crumb topping. Bake at 350° for 25-30 minutes or until a toothpick inserted near the center comes out clean. Cool in pans for 5 minutes before removing to wire racks.

Combine glaze ingredients; drizzle over muffins. Serve warm.
YIELD: about 2 dozen.

carol stevison
AKRON, OHIO

Offer these at special celebrations—and watch folks come back for more! The crumb topping and sweet glaze complement the lemony muffin.

YEAST alternatives

For best results, our home economists recommend using the type of yeast called for in a recipe. But in a pinch, active dry yeast can be substituted for quick-rise yeast in equal parts. When using active dry yeast, first dissolve it in warm water before adding it to other ingredients. Use 1/4 cup of warm water (110°-115°) to dissolve each 1/4-ounce package of active dry yeast. The dough will need to rise two times before baking, once after kneading and once after shaping.

SIMPLY-A-MUST DINNER ROLLS

PREP: 40 min. + rising | BAKE: 10 min.

5-1/2 to 6 cups all-purpose flour
1/2 cup sugar
1 tablespoon quick-rise yeast
2 teaspoons salt
1 cup 2% milk
1/2 cup canola oil
3 eggs
2 tablespoons butter, melted

In a large bowl, combine 3 cups flour, sugar, yeast and salt. In a small saucepan, heat milk and oil to 120°-130°. Add to dry ingredients; beat just until moistened. Add eggs; beat until smooth. Stir in enough remaining flour to form a soft dough (dough will be sticky).

Turn onto a floured surface; knead until smooth and elastic, about 6-8 minutes. Cover and let rest for 10 minutes. Divide dough into thirds. Roll each portion into a 12-in. circle; brush with butter. Cut each circle into 12 wedges.

Roll up wedges from the wide end and place point side down 2 in. apart on baking sheets coated with cooking spray. Curve ends to form crescents. Cover and let rise until nearly doubled, about 30 minutes.

Bake at 400° for 10-12 minutes or until golden brown. Remove rolls from pans to wire racks.
YIELD: 3 dozen.

michelle minaker
TWO RIVERS, WISCONSIN

I make these fluffy, buttery rolls every year for holiday meals. They always turn out velvety and crisp and leftovers work wonderfully for mini sandwiches.

FINNISH WHEAT ROLLS

PREP: 15 min. + rising | **BAKE:** 25 min.

2 packages (1/4 ounce *each*) active dry yeast
2 cups warm water (110° to 115°)
1 cup butter, melted
1/4 cup dried parsley flakes
1 tablespoon dried rosemary, crushed
2 teaspoons salt
1 teaspoon rubbed sage
1 teaspoon dried thyme
2-3/4 cups whole wheat flour
3 to 3-1/2 cups all-purpose flour
Additional melted butter

In a large bowl, dissolve the yeast in warm water. Add the butter, parsley, rosemary, salt, sage, thyme and whole wheat flour. Beat until smooth. Stir in enough all-purpose flour to form a soft dough.

Turn onto a floured surface; knead until smooth and elastic, about 6-8 minutes. Place in a greased bowl, turning once to grease top. Cover and let rise in a warm place until doubled, about 30 minutes.

Punch dough down. Turn onto a lightly floured surface; divide into 24 pieces. Shape each into a ball. Place 2 in. apart on greased baking sheets. Cover and let rise in a warm place until doubled, about 30 minutes.

Brush with additional melted butter. Bake at 425° for 25-30 minutes or until golden brown. Remove from pans to wire racks. Serve warm.

YIELD: 2 dozen.

tarya mannonen-cameron

SEATTLE, WASHINGTON

When I came to the United States from Finland to go to college, I missed the traditional breads we enjoy back home. I came up with this recipe to recapture those fabulous flavors.

NUT-TOPPED STRAWBERRY RHUBARB MUFFINS

PREP: 25 min. | **BAKE:** 20 min. + cooling

2-3/4 cups all-purpose flour
1-1/3 cups packed brown sugar
2-1/2 teaspoons baking powder
1/2 teaspoon baking soda
1/2 teaspoon ground cinnamon
1/4 teaspoon salt
1 egg
1 cup buttermilk
1/2 cup canola oil
2 teaspoons vanilla extract
1 cup chopped fresh strawberries
3/4 cup diced fresh *or* frozen rhubarb

TOPPING:
1/2 cup chopped pecans
1/3 cup packed brown sugar
1/2 teaspoon ground cinnamon
1 tablespoon cold butter

In a large bowl, combine the first six ingredients. In another bowl, whisk the egg, buttermilk, oil and vanilla. Stir into dry ingredients just until moistened. Fold in strawberries and rhubarb. Fill greased or paper-lined muffin cups two-thirds full.

In a small bowl, combine the pecans, brown sugar and cinnamon. Cut in butter until mixture resembles coarse crumbs. Sprinkle over batter.

Bake at 400° for 20-25 minutes or until a toothpick inserted near the center comes out clean. Cool for 5 minutes before removing from pans to wire racks. Serve warm.
YIELD: 1-1/2 dozen.

audrey stallsmith
HADLEY, PENNSYLVANIA

A crispy, sugar topping highlights these tender muffins that are filled with two favorite spring foods—rhubarb and strawberries. The treats are wonderful for a brunch buffet or a grab-and-go breakfast.

CHERRY CHIP MUFFINS

PREP/TOTAL TIME: 30 min.

1-1/2 cups all-purpose flour
1/2 cup sugar
2 teaspoons baking powder
1/2 teaspoon salt
1 egg
1/2 cup milk
1/4 cup canola oil
1 jar (10 ounces) red maraschino cherries
3/4 cup miniature semisweet chocolate chips
1/2 cup chopped pecans
1 cup confectioners' sugar
Softened cream cheese, optional

In a large bowl, combine the flour, sugar, baking powder and salt. In another bowl, whisk the egg, milk and oil; stir into dry ingredients just until moistened. Drain cherries, reserving 2 tablespoons of juice for glaze (discard remaining juice or save for another use). Chop cherries; fold the chips, pecans and cherries into the batter.

Drop by tablespoonfuls into greased or paper-lined heart-shaped or miniature muffin cups. Bake at 375° for 10-13 minutes or until a toothpick inserted near the center comes out clean.

Cool for 10 minutes; remove from pans to wire racks. Combine confectioners' sugar and reserved cherry juice to make a thin glaze; drizzle over muffins. Serve with cream cheese if desired.

YIELD: about 4 dozen.

shirley glaab
HATTIESBURG, MISSISSIPPI

These pretty muffins are perfect for Christmas morning, Valentine's Day or any occasion when you want to treat someone special to sweet treat. Drizzled with pink icing, they look adorable and taste wonderful.

BUTTERY CROISSANTS

PREP: 1 hour + chilling | **BAKE:** 15 min./batch

1-1/2 cups butter, softened
1/3 cup all-purpose flour
DOUGH:
1 package (1/4 ounce) active dry yeast
1/4 cup warm water (110° to 115°)
1 cup warm 2% milk (110° to 115°)
1/4 cup sugar
1 egg
1 teaspoon salt
3-1/2 to 3-3/4 cups all-purpose flour

In a small bowl, beat butter and flour until combined; spread into a 12-in. x 6-in. rectangle on a piece of waxed paper. Cover with another piece of waxed paper; refrigerate for at least 1 hour.

In a large bowl, dissolve yeast in warm water. Add the milk, sugar, egg, salt and 2 cups flour; beat until smooth. Stir in enough remaining flour to form a soft dough. Turn onto a floured surface; knead until smooth and elastic, about 6-8 minutes.

Roll dough into a 14-in. square. Remove top sheet of waxed paper from butter; invert onto half of dough. Remove waxed paper. Fold dough over butter; seal edges.

Roll into a 20-in. x 12-in. rectangle. Fold into thirds. Repeat rolling and folding twice. (If butter softens, chill after folding.) Wrap in plastic wrap; refrigerate overnight.

Unwrap dough. On a lightly floured surface, roll into a 25-in. x 20-in. rectangle. Cut into 5-in. squares. Cut each square diagonally in half, forming two triangles.

Roll up triangles from the wide end; place 2 in. apart with point down on ungreased baking sheets. Curve ends down to form crescent shape. Cover and let rise until doubled, about 45 minutes.

Bake at 375° for 12-14 minutes or until golden brown. Remove to wire racks. Serve warm.

YIELD: about 3 dozen.

loraine meyer
BEND, OREGON

A traditional dinner roll like this is always welcome at holiday dinners. The recipe makes a big batch, so it's great when you're entertaining.

SOUTHWEST SURPRISE BREAD

PREP: 30 min. + rising | **BAKE:** 40 min. + cooling

- 2 packages (1/4 ounce *each*) active dry yeast
- 2 cups warm 2% milk (110° to 115°)
- 1 can (16 ounces) spicy fat-free refried beans
- 2 tablespoons sugar
- 2 tablespoons butter, melted
- 2 teaspoons salt
- 5 to 6 cups all-purpose flour

In a large bowl, dissolve yeast in warm milk. Add the beans, sugar, butter, salt and 2 cups flour. Beat until smooth. Stir in enough remaining flour to form a firm dough.

Turn onto a lightly floured surface; knead dough until smooth and elastic, about 6-8 minutes. Place in a bowl coated with cooking spray, turning once to coat the top. Cover and let rise in a warm place until doubled, about 1 hour.

Punch dough down. Turn onto a lightly floured surface; divide in half. Shape into loaves. Place in two 9-in. x 5-in. loaf pans coated with cooking spray. Cover and let rise until doubled, about 30 minutes.

Bake at 350° for 40-45 minutes or until golden brown. Remove from pans to wire racks to cool.

YIELD: 2 loaves (16 slices each).

sandra lee herr
STEVENS, PENNSYLVANIA

Fat-free refried beans are the surprise ingredient in these soft, high-rising loaves featuring just a hint of heat. We serve this alongside our favorite Mexican dishes.

SWISS ONION BREAD

PREP: 30 min. + rising | **BAKE:** 25 min.

- 2 packages (1/4 ounce *each*) active dry yeast
- 1-1/2 cups warm water (110° to 115°), *divided*
- 1 teaspoon plus 1/4 cup sugar, *divided*
- 1/2 cup butter, melted
- 1 medium onion, finely chopped
- 1 egg
- 2 teaspoons salt
- 1/4 teaspoon ground mustard
- 6-3/4 to 7-1/4 cups bread *or* all-purpose flour
- 3/4 cup shredded Swiss cheese

FILLING:
- 3/4 cup finely chopped onion
- 1/4 cup shredded Swiss cheese
- 3 tablespoons butter
- 1 tablespoon poppy seeds
- 1 teaspoon paprika
- 1/2 teaspoon salt

EGG WASH:
- 1 egg yolk
- 2 teaspoons water
- Additional poppy seeds, optional

In a large bowl, dissolve yeast in 1/2 cup warm water. Add 1 teaspoon sugar; let stand for 5 minutes. Add the butter, onion, egg, salt, mustard, 3 cups flour and remaining water and sugar. Beat until smooth. Stir in cheese and enough remaining flour to form a soft dough.

Turn onto a floured surface; knead until smooth and elastic, about 8-10 minutes. Place in a greased bowl, turning once to grease top. Cover and let rise in a warm place until doubled, about 45 minutes.

Punch dough down. Turn onto a lightly floured surface; divide in half. Roll each portion into a 18-in. x 10-in. rectangle. Cut in half lengthwise. Combine filling ingredients; spread to within 1/2 in. of edges. Roll up each, jelly-roll style, starting with a long side; pinch seams to seal. Place two ropes, side by side, on a greased baking sheet. Twist ropes together; pinch ends to seal and tuck under. Repeat with remaining dough.

Cover and let rise in a warm place until doubled, about 45 minutes. Beat egg yolk and water; brush over twists. Sprinkle with additional poppy seeds if desired.

Bake at 375° for 25-35 minutes or until golden brown. Remove from pans to wire racks to cool. Store in the refrigerator.

YIELD: 2 loaves (16 slices each).

martha smith
CANTON, OHIO

Our granddaughter, Lena, used this recipe as part of her 4-H project, and it was well received. The slight crunch from poppy seeds pairs well with the creamy Swiss cheese.

THREE-GRAIN WILD RICE BREAD

PREP: 20 min. + rising | **BAKE:** 35 min.

- 1 package (1/4 ounce) active dry yeast
- 1/3 cup warm water (110° to 115°)
- 2 cups warm 2% milk (110° to 115°)
- 2 cups whole wheat flour
- 1/2 cup rye flour
- 1/2 cup quick-cooking oats
- 1/2 cup honey
- 2 tablespoons butter, melted
- 2 teaspoons salt
- 4 to 4-1/2 cups bread *or* all-purpose flour
- 1 cup cooked wild rice, cooled to room temperature
- 1 egg
- 1 tablespoon cold water

In a large bowl, dissolve the yeast in warm water. Add the milk, whole wheat flour, rye flour, oats, honey, butter, salt and 2 cups bread flour. Beat until smooth. Stir in wild rice and enough remaining bread flour to form a stiff dough.

Turn onto a floured surface; knead until smooth and elastic, about 8-10 minutes. Place in a greased bowl, turning once to grease top. Cover and let rise in a warm place until doubled, about 1-1/2 hours.

Punch dough down. Turn onto a lightly floured surface; divide in half. Shape into loaves. Transfer to two greased 9-in. x 5-in. loaf pans. Cover and let rise until doubled, about 30 minutes.

Beat the egg and cold water; brush over loaves. Bake at 375° for 35-40 minutes or until golden brown. Remove from pans to wire racks to cool.

YIELD: 2 loaves (16 slices each).

kim l'hote
VIOLA, WISCONSIN

Wild rice really shines in this one-of-a-kind recipe. The first time I made this bread, I knew I'd found a favorite. Try adding some caraway and fennel seeds for extra flavor.

ITALIAN SWEET BREAD

PREP: 10 min. + rising | **BAKE:** 20 min.

1 cup warm 2% milk (70° to 80°)
1 egg, lightly beaten
2 tablespoons butter, softened
1/4 cup sugar
1 teaspoon salt
3 cups all-purpose flour
2 teaspoons active dry yeast

EGG WASH:
1 egg
1 tablespoon water
Italian seasoning, optional

In bread machine pan, place the first seven ingredients in the order suggested by the manufacturer. Select dough setting (check dough after 5 minutes of mixing; add 1 to 2 tablespoons of water or flour if needed).

When the cycle is completed, turn dough onto a floured surface. Divide in half. Shape each portion into a ball; flatten slightly. Place in two greased 9-in. round baking pans. Cover and let rise until doubled, about 45 minutes.

Beat egg and water; brush over the dough. Sprinkle with Italian seasoning if desired. Bake at 350° for 20-25 minutes or until golden brown. Remove from pans to wire racks to cool.

YIELD: 2 loaves (16 slices each).

kim ooms
COTTAGE GROVE, MINNESOTA

This golden brown bread offers satisfying sweetness in every slice. The hearty round loaves rise well and cut beautifully. With an egg wash and a sprinkling of Italian seasoning, they look pretty, too.

UPSIDE-DOWN PEACH MUFFINS

PREP: 15 min. | **BAKE:** 30 min.

- 1 cup milk
- 1/4 cup canola oil
- 2 eggs
- 2 cups all-purpose flour
- 1-1/2 cups sugar
- 1 tablespoon baking powder
- 1/2 teaspoon salt
- 6 tablespoons butter, softened
- 1 cup plus 2 tablespoons packed brown sugar
- 3 cups sliced peeled ripe peaches

In a small bowl, beat the milk, oil and eggs until smooth. Combine the flour, sugar, baking powder and salt; add to the egg mixture and mix well.

In each of 18 greased muffin cups, place 1 teaspoon of butter and 1 tablespoon brown sugar. Bake at 375° for 5 minutes.

Arrange peaches in the muffin cups. Fill each half full with batter. Bake at 375° for 25 minutes or until a toothpick inserted near the center comes out clean. Immediately invert onto wire racks. Serve warm.
YIELD: 1-1/2 dozen.

geraldine grisdale
MT. PLEASANT, MICHIGAN

If you're looking for something small and sweet to take to a gathering, give these peach muffins a try. They make lovely individual servings for a breakfast buffet or ladies' luncheon.

HERB POTATO ROLLS

PREP: 30 min. + rising | **BAKE:** 30 min.

- 5 to 5-1/2 cups all-purpose flour
- 1 cup mashed potato flakes
- 2 packages (1/4 ounce *each*) active dry yeast
- 1 tablespoon sugar
- 1 tablespoon minced chives
- 2 teaspoons salt
- 2 teaspoons minced fresh parsley
- 2 cups milk
- 1/2 cup sour cream
- 2 eggs

In a large bowl, combine 3 cups flour, potato flakes, yeast, sugar, chives, salt and parsley. In a small saucepan, heat milk and sour cream to 120°-130°; add to dry ingredients. Beat on medium speed for 2 minutes. Add eggs and 1/2 cup flour; beat 2 minutes longer. Stir in enough remaining flour to form a soft dough.

Turn onto a floured surface; knead until smooth and elastic, about 6-8 minutes. Place in a greased bowl, turning once to grease top. Cover and let rise in a warm place until doubled, about 45 minutes.

Punch dough down. Turn onto a lightly floured surface; divide into 24 pieces. Shape each into a roll. Place in a greased 13-in. x 9-in. baking pan. Cover and let rise until doubled, about 35 minutes.

Bake at 375° for 30-35 minutes or until golden brown. Remove to wire racks.
YIELD: 2 dozen.

lonna smith
WOODRUFF, WISCONSIN

These dinner rolls are perfectly seasoned, rise high and bake up fluffy and golden brown. The recipe is from my grandma who enjoyed them as a child in Germany. I practiced for years before I finally mastered the recipe!

TENDER rolls

To make rolls that are soft and tender, use milk as the liquid, which will add tenderness to the dough and form a soft crust. Brush the tops of the rolls with melted butter after baking to produce a pretty sheen.

p. 262

p. 259

p. 269

big-batch
desserts

WALNUT CHIP COOKIES

PREP: 25 min. | BAKE: 10 min./batch

2 cups butter, softened

2 cups sugar

2 cups packed brown sugar

4 eggs

2 ounces unsweetened chocolate, melted

2 teaspoons vanilla extract

5 cups quick-cooking oats

4 cups all-purpose flour

2 teaspoons baking soda

2 teaspoons baking powder

1 teaspoon salt

4 cups (24 ounces) semisweet chocolate chips

3 cups chopped walnuts

In a large bowl, cream butter and sugars until light and fluffy. Add the eggs, one at a time, beating well after each addition. Beat in melted chocolate and vanilla.

Place half of the oats at a time in a blender; cover and process until powdery. Combine the oats, flour, baking soda, baking powder and salt; gradually add to creamed mixture and mix well.

Transfer to a large bowl if necessary. Stir in the chocolate chips and nuts. Roll into 1-1/4-in. balls.

Place 2 in. apart on lightly greased baking sheets. Bake at 375° for 7-9 minutes or until edges are firm (do not overbake). Remove to wire racks to cool.

YIELD: about 12 dozen.

joy hanje
GAYLORD, MICHIGAN

No one can resist these rich cookies with their double dose of sweetness. Melted chocolate is mixed into the dough, then chocolate chips, oats and walnuts are added. Yum!

FROSTED BROWNIES

PREP: 20 min. + cooling | BAKE: 25 min.

4 ounces unsweetened chocolate, chopped

1 cup canola oil

2 cups sugar

4 eggs

1 teaspoon vanilla extract

1 cup all-purpose flour

1/4 teaspoon salt

1 cup chopped walnuts

FROSTING:

2 tablespoons butter

2 ounces unsweetened chocolate

2-1/2 cups confectioners' sugar

1/4 cup milk

1 teaspoon vanilla extract

In a large microwave-safe bowl, heat chocolate until melted. Add oil and sugar; mix well. Stir in eggs and vanilla. Add flour and salt; mix well. Stir in the nuts. Pour into a greased 13-in. x 9-in. baking pan.

Bake at 350° for 25-30 minutes or until a toothpick inserted near the center comes out with moist crumbs (do not overbake). Cool on a wire rack.

For frosting, melt butter and chocolate; stir until smooth. Cool to room temperature. In a bowl, combine the chocolate mixture, confectioners' sugar, milk and vanilla until smooth. Frost brownies.

YIELD: 2-1/2 dozen.

pat yaeger
NAPLES, FLORIDA

You can't go wrong with this classic treat. These fudgy frosted squares travel well to potlucks and picnics and are sure to be one of the first items to disappear.

TOASTED BUTTER PECAN CAKE

PREP: 25 min. | **BAKE:** 25 min. + cooling

    1 cup plus 2 tablespoons butter, softened,
      divided
2-2/3 cups chopped pecans
    2 cups sugar
    4 eggs
    2 teaspoons vanilla extract
    3 cups all-purpose flour
    2 teaspoons baking powder
  1/2 teaspoon salt
    1 cup 2% milk
FROSTING:
    2 packages (one 8 ounces, one 3 ounces)
      cream cheese, softened
  2/3 cup butter, softened
6-1/2 cups confectioners' sugar
1-1/2 teaspoons vanilla extract
    1 to 2 tablespoons 2% milk

In a small heavy skillet, melt 2 tablespoons butter. Add pecans; cook over medium heat until toasted, about 4 minutes. Set mixture aside to cool.

In a large bowl, cream the sugar and remaining butter until light and fluffy. Add eggs, one at a time, beating well after each addition. Beat in vanilla. Combine the flour, baking powder and salt; add to creamed mixture alternately with milk. Beat just until combined. Fold in 2 cups reserved pecans.

Spread evenly into three greased and waxed paper-lined 9-in. round baking pans. Bake at 350° for 25-30 minutes or until a toothpick inserted near the center comes out clean. Cool for 10 minutes before removing from pans to wire racks to cool completely.

For frosting, in a large bowl, beat the cream cheese, butter, confectioners' sugar and vanilla until smooth. Beat in enough milk to achieve spreading consistency. Spread frosting between layers and over top and sides of cake. Sprinkle with remaining pecans. Store in the refrigerator.

YIELD: 12-16 servings.

phyllis edwards
FORT VALLEY, GEORGIA

If you like butter pecan ice cream, you'll love this cake. Loads of nuts are folded into the batter, and more are sprinkled over the delectable frosting.

FROSTED cakes

When transporting a frosted cake to a potluck, place it in the bowl of a salad spinner. The bowl is the perfect size and will ensure the frosting is protected.

CARAMEL-SWIRL CHEESECAKE DESSERT

PREP: 40 min. | **BAKE:** 40 min. + chilling

1/2 cup butter, softened
3 tablespoons sugar
1 teaspoon vanilla extract
1 cup all-purpose flour
1/3 cup flaked coconut, lightly toasted

FILLING:
3 packages (8 ounces *each*) cream cheese, softened
1 cup ricotta cheese
3/4 cup sugar
2 tablespoons all-purpose flour
1 cup heavy whipping cream
3 teaspoons vanilla extract
3 eggs, lightly beaten
1/3 cup caramel ice cream topping

In a small bowl, cream butter and sugar until light and fluffy. Beat in vanilla. Combine flour and coconut; gradually beat into creamed mixture.

Press into a lightly greased 13-in. x 9-in. baking dish. Bake at 350° for 10-12 minutes or until lightly browned. Cool on a wire rack.

For filling, in a large bowl, beat cream cheese and ricotta until blended. Add sugar and flour and mix well. Combine cream and vanilla; gradually beat into cream cheese mixture. Add eggs; beat on low speed just until combined.

Spread filling over crust. Drizzle with caramel topping; gently cut through filling with a knife to swirl.

Bake at 350° for 40-45 minutes or until center is almost set. Cool on a wire rack for 1-1/2 hours. Cover and refrigerate for at least 6 hours before serving.
YIELD: 12-15 servings.

gilda lester
MILLSBORO, DELAWARE

A rich ricotta-cream cheese filling and a luscious caramel drizzle make this dessert extra delicious. These heavenly bars are a welcome delight at picnics and birthday parties.

MIXED NUT BARS

PREP: 10 min. | **BAKE:** 20 min. + cooling

1-1/2 cups all-purpose flour
3/4 cup packed brown sugar
1/4 teaspoon salt
1/2 cup plus 2 tablespoons cold butter, *divided*
1 cup butterscotch chips
1/2 cup light corn syrup
1 can (11-1/2 ounces) mixed nuts

In a small bowl, combine the flour, brown sugar and salt. Cut in 1/2 cup butter until mixture resembles coarse crumbs. Press into a greased 13-in. x 9-in. baking pan. Bake at 350° for 10 minutes.

Meanwhile, in a microwave, melt butterscotch chips and remaining butter; stir until smooth. Stir in corn syrup.

Sprinkle the nuts over crust; top with butterscotch mixture. Bake 10 minutes longer or until set. Cool on a wire rack. Cut into bars.

YIELD: about 3-1/2 dozen.

bobbi brown
WAUPACA, WISCONSIN

One pan of these sweet bars goes a long way. They get a kid-pleasing flavor from butterscotch chips.

COULDN'T BE SIMPLER BARS

PREP: 10 min. | **BAKE:** 25 min. + cooling

1/2 cup butter, melted
1 cup graham cracker crumbs (about 16 squares)
1 cup flaked coconut
1 cup (6 ounces) semisweet chocolate chips
1 cup butterscotch chips
1 can (14 ounces) sweetened condensed milk
1 cup chopped walnuts

Pour butter into a greased 13-in. x 9-in. baking pan. Sprinkle with crumbs and coconut. Top with chips. Pour milk over all. Sprinkle with walnuts.

Bake at 350° for 23-28 minutes or until browned and bubbly. Cool completely on a wire rack before cutting.

YIELD: about 3-1/2 dozen.

kerry bouchard
AUGUSTA, MONTANA

I get lots of compliments every time I take these chewy bars to a gathering or serve them to guests.

CRISP PEPPERMINT PATTIES

PREP: 15 min. + chilling | **BAKE:** 10 min./batch

1 cup butter-flavored shortening
1/2 cup sugar
1/2 cup packed brown sugar
2 eggs
1 package (12 ounces) chocolate-covered peppermint patties, melted
1 teaspoon vanilla extract
2-1/3 cups all-purpose flour
1 teaspoon baking soda
1/2 teaspoon salt

In a large bowl, cream shortening and sugars until light and fluffy. Beat in the eggs, melted peppermint patties and vanilla. Combine the flour, baking soda and salt; gradually add to creamed mixture and mix well. Cover and refrigerate for 30 minutes or until easy to handle.

Drop by rounded teaspoonfuls 2 in. apart onto ungreased baking sheets. Bake at 375° for 8-10 minutes or until the surface cracks. Cool for 1-2 minutes before removing the cookies to wire racks.

YIELD: 5 dozen.

deborah kay collins
MANSFIELD, OHIO

Mint lovers will delight in every bite of these original crisp cookies. They not only taste wonderful, they're attractive as well.

BIG-BATCH BUTTERSCOTCH COOKIES

PREP: 20 min. | **BAKE:** 10 min./batch

1-1/2 cups butter, softened
   3 cups packed brown sugar
   3 eggs
   1 tablespoon vanilla extract
5-1/4 cups all-purpose flour
   1 tablespoon baking powder
1-1/2 teaspoons baking soda
  1/2 teaspoon cream of tartar

In a large bowl, cream butter and brown sugar until light and fluffy. Add eggs, one at a time, beating well after each addition. Beat in vanilla. Combine the flour, baking powder, baking soda and cream of tartar; gradually add to the creamed mixture and mix well (bowl will be full.)

Drop by level tablespoonfuls 2 in. apart onto ungreased baking sheets. Bake at 350° for 10-12 minutes or until golden brown. Remove to wire racks to cool.
YIELD: about 20 dozen.

joanne riechman
MCCOMB, OHIO

My mom and I created this butterscotch recipe years ago. No matter where we take these crowd-pleasing cookies, we always get rave reviews!

STRAWBERRY CREAM CAKE

PREP: 45 min. | **BAKE:** 35 min. + cooling

   6 eggs, *separated*
1-1/2 cups sugar, *divided*
   3 tablespoons lemon juice
   3 tablespoons canola oil
   2 tablespoons water
1-3/4 cups all-purpose flour
  1/2 teaspoon salt
   2 cups heavy whipping cream
  1/2 cup confectioners' sugar
  1/2 teaspoon vanilla extract
   3 cups sliced fresh strawberries
   2 cups whole fresh strawberries

ABOUT strawberries

When buying strawberries, pick the plumpest and most fragrant berries. They should be firm, bright and fresh-looking, with no mold or bruised spots. Do not wash or hull berries until you are ready to use them. Refrigerate unwashed berries as soon as possible.

Place egg whites in a large bowl; let stand at room temperature for 30 minutes.

In another bowl, beat egg yolks until slightly thickened. Gradually add 3/4 cup sugar, beating until thick and lemon-colored. Beat in the lemon juice, oil and water. Combine the flour and salt; add to the yolk mixture.

Beat egg whites on medium speed until soft peaks form. Gradually add remaining sugar, 1 tablespoon at a time, beating on high until stiff glossy peaks form. Fold a fourth of the egg whites into the batter, then fold in remaining whites.

Gently spoon into an ungreased 10-in. tube pan. Cut through batter with a knife to remove air pockets. Bake on the lowest oven rack at 325° for 35-40 minutes or until cake springs back when lightly touched. Immediately invert pan; cool completely.

In a large bowl, beat cream until it begins to thicken. Add the confectioners' sugar and vanilla; beat until stiff peaks form.

Run a knife around sides and center tube of pan; remove cake. Cut into three horizontal layers. Place one layer on a serving plate; top with some of the whipped cream and sliced strawberries. Repeat. Top with remaining cake layer; spread remaining whipped cream over top and sides of cake. Arrange remaining sliced berries on sides of cake.

Cut whole berries in half; arrange on cake top. Store in the refrigerator.
YIELD: 12 servings.

agnes deleon
MELROSE, MONTANA

I can't tell you how many times I've made everyone ooh and aah when they see this beautiful dessert. It is wonderful for just about any occasion.

BERRY-TOPPED WHITE CUPCAKES

PREP: 30 min. | **BAKE:** 20 min. + cooling

5 egg whites

1/2 cup plus 2 tablespoons butter, softened

1 cup sugar, *divided*

3/4 teaspoon vanilla extract

2-1/4 cups cake flour

2-1/4 teaspoons baking powder

1/2 teaspoon salt

3/4 cup milk

ICING:

4 ounces cream cheese, softened

1/3 cup butter, softened

2 cups confectioners' sugar

1/2 teaspoon lemon juice

Assorted fresh fruit

Place egg whites in a large bowl; let stand at room temperature for 30 minutes. In another bowl, cream butter and 3/4 cup sugar until light and fluffy. Beat in vanilla. Combine the flour, baking powder and salt; add to creamed mixture alternately with milk, beating well after each addition.

Beat egg whites on medium speed until soft peaks form. Gradually beat in remaining sugar, about 2 tablespoons at a time, on high until stiff glossy peaks form and sugar is dissolved. Fold a fourth of the egg whites into batter; fold in remaining whites.

With a spoon, gently fill foil– or paper-lined muffin cups two-thirds full. Bake at 350° for 18-22 minutes. Cool for 10 minutes before removing from pans to wire racks to cool completely.

For icing, in a small bowl, beat cream cheese and butter until smooth. Gradually beat in confectioners' sugar and lemon juice. Spread over cupcakes. Top with fruit.

YIELD: 22 cupcakes.

judith kenninger
BROWNSBURG, INDIANA

Guests just love these yummy white cupcakes that are topped with a cream cheese frosting. The strawberry-blueberry garnish makes them a perfect treat for a patriotic-themed party on Memorial Day or the Fourth of July.

CREAM CHEESE BROWNIES

PREP: 20 min. | **BAKE:** 35 min. + cooling

2 packages (8 ounces *each*) cream cheese, softened

2 cups sugar, *divided*

3 tablespoons milk

1 cup butter, softened

2/3 cup instant hot cocoa mix

4 eggs

2 teaspoons vanilla extract

1-1/2 cups all-purpose flour

1 cup chopped nuts

In a small bowl, beat the cream cheese, 1/2 cup sugar and milk until fluffy; set aside. In a large bowl, cream the butter, cocoa mix and remaining sugar until light and fluffy. Beat in eggs and vanilla. Stir in flour and nuts and mix well.

Pour half into a greased 13-in. x 9-in. baking pan. Spread with the cream cheese mixture. Top with remaining batter. Cut through batter with a knife to swirl the cream cheese.

Bake at 350° for 35-40 minutes or until a toothpick inserted near the center comes out clean. Cool on a wire rack. Cut into bars.
YIELD: 2-1/2 dozen.

carolyn reed
NORTH ROBINSON, OHIO

A good friend from church shared this recipe with me. Cream cheese lends itself well in these moist and chewy brownies that are finger-lickin' good!

ORANGE SPONGE CAKE

PREP: 40 min. | **BAKE:** 45 min. + cooling

amy sauser
OMAHA, NEBRASKA

6 eggs, *separated*
1-1/3 cups cake flour
1-1/2 cups sugar, *divided*
1/4 teaspoon salt
1/2 cup orange juice
3 teaspoons grated orange peel
3/4 teaspoon cream of tartar

GLAZE:
1/3 cup butter, cubed
2 cups confectioners' sugar
3 to 5 teaspoons water
1-1/2 teaspoons vanilla extract

Place egg whites in a large bowl; let stand at room temperature for 30 minutes. Sift the flour, 1/3 cup sugar and salt together twice; set aside.

In another bowl, beat egg yolks on high speed for 5 minutes or until thick and lemon-colored. Gradually beat in 2/3 cup sugar. Add orange juice and peel; beat 3 minutes longer. Gradually add flour mixture and mix well.

Add cream of tartar to egg whites; beat on medium speed until soft peaks form. Gradually beat in the remaining sugar, 1 tablespoon at a time, on high until stiff peaks form. Fold into batter.

Gently spoon into an ungreased 10-in. tube pan. Cut through batter with a knife to remove air pockets. Bake on the lowest oven rack at 325° for 45-55 minutes or until cake springs back when lightly touched. Immediately invert pan; cool completely, about 1 hour.

Run a knife around sides and center tube of pan. Remove cake to a serving plate. For glaze, melt butter in a small saucepan; remove from the heat. Add confectioners' sugar, water and vanilla; stir until smooth. Pour over cake, allowing it to drizzle down sides.

YIELD: 12 servings.

My dad requested this cake every year for his birthday. For a wedding present, my Aunt Marilyn included this cherished recipe in a family cookbook she made for me.

BOSTON CREAM PIE

PREP: 45 min. + chilling | **BAKE:** 1 hour

clara honeyager
MUKWONAGO, WISCONSIN

4 packages (18-1/4 ounces *each*) yellow cake mix
11 cups cold milk
4 packages (5.1 ounces *each*) instant vanilla pudding mix
4 jars (16 ounces *each*) hot fudge ice cream topping, warmed
96 maraschino cherries with stems, optional

Prepare and bake cakes according to package directions, using four greased 13-in. x 9-in. baking pans. Cool completely on wire racks.

Meanwhile, in a large bowl, beat milk and pudding mixes on low for 2-3 minutes. Cover and chill for at least 30 minutes. Cut each cake into 24 pieces; split each piece horizontally. Place about 1 heaping tablespoon of pudding between layers. Spread each with 1 tablespoon fudge topping and garnish with a cherry if desired.

YIELD: 96 servings.

This classic dessert can be made without much fuss. It's pretty and tasty, and it's always quickly gobbled up at picnics and potlucks.

OLD-FASHIONED JAM CAKE

PREP: 25 min. + standing | **BAKE:** 40 min. + cooling

- 1 cup raisins
- 1 can (8 ounces) crushed pineapple, undrained
- 1 cup butter, softened
- 1 cup sugar
- 4 eggs
- 3 cups all-purpose flour
- 1/3 cup baking cocoa
- 1 teaspoon baking soda
- 1 teaspoon ground cinnamon
- 1 teaspoon ground nutmeg
- 1/2 teaspoon ground cloves
- 1 jar (12 ounces) *or* 1 cup blackberry jam
- 2/3 cup buttermilk
- 1 cup chopped pecans

CARAMEL ICING:
- 1 cup butter, cubed
- 2 cups packed brown sugar
- 1/2 cup 2% milk
- 3-1/2 to 4 cups confectioners' sugar

In a small bowl, combine the raisins and pineapple; let stand for at least 30 minutes.

In a large bowl, cream butter and sugar until light and fluffy. Add eggs, one at a time, beating well after each addition. Combine dry ingredients; gradually add to creamed mixture alternately with jam and buttermilk, beating well after each addition. Stir in raisin mixture and nuts.

Spread into two greased and floured 9-in. round baking pans. Bake at 350° for 40-45 minutes or until a toothpick inserted near the center comes out clean. Cool for 10 minutes before removing from pans to wire racks to cool completely.

For icing, in a large saucepan, melt butter over medium heat. Stir in brown sugar and milk. Bring to a boil. Remove from the heat; cool until just warm. Pour into a large bowl; beat in enough confectioners' sugar to achieve a spreading consistency. Spread frosting between layers and over the top and sides of cake.

YIELD: 12-16 servings.

janet robinson
LAWRENCEBURG, KENTUCKY

I remember my Aunt Murna telling me she made this cake often when she was a young girl. Through the years, she made improvements to it, and her cake become a real family favorite. It has

RANGER COOKIES

PREP: 25 min. | **BAKE:** 10 min./batch

- 1 cup shortening
- 1 cup sugar
- 1 cup packed brown sugar
- 2 eggs
- 1 teaspoon vanilla extract
- 2 cups all-purpose flour
- 1 teaspoon baking soda
- 1/2 teaspoon baking powder
- 1/2 teaspoon salt
- 2 cups quick-cooking oats
- 2 cups crisp rice cereal
- 1 cup flaked coconut

In a large bowl, cream the shortening and sugars until light and fluffy. Beat in eggs and vanilla. Combine the flour, baking soda, baking powder and salt; gradually add to creamed mixture and mix well. Stir in the oats, cereal and coconut.

Drop by rounded tablespoonfuls 2 in. apart onto ungreased baking sheets. Bake at 350° for 7-9 minutes or until golden brown. Remove to wire racks.

YIELD: 7-1/2 dozen.

mary lou boyce
WILMINGTON, DELAWARE

These golden-brown cookies are crispy on the outside and cake-like on the inside. The recipe yields a large batch, so it's the perfect treat to send with the kids to school, camp or any gathering with friends.

DRY ingredients

Spoon dry ingredients such as flour, sugar or cornmeal into a dry measuring cup over a canister or waxed paper. Fill the cup to overflowing, then level by sweeping a metal spatula across the top.

SPECIAL PLEASURE CHOCOLATE CHEESECAKE

PREP: 20 min. | **BAKE:** 40 min. + chilling

- 1 package (18 ounces) ready-to-bake refrigerated triple-chocolate cookie dough
- 1 package (8 ounces) milk chocolate toffee bits
- 1 package (9-1/2 ounces) Dove dark chocolate candies
- 3 packages (8 ounces *each*) cream cheese, softened
- 1 can (14 ounces) sweetened condensed milk
- 3/4 cup (6 ounces) vanilla yogurt
- 4 eggs, lightly beaten
- 1 teaspoon vanilla extract

Whipped cream

Let dough stand at room temperature for 5-10 minutes to soften. Press nine portions of dough into an ungreased 13-in. x 9-in. baking dish (save remaining dough for another use). Set aside 2 tablespoons toffee bits for garnish; sprinkle remaining toffee bits over dough.

In a small microwave-safe bowl, heat chocolate candies at 70% power for 15 seconds; stir. Microwave in 5-second intervals until melted; stir until smooth.

In a large bowl, beat the cream cheese, milk and yogurt until smooth. Add eggs; beat on low speed just until combined. Fold in vanilla and melted chocolate. Pour over the crust.

Bake at 350° for 40-45 minutes or until center is almost set. Cool on a wire rack. Refrigerate for 4 hours or overnight. Garnish with whipped cream and reserved toffee bits. Refrigerate leftovers.

YIELD: 24 servings.

benjamin & sue ellen clark
WARSAW, NEW YORK

When I have time, I enjoy making cheesecakes. I love this fail-proof dessert because it's so easy to prepare and has just the right mix of ingredients to make it a special pleasure at any celebration.

CHOCOLATE-PEANUT BUTTER CUPCAKES

PREP: 30 min. | **BAKE:** 20 min. + cooling

> 1 package (18-1/4 ounces) chocolate cake mix
> 1-1/4 cups water
> 1/2 cup peanut butter
> 1/3 cup canola oil
> 3 eggs
> 24 miniature peanut butter cups

FROSTING:

> 6 ounces semisweet chocolate, chopped
> 2/3 cup heavy whipping cream
> 1/3 cup peanut butter
> Additional miniature peanut butter cups, chopped

In a large bowl, combine the cake mix, water, peanut butter, oil and eggs; beat on low speed for 30 seconds. Beat on medium for 2 minutes or until smooth.

Fill paper-lined muffin cups half full. Place a peanut butter cup in the center of each cupcake. Cover each cupcake with 1 tablespoonful batter.

Bake at 350° for 18-22 minutes or until a toothpick inserted near the center comes out clean. Cool for 10 minutes before removing from pans to wire racks to cool completely.

Place chocolate in a small bowl. In a small saucepan, bring cream just to a boil. Pour over chocolate; whisk until smooth. Stir in peanut butter. Cool, stirring occasionally, to room temperature or until ganache reaches a spreading consistency, about 10 minutes.

Spread over cupcakes; immediately sprinkle with additional peanut butter cups. Let stand until set.

YIELD: 2 dozen.

taste of home test kitchen

Chocolate and peanut butter connoisseurs will give these luscious bites a thumbs up! This classic combination makes them a welcome addition to any party or celebration.

CHEESE-FILLED SHORTBREAD TARTLETS

PREP: 25 min. + chilling | **BAKE:** 20 min./batch + cooling

1 package (8 ounces) cream cheese, softened
1 cup sweetened condensed milk
1/3 cup lemon juice
1 teaspoon vanilla extract
1 cup butter, softened
1-1/2 cups all-purpose flour
1/2 cup confectioners' sugar
1 tablespoon cornstarch
Fresh raspberries and mint sprigs, optional

In a small bowl, beat cream cheese until smooth. Gradually beat in the milk, lemon juice and vanilla. Cover and refrigerate for 8 hours or overnight.

In another bowl, beat the butter, flour, confectioners' sugar and cornstarch until smooth. Roll into 1-in. balls. Place in greased miniature muffin cups; press onto the bottom and up the sides. Prick with a fork.

Bake at 325° for 20-25 minutes or until golden brown. Immediately run a knife around each tart to loosen completely. Cool in pans on wire racks.

Pipe or spoon 1 tablespoon cheese filling into each tart shell. Cover and refrigerate until set. Just before serving, garnish with raspberries and mint if desired.
YIELD: 3 dozen.

cathy walerius
MOUND, MINNESOTA

These bite-size treats are a nice addition to a dessert buffet. You can store baked unfilled tart shells in an airtight container at room temperature overnight or in the freezer for a few weeks.

COOKIES FOR A CROWD

PREP: 20 min. | **BAKE:** 10 min./batch

4 cups shortening
4 cups peanut butter
4 cups packed brown sugar
4 cups sugar
8 eggs
4 teaspoons vanilla extract
10 cups all-purpose flour
4 teaspoons baking soda
4 teapoons salt
1 cup chopped salted peanuts, optional

In a large bowl, cream the shortening, peanut butter and sugars until light and fluffy. Add the eggs one, at a time, beating well after each addition. Stir in vanilla. Combine the flour, baking soda and salt; add to creamed mixture and mix well. Stir in peanuts if desired.

Drop by rounded teaspoonfuls 2 in. apart onto ungreased baking sheets. Flatten with a fork if desired. Bake at 350° for 10-12 minutes or until set.
YIELD: about 20 dozen.

mary green
MISHICOT, WISCONSIN

As a cook at a 4-H camp, I'm a pro at whipping up delectable treats to serve a crowd. My campers go wild over these crisp cookies with an excellent peanutty flavor.

POUND CAKE

PREP: 20 min. | **BAKE:** 1 hour + cooling

2 cups butter, softened
4 cups confectioners' sugar
6 eggs
1 teaspoon almond extract
3 cups all-purpose flour
1/2 teaspoon salt
Fresh raspberries and whipped cream, optional

In a large bowl, cream butter and confectioners' sugar until light and fluffy, about 5 minutes. Add eggs, one at a time, beating well after each addition. Stir in extract. Combine flour and salt; gradually add to creamed mixture. Beat just until combined.

Transfer to two greased 8-in. x 4-in. loaf pans. Bake at 325° for 60-70 minutes or until a toothpick inserted near the center comes out clean. Cool for 10 minutes before removing from pans to wire racks. Serve with raspberries and whipped cream if desired.
YIELD: 2 cakes (12 servings each).

margie dalton
CHICAGO, ILLINOIS

This pound cake is a treasured third generation family recipe. It's rich, buttery and has a lovely golden-brown crust.

CHOCOLATE-COVERED CHEESECAKE SQUARES

PREP: 1 hour | **BAKE:** 35 min. + freezing

1 cup graham cracker crumbs
1/4 cup finely chopped pecans
1/4 cup butter, melted

FILLING:
2 packages (8 ounces *each*) cream cheese, softened
1/2 cup sugar
1/4 cup sour cream
2 eggs, lightly beaten
1/2 teaspoon vanilla extract

COATING:
24 ounces semisweet chocolate, chopped
3 tablespoons shortening

Line a 9-in. square baking pan with foil and grease the foil. In a small bowl, combine the graham cracker crumbs, pecans and butter. Press into prepared pan; set aside.

In a large bowl, beat the cream cheese, sugar and sour cream until smooth. Add eggs; beat on low speed just until combined. Stir in vanilla. Pour over crust.

Bake at 325° for 35-40 minutes or until center is almost set. Cool on a wire rack. Refrigerate until chilled. Freeze overnight.

In a microwave, melt chocolate and shortening; stir until smooth. Cool slightly.

Using foil, lift cheesecake out of pan. Gently peel off foil; cut into 49 squares. Remove a few pieces at a time for dipping; keep remaining squares refrigerated until ready to dip.

Using a toothpick, completely dip squares, one at a time, in melted chocolate; allow excess to drip off. Place on waxed paper-lined baking sheets; spoon about 1 teaspoon chocolate over each. (Reheat chocolate if needed to finish dipping.) Let stand for 20 minutes or until set. Store in an airtight container in the refrigerator or freezer.

YIELD: 49 squares.

esther neustaeter
LA CRETE, ALBERTA

Satisfy your cheesecake craving with these bite-size delights! They're party favorites and perfect for holiday dessert trays.

PEANUT BUTTER 'N' JELLY BARS

PREP: 10 min. | **BAKE:** 15 min. + cooling

1 tube (16-1/2 ounces) refrigerated peanut butter cookie dough
1/2 cup peanut butter chips
1 can (16 ounces) buttercream frosting
1/4 cup creamy peanut butter
1/4 cup seedless raspberry jam *or* grape jelly

Let the dough stand at room temperature for 5-10 minutes to soften. Press dough into an ungreased 13-in. x 9-in. baking dish; sprinkle with peanut butter chips.

Bake at 375° for 15-18 minutes or until lightly browned and edges are firm to the touch. Cool on a wire rack.

In a small bowl, beat frosting and peanut butter until smooth. Spread over bars. Drop jam by teaspoonfuls over frosting; cut through frosting with a knife to swirl the jam.

YIELD: 2 dozen.

carolyn mulloy
DAVISON, MICHIGAN

My two young sons are crazy about these simple cookie bars. And as a busy on-the-go mom, no-fuss preparation makes this one scrumptious dessert I can rely on.

CHEESECAKE WITH RASPBERRY SAUCE

PREP: 1 hour | **BAKE:** 50 min. + chilling

1-3/4 cups graham cracker crumbs
1/4 cup sugar
1/3 cup butter, melted

FILLING:
5 packages (8 ounces *each*) cream cheese, softened
1 cup sugar
1 cup (8 ounces) sour cream
1/2 cup heavy whipping cream
2 teaspoons vanilla extract
7 eggs, lightly beaten

SAUCE/TOPPING:
1 package (12 ounces) frozen unsweetened raspberries, thawed
1/2 cup sugar
2 cups heavy whipping cream
1/2 cup confectioners' sugar
1 teaspoon vanilla extract

Place a greased 10-in. springform pan on a double thickness of heavy-duty foil (about 18 in. square). Securely wrap foil around pan.

In a small bowl, combine cracker crumbs and sugar; stir in the butter. Press onto the bottom and 1 in. up the sides of prepared pan. Place on a baking sheet. Bake at 350° for 5-8 minutes. Cool on a wire rack.

In a large bowl, beat cream cheese and sugar until smooth. Beat in the sour cream, heavy cream and vanilla. Add eggs; beat on low speed just until combined. Pour into crust. Place springform pan in a large baking pan; add 1 in. of hot water to larger pan.

Bake at 350° for 50-60 minutes or until center is just set and top appears dull. Remove springform pan from water bath. Cool on a wire rack for 10 minutes. Carefully run a knife around edge of pan to loosen. Cool 1 hour longer. Refrigerate overnight.

For sauce, place raspberries and sugar in a food processor; cover and process until blended. For topping, in a small bowl, beat heavy cream until it begins to thicken. Add confectioners' sugar and vanilla; beat until soft peaks form. Serve the cheesecake with raspberry sauce and topping.

YIELD: 16 servings.

jeanette volker
WALTON, NEBRASKA

It's a family tradition to make this delectable cheesecake as the finale for our Christmas dinner.

AVOID cracks

To prevent cracks in a cheesecake, avoid overbeating after adding the eggs; beat on low just until blended. Don't overbake. When done, the edges should be puffed; the center set but still soft. The center will firm upon cooling.

DOUBLE CHOCOLATE BARS

PREP/TOTAL TIME: 20 min.

1 package (16 ounces) cream-filled chocolate sandwich cookies, crushed

3/4 cup butter, melted

1 can (14 ounces) sweetened condensed milk

2 cups (12 ounces) miniature semisweet chocolate chips, *divided*

Combine cookie crumbs and butter; pat onto the bottom of an ungreased 13-in. x 9-in. baking pan.

In a microwave, melt the milk and 1 cup chocolate chips; stir until smooth. Pour over crust. Sprinkle with remaining chips.

Bake at 350° for 10-12 minutes or until chips begin to melt but do not lose their shape. Cool on a wire rack.

YIELD: about 4 dozen.

nancy clark
ZEIGLER, ILLINOIS

A friend brought these fudgy bars to a potluck a few years ago to tempt me with yet another chocolate treat. They are simple to make, and cleanup is a breeze. They're very rich, though, so be sure to cut them into bite-size pieces.

MARBLED CHOCOLATE PEANUT COOKIES

PREP: 20 min. | **BAKE:** 15 min./batch

PEANUT BUTTER DOUGH:
1 cup butter, softened
1 cup peanut butter
1-1/4 cups sugar
1-1/4 cups packed brown sugar
3 eggs
2 teaspoons vanilla extract
2-1/2 cups all-purpose flour
1/2 teaspoon baking soda
1/2 teaspoon salt
1 cup chopped peanuts

CHOCOLATE DOUGH:
1 cup butter, softened
1 cup packed brown sugar
3/4 cup sugar
3 eggs
2 teaspoons vanilla extract
2-1/2 cups all-purpose flour
1/2 cup baking cocoa
1/2 teaspoon baking soda
1/2 teaspoon salt
2 cups (12 ounces) semisweet chocolate chips

In a large bowl, cream the butter, peanut butter and sugars until light and fluffy. Add eggs, one at a time, beating well after each addition. Beat in vanilla. Combine the flour, baking soda and salt; gradually add to the creamed mixture and mix well. Stir in peanuts; set aside.

For the chocolate dough, in another bowl, cream the butter and sugars until light and fluffy. Add eggs, one at a time, beating well after each addition. Beat in the vanilla. Combine the flour, cocoa, baking soda and salt; gradually add to the creamed mixture and mix well. Stir in the chocolate chips. Gently fold in the peanut butter dough until slightly marbled.

Drop by heaping tablespoonfuls 3 in. apart onto greased baking sheets. Bake at 350° for 14-16 minutes or until lightly browned and firm. Remove to wire racks to cool completely.

YIELD: 9-1/2 dozen.

shirley de lange
BYRON CENTER, MICHIGAN

This recipe came about by accident when I was making both my husband's favorite peanut butter cookies and my favorite chocolate cookies. I had two small portions of dough left over and decided to combine them into one flavor-filled cookie. They were a hit!

CARAMEL PECAN BARS

PREP: 15 min. | **BAKE:** 20 min. + cooling

1 cup butter, cubed
2-1/4 cups packed brown sugar
2 eggs
2 teaspoons vanilla extract
1-1/2 cups all-purpose flour
2 teaspoons baking powder
2 cups chopped pecans
Confectioners' sugar, optional

In a large saucepan, heat butter and brown sugar over medium heat until the sugar is dissolved. In a small bowl, beat the eggs, vanilla and butter mixture. Combine flour and baking powder; gradually add to the butter mixture and mix well. Stir in pecans.

Spread into a greased 13-in. x 9-in. baking pan. Bake at 350° for 20-25 minutes or until a toothpick inserted near the center comes out with moist crumbs and edges are crisp. Cool on a wire rack. Dust with confectioners' sugar if desired. Cut into bars.

YIELD: 4 dozen.

emma manning
CROSSETT, ARKANSAS

This recipe won first place at a baking contest held where I work. These rich bars really capture the flavor of pecan pie.

NUTTY BUTTER MUNCHIES

PREP: 15 min. | **BAKE:** 10 min./batch

- 1 cup butter, softened
- 1/2 cup chunky peanut butter
- 1 cup sugar
- 1 cup packed brown sugar
- 3 eggs
- 1 teaspoon vanilla extract
- 1/2 teaspoon almond extract
- 3 cups all-purpose flour
- 1/2 teaspoon baking soda
- 1/2 teaspoon salt
- 1-1/2 cups chopped pecans
- 1/2 cup salted peanuts

In a large bowl, cream the butter, peanut butter and sugars until light and fluffy. Add eggs, one at a time, beating well after each addition. Beat in extracts. Combine the flour, baking soda and salt; gradually add to the creamed mixture and mix well. Stir in nuts.

Drop by tablespoonfuls 2 in. apart onto greased baking sheets. Flatten with a glass dipped in sugar. Bake at 350° for 10-12 minutes or until the edges are lightly browned. Remove to wire racks to cool.

YIELD: 8-1/2 dozen.

zenola frazier
TALLULAH, LOUISIANA

I developed this recipe for a crisp cookie to satisfy my sweet tooth. Everyone else loves them, too!

ZINFANDEL STRAWBERRY TRIFLE

PREP/TOTAL TIME: 25 min.

- 1-1/2 cups Zinfandel wine *or* grape juice
- 1/2 cup sugar, *divided*
- 1 quart fresh strawberries, sliced
- 1 teaspoon vanilla extract
- 2 loaves (10-3/4 ounces *each*) frozen pound cake, thawed
- 2 cups heavy whipping cream

Additional fresh strawberries

In a large saucepan, combine wine and 1/3 cup sugar. Bring to a boil; cook until liquid is reduced to about 1/2 cup. Set saucepan in ice water and stir the mixture for 3 minutes. Stir in strawberries and vanilla.

Meanwhile, cut one cake in half widthwise (save the other half for another use). Cube remaining cake; set aside.

In a small bowl, beat cream until it begins to thicken. Add remaining sugar; beat until soft peaks form.

In a 3-qt. trifle bowl or glass serving bowl, layer a third of the cake cubes, strawberry mixture and whipped topping. Repeat twice. Chill cake until serving. Garnish with the additional strawberries.

YIELD: 15 servings.

nicole clayton
PRESCOTT, ARIZONA

A friend gave me the recipe for this mouthwatering trifle. It's so easy to make and looks really special on a buffet table.

CHOCOLATE BLISS MARBLE CAKE

PREP: 40 min. | **BAKE:** 30 min. + cooling

5 egg whites
1/4 cup baking cocoa
1/4 cup hot water
1 cup sugar, *divided*
1 cup fat-free milk
3 tablespoons canola oil
1 teaspoon vanilla extract
3/4 teaspoon almond extract
2-1/2 cups all-purpose flour
3 teaspoons baking powder
1/2 teaspoon salt
1-1/2 cups reduced-fat whipped topping
4 ounces semisweet chocolate
1-1/2 cups fresh raspberries

Let egg whites stand at room temperature for 30 minutes. Dissolve cocoa in water; let stand until cool.

In a large bowl, beat 3/4 cup sugar, milk, oil and extracts until well blended. Combine the flour, baking powder and salt; gradually beat into sugar mixture until blended.

In another bowl with clean beaters, beat egg whites on medium speed until soft peaks form. Beat in remaining sugar, 1 tablespoon at a time, on high until stiff peaks form. Gradually fold into batter. Remove 2 cups batter; stir in reserved cocoa mixture.

Coat a 10-in. fluted tube pan with cooking spray. Alternately spoon the plain and chocolate batters into pan. Cut through batter with a knife to swirl.

Bake at 350° for 30-35 minutes or until a toothpick inserted near the center comes out clean. Cool for 10 minutes before removing from pan to a wire rack to cool completely.

For topping, in a microwave, melt whipped topping and chocolate; stir until smooth.

Place cake on a serving plate. Drizzle with topping. Arrange raspberries in center of cake.
YIELD: 16 servings.

josephine piro
EASTON, PENNSYLVANIA

This cake is served at all of our family parties. It's low in fat, but tastes delicious.

FLUTED tube cakes

Fluted tube pans should be well greased and floured before adding the batter. After the cake tests done, transfer the pan to a wire rack and allow to cool for only 10 minutes before removing the cake from the pan.

LEMON CHIFFON CAKE

PREP: 25 min. | **BAKE:** 50 min. + cooling

    7 eggs, *separated*
    2 cups all-purpose flour
1-1/2 cups sugar
    3 teaspoons baking powder
    1 teaspoon salt
  3/4 cup water
  1/2 cup canola oil
    4 teaspoons grated lemon peel
    2 teaspoons vanilla extract
  1/2 teaspoon cream of tartar

LEMON FROSTING:
  1/3 cup butter, softened
    3 cups confectioners' sugar
4-1/2 teaspoons grated lemon peel
Dash salt
  1/4 cup lemon juice

Place egg whites in a large bowl; let stand at room temperature for 30 minutes.

In another bowl, combine the flour, sugar, baking powder and salt. Whisk the egg yolks, water, oil, lemon peel and vanilla; add to dry ingredients and beat until well blended. Add cream of tartar to egg whites; beat on medium speed until soft peaks form. Fold into batter.

Gently spoon into an ungreased 10-in. tube pan. Cut through batter with a knife to remove air pockets. Bake on the lowest oven rack at 325° for 50-55 minutes or until the top springs back when lightly touched. Immediately invert pan; cool completely, about 1 hour.

Run a knife around sides and center tube of pan. Remove cake to a serving plate. In a small bowl, combine frosting ingredients; beat until smooth. Frost top of cake.
YIELD: 12-16 servings.

trisha kammers
CLARKSTON, WASHINGTON

This light, airy cake was my dad's top choice for birthdays and other celebrations. The lemon frosting on top makes it over-the-top indulgent.

CARROT CAKE BARS

PREP: 35 min. | **BAKE:** 20 min. + cooling

 3 eggs
1-1/4 cups canola oil
 2 cups all-purpose flour
 2 cups sugar
 2 teaspoons ground cinnamon
 1 teaspoon baking powder
 1/2 teaspoon baking soda
 1/4 to 1/2 teaspoon salt
 1 jar (6 ounces) carrot baby food
 1 container (3-1/2 ounces) applesauce
   baby food
 1 container (3-1/2 ounces) apricot
   baby food
 1/2 cup chopped walnuts, optional

FROSTING:
 1 package (8 ounces) cream cheese,
   softened
 1/2 cup butter, softened
 1 teaspoon vanilla extract
3-3/4 cups confectioners' sugar

In a large bowl, beat the eggs and oil for 2 minutes. Combine the flour, sugar, cinnamon, baking powder, baking soda and salt; add to egg mixture. Add baby foods; mix well. Stir in walnuts if desired. Transfer to a greased 15-in. x 10-in. x 1-in. baking pan.

Bake at 350° for 20-25 minutes or until a toothpick inserted near the center comes out clean. Cool on a wire rack.

For frosting, in a small bowl, beat cream cheese and butter until light and fluffy. Beat in vanilla. Gradually beat in confectioners' sugar. Frost cake and cut into bars. Store in the refrigerator.

YIELD: 3 dozen.

agnes ward
STRATFORD, ONTARIO

A friend served these moist, tender cake bars at an outdoor party, and everyone raved about the taste. I'll often bake a big panful and freeze some for those days when I crave something sweet.

HONEY MAPLE COOKIES

PREP: 20 min. | **BAKE:** 10 min./batch

 1 cup shortening
 3/4 cup honey
 3/4 cup maple syrup
 2 eggs
 1 teaspoon vanilla extract
2-1/2 cups all-purpose flour
 1 teaspoon baking soda
 1 teaspoon salt
 2 cups (12 ounces) semisweet chocolate
   chips
 1 cup chopped pecans

In a large bowl, beat shortening until light and fluffy. Add honey and syrup, a little at a time, beating well after each addition. Add eggs, one at a time, beating well after each addition (mixture will appear curdled). Beat in vanilla. Combine the flour, baking soda and salt. Gradually add to honey mixture and mix just until moistened. Stir in the chocolate chips and pecans.

Drop by rounded tablespoonfuls onto greased baking sheets. Bake at 350° for 8-10 minutes or until golden brown. Remove to wire racks.

YIELD: 5 dozen.

barbara kuder
TRIBUNE, KANSAS

Honey and maple syrup make these chocolate chip cookies stand out from the rest. They're always a welcome treat at classroom and charity bake sales.

CLASSIC CARROT CAKE

PREP: 30 min. | **BAKE:** 35 min. + cooling

- 1 can (8 ounces) unsweetened crushed pineapple
- 2 cups shredded carrots
- 4 eggs
- 1 cup sugar
- 1 cup packed brown sugar
- 1 cup canola oil
- 2 cups all-purpose flour
- 2 teaspoons baking soda
- 2 teaspoons ground cinnamon
- 1/4 teaspoon salt
- 3/4 cup chopped walnuts

FROSTING:
- 2 packages (8 ounces *each*) cream cheese, softened
- 1/4 cup butter, softened
- 2 teaspoons vanilla extract
- 1-1/2 cups confectioners' sugar

Drain pineapple, reserving 2 tablespoons juice (discard remaining juice or save for another use). In a large bowl, beat the carrots, eggs, sugars, oil, pineapple and reserved juice until well blended. In a small bowl, combine the flour, baking soda, cinnamon and salt; gradually beat into pineapple mixture until blended. Stir in the chopped walnuts.

Transfer to a greased 13-in. x 9-in. baking dish. Bake at 350° for 35-40 minutes or until a toothpick inserted near the center comes out clean. Cool on a wire rack.

For frosting, in a large bowl, beat cream cheese and butter until smooth. Beat in vanilla. Gradually beat in confectioners' sugar until smooth. Spread over cake.

YIELD: 12 servings.

cheri eby
GUNNISON, COLORADO

You'll love the texture and flavor in this pretty, moist cake. The cream cheese frosting adds just the right amount of sweetness.

STICKY situation

To easily remove marshmallow creme from a jar, place the jar in a pan of very hot water. When cool, replace the water once or twice, then spoon out with a wooden spoon.

S'MORE BARS

PREP: 20 min. | **BAKE:** 25 min. + cooling

- 1/2 cup butter, softened
- 3/4 cup sugar
- 1 egg
- 1 teaspoon vanilla extract
- 1-1/3 cups all-purpose flour
- 3/4 cup graham cracker crumbs
- 1 teaspoon baking powder
- 1/8 teaspoon salt
- 5 milk chocolate candy bars (1.55 ounces *each*)
- 1 cup marshmallow creme

In a large bowl, cream the butter and sugar until light and fluffy. Add egg and vanilla; beat well. Combine the flour, cracker crumbs, baking powder and salt; gradually add to the creamed mixture. Set aside 1/2 cup for the topping.

Press remaining mixture into a greased 9-in. square baking pan. Place candy bars over crust; spread with marshmallow creme. Crumble remaining graham cracker mixture over top.

Bake at 350° for 25-30 minutes or until golden brown. Cool on a wire rack. Cut into bars. Store in an airtight container.

YIELD: 1-1/2 dozen.

lisa moriarty
WILTON, NEW HAMPSHIRE

Once school starts, it can be hard for kids to let go of summer. But these rich, gooey, great-tasting bars will bring back sweet campfire memories—and smiles—whether they're served for dessert or as an after-school snack.

JAM-TOPPED MINI CHEESECAKES

PREP/TOTAL TIME: 30 min. + chilling

1 cup graham cracker crumbs
3 tablespoons butter, melted
1 package (8 ounces) cream cheese, softened
1/3 cup sugar
1 teaspoon vanilla extract
1 egg, lightly beaten
Assorted jams, warmed

In a small bowl, combine graham cracker crumbs and butter. Press gently onto the bottom of 12 paper-lined muffin cups. In another small bowl, beat the cream cheese, sugar and vanilla until smooth. Add the egg; beat on low until just combined. Spoon over the crusts.

Bake at 350° for 15-16 minutes or until center is set. Cool for 10 minutes before removing from pan to a wire rack to cool completely. Refrigerate for at least 1 hour.

Remove paper liners; top each cheesecake with 1 teaspoon jam.

YIELD: 1 dozen.

taste of home test kitchen

Presto! Our expert home economists turned luscious cheesecake into finger food in just 15 minutes. For fun, experiment with other types of jams and preserves such as strawberry or apricot.

BERRY CREAM PIE

PREP: 15 min. | **COOK:** 15 min. + chilling

FILLING:
1/2 cup sugar
3 tablespoons cornstarch
3 tablespoons all-purpose flour
1/2 teaspoon salt
2 cups 2% milk
1 egg, lightly beaten
1/2 teaspoon vanilla extract
1/2 teaspoon almond extract, optional
1/2 cup heavy whipping cream
1 pastry shell (9 inches), baked

GLAZE:
1/2 cup crushed strawberries
1/2 cup water
1/4 cup sugar
2 teaspoons cornstarch
1-1/2 cups quartered strawberries
1-1/2 cups fresh raspberries

In a large saucepan, combine the sugar, cornstarch, flour and salt; gradually stir in milk until smooth. Cook and stir over medium-high heat until thickened and bubbly. Reduce heat; cook and stir 2 minutes more.

Remove from the heat and stir a small amount of hot filling into egg; return all to the saucepan, stirring constantly. Bring to a gentle boil; cook and stir for 2 minutes. Remove from the heat; gently stir in vanilla and almond extract if desired. Cool to room temperature.

In a small bowl, beat cream until stiff peaks form; fold into filling. Pour into pastry shell. Chill for at least 2 hours.

About 2 hours before serving, prepare glaze. In a large saucepan, combine crushed strawberries and water; cook for 2 minutes. Combine sugar and cornstarch; gradually add to the pan. Cook and stir until thickened and clear; strain. Cool for 20 minutes.

Meanwhile, arrange quartered strawberries and raspberries over filling; pour glaze evenly over berries. Refrigerate for 1 hour.

YIELD: 8 servings.

sue yaeger
BOONE, IOWA

I found this recipe in a very old cookbook, and I made it for a family gathering. The pie was gone in no time. It's a perfect summertime treat.

RASPBERRY CHOCOLATE CAKE

PREP: 45 min. + standing | **BAKE:** 35 min. + cooling

- 3 cups sugar
- 2-3/4 cups all-purpose flour
- 1 cup baking cocoa
- 2 teaspoons baking soda
- 1-1/2 teaspoons salt
- 3/4 teaspoon baking powder
- 1-1/4 cups buttermilk
- 3/4 cup canola oil
- 3 teaspoons vanilla extract
- 3 eggs
- 1-1/2 cups strong brewed coffee, room temperature

FILLING:
- 3 tablespoons all-purpose flour
- 6 tablespoons milk
- 6 tablespoons shortening
- 3 tablespoons butter, softened
- 3 cups confectioners' sugar
- 2 tablespoons raspberry liqueur
- 1/4 teaspoon salt
- 2 drops red food coloring, optional
- 4 tablespoons seedless raspberry jam, melted

FROSTING:
- 1 package (8 ounces) cold cream cheese
- 1/3 cup butter, softened
- 1/2 cup baking cocoa
- 1 tablespoon raspberry liqueur
- 4 cups confectioners' sugar

Line three greased 9-in. round baking pans with waxed paper and grease paper; set aside. In a large bowl, combine the first six ingredients. Combine the buttermilk, oil and vanilla; add to the dry ingredients. Add eggs, one at a time, beating well after each addition; beat for 2 minutes. Gradually add coffee (batter will be thin).

Pour batter into prepared pans. Bake at 350° for 35-40 minutes or until a toothpick inserted near the center comes out clean. Cool for 10 minutes before removing from pans to wire racks to cool completely; discard waxed paper.

For filling, in a small saucepan, whisk together flour and milk until smooth. Cook over medium heat for 1 minute or until thickened, stirring constantly. Remove from the heat and let stand until cool.

In a large bowl, cream shortening and butter until light and fluffy. Gradually add confectioners' sugar and mix well. Gradually add cooled milk mixture; beat for 4 minutes or until light and fluffy. Beat in liqueur, salt and food coloring if desired.

Level tops of cakes if necessary. Place one layer on a serving plate; spread with about 2 tablespoons jam. Place remaining layers on waxed paper; spread one of the remaining layers with remaining jam. Let cake stand for 30 minutes.

Spread 1/2 cup filling over cake on the plate to within 1/4 in. of edges. Top with jam-covered cake, then spread with remaining filling. Top with remaining cake layer.

In a large bowl, beat cream cheese and butter until smooth. Beat in cocoa and liqueur. Gradually beat in confectioners' sugar until light and fluffy. Frost top and sides of cake. Store in the refrigerator.

YIELD: 16 servings.

marlene sanders
PARADISE, TEXAS

I get rave reviews whenever I make this cake. The layers are so impressive, and the raspberry filling is heavenly.

CAKE layers

Stacking layers for a layered cake is easier when they are level. When the cake is cool, use a long serrated knife to slice the high spot from the bottom layer of the two-layer or the bottom and middle layers of a three-layer cake. You can trim off the crown of the top layer or leave it for a domed effect.

PECAN PIE FOR A CROWD

PREP: 15 min. | **BAKE:** 40 min. + cooling

- 12 eggs, lightly beaten
- 1 cup dark brown sugar
- 5 cups sugar
- 2 cups dark corn syrup
- 1-1/3 cups honey
- 1 cup butter, melted
- 3 tablespoons vanilla extract
- 12 to 15 cups chopped pecans
- 8 unbaked pastry shells (9 inches)

In large bowls, combine the first seven ingredients. Add pecans. Pour 2-1/4 cups filling into each pastry shell.

Bake at 300° for 40-50 minutes or until set (cover the edges with foil during the last 15 minutes to prevent overbrowning if necessary). Cool on a wire rack. Refrigerate any leftovers.

YIELD: 8 pies (8 servings each).

louise covington
BENNETTSVILLE, SOUTH CAROLINA

Honey gives these pies a unique delicious flavor. I sometimes add chocolate for a special twist. This will be your go-to recipe when you need a fantastic dessert to feed a crowd!

BLACK WALNUT BROWNIES

PREP: 10 min. | **BAKE:** 30 min. + cooling

- 1 cup sugar
- 1/4 cup canola oil
- 2 eggs
- 1 teaspoon vanilla extract
- 1/2 cup all-purpose flour
- 2 tablespoons baking cocoa
- 1/2 teaspoon salt
- 1/2 cup chopped black walnuts

In a small bowl, beat sugar and oil until blended. Beat in eggs and vanilla. Combine the flour, cocoa and salt; gradually add to sugar mixture and mix well. Stir in walnuts.

Pour into a greased 8-in. square baking pan. Bake at 350° for 30-35 minutes or until a toothpick inserted near the center comes out clean. Cool on a wire rack.

YIELD: 16 servings.

catherine berra bleem
WALSH, ILLINOIS

These brownies, studded with big chunks of black walnuts, are crisp on top and chewy inside. Our friends have given this treat rave reviews, especially those who live in areas where black walnuts are hard to find.

MINTY CREAM CHEESE BARS

PREP: 25 min. | **BAKE:** 25 min. + cooling

- 2 cups (12 ounces) semisweet chocolate chips
- 6 tablespoons butter, cubed
- 3/4 teaspoon mint extract
- 2 cups crushed cream-filled chocolate sandwich cookies (about 20 cookies)
- 2 cups chopped walnuts
- 2 packages (8 ounces *each*) cream cheese, softened
- 1/2 cup sugar
- 4 eggs
- 2 tablespoons cold brewed coffee
- 1/4 cup all-purpose flour

paula marchesi
LENHARTSVILLE, PENNSYLVANIA

You're going to love the way chocolate and mint come together in these easy, creamy bars. They're sure to be family favorites!

MINT topping

Give these cheesecake-like bars a delicious new twist with a minty topping. Instead of sprinkling the bars with the reserved crumb mixture, melt 1 cup mint chocolate chips in the microwave. Stir the chips until cool. Once the bars have cooled, spread the melted chips over the top.

In a large microwave-safe bowl, melt the chocolate chips and butter; stir until smooth. Stir in the extract until smooth. Stir in cookie crumbs and walnuts (the mixture will be very moist).

Set aside 2 cups of the crumb mixture for topping. Press remaining crumb mixture onto the bottom of an ungreased 13-in. x 9-in. baking pan. Bake at 350° for 10-12 minutes or until lightly browned.

Meanwhile, in a large bowl, beat cream cheese and sugar until smooth. Add eggs, one at a time, beating well after each addition. Beat in coffee. Gradually add flour just until combined.

Spread over crust. Sprinkle with reserved crumb mixture. Bake for 25-27 minutes or until set. Cool on a wire rack. Cut into bars.

YIELD: about 2-1/2 dozen.

BACK-TO-SCHOOL COOKIES

PREP: 30 min. | BAKE: 10 min./batch

1 cup butter-flavored shortening
1 cup creamy peanut butter
2 cups packed brown sugar
4 egg whites
1 teaspoon vanilla extract
2 cups all-purpose flour
1 teaspoon baking soda
1/2 teaspoon baking powder
2 cups crisp rice cereal
1-1/2 cups chopped nuts
1 cup flaked coconut
1 cup quick-cooking oats

In a large bowl, cream the shortening, peanut butter and brown sugar until light and fluffy. Beat in egg whites and vanilla. Combine the flour, baking soda and baking powder; gradually add to creamed mixture and mix well. Stir in the cereal, nuts, coconut and oats.

Drop by rounded tablespoonfuls 2 in. apart onto ungreased baking sheets. Flatten the cookies with a fork, forming a crisscross pattern. Bake cookies at 375° for 7-8 minutes. Remove to wire racks.

YIELD: 6-1/2 dozen.

frances pierce
WADDINGTON, NEW YORK

Pull this recipe from your files the next time you need to send the kids off with a sweet treat to share with classmates. The peanut butter cookies are great for bake sales, too.

p. 289

p. 287

p. 301

seasonal
specialties

CANDY CORN CHEESE SPREAD

PREP: 15 min. | **BAKE:** 40 min. + standing

- 3/4 cup finely crushed yellow tortilla chips
- 2 tablespoons butter, melted
- 1 package (8 ounces) cream cheese, softened
- 4 tablespoons sour cream, *divided*
- 1 egg, lightly beaten
- 1 garlic clove, minced
- 3/4 teaspoon chili powder, *divided*
- 1/4 teaspoon ground cumin
- 1 can (4 ounces) chopped green chilies
- 1 cup (4 ounces) shredded Mexican cheese blend

Assorted crackers

Press parchment paper onto the bottom of a 1-qt. round baking dish. In a bowl, combine the crushed chips and butter; press into a prepared dish. Bake, uncovered, at 325° for 10 minutes.

Meanwhile, in a small bowl, combine the cream cheese, 2 tablespoons sour cream, egg, garlic, 1/4 teaspoon chili powder and cumin. Stir in the chilies and cheese blend. Spoon evenly over warm crust.

Bake at 325° for 40-45 minutes or until the top is lightly browned and a thermometer inserted near the center reads 160°. Let stand for 10 minutes; run a knife around edge and invert onto a serving platter. Carefully remove parchment paper.

Place remaining sour cream in a heavy-duty resealable plastic bag; cut a small hole in a corner of bag. Pipe a large candy corn shape; sprinkle with remaining chili powder. Serve with crackers.

YIELD: 2 cups.

taste of home test kitchen

This yummy cheese spread is perfect for Halloween gatherings. It can be served warm, at room temperature or even chilled. It has lots of Tex-Mex flavor that is sure to please your guests.

SWEET POTATO CASSEROLE

PREP: 45 min. | **BAKE:** 40 min.

- 6 medium sweet potatoes
- 1/2 cup butter, cubed
- 3/4 cup sugar
- 1 can (20 ounces) crushed pineapple, drained
- 2 eggs, beaten
- 1 teaspoon vanilla extract
- 1/2 teaspoon ground nutmeg
- 1/2 teaspoon salt
- 15 large marshmallows

Place sweet potatoes in a large kettle and cover with water; bring to a boil. Boil gently until potatoes can easily be pierced with the tip of a sharp knife, about 30-45 minutes. Drain; cool slightly.

Peel potatoes and place in a large bowl; mash. Stir in butter and sugar until butter is melted. Add pineapple, eggs, vanilla, nutmeg and salt.

Spoon into a greased 2-qt. baking dish. Top with marshmallows. Bake, uncovered, at 350° for 40-45 minutes or until a knife inserted near the center comes out clean.

YIELD: 8 servings.

ruth leach
SHREVEPORT, LOUISIANA

Pineapple, sugar and marshmallows lend a sweet touch to these spuds. I like to make this casserole for family get-togethers and special dinners at home.

PUMPKIN CHEESECAKE DELUXE

PREP: 35 min. | **BAKE:** 1 hour + chilling

- 3/4 cup chopped pecans, toasted
- 32 gingersnap cookies, coarsely crushed
- 3 tablespoons brown sugar
- 6 tablespoons butter, melted

FILLING:
- 3 packages (8 ounces *each*) cream cheese, softened
- 1 cup packed brown sugar
- 1-1/2 cups canned pumpkin
- 1/2 cup heavy whipping cream
- 1/4 cup maple syrup
- 3 teaspoons vanilla extract
- 1 teaspoon ground cinnamon
- 1/2 teaspoon ground ginger
- 1/4 teaspoon ground cloves
- 4 eggs, lightly beaten

Sweetened whipped cream, optional
Pecan brittle, optional

Place a greased 9-in. springform pan on a double thickness of heavy-duty foil; securely wrap foil around pan. Place pecans in a food processor; cover and process until ground. Add the gingersnaps, brown sugar and butter; cover and pulse until blended. Press onto the bottom and 2 in. up the sides of prepared pan; set aside.

In a large bowl, beat cream cheese and brown sugar until smooth. Beat in the pumpkin, cream, syrup, vanilla and spices. Add eggs; beat on low speed just until combined. Pour into crust. Place springform pan in a large baking pan; add 1 in. of hot water to larger pan.

Bake at 325° for 60-70 minutes or until center is just set and top appears dull. Remove pan from water bath. Cool on wire rack for 10 minutes. Carefully run a knife around edge of pan to loosen; cool 1 hour longer. Chill overnight.

Garnish with whipped cream and pecan brittle if desired.

YIELD: 12 servings.

andrea quiroz
CHICAGO, ILLINOIS

I developed this recipe out of my love for cheesecake and my family's love for pumpkin pie. I made it for Thanksgiving, and every morsel was devoured. They wished I had made two!

ROASTED GARLIC AND SWEET POTATO SOUP

PREP: 1 hour + cooling | **COOK:** 15 min.

1 whole garlic bulb

3 teaspoons olive oil, *divided*

2-1/2 pounds sweet potatoes (about 4 large), peeled and cut into 1/2-inch slices

2 large onions, cut into wedges

6 cups reduced-sodium chicken broth, *divided*

2 tablespoons minced fresh parsley

1 tablespoon minced fresh thyme *or* 1 teaspoon dried thyme

1/4 teaspoon salt

1/8 teaspoon pepper

Remove papery outer skin from garlic bulb (do not peel or separate cloves). Cut top off bulb; brush with 1/2 teaspoon oil. Wrap in heavy-duty foil.

Place the sweet potatoes and onions in a 15-in. x 10-in. x 1-in. baking pan coated with cooking spray. Drizzle with remaining oil; toss to coat.

Bake the garlic and vegetables at 425° for 30-35 minutes. Cool for 10-15 minutes.

Place 1-1/2 cups broth, parsley, thyme, salt and pepper in a blender. Squeeze softened garlic into mixture; cover and process until smooth. Transfer to a large saucepan.

In batches, process the sweet potatoes, onions and remaining broth until smooth; add to the garlic mixture. Cook, stirring occasionally, until heated through.

YIELD: 10 servings (2-1/2 quarts).

kathy rairigh
MILFORD, INDIANA

My garden produced a bumper crop of sweet potatoes so I created this recipe to help use them up. Your holiday guests will love the creamy texture and flavors of garlic and thyme in this warm soup.

HOLIDAY GREEN BEANS

PREP: 40 min. | **BAKE:** 15 min.

- 8 cups cut fresh green beans (about 2 pounds)
- 1/2 pound sliced fresh mushrooms
- 2 tablespoons butter
- 2 tablespoons all-purpose flour
- 1 teaspoon dried minced onion
- 1/2 teaspoon pepper
- 1/2 cup fat-free milk
- 1 cup reduced-fat sour cream
- 1 teaspoon Worcestershire sauce
- 1-1/2 cups (6 ounces) shredded reduced-fat Swiss cheese

TOPPING:
- 1/3 cup slivered almonds
- 1/3 cup crushed cornflakes
- 1 tablespoon butter, melted

Place the beans in a Dutch oven and cover with water; bring to a boil. Cover and cook for 3-5 minutes or until crisp-tender; drain and set aside.

In a large skillet, saute mushrooms in butter until tender. Stir in the flour, onion and pepper until blended. Gradually stir in milk. Bring to a boil; cook and stir for 1-2 minutes or until thickened. Remove from the heat; stir in sour cream and Worcestershire sauce. Stir in the beans and cheese until blended.

Transfer to an 11-in. x 7-in. baking dish coated with cooking spray (dish will be full). Combine topping ingredients; sprinkle over the top.

Bake, uncovered, at 400° for 12-16 minutes or until bubbly and heated through.

YIELD: 12 servings.

laura fall-sutton
BUHL, IDAHO

Try this perked-up green bean casserole this year, and you'll never go back to the old stuff. No one will ever know it's light!

FRIGHTFULLY GOOD CAKES

PREP: 50 min. + standing

- 1 loaf (10-3/4 ounces) frozen pound cake, thawed
- 1 can (16 ounces) vanilla frosting
- Green, orange and black paste food coloring
- 4 ounces white candy coating, chopped
- Halloween candies and miniature marshmallows

Level top of the cake; cut into 1/2-in. slices. Place on a wire rack over a baking sheet.

Spoon frosting into a microwave-safe bowl; microwave, uncovered, on high for 20 seconds. Stir; repeat until frosting no longer holds a peak. (Do not overheat.) Tint some of the frosting with green and/or orange food coloring. Slowly pour frosting over cakes, coating top and sides. If necessary, use frosting drippings and reheat. Let stand for 30 minutes or until set.

For words, melt white coating in a microwave-safe bowl; stir until smooth. Tint with food coloring. Transfer to a pastry or plastic bag; cut a hole in the corner of bag. Pipe words onto waxed paper. Let stand for 15 minutes or until set. Carefully remove from paper and position on cakes. Add faces, candies and marshmallows as desired.

YIELD: 14 servings.

taste of home test kitchen
If there is one word to describe these one- or two-bite cakes, it is EASY! Embellish them with a variety of colorful Halloween candies.

SAUSAGE CORN BREAD DRESSING

PREP: 30 min. | **BAKE:** 50 min.

1 cup all-purpose flour
1 cup cornmeal
1/4 cup sugar
3 teaspoons baking powder
1 teaspoon salt
1 cup buttermilk
1/4 cup unsweetened applesauce
2 egg whites

DRESSING:
1 pound turkey Italian sausage links, casings removed
4 celery ribs, chopped
1 medium onion, chopped
1 medium sweet red pepper, chopped
2 medium tart apples, chopped
1 cup chopped roasted chestnuts
3 tablespoons minced fresh parsley
2 garlic cloves, minced
1/2 teaspoon dried thyme
1/2 teaspoon pepper
1 cup reduced-sodium chicken broth
1 egg white

For the corn bread, combine the first five ingredients in a large bowl. Combine the buttermilk, applesauce and egg whites; stir into dry ingredients just until moistened.

Pour into an 8-in. square baking dish coated with cooking spray. Bake at 400° for 20-25 minutes or until a toothpick inserted near the center comes out clean. Cool on a wire rack.

In a large nonstick skillet, cook the sausage, celery, onion and red pepper over medium heat until meat is no longer pink; drain. Transfer to a large bowl. Crumble corn bread over mixture. Add the apples, chestnuts, parsley, garlic, thyme and pepper. Stir in broth and egg white.

Transfer to a 13-in. x 9-in. baking dish coated with cooking spray. Cover and bake at 325° for 40 minutes. Uncover; bake 10 minutes longer or until lightly browned.

YIELD: 16 servings.

rebecca baird
SALT LAKE CITY, UTAH

The phrases "holiday dinner" and "low-fat" are seldom used together, unless this corn bread stuffing is on the menu. Made with turkey sausage, herbs, fruit and veggies, this recipe lets you enjoy all the trimmings without any of the guilt.

EASY HALLOWEEN SLOPPY JOES

PREP: 5 min. | **COOK:** 45 min.

1 pound ground beef
1 large onion, chopped
1-1/2 cups ketchup
3/4 cup sweet pickle relish
1/2 cup packed brown sugar
8 hamburger buns, split
8 slices process American cheese
2 baby dill pickles, sliced

In a large skillet, cook beef and onion over medium heat until the meat is no longer pink; drain. Stir in the ketchup, relish and brown sugar. Cover and simmer for 30 minutes or until heated through.

Spoon over hamburger bun halves. Cut each slice of cheese diagonally. Cut one piece diagonally again. Use two smaller triangles as eyes and large triangle as mouth. Put 1 slice pickle on each eye.

YIELD: 8 servings.

patricia pidgeon
SYCAMORE, ILLINOIS

My grandma served these sandwiches every time I visited, and I continued the tradition when I had children of my own. My grandkids enjoy them now, too. The recipe calls for inexpensive ingredients, so it's great for a party.

CARAMEL APPLE MUFFINS

PREP: 25 min. | **BAKE:** 20 min.

- 2 cups all-purpose flour
- 3/4 cup sugar
- 2 teaspoons baking powder
- 2-1/2 teaspoons ground cinnamon
- 1/2 teaspoon salt
- 1 egg
- 1 cup 2% milk
- 1/4 cup butter, melted
- 2 teaspoons vanilla extract
- 1/2 cup chopped peeled tart apple
- 12 caramels, chopped

TOPPING:
- 1/2 cup packed brown sugar
- 1/4 cup quick-cooking oats
- 3 tablespoons butter, melted
- 1 teaspoon ground cinnamon

In a large bowl, combine the flour, sugar, baking powder, cinnamon and salt. In another bowl, whisk the egg, milk, butter and vanilla. Stir the mixture into the dry ingredients just until moistened. Fold in the apple and caramels.

Fill paper-lined muffin cups three-fourths full. Combine topping ingredients; sprinkle over batter.

Bake at 350° for 20-25 minutes or until a toothpick inserted in the cake portion comes out clean. Cool for 5 minutes before removing from pans to wire racks. Serve warm.
YIELD: 14 muffins.

therese puckett
SHREVEPORT, LOUISIANA

Anyone who loves caramel apples will love these muffins. They are terrific served with breakfast or simply with coffee.

HAUNTED POTPIE

PREP: 30 min. | **BAKE:** 50 min.

- 4 cups cubed cooked chicken
- 4 cups frozen cubed hash brown potatoes, thawed
- 1 package (16 ounces) frozen mixed vegetables, thawed and drained
- 1 can (10-3/4 ounces) condensed cream of chicken soup, undiluted
- 1 can (10-3/4 ounces) condensed cream of onion soup, undiluted
- 1 cup (8 ounces) sour cream
- 2/3 cup milk
- 2 tablespoons all-purpose flour
- 1/2 teaspoon salt
- 1/2 teaspoon pepper
- 1/4 teaspoon garlic powder
- 3 slices rye bread
- 1 sheet frozen puff pastry, thawed

In a large bowl, combine the first 11 ingredients. Transfer to a greased 13-in. x 9-in. baking dish. Place bread in a food processor, cover and process to make crumbs; sprinkle over chicken mixture. Bake at 350° for 40-45 minutes or until bubbly.

Meanwhile, on a lightly floured surface, unfold pastry sheet. Using a small floured ghost-shaped cookie cutter, cut out 12 ghosts. Place on an ungreased baking sheet. Remove potpie from the oven; set aside and keep warm. Bake ghosts at 400° for 10 minutes or until puffy and golden brown. Place on top of potpie; serve immediately.

YIELD: 12 servings.

taste of home test kitchen

Convenience items such as frozen hash browns, frozen veggies and puff pastry make this potpie quick and easy to make. The rye bread crumbs add an interesting twist.

PUMPKIN PIES FOR A GANG

PREP: 50 min. | **BAKE:** 1 hour + cooling

- 4 packages (15 ounces *each*) refrigerated pie pastry
- 16 eggs, lightly beaten
- 4 cans (29 ounces *each*) solid-pack pumpkin
- 1/2 cup dark corn syrup
- 9 cups sugar
- 1-1/4 cups all-purpose flour
- 1 cup nonfat dry milk powder
- 4 teaspoons salt
- 4 teaspoons *each* ground ginger, cinnamon and nutmeg
- 1 teaspoon ground cloves
- 8 cups 2% milk

Unroll pastry; line eight 9-in. pie plates with one sheet of pastry. Flute edges; set aside. In very large bowl, combine the eggs, pumpkin and corn syrup. In another large bowl, combine the dry ingredients; place half in each of two large bowls. Stir half of the pumpkin mixture into each bowl. Gradually stir in milk until smooth.

Pour into pie shells. Bake at 350° for 60-70 minutes or until a knife inserted near the center comes out clean. Cool on wire racks. Store in the refrigerator.

YIELD: 8 pies (6-8 servings each).

edna hoffman
HEBRON, INDIANA

When I think of cooking for a crowd this time of year, pumpkin pie always comes to mind. Guests love this traditional treat, and the recipe is perfect for a large gathering...it fills eight pie shells!

GINGERBREAD PUMPKIN TRIFLE

PREP: 35 min. | **BAKE:** 25 min. + chilling

- 1/2 cup shortening
- 1/3 cup sugar
- 1 cup molasses
- 1 egg
- 2-1/3 cups all-purpose flour
- 1 teaspoon baking soda
- 1 teaspoon ground ginger
- 1 teaspoon ground cinnamon
- 3/4 teaspoon salt
- 3/4 cup hot water

FILLING/TOPPING:
- 2 cups cold milk
- 1 package (3.4 ounces) instant vanilla pudding mix
- 1 can (15 ounces) solid-pack pumpkin
- 1/2 cup packed brown sugar
- 1 teaspoon vanilla extract
- 1/2 teaspoon ground cinnamon
- 2 cups heavy whipping cream
- 1/3 cup sugar
- 1 teaspoon rum extract

In a large bowl, cream shortening and sugar until light and fluffy. Beat in molasses and egg. Combine the flour, baking soda, ginger, cinnamon and salt; add to creamed mixture alternately with water, beating well after each addition.

Pour into a greased 13-in. x 9-in. baking pan. Bake at 350° for 25-30 minutes or until a toothpick inserted near center comes out clean. Cool on a wire rack. Cut gingerbread into 1/2-in. to 1-in. cubes; set aside.

In a large bowl, whisk milk and pudding mix for 2 minutes. Let stand for 2 minutes or until soft-set. Combine the pumpkin, brown sugar, vanilla and cinnamon; stir into pudding. In another bowl, beat cream until it begins to thicken. Add sugar and extract; beat until stiff peaks form.

Set aside 1/4 cup gingerbread cubes. In a 4-qt. trifle bowl or glass serving bowl, layer a third of the remaining gingerbread cubes; top with a third of the pumpkin mixture and whipped cream. Repeat the layers twice. Crumble reserved gingerbread; sprinkle over top. Cover and refrigerate for at least 1 hour before serving.

YIELD: 16 servings.

deborah hahn
BELLE, MISSOURI

I like to spice up special dinners with this dessert featuring two popular fall flavors. A fun and yummy alternative to pumpkin pie, this is my favorite potluck contribution. It will become yours, too!

CRIMSON CRANBERRY PUNCH

PREP: 20 min. + freezing

- 1/2 cup frozen cranberries
- 3-1/2 cups cold water
- 1 bottle (48 ounces) white grape juice, chilled
- 2 cans (12 ounces *each*) frozen cranberry juice concentrate, thawed
- 4 cans (12 ounces *each*) diet lemon-lime soda, chilled
- 3 orange slices
- 3 lemon slices

MAKING an ice ring

Fill a ring mold halfway with water. Freeze until solid. Top with your choice of fruit. Add enough water to almost cover fruit. Freeze until solid. Unmold by wrapping the bottom of the mold with a hot, damp dishcloth. Turn out onto a baking sheet; place in punch bowl fruit side up.

Place the cranberries in a 4-1/2-cup ring mold coated with cooking spray. Slowly pour a small amount of cold water into the mold to barely cover berries; freeze until solid. Add remaining water; freeze until solid.

Just before serving, combine grape juice and cranberry juice concentrate in a large punch bowl; stir in soda. Unmold ice ring; place the fruit side up in punch bowl. Add orange and lemon slices.

YIELD: 5 quarts.

judie white
FLORIEN, LOUISIANA

You can stir up this punch quickly because it calls for only a few ingredients. The pretty ice ring keeps it cold and refreshing.

FESTIVE BEAN 'N' PEPPER BUNDLES

PREP: 25 min. | **BAKE:** 15 min.

- 1 pound fresh green beans, trimmed
- 1 pound fresh wax beans, trimmed
- 2 tablespoons chicken bouillon granules
- 1/2 teaspoon garlic powder
- 3 medium zucchini
- 2 medium sweet red peppers, julienned
- 1/4 cup butter, melted

In a large saucepan, combine the beans, bouillon and garlic powder; cover with water. Bring to a boil. Cook, uncovered, for 8-10 minutes or until crisp-tender; drain.

Cut zucchini into 1/2-in. slices. Hollow out centers, leaving 1/4-in. rings; discard the centers. Thread beans and peppers through squash rings.

Place in a greased 15-in. x 10-in. x 1-in. baking pan; drizzle with butter. Cover and bake at 350° for 15-20 minutes or until zucchini is crisp-tender.

YIELD: 12-15 servings.

judith krucki
LAKE ORION, MICHIGAN

This is a beautiful way to prepare vegetables for a special holiday meal. The flavor pairs well with a variety of entrees.

TURKEY WITH FESTIVE FRUIT STUFFING

PREP: 40 min. | **BAKE:** 3-3/4 hours + standing

3 celery ribs, chopped
2 medium onions, chopped
3/4 cup butter, *divided*
5 cups unseasoned stuffing cubes
1-1/2 cups chopped peeled tart apples (about 2 medium)
1 cup chopped walnuts
1/2 cup raisins
1/2 cup dried cranberries
1/4 cup egg substitute
1 teaspoon salt
1/4 teaspoon pepper
1 to 2 cups chicken broth
1 turkey (14 pounds)

In a large skillet, saute celery and onions in 1/2 cup butter until tender. Transfer to a large bowl; stir in the stuffing cubes, apples, walnuts, raisins and cranberries. Stir in the egg substitute, salt, pepper and enough broth to reach desired moistness.

Just before baking, loosely stuff turkey with stuffing. Skewer turkey openings; tie drumsticks together. Place breast side up on a rack in a roasting pan. Melt remaining butter; brush over turkey.

Bake, uncovered, at 325° for 3-3/4 to 4-1/4 hours or until a meat thermometer reads 180° for turkey and 165° for stuffing, basting occasionally with pan drippings. (Cover loosely with foil if turkey browns too quickly.)

Cover turkey and let stand for 20 minutes before removing stuffing and carving turkey. If desired, thicken pan drippings for gravy.
YIELD: 14 servings (10 cups stuffing).

elaine helmick
PARADISE, CALIFORNIA

A dear friend shared this Thanksgiving staple with me. Apples, cranberries and raisins make every bite moist and fruity.

OLIVE & ROASTED PEPPER BRUSCHETTA

PREP/TOTAL TIME: 15 min.

1/2 cup grated Romano cheese
1/2 cup chopped pitted green olives
1/2 cup chopped roasted sweet red peppers
  2 teaspoons olive oil
1/2 teaspoon dried basil
 16 slices French bread baguette
    (1/2 inch thick), toasted

In a small bowl, combine the first five ingredients. Top each bread slice with 1 tablespoon olive mixture.
YIELD: 16 appetizers.

jennifer mathis
HILTON HEAD, SOUTH CAROLINA

I've tried many versions of bruschetta, but I think this recipe contains the perfect blend of ingredients. It's a great appetizer for a holiday cocktail party.

HOLIDAY CHEESECAKE

PREP: 30 min. | **BAKE:** 1-1/2 hours + chilling

1-1/2 cups graham cracker crumbs
1/2 cup pecans, toasted and finely chopped
2 tablespoons light brown sugar
6 tablespoons butter, melted

FILLING:
4 packages (8 ounces *each*) cream cheese, softened
1 cup sugar
3 teaspoons vanilla extract
4 eggs, lightly beaten
1 cup (6 ounces) miniature semisweet chocolate chips

TOPPING:
2 cups (16 ounces) sour cream
1/4 cup sugar
Assorted candies

Place an ungreased 9-in. springform pan on a double thickness of heavy-duty foil (about 18 in. square). Securely wrap foil around pan.

In a small bowl, combine cracker crumbs, pecans and brown sugar; stir in butter. Press onto bottom and 1-1/2 in. up the sides of prepared pan. Place on a baking sheet. Bake at 350° for 5 minutes. Cool on a wire rack.

In a large bowl, beat the cream cheese, sugar and vanilla until smooth. Add eggs; beat on low speed just until combined. Fold in chocolate chips. Pour into crust. Place in a larger baking pan; add 1 in. of hot water to larger pan.

Bake at 325° for 1-1/2 hours or until center is just set and top appears dull. In a small bowl, combine sour cream and sugar until smooth; spoon over hot cheesecake and spread to cover. Bake for 5 minutes longer or until topping is just set.

Remove springform pan from water bath. Cool on a wire rack for 10 minutes. Carefully run a knife around edge of pan to loosen; cool 1 hour longer. Refrigerate overnight. Garnish with candies.

YIELD: 16 servings.

taste of home test kitchen

Make Christmas dazzle with this showstopping cheesecake. Each slice is overloaded with fun, festive candy toppings.

ROSEMARY MASHED POTATOES

PREP/TOTAL TIME: 30 min.

8 large potatoes (about 4 pounds), peeled and quartered
1-1/2 teaspoons salt, *divided*
3/4 cup heavy whipping cream
1/4 cup butter, cubed
1/2 teaspoon minced fresh rosemary
1/4 teaspoon ground nutmeg
1/4 teaspoon pepper

Place the potatoes in a Dutch oven; add 1 teaspoon salt. Cover with water. Bring to a boil. Reduce the heat; cover and simmer for 15-20 minutes or until tender. Drain.

Place potatoes in a large bowl. Add the cream, butter, rosemary, nutmeg, pepper and remaining salt; beat until smooth.

YIELD: 12 servings.

sue gronholz
BEAVER DAM, WISCONSIN

These special-occasion mashed potatoes call for whipping cream instead of milk. I must admit that I was a little shocked when a good friend suggested this, but I have to agree that it certainly makes ordinary mashed potatoes taste exceptional.

ANISE SUGAR COOKIES

PREP: 40 min. | **BAKE:** 10 min./batch

1 cup butter, softened
1-1/2 cups sugar
2 eggs
1/4 to 1/2 teaspoon anise extract
3 cups all-purpose flour
1 to 1-1/2 teaspoons aniseed
1 teaspoon salt
1 teaspoon baking powder
1 teaspoon baking soda
Frosting and coarse sugar, optional

In a large bowl, cream butter and sugar until light and fluffy. Beat in eggs and extract. Combine the flour, aniseed, salt, baking powder and baking soda; gradually add to creamed mixture and mix well.

Shape batter into 1-in. balls; place on greased baking sheets. Flatten with a glass dipped in sugar.

Bake at 375° for 6-7 minutes or until set. Cool on wire racks. If desired, frost cookies and sprinkle with coarse sugar.

YIELD: 9 dozen.

paula marchesi
LENHARTSVILLE, PENNSYLVANIA

As much as I love giving away my baked Christmas treats, I always keep a batch or two of these frosted sugar cookies for myself. The light anise flavor and melt-in-your-mouth texture make them a perfect after-dinner treat.

CHICKEN, PEAR & GORGONZOLA TARTS

PREP: 30 min. | **COOK:** 5 min.

8 bacon strips
1-1/2 teaspoons brown sugar
1/4 teaspoon ground cinnamon
3/4 cup finely chopped cooked chicken breast
1/3 cup pear nectar
1/4 cup finely chopped dried pears
3 tablespoons apricot preserves
2 teaspoons butter
1/4 teaspoon salt
1/4 teaspoon pepper
2 packages (1.9 ounces *each*) frozen miniature phyllo tart shells
1/3 cup crumbled Gorgonzola cheese

Place the bacon in a 15-in. x 10-in. x 1-in. baking pan; broil 4 in. from the heat for 4-6 minutes on each side or until crisp. Combine brown sugar and cinnamon; sprinkle over bacon. Broil 1 minute longer or until bacon is glazed and bubbly. Drain on paper towels. Cool slightly and crumble.

In a small skillet, combine the chicken, pear nectar, pears, preserves, butter, salt and pepper. Bring to a boil; cook, stirring occasionally, for 3-4 minutes or until thickened. Spoon about 1 teaspoonful of filling into each tart shell; place tarts on a baking sheet. Sprinkle tarts with the bacon and cheese.

Bake at 350° for 5-7 minutes or until heated through. Serve warm.

YIELD: 2-1/2 dozen.

kathleen boulanger
WILLISTON, VERMONT

I've been experimenting with candied bacon and tried incorporating it into some of my favorite recipes. These fancy little bites are a hit wherever I take them.

SANTA CLAUS CUTOUTS

PREP: 25 min. + chilling | **BAKE:** 10 min./batch + cooling

1 cup butter, softened
1 package (3 ounces) cream cheese,
    softened
1 cup sugar
1 egg
1 teaspoon vanilla extract
2-1/2 cups all-purpose flour
1/4 teaspoon salt
White, red and blue candy coating disks

In a large bowl, cream the butter, cream cheese and sugar until light and fluffy. Beat in egg and vanilla. Combine flour and salt; gradually add to creamed mixture and mix well. Cover and refrigerate for 1-2 hours or until firm.

On a lightly floured surface, roll out dough to 1/4-in. thickness. Cut with a floured 3-in. Santa cookie cutter. Place 1 in. apart on greased baking sheets. Bake at 375° for 6-8 minutes or until edges are lightly browned. Cool for 1 minute before removing cookies to wire racks to cool completely.

Melt white candy coating; using a clean paintbrush, add a beard, mustache, eyebrows, hat brim and pom-pom to each Santa. Melt red coating; add hat, nose and mouth. Melt blue coating; add eyes. Store in an airtight container.

YIELD: about 3 dozen.

jane brown
GREENSBURG, INDIANA

Santa turns out to be a handsome fellow when I use my favorite cutout cookie recipe. Painting on the candy coating allows for detailed decorating. My 14 shoe boxes of shaped cutters tell you how much I enjoy making cookies!

DELIGHTFUL HOLIDAY BREAD

PREP: 40 min. + rising | **BAKE:** 30 min.

2 packages (1/4 ounce *each*) active dry yeast

1-3/4 cups warm water (110° to 115°)

2 eggs

3 tablespoons sugar

2 tablespoons almond extract

2 tablespoons canola oil

1-1/2 teaspoons salt

5-3/4 to 6-1/4 cups all-purpose flour

TOPPING:

1 egg

1 tablespoon water

5 teaspoons sugar

3 tablespoons sliced almonds

In a large bowl, dissolve the yeast in warm water. Add the eggs, sugar, extract, oil, salt and 4 cups flour; beat until smooth. Stir in enough remaining flour to form a soft dough (dough will be sticky).

Turn onto a lightly floured surface; knead until smooth and elastic, about 6-8 minutes. Place in a large bowl coated with cooking spray; turn once to coat top. Cover and let rise until doubled, about 1 hour.

Punch dough down; turn onto a lightly floured surface. Divide into thirds; shape each portion into a 20-in. rope. Place ropes on a large baking sheet coated with cooking spray; braid. Pinch ends together, forming a round loaf. Cover and let rise until doubled, about 40 minutes.

Beat egg and water; brush over loaf. Sprinkle with sugar and almonds. Bake at 350° for 30-35 minutes or until golden brown. Remove to a wire rack.

YIELD: 1 loaf (24 slices).

cheri neustifter
STURTEVANT, WISCONSIN

The first time I made this braided bread for Christmas, everyone loved it. In fact, when my sister-in-law came for a visit the following July, she asked me to teach her to make it.

HOLIDAY APPETIZER PUFFS

PREP: 20 min. | **BAKE:** 25 min.

1 cup water
1/2 cup butter, cubed
1/2 teaspoon salt
1 cup all-purpose flour
4 eggs

FILLING:
1 package (8 ounces) cream cheese, softened
1/4 cup mayonnaise
1 can (6 ounces) crabmeat, drained and cartilage removed
1/2 cup shredded Swiss cheese
1 tablespoon minced chives
1 teaspoon garlic salt
1 teaspoon Worcestershire sauce
1/4 teaspoon pepper

In a small saucepan, bring the water, butter and salt to a boil. Add flour all at once and stir until a smooth ball forms. Remove from the heat; let stand for 5 minutes. Add eggs, one at a time, beating well after each addition. Continue beating until mixture is smooth and shiny.

Drop by rounded teaspoonfuls 2 in. apart onto greased baking sheets. Bake at 400° for 25-30 minutes or until golden brown. Remove to wire racks. Immediately cut a slit in puffs to allow steam to escape. When cool, split puffs open; remove tops and set aside. Discard soft dough from inside.

In a small bowl, beat cream cheese and mayonnaise until smooth. Stir in the remaining filling ingredients. Just before serving, spoon the filling into puffs; replace the tops.

YIELD: 4 dozen.

kathy fielder
DALLAS, TEXAS

These golden puffs are so versatile. Instead of the crab filling, you can also use your favorite chicken or tuna salad.

CRANBERRY BOG BARS

PREP: 25 min. | **BAKE:** 25 min. + cooling

1-1/4 cups butter, softened, *divided*
1-1/2 cups packed brown sugar, *divided*
3-1/2 cups old-fashioned oats, *divided*
1 cup all-purpose flour
1 can (14 ounces) whole-berry cranberry sauce
1/2 cup finely chopped pecans

In a large bowl, cream 1 cup butter and 1 cup brown sugar until light and fluffy. In another bowl, combine 2-1/2 cups oats and flour. Gradually add to the creamed mixture until crumbly. Press into a greased 13-in. x 9-in. baking pan. Spread crust with the cranberry sauce.

In a microwave-safe bowl, melt remaining butter; stir in the pecans and the remaining brown sugar and oats. Sprinkle over the cranberry sauce. Bake at 375° for 25-30 minutes or until lightly browned. Cool on a wire rack. Cut into bars.

YIELD: 3 dozen.

sally wakefield
BRUCETON MILLS, WEST VIRGINIA

Sweet and chewy, these fun bars feature a host of fall flavors. I like to sprinkle them with confectioners' sugar before serving.

PERFECT bars

To easily lift bars out of a pan, bake the bars in a foil-lined pan—greasing it according to the recipe's directions. Use the foil to lift bars out of the pan after they've cooled. Use a serrated knife to cut the bars straight downward.

MINT COOKIES 'N' CREAM BROWNIES

PREP: 25 min. | **BAKE:** 25 min. + cooling

1/2 cup butter, softened
1 cup sugar
4 eggs
1-1/2 cups chocolate syrup
1 cup all-purpose flour
6 mint cream-filled chocolate sandwich cookies, chopped

MINT CREAM:
1/2 cup butter, softened
2 cups confectioners' sugar
1 tablespoon 2% milk
1/4 to 1/2 teaspoon mint extract
2 drops green food coloring
Additional mint cream-filled chocolate sandwich cookies, crushed

In a large bowl, cream the butter and sugar until light and fluffy. Add the eggs, one at a time, beating well after each addition. Beat in chocolate syrup, then flour, just until blended. Fold in the chopped cookies.

Pour into a greased 13-in. x 9-in. baking pan. Bake at 350° for 25-30 minutes or until a toothpick inserted near the center comes out clean (do not overbake). Cool completely on a wire rack.

For mint cream, in a small bowl, cream butter and confectioners' sugar until light and fluffy. Beat in the milk, extract and food coloring. Frost brownies; sprinkle with crushed cookies. Cut into squares.

YIELD: 3-1/2 dozen.

janell traubel
BOISE, IDAHO

I created this recipe for my sons who love the flavors of mint and chocolate. The creamy mint frosting is a delicious complement to the fudgy brownie.

O'LARRY'S SKILLET POTATOES

PREP/TOTAL TIME: 30 min.

2 pounds potatoes, cut into 1/2-inch cubes
1 medium onion, finely chopped
1 medium sweet red pepper, chopped
1 teaspoon Caribbean jerk seasoning
1 teaspoon salt
1/4 cup olive oil
2 garlic cloves, minced

Place potatoes in a large saucepan and cover with water. Bring to a boil. Reduce heat; cover and simmer for 5-10 minutes or until almost tender. Drain.

In a large skillet, saute the potatoes, onion, red pepper, jerk seasoning and salt in oil until the potatoes are golden brown and vegetables are tender. Add the garlic; cook 1 minute longer.

YIELD: 10 servings.

kerry barnett-amundson
OCEAN PARK, WASHINGTON

My husband, Larry, uses all fresh ingredients when he prepares his famous O'Larry's Skillet Potatoes. These zippy spuds have colorful bits of red pepper.

GLAZED CORNED BEEF DINNER

PREP: 20 min. | **COOK:** 8-1/4 hours

- 8 medium red potatoes, quartered
- 2 medium carrots, sliced
- 1 medium onion, sliced
- 1 corned beef brisket with spice packet (3 pounds)
- 1-1/2 cups water
- 4 orange peel strips (3 inches)
- 3 tablespoons orange juice concentrate
- 3 tablespoons honey
- 1 tablespoon Dijon mustard

Place the potatoes, carrots and onion in a 5-qt. slow cooker. Cut brisket in half; place over vegetables. Add the water, orange peel and contents of spice packet.

Cover and cook on low for 8-9 hours or until meat and vegetables are tender.

Using a slotted spoon, transfer corned beef and vegetables to a 13-in. x 9-in. baking dish. Discard orange peel.

Combine the orange juice concentrate, honey and mustard; pour over meat. Bake, uncovered, at 375° for 15-20 minutes, basting occasionally.

YIELD: 8 servings.

shannon strate

SALT LAKE CITY, UTAH

This recipe is so tasty that it's the only way my family will eat corned beef. The glaze is the kicker!

SIX-FRUIT SALAD

PREP/TOTAL TIME: 10 min.

2 cups fresh strawberries, quartered
1 cup cubed honeydew
1/2 cup fresh blueberries
1 large apple, chopped
1 large navel orange, peeled and chopped
1 large ripe banana, cut into 1/4-inch slices
1/2 cup orange juice

In a large bowl, combine the fruit. Drizzle with orange juice and stir gently. Serve the salad immediately.

YIELD: 8 servings.

paula baglole
SUMMERSIDE, PRINCE EDWARD ISLAND

People always offer compliments when I take this salad to covered-dish suppers. The refreshing medley of fruits and berries is also a favorite treat for breakfast or brunch.

LEMON BASIL CUPCAKES

PREP: 30 min. | **BAKE:** 20 min. + cooling

1 cup butter, softened
2 cups sugar
3 eggs
3/4 teaspoon vanilla extract
1/2 teaspoon grated lemon peel
3-1/2 cups all-purpose flour
2 teaspoons baking powder
1 teaspoon baking soda
2 cups (16 ounces) sour cream
1 jar (10 ounces) lemon curd

LEMON SYRUP:
1 cup water
3/4 cup sugar
1/3 cup lemon juice
5 fresh basil leaves
1 lemon peel strip (1-1/2 inches x 1/2 inch)

LEMON MOUSSE FROSTING:
2 cups confectioners' sugar
3 tablespoons butter, softened
1/2 teaspoon vanilla extract
1/4 teaspoon grated lemon peel
1/8 teaspoon lemon extract
1-1/4 cups heavy whipping cream, whipped

GARNISH:
2 teaspoons light corn syrup
1/4 cup sugar
1 new small paintbrush
24 fresh basil leaves

In a bowl, cream butter and sugar until light and fluffy. Add eggs, one at a time, beating well after each addition. Beat in vanilla and lemon peel. Combine the flour, baking powder and baking soda; add to the creamed mixture alternately with the sour cream, beating well after each addition.

Fill paper-lined muffin cups three-fourths full. Bake at 350° for 20-25 minutes or until a toothpick inserted near the center comes out clean. Cool for 10 minutes before removing from pans to wire racks to cool.

Cut a small hole in the corner of a pastry or plastic bag; insert a small round pastry tip. Fill with lemon curd. Push the tip through the top of each cupcake to fill.

For syrup, in a small saucepan, combine the water, sugar, lemon juice, basil and lemon peel. Bring to a boil; cook until liquid is reduced to 1 cup. Strain; discard basil and peel. Cool completely.

In a bowl, beat the confectioners' sugar, butter, 3 tablespoons lemon syrup, vanilla, lemon peel and extract until smooth. Fold in whipped cream. Frost cupcakes. (Refrigerate remaining syrup for another use.)

Place corn syrup and sugar in small bowls. Dip paintbrush in corn syrup; brush over a basil leaf. Coat leaf with sugar. Repeat. Garnish cupcakes with basil leaves. Store cupcakes in the refrigerator.
YIELD: 2 dozen.

julie ohnstad
MARIETTA, GEORGIA

These light and tender lemon cupcakes are a delightful treat for showers, luncheons, bake sales or classroom parties. You'll see faces light up after just one bite. Garnish each one with a candied fresh basil leaf for extra charm.

MINI MUFFULETTA

PREP: 25 min. + chilling

1 jar (10 ounces) pimiento-stuffed olives, drained and chopped
2 cans (4-1/4 ounces *each*) chopped ripe olives
2 tablespoons balsamic vinegar
1 tablespoon red wine vinegar
1 tablespoon olive oil
3 garlic cloves, minced
1 teaspoon dried basil
1 teaspoon dried oregano
6 French rolls, split
1/2 pound thinly sliced hard salami
1/4 pound sliced provolone cheese
1/2 pound thinly sliced cotto salami
1/4 pound sliced part-skim mozzarella cheese

In a large bowl, combine the first eight ingredients; set aside. Hollow out the tops and bottoms of the rolls, leaving 3/4-in. shells (discard removed bread or save for another use).

Spread the olive mixture over tops and bottoms of rolls. On roll bottoms, layer the hard salami, provolone cheese, cotto salami and mozzarella cheese. Replace tops.

Wrap tightly in plastic wrap. Refrigerate overnight. Cut each into six wedges; secure with toothpicks.
YIELD: 3 dozen.

gareth craner
MINDEN, NEVADA

Folks love these hearty little sandwich wedges. The recipe is great for a party and can be prepared a day in advance.

PINEAPPLE CHEESECAKE

PREP: 40 min. | **BAKE:** 70 min. + chilling

1-1/4 cups graham cracker crumbs
1/4 cup sugar
1/3 cup butter, melted

FILLING:
3 packages (8 ounces *each*) cream cheese, softened
1/4 cup sugar
1-1/2 cups (12 ounces) sour cream
3/4 cup sweetened condensed milk
3 to 4 teaspoons grated orange peel
3 teaspoons vanilla extract
5 eggs, *separated*

TOPPING:
1/4 cup sugar
4 tablespoons cold water, *divided*
1 can (20 ounces) crushed pineapple, drained
1 tablespoon cornstarch

In a small bowl, combine the graham cracker crumbs, sugar and butter. Press onto the bottom of a greased 10-in. springform pan; set aside.

In a large bowl, beat cream cheese and sugar until smooth. Beat in the sour cream, milk, orange peel and vanilla. Add the egg yolks; beat on low speed just until the mixture is combined.

In a small bowl, beat egg whites until stiff peaks form; fold into cream cheese mixture. Pour over crust.

Place pan on a baking sheet. Bake at 325° for 70-75 minutes or until center is almost set. Cool on a wire rack for 10 minutes. Carefully run a knife around edge of pan to loosen; cool 1 hour longer. Cover and refrigerate for at least 6 hours or overnight.

For topping, combine the sugar and 2 tablespoons water in a small saucepan. Bring to a boil over medium heat; cook for 2 minutes. Stir in pineapple. In a small bowl, combine cornstarch and remaining water until smooth; stir into pineapple mixture. Bring to a boil; cook and stir for 2 minutes or until thickened. Cool completely. Spread the topping over the cheesecake. Store cake in the refrigerator.

YIELD: 12 servings.

lorraine caland
THUNDER BAY, ONTARIO

With its make-ahead convenience, this fruit-topped cheesecake often appears on my holiday menus. It never fails to impress guests.

BROCCOLI RICE CASSEROLE

PREP: 15 min. | **BAKE:** 30 min.

1-1/2 cups water
1/2 cup butter, cubed
1 tablespoon dried minced onion
2 cups uncooked instant rice
1 package (16 ounces) frozen chopped broccoli, thawed
1 can (10-3/4 ounces) condensed cream of mushroom soup, undiluted
1 jar (8 ounces) process cheese sauce

In a large saucepan, bring the water, butter and onion to a boil. Stir in rice. Remove from the heat; cover and let stand for 5 minutes or until water is absorbed.

Stir in the broccoli, soup and cheese sauce. Transfer to a greased 2-qt. baking dish. Bake, uncovered, at 350° for 30-35 minutes or until bubbly.

YIELD: 8 servings.

jennifer fuller
BALLSTON SPA, NEW YORK

When I was little, serving this dish was the only way my mother could get me to eat broccoli. It's an excellent recipe to serve anytime and is especially good with poultry.

HOLIDAY BRUNCH CASSEROLE

PREP: 15 min. + chilling | **BAKE:** 30 min. + standing

- 4 cups frozen shredded hash brown potatoes
- 1 pound bulk pork sausage, cooked and drained
- 1/2 pound sliced bacon, cooked and crumbled
- 1 medium green pepper, chopped
- 2 cups (8 ounces) shredded cheddar cheese, *divided*
- 1 green onion, chopped
- 1 cup reduced-fat biscuit/baking mix
- 1/2 teaspoon salt
- 4 eggs
- 3 cups milk

In a large bowl, combine the hash browns, sausage, bacon, green pepper, 1 cup cheese and onion. Transfer to a greased 13-in. x 9-in. baking dish.

In another bowl, whisk the biscuit mix, salt, eggs and milk; pour over the top. Sprinkle with remaining cheese. Cover and refrigerate overnight.

Remove from the refrigerator 30 minutes before baking. Bake, uncovered, at 375° for 30-35 minutes or a knife inserted near the center comes out clean. Let stand for 10 minutes before cutting.

YIELD: 12 servings.

nelda cronbaugh
BELLE PLAINE, IOWA

If you'll be having overnight company during the holidays, you may want to consider this hearty casserole. Your guests will be impressed with its bountiful filling and scrumptious flavor.

GLAZED EASTER HAM

PREP: 15 min. | **BAKE:** 2 hours + standing

- 1 fully cooked bone-in ham (8 to 10 pounds)
- 1/4 cup packed brown sugar
- 1/4 cup orange juice
- 2 tablespoons honey
- 1 tablespoon stone-ground mustard
- 2 teaspoons dried basil
- 1 teaspoon grated orange peel
- 1/8 teaspoon ground cloves

Place ham on a rack in a shallow roasting pan. Score the surface of the ham, making diamond shapes 1/2 in. deep. Bake at 325° for 1-3/4 hours.

In a small bowl, combine the remaining ingredients. Spoon over ham. Bake 15-30 minutes longer or until a meat thermometer reads 140°. Let stand for 10-15 minutes before slicing.

YIELD: 12-16 servings.

sue gronholz
BEAVER DAM, WISCONSIN

Baked ham is an Easter tradition at our house. The glaze features my dried homegrown basil. My large family loves ham, and this recipe always satisfies our hearty appetites.

DIJON SCALLOPED POTATOES

PREP: 25 min. | **BAKE:** 50 min. + standing

- 2/3 cup chopped onion
- 2 teaspoons canola oil
- 1 can (14-1/2 ounces) chicken broth
- 2 packages (3 ounces *each*) cream cheese, cubed
- 1 tablespoon Dijon mustard
- 3 medium russet potatoes, peeled and thinly sliced
- 2 medium sweet potatoes, peeled and thinly sliced
- 1-1/2 to 2 cups crushed butter-flavored crackers
- 3 tablespoons grated Parmesan cheese
- 2 tablespoons butter, melted
- 2 teaspoons minced fresh parsley

In a Dutch oven, saute the onion in oil until tender. Reduce heat to medium; stir in the broth, cream cheese and mustard until blended. Remove mixture from the heat. Stir in the potatoes.

Transfer to a 13-in. x 9-in. baking dish coated with cooking spray. Combine the crushed crackers, cheese and butter; sprinkle over the top.

Bake casserole, uncovered, at 350° for 50-60 minutes or until the potatoes are tender. Sprinkle with parsley. Let stand for 10 minutes before serving.

YIELD: 8 servings.

carolyn putnam
NORWALK, OHIO

My family enjoys this creamy and colorful recipe for cheesy potatoes. It has both sweet and white potatoes, lots of rich, buttery flavor and a pretty, golden-crumb topping.

SURPRISE MONKEY BREAD

PREP: 25 min. | **BAKE:** 40 min.

- 1 cup packed brown sugar
- 1/2 cup butter, cubed
- 2 tubes (12 ounces *each*) refrigerated flaky buttermilk biscuits
- 1/2 cup sugar
- 1 tablespoon ground cinnamon
- 1 package (8 ounces) cream cheese, cut into 20 cubes
- 1-1/2 cups chopped walnuts

In a small microwave-safe bowl, heat brown sugar and butter on high for 1 minute or until sugar is dissolved; set aside.

Flatten each biscuit into a 3-in. circle. Combine sugar and cinnamon; sprinkle 1/2 teaspoon in the center of each biscuit. Top with a cream cheese cube. Fold dough over filling; pinch edges to seal tightly.

Sprinkle 1/2 cup walnuts into a 10-in. fluted tube pan coated with cooking spray. Layer with half of the biscuits, cinnamon-sugar and butter mixture and 1/2 cup walnuts. Repeat layers.

Bake at 350° for 40-45 minutes or until golden brown. Immediately invert onto a serving platter. Serve bread warm. Refrigerate any leftovers.

YIELD: 1 loaf (12 servings).

lois rutherford
ELKTON, FLORIDA

Cream cheese adds a luscious touch to this glorified monkey bread. When my neighbor has her annual holiday brunch, this is one recipe that's always requested.

BROWN sugar

When a recipe calls for brown sugar, it should always be firmly packed. The moisture in brown sugar tends to trap air between the crystals, so it should be firmly packed when measuring.

STRAWBERRY CUSTARD PIES

PREP: 35 min. + chilling

4-1/2 cups sugar

3/4 cup cornstarch

4-1/2 cups cold water

3 packages (3 ounces *each*) strawberry gelatin

1 tablespoon lemon juice

6 packages (3 ounces *each*) cook-and-serve vanilla pudding mix

6 pastry shells (9 inches), baked

3 pounds fresh strawberries, halved

Whipped cream, optional

In a large saucepan, combine the sugar and cornstarch; gradually stir in water until smooth. Bring to a boil; cook and stir for 2 minutes or until thickened. Remove from the heat. Stir in the gelatin and lemon juice until the gelatin is dissolved. Cool mixture to room temperature.

Prepare the pudding mixes according to package directions. Pour into pastry shells. Top with the strawberries. Carefully spoon gelatin mixture over berries. Refrigerate until set. Garnish pies with the whipped cream if desired.

YIELD: 6 pies (8 servings each).

caroline park
PRITCHARD, BRITISH COLUMBIA

These luscious pies were a specialty at a restaurant where I used to work. They feature such a big, fresh berry taste that I've had many requests to bring them to large gatherings.

HOT DOGS WITH THE WORKS

PREP/TOTAL TIME: 15 min.

1-1/2 cups (6 ounces) shredded pepper Jack cheese

3/4 cup chopped seeded tomato

3 tablespoons chopped onion

2 tablespoons sweet pickle relish

8 hot dogs

8 hot dog buns

In a small bowl, combine the cheese, tomato, onion and relish. Place hot dogs in buns; top with cheese mixture.

Wrap each hot dog in a double thickness of heavy-duty foil (about 12 in. x 10 in.). Grill, covered, over medium-hot heat for 8-10 minutes or until heated through. Open foil carefully to allow steam to escape.

YIELD: 8 servings.

maria regakis
SOMERVILLE, MASSACHUSETTS

What screams summer more than grilled hot dogs? I place the hot dogs in the buns before topping them with this zesty cheese sauce and grilling them in a double layer of foil.

THERMOS hot dogs

Before heading out for a weekend picnic, place hot dogs in a thermos and cover them with boiling water. When it's time to eat, the hot dogs are piping hot.

STEAK AND VEGETABLE KABOBS

PREP: 15 min. + marinating | **GRILL:** 10 min.

1/4 cup packed brown sugar

1/4 cup lemon juice

1/4 cup canola oil

1/4 cup soy sauce

2 garlic cloves, minced

3 whole cloves

Dash dried basil

2-1/2 pounds beef top sirloin steak, cut into 1-1/4 inch pieces

24 cherry tomatoes

24 large fresh mushrooms

1 large green *or* sweet red pepper, cut into 1-1/2-inch cubes

2 small zucchini squash, cut into 1-inch slices

1 medium onion, cut into wedges

Hot cooked rice

In a large bowl, combine the first seven ingredients; set aside. On metal or soaked wooden skewers, alternately thread meat and vegetables.

Place in a large glass dish. Pour marinade over kabobs; cover and refrigerate for 6 hours or overnight, turning several times. Discard cloves.

Grill over medium-hot heat until the meat reaches desired doneness and vegetables are tender. Serve with rice.

YIELD: 10 servings.

lorri cleveland

KINGSVILLE, OHIO

You can spend your day out of the kitchen by assembling these kabobs in the morning, then letting them marinate all day. Then all that's left to do is to let them sizzle on the grill before dinnertime.

CHICKEN SALAD FOR 50

PREP: 40 min. + chilling

- 9 cups cubed cooked chicken
- 9 cups cooked small pasta shells
- 8 cups chopped celery
- 8 cups seedless green grapes halves
- 18 hard-cooked eggs, chopped
- 2 cans (20 ounces *each*) pineapple tidbits, drained

DRESSING:

- 4 cups mayonnaise
- 2 cups (16 ounces) sour cream
- 2 cups whipped topping
- 1/4 cup lemon juice
- 1/4 cup sugar
- 1-1/2 teaspoons salt
- 2 cups cashew halves

In two very large bowls, combine the first six ingredients. In another large bowl, whisk the first six dressing ingredients. Pour over the chicken mixture; toss to coat. Cover and refrigerate for at least 1 hour. Stir in cashews just before serving.

YIELD: 50 servings (1 cup each).

florence vold
STORY CITY, IOWA

I got lots of recipe requests when I served this classic at a women's luncheon. The creamy dressing, grapes and cashews make it extra special.

GRILLED THIGHS AND DRUMSTICKS

PREP: 10 min. + marinating | **GRILL:** 30 min.

2-1/2 cups packed brown sugar
2 cups water
2 cups cider vinegar
2 cups ketchup
1 cup canola oil
4 tablespoons salt
3 tablespoons prepared mustard
4-1/2 teaspoons Worcestershire sauce
1 tablespoon soy sauce
1 teaspoon pepper
1 teaspoon Liquid Smoke, optional
10 pounds bone-in chicken thighs and
chicken drumsticks
1/2 teaspoon seasoned salt

In a large bowl, combine the first 11 ingredients. Pour into two large resealable plastic bags; add the chicken. Seal the bags and turn to coat; refrigerate overnight.

Drain and discard marinade. Prepare grill for indirect heat. Using long-handled tongs, moisten a paper towel with cooking oil and lightly coat the grill rack. Sprinkle chicken with seasoned salt. Grill chicken skin side down, covered, over indirect medium heat for 15-20 minutes on each side or until a meat thermometer reads 180°.
YIELD: 12-14 servings.

brenda beachy
BELVIDERE, TENNESSEE

This chicken is juicy, has great barbecue flavor and makes a big batch, so it's perfect for any outdoor party or potluck.

OLD-FASHIONED LEMONADE

PREP/TOTAL TIME: 15 min. + chilling

2 to 2-1/2 cups sugar
5 cups water, *divided*
1 tablespoon grated lemon peel
1-3/4 cups lemon juice (about 6 lemons)

In a large saucepan, combine sugar, 1 cup water and lemon peel. Cook and stir over medium heat until sugar is dissolved, about 4 minutes.

Remove from the heat. Stir in lemon juice and remaining water. Pour into a pitcher and refrigerate until chilled. Serve over ice.
YIELD: 2 quarts.

tammi simpson
GREENSBURG, KENTUCKY

Memorial Day and Fourth of July gatherings just wouldn't be the same without homemade lemonade. The fresh-squeezed taste of this sweet-tart beverage makes it a winner.

WATERMELON GRAPE SALAD

PREP/TOTAL TIME: 30 min.

10 cups cubed seedless watermelon
10 cups seedless red grapes
1-1/4 cups white grape juice
5 teaspoons minced fresh tarragon
5 teaspoons honey

In several large bowls, combine watermelon and grapes. In small bowl, whisk the grape juice, tarragon and honey. Pour over fruit and toss to coat. Serve immediately in a watermelon boat or large bowl.
YIELD: 20 servings.

sue gronholz
BEAVER DAM, WISCONSIN

Infused with tarragon and honey, this fresh fruit salad stands out from the rest.

LAYERED SUMMERTIME SALAD

PREP/TOTAL TIME: 30 min.

- 2 cups uncooked gemelli *or* spiral pasta
- 1 cup mayonnaise
- 2 tablespoons lemon juice
- 1 teaspoon sugar
- 1/2 teaspoon garlic powder
- 1/2 cup sliced green onions
- 4 bacon strips, cooked and crumbled, *divided*
- 4 cups torn romaine
- 1 cup fresh snow peas, trimmed and halved
- 1 cup fresh cauliflowerets
- 1 cup fresh broccoli florets
- 1 large sweet red pepper, chopped
- 1/2 cup shredded Swiss cheese

Cook pasta according to package directions. Meanwhile, in a small bowl, combine the mayonnaise, lemon juice, sugar and garlic powder; set aside. Drain the pasta and rinse in cold water; toss with the onions and half of the bacon.

In a large salad bowl, layer half of the romaine, pasta mixture, peas, cauliflower, broccoli, red pepper, mayonnaise mixture and cheese. Repeat layers. Sprinkle with remaining bacon. Cover and refrigerate until serving.

YIELD: 16 servings.

betty fulks
ONIA, ARKANSAS

Luscious layers of pasta and veggies make up this super summer salad that can be made ahead for warm-weather picnics and deck parties. It makes enough to feed a crowd.

SOUTHWESTERN BURGERS

PREP/TOTAL TIME: 30 min.

- 1 can (4 ounces) chopped green chilies
- 1/4 cup Worcestershire sauce
- 1/2 teaspoon hickory Liquid Smoke, optional
- 1/2 cup crushed butter-flavored crackers (about 12 crackers)
- 4-1/2 teaspoons chili powder
- 3 teaspoons ground cumin
- 1/2 teaspoon salt
- 1/2 teaspoon pepper
- 2 pounds lean ground beef (90% lean)
- 1/2 pound bulk pork sausage
- 8 slices pepper Jack cheese
- 8 sesame seed hamburger buns, split

Lettuce leaves, optional

In a large bowl, combine the first eight ingredients. Crumble beef and sausage over the mixture and mix well. Shape into eight patties.

Grill, covered, over medium heat for 5-7 minutes on each side or until no longer pink. Top with cheese. Grill 1 minute longer or until cheese is melted.

Grill buns, cut side down, for 1-2 minutes or until toasted. Serve burgers on buns with lettuce if desired.

YIELD: 8 servings.

robert hodges
SAN DIEGO, CALIFORNIA

Whether you're tailgating at the ballpark or hanging out on the patio with friends, these southwestern-style burgers are great on the grill. Sometimes I make six patties rather than eight because I like my burgers bigger and better!

GRILLED burgers

To keep grilled burgers from drying out, be careful not to overhandle the meat before cooking. If you add seasonings to the ground beef, gently mix them in with two forks just until combined. Then shape into 4-inch round patties about 1/2 inch thick (beef plumps when it cooks). Also, avoid flattening the burgers with a spatula as they cook as this will press out the juices that keep the burgers moist.

SUMMER VEGGIE SUBS

PREP/TOTAL TIME: 30 min. + standing

- 4 medium sweet red peppers
- 1/2 cup fat-free mayonnaise
- 2 tablespoons minced fresh basil
- 1 tablespoon minced fresh parsley
- 1 tablespoon minced fresh tarragon
- 2 loaves French bread (1 pound *each*), halved lengthwise
- 2 cups fresh baby spinach
- 2 cups thinly sliced cucumbers
- 2 cups alfalfa sprouts
- 4 medium tomatoes, sliced
- 2 medium ripe avocados, peeled and sliced
- 3/4 pound thinly sliced deli turkey
- 6 slices reduced-fat Swiss cheese, halved

Broil peppers 4 in. from the heat until skins blister, about 5 minutes. With tongs, rotate peppers a quarter turn. Broil and rotate until all the sides are blistered and blackened. Immediately place peppers in a large bowl; cover and let stand for 15-20 minutes.

Peel off and discard charred skin. Remove stems and seeds. Julienne peppers.

Combine the mayonnaise, basil, parsley and tarragon; spread over bread bottoms. Top with the spinach, cucumbers, sprouts, roasted peppers, tomatoes, avocados, turkey and cheese. Replace tops. Cut each loaf into six slices.

YIELD: 12 servings.

jennie todd
LANCASTER, PENNSYLVANIA

A local park near our home holds free outdoor concerts during the summer. I always arrive with these subs in tow. They're perfect for any outdoor gathering. Omit the turkey if you prefer a meatless sub.

PATRIOTIC CUPCAKES

PREP: 15 min. | BAKE: 20 min. + cooling

    1 package (18-1/4 ounces) white cake mix
1/2 teaspoon blue food coloring
1/2 teaspoon red food coloring
    1 can (16 ounces) vanilla frosting
Red, white and blue sprinkles

Prepare the cake mix batter according to package directions for cupcakes.

In a small bowl, combine 1-1/3 cups batter and the blue food coloring. In another bowl, combine 1-1/3 cups batter and the red food coloring. Leave the remaining batter plain.

Fill paper-lined muffin cups with 2 tablespoons red batter, 2 tablespoons plain batter and 2 tablespoons blue batter. Bake at 350° for 20-24 minutes or until a toothpick inserted near the center comes out clean. Cool for 10 minutes before removing from the pans to wire racks to cool completely. Frost with the vanilla frosting; decorate with the sprinkles.

YIELD: 1-1/2 dozen.

jodi rugg
AURORA, ILLINOIS

These festive cupcakes are sure to be the star of your Fourth of July menu. You can use different food coloring and sprinkles to suit any season or holiday.

HONEY-GRILLED CHICKEN BREASTS

PREP: 15 min. + marinating | **GRILL:** 10 min.

- 1/2 cup orange juice
- 1/3 cup honey
- 1/4 cup lemon juice
- 1/4 cup reduced-sodium soy sauce
- 2 tablespoons minced fresh gingerroot
- 12 garlic cloves, minced
- 1/2 teaspoon pepper
- 1/4 teaspoon salt
- 8 boneless skinless chicken breast halves (6 ounces *each*)

In a small bowl, combine the first eight ingredients. Pour 1/2 cup marinade into a large resealable plastic bag; add the chicken. Seal the bag and turn to coat; refrigerate for 8 hours or overnight. Cover and refrigerate remaining marinade.

Drain and discard marinade. Using long-handled tongs, moisten a paper towel with cooking oil and lightly coat the grill rack. Grill, covered, over medium heat or broil 4 in. from the heat for 5-7 minutes on each side or until a meat thermometer reads 170°, basting frequently with reserved marinade.

YIELD: 8 servings.

jennifer petersen
MURRAY, UTAH

Orange juice and soy sauce make a tasty combination in this recipe from my mother-in-law. The longer this chicken marinates, the fuller the flavor!

PICNIC PASTA SALAD

PREP/TOTAL TIME: 25 min.

- 1 package (12 ounces) tricolor spiral pasta
- 1 package (10 ounces) refrigerated tricolor tortellini
- 1 jar (7-1/2 ounces) marinated artichoke hearts, undrained
- 1/2 pound fresh broccoli florets (about 1-3/4 cups)
- 12 ounces provolone cheese, cubed
- 12 ounces hard salami, cubed
- 1 medium sweet red pepper, chopped
- 1 medium green pepper, chopped
- 1 can (15 ounces) garbanzo beans *or* chickpeas, rinsed and drained
- 2 cans (2-1/4 ounces *each*) sliced ripe olives, drained
- 1 medium red onion, chopped
- 4 garlic cloves, minced
- 2 envelopes Italian salad dressing mix

Cook spiral pasta and tortellini according to package directions. Drain and rinse in cold water. Place in a large bowl; add artichokes, broccoli, provolone cheese, salami, peppers, beans, olives, onion and garlic.

Prepare salad dressing according to the package directions; pour over salad and toss to coat. Serve immediately or cover and refrigerate until serving.

YIELD: 14-16 servings.

felicia fiocchi
VINELAND, NEW JERSEY

My family is not big on traditional pasta salads made with mayonnaise, but they love this colorful version that uses Italian dressing. It's now a staple for all our family reunions.

EASY cheese

When a recipe calls for cubed cheese, cut up string cheese or cheese stick snacks instead of a block of cheese. Since the cheese is individually wrapped, you can open only the number of packages you need, and you won't end up with an open block of cheese that might spoil before being used.

general recipe index

alphabetical recipe index